THE ALPINE JOURNAL

2006

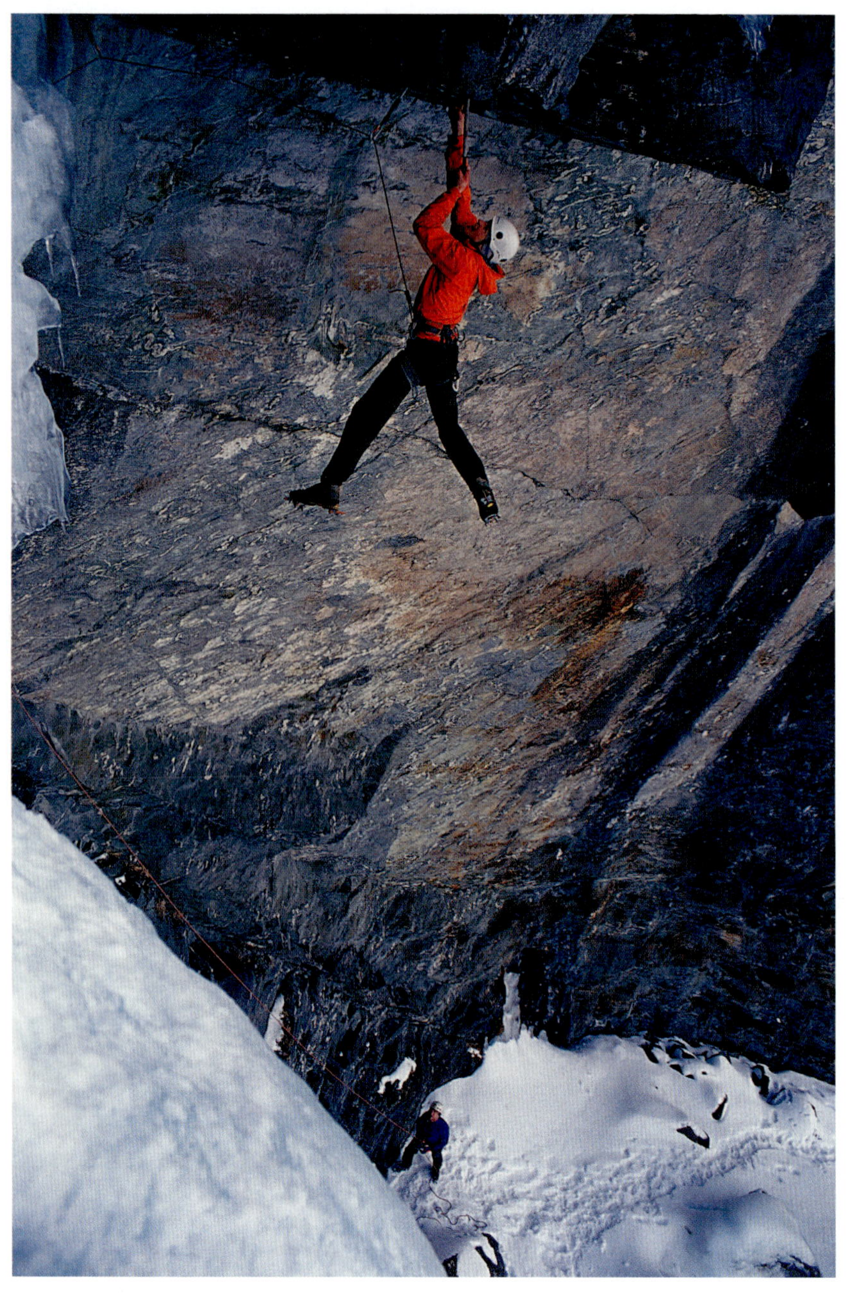

Kester Brown on the first ascent of *Northern Exposure* (M11) in Queenstown's Wye Creek, New Zealand. Photo: Jason Naran. (*Kester Brown collection*)

THE ALPINE JOURNAL 2006

The Journal of the Alpine Club

A record of mountain adventure
and scientific observation

Edited by Stephen Goodwin

Assistant Editors:
Paul Knott and Geoffrey Templeman

Production Editor: Johanna Merz

Volume 111

No 355

Supported by the
Mount Everest Foundation

Published jointly by
THE ALPINE CLUB & THE ERNEST PRESS

THE ALPINE JOURNAL 2006
Volume 111 No 355

Address all editorial communications to the Hon Editor :
Stephen Goodwin, 1 Ivy Cottages, Edenhall, Penrith, CA11 8SN
e-mail : sg@stephengoodwin.demon.co.uk
Address all sales and distribution communications to:
Cordée, 3a De Montfort Street, Leicester, LE1 7HD

Back numbers:
Apply to the Alpine Club, 55 Charlotte Road, London, EC2A 3QF
or, for 1969 to date, apply to Cordée, as above.

First published in 2006 jointly by the Alpine Club and the Ernest Press
Typesetting by Johanna Merz

A CIP catalogue record for this book is
available from the British Library

ISBN 0 948153 85 7

Foreword

One of the most engaging 'mountaineering' books of 2005, if not of a good many more years than that, was a slim volume entitled *Playing*, a collection of letters by Robin Hodgkin describing his climbing adventures in the 1930s and '40s. Writing to his mother while on the approach to Masherbrum in 1938 he describes the arrangements made for getting mail home: 'Letters will thus take 3-4 weeks from the mountain to England; so we will never be much out of touch.'

Halcyon days; when going on a trip ('expedition' or 'holiday', call it what you will) meant living in the here and now without any pang of guilt that one should be contacting home or office, let alone informing the worldwide web of one's daily doings. Of course you don't have to carry a 'phone or check emails, but the mere existence of the opportunity has changed the realities of being in or out of touch. It would be hard to argue today, as the youthful Hodgkin blithely assumed, that news exchanged barely once a month amounted to be being 'never much out of touch'.

One of the benefits of 'slow news' is that when it does eventually emerge it is likely to be in a considered and digestible form. Contrast this to the bombardment of the senses from Everest last May. One day's headlines proclaiming the youngest or oldest ascensionist was trumped the next by a dying man seemingly ignored by his fellows, only to be followed by a report of a Sherpa stripping naked on the summit, and next day of a 'dead' man walking back into base camp. As old hacks would say of their most improbable-but-true scoops: 'You couldn't make it up!'

Rather overlooked was the death of three Sherpas in the Khumbu icefall in a sérac collapse on 21 April. The icefall has seemed a relatively benign beast in recent years, but this tragedy was a reminder that the true cost of the Everest ego trip goes well beyond the client's £40,000. Does anyone still ponder, as Eric Shipton did in 1951, the morality of subjecting employees to such a risk? And today in pursuit of what?

It is tempting to say that the annual circus on Everest has nothing to do with *real* mountaineering and to get on with our own climbing games in smug superiority. Except that to the general public getting to the top of Everest should be the zenith of any mountaineer's ambition. Everest, the Eiger and Matterhorn, and at a parochial level Ben Nevis, are the public face of mountaineering and what goes on there defines how we are seen.

As a correspondent to the *Daily Telegraph* letters page wrote after it was reported that 40 mountaineers had passed by Englishman David Sharp as he lay dying 300 metres below the summit: 'Never again will I look upon Everest climbers as heroes, but as the antithesis of the Good Samaritan.' The full story of who might have done what to help Sharp will undoubtedly prove more complex and nuanced – a suitable subject for 'slow news'. But no amount of later detail is likely to dispel the impression that springtime on Everest has become a deadly farce.

Can anything be done to restore a sense of dignity to Everest, and to ourselves who are in a sense demeaned by what goes on there? Closing the mountain altogether is the ideal, along with dropping the colonialist name, leaving the mother goddess Miyo-Lungsangma to watch over her domain in peace. But we know that is a dream, and of itself a kind of colonialist solution. China isn't troubled by Westerners paying fistfuls of dollars to expire in highest Tibet while for Nepal the mountain is a cash cow, supporting a whole web of livelihoods. The vested interests stretch around the world, from commercial operators, gear manufacturers, sponsors and even charities, to mountain guides, with not a few AC members involved along the way.

So if the circus is to go on perhaps the best thing we can attempt is to instil a little of that old-fashioned virtue, the comradeship of the rope. This might be derided as the kind of unworldly exhortation you might expect from the Alpine Club, but in fact it is laid down in the Tyrol Declaration of 2002 (International Year of Mountains) under the stamp of the UIAA. One of the signatories was our then president, Doug Scott, who argues in this *AJ* that there can be no 'morality-free zone' on Everest.

The Tyrol document represents a kind of industry best practice – the sort of thing that might be cited in a court of law if a sick person had been abandoned on a mountainside. And regrettably Everest accidents have reached the courts. Scott and co declared: 'Helping someone in trouble has absolute priority over reaching goals we set for ourselves in the mountains. Saving a life or reducing damage to an injured person's health is far more valuable than the hardest of first ascents.'

Maybe expeditions, particularly commercial operations, could be pressured into signing up to the Tyrol principles in the same way that trekking and climbing agencies have come on board with commitments to better rates of pay and adequate clothing and shelter for porters? As a further incentive, Sherpas should be confident that if they rescue a stricken climber there is a formalised 'bounty' system in place, perhaps backed by insurance, guaranteeing payment commensurate with a summit bonus. Bounties and coercion are second best to simple human decency and nor, of course, will they make mountaineers seem any less insane in the eyes of Joe Public. On the latter, though, we are probably irredeemable.

But that's enough of Everest. This 111th volume of the *Alpine Journal* focuses on what we ourselves believe mountaineering to be about, with accounts of exploratory climbing, particularly in Tibet, and of three of the real stand-out achievements of 2005 – the Arrans and friends on Angel Falls, House and Anderson on Nanga Parbat's Rupal Face and the first, generally accepted, ascent of the north face of Cerro Torre, though Cesare Maestri still begs to differ. My heartfelt thanks to the correspondents who have made this 2006 *AJ* possible, and to my invaluable production editor, Johanna Merz, and assistant editors Paul Knott and Geoffrey Templeman.

Stephen Goodwin

Contents

Illustrations

Tibet

Jim Curran *Everest and the Rongbuk Glacier* 2005
Oil on canvas
Private collection

3. Kajaqiao, pronounced 'Chachacho', named for its likeness to hands raised in prayer. Fowler and Watts reached the summit via the west face and north-west ridge, prominent in this photo. (*Mick Fowler*)

MICK FOWLER

Through Permits and Powder

A first ascent of Kajaqiao

Chris Watts and I peered curiously out of the window of our hotel in Nagchu, a fair sized town at an uncomfortable altitude of about 4500m on the Tibetan plateau. The temperature hovered stubbornly below freezing and a dusting of snow blew around the courtyard. On the pavement a group of well-muffled yak herders with eye-catching fox fur hats leaned hard into the biting wind. It was 17 October, still a few months to go before winter. At 6447m, the summit of Kajaqiao, the mountain we had come to climb, was about 2000m higher than this. What would the conditions be like up there, we wondered?

Kajaqiao is situated in the Nyainqentanglha East range of mountains about two days' drive east of Lhasa. This is officially a closed part of Tibet and so numerous permits are required to secure access. Permits tend not to be issued until the last minute with the result that visits to this area entail a fair bit of pre-trip anxiety. In 2004, it was not until 17 hours before our flight was due to leave London that we finally had to acknowledge that we had failed on the bureaucratic challenge. But we sensed there was something very special here which would make it all worthwhile in the end. And so we persevered. By mid-2005 the China Tibet Mountaineering Association (CTMA) had secured permits from the police, army, local governor, Beijing bureaucrats and sundry others. Armed with nine separate permits we now looked out at the Nagchu street scene, waited for our liaison officer to return and kept our fingers crossed that no bureaucrat would stand in the way of our reaching the mountain of our dreams.

It was a photograph taken by the Japanese explorer Tamotsu (Tom) Nakamura that first gave Chris and me the irrepressible urge to visit this part of the world. Not only did the mountains look fantastic, but also the ethnic interest looked considerable. Adam Thomas and Phil Amos were amongst the select group of westerners who had been there before. Their enthusiasm and will to return was such that we readily decided to team up. And so, after a year and a half of bureaucratic challenges, the four of us, together with Jimi our liaison officer, and Tenzing from the CTMA, were on the way. In the meantime, Tom, in his characteristically helpful manner, had forwarded detailed maps and photographs taken by two Japanese reconnaissance expeditions.

The 250km of dirt track from Nagchu to the regional centre of Lhari was notable for wild scenery, yaks, and a new respect on my part for four-wheel drive vehicles. We passed mud hut villages, a few tents of nomads and several impressively large piles of beer bottles. After a full day's driving,

4. Kajaqiao (6447m) (*left*) and Manamcho (6264m) (*right*) in the Nyainqentanglha East, Tibet. (*Mick Fowler*)

5. Yak steak anyone? Pavement butcher's in Lhari, eastern Tibet. (*Mick Fowler*)

it was something of a surprise when the dirt track transformed to a concrete dual carriageway with street-lamps down the centre and lock-up shop units on either side. This continued for a mile or so and then stopped as suddenly as it had started. There was no doubt about it, the Chinese influence had well and truly come to Lhari. On the pavement a group of nomads with traditional wrap-around yak skin coats and red braids in their jet black hair were busy cutting up a yak with an axe. The head had been removed and hung forlornly on pristine metal railings. It seemed a fine symbol of two cultures in incongruous co-existence.

We had reason to believe that Lhari could be the bureaucratic crux. A Swiss team en route for Kajaqiao had been turned back here in 2004 and we could do little but keep our fingers crossed as a stern looking policeman peered closely at the variety of official permits Tenzing placed in front of him. The officer appeared mystified, but no matter, to our relief I left clutching a letter asking the headman of the local village to arrange for our equipment to be carried to our base camp. It seemed odd that a police letter was necessary effectively instructing the headman to help. However, it was explained to us that the lucrative business of collecting caterpillar fungus in the spring gave the local communities so much income that they might not be interested in portering for us without a little 'persuasion' from the authorities. The fungus is a popular Chinese aphrodisiac, as Dick Isherwood related in an account in last year's *AJ* of an attempt on Haizi Shan in Sichuan.

About 35km from Lhari, the village of Tatse sits on meadows above the beautiful Yi'ong Tsangpo river. It has a population of about 40 and is dominated by an immaculately kept monastery. The locals remembered the Japanese reconnaissance trips and also a Japanese attempt on Kajaqiao. The younger people in particular were friendly and very interested in what we were planning to do. They told us that Kajaqiao is pronounced 'Chachacho' and that the mountain is named after its likeness to hands drawn together in prayer. An elderly woman expressed concern that it would snow forever if anyone ever stood on the summit but the younger occupants were enthusiastic at the prospect of helping us. Since the introduction of motor vehicles, yaks and horses are rarely used for carrying and it was decided that portering would be best.

'I think 10 will be enough,' announced Tenzing.

We looked around at the enormous amount of gear that Tenzing and Jimi had brought. There were at least three huge gas cylinders, a massive marquee-style tent, several large yak steaks, crates of beer…and on it went. Ten porters seemed ridiculously inadequate. Tenzing clearly registered the look of concern on our faces.

'We will have base camp here,' he reassured us pointing to the meadows next to the river.

This was all very curious. With security in mind we had specifically clarified that Tenzing and Jimi would be staying at our base camp.

Something had clearly been lost in translation but there wasn't much we could do about it now. CTMA policy, it seemed, was to have base camp at the roadside wherever possible.

The porters arrived on motorbikes, which was something of a first in my experience. The first part of the walk-in then involved a mile or two of them roaring away on their bikes with us trailing far behind. After six hours or so we had arrived at the site of the base camp used by the Japanese. The only evidence of their passing was a couple of rudimentary tent platforms that we gratefully occupied. The porters had been excellent and, as our heads throbbed painfully at the 4800m altitude, we were more than grateful for the help they gave us to build a kitchen shelter.

We awoke to some 25cm of snow. It was considerably colder than we expected, to the extent that the eggs that the porters had caringly carried had frozen solid – and were to stay that way for the duration.

Our acclimatisation explorations revealed the head of the valley to be dominated by two mountains: Kajaqiao at 6447m and Manamcho at 6264m. Both looked inspirational but seriously snow-plastered. The amount of snow was a real concern. The initial 25cm dump had been added to regularly and by the time we were ready to attempt an ascent a metre of new snow must have fallen. This wouldn't have been so bad with plenty of freeze and thaw but with the temperature continually below freezing the snow simply accumulated as deep powder. We had not brought snowshoes with the result that travelling around was absolutely knackering.

Bad weather and deep snow slowed us to such an extent that it took two days of heavy panting to get from base camp to the foot of our chosen line at about 5300m. Clouds had prevented us from getting a good view while we were acclimatising but now we could see that the west face above us sported a series of left-trending shallow couloirs leading up to the crest of the north-west ridge. The overall angle was not too steep but it was difficult to judge the difficulties.

Our first bivouac on the face was a remarkably good find. Perched on the crest of a projecting rib of rounded slabs, I was surprised that we managed to cut a very comfortable tent-sized platform. The day had been an exhausting one, largely because of the vast amounts of soft snow that had accumulated on ramp lines on the lower part of the face. Technical wading, which is the best way I can describe it, is not my favourite style of climbing. But at least we were making progress and as the evening sun bathed us we relaxed in the tent and soaked up the view. And increasingly impressive it was too. The skyline to the west was opening up with a myriad of teeth-like unclimbed peaks whilst down below we could see Adam and Phil as tiny dots moving almost imperceptibly across the huge expanse of snow and ice bordering the west side of Kajaqiao and Manamcho. They looked very small and insignificant against such a vast and majestic backdrop.

Above it was steeper, which was good in that the deep snow that had plagued us so far would not stick. The problem, though, was that easy-looking sections were in fact granite slabs covered with a thick dusting of powder. Our day proceeded cautiously. It wasn't that there was anything particularly difficult but it all felt horribly precarious and insecure. At one point I was reduced to a gibbering 'watch me' call on ground on which we would have moved together if the snow had been nicely frozen. But this part of the world seemed not to be over endowed with nicely frozen snow. By dint of judicious route-finding the day progressed safely, if slowly, ending with an open bivouac on the left-bounding rib of the main couloir line.

'This is a crap bivouac ledge,' announced Chris emphatically.

We had already put a lot of effort into it but I had to admit Chris's comment was disturbingly apt. What had looked a promising possibility was ruined by an immovable block. There was nothing for it but to fashion a narrow nose-to-tail ledge out of a thin snow band. Fortunately the clouds that had swirled around for much of the day had lifted and a glorious evening had developed. We were even able to sit side by side with the stove hanging between us whilst we brewed up and endured our evening meal of Chinese baby powder and curious fruit flavoured sausages. This was one of two menu options, the other being noodles with flavouring sachet. Both were very light but sufficiently unappetising for us frequently to fail to finish our portions. On the bright side this meant that the food was lasting longer than we expected – which was very handy because all this grappling with powdery snow was taking longer than planned. Despite the discomfort factor being fairly high, we both snuggled down contentedly, soaking up the remarkable view and looking forward to a good night's sleep.

It was some hours later that I awoke with a start. I had been wrapped cosily in the tent fabric but now it was billowing around me like a huge sail and spindrift was blowing into my sleeping bag. Moving too hastily to rewrap myself resulted in my end of the ledge collapsing and me spending the rest of the night perched uncomfortably on the remains. Chris woke briefly to curse the spindrift runnel pouring directly onto his head before settling down and snoring loudly. By daybreak I had given him a good kicking on several occasions with no positive response. However he did feel he had not had a good night's sleep, which was comforting in a perverse sort of way.

Experience and determination are probably the two key factors that dictate success or failure in the greater ranges. With a bleak and windy dawn both were tested to the full and it was a hesitant and weary team that scrabbled and dithered over the best line. This sort of climbing is so difficult to grade and describe. To begin with it was similar to the insecure scrabbling of the day before. Above, though, we could see the angle increased slightly which could make things much more difficult. But mountains are nothing if not surprising; the steeper ground was closer to the windswept ridge and as the angle increased the snow conditions improved. We were able to move faster and by afternoon were enduring a character-building crosswind on the ridge. The choice was difficult. On the windward side the wind was fierce and the

6. Chris Watts on Kajaqiao's west face, day three, pitch four. (*Mick Fowler*)

7. Bivvi three, with unclimbed Manamcho beyond. (*Mick Fowler*)

ground technical whereas on the lee side excitingly steep powder snow presented its fair share of problems. We alternated uncomfortably, reaching an easing of the angle above a prominent sérac an hour or so before nightfall.

'Time for a snow-hole,' Chris shouted above the sound of the roaring wind.

Snow-holes have always distressed me. Perhaps it is because I have never had the time to dig out a nice spacious one, or perhaps I have latent claustrophobic tendencies which only surface when I am surrounded by snow on all sides. Chris, however, had such enthusiasm that I found myself reluctantly digging into the slope and going so far as to lie on my stomach and hug vast quantities of snow against my body in my efforts to clear out what I had dug. Inevitably snow ended up inside my clothing and I became damp. The calm atmosphere in the hole was encouraging. After an hour Chris pronounced it big enough, produced his sleeping mat and bag and settled down. I peered in. Length and width looked okay but the ceiling was flat and only about 40cm high. Hesitantly I decided to test my feelings before committing. It felt awful. A quick bit of experimenting revealed that even the weedy Fowler shoulders were broad enough to dislodge copious quantities of snow from the roof when I turned over. The snow tended to fall in my face and down my neck. I was beginning to feel really cold.

'No way. Sorry Chris. Can't do it.'

For me the last hour or so had been a complete waste of time and energy. I now felt a fast-rising need to arrange something safe for myself, otherwise it was all going to go horribly wrong. Chris, who somehow appeared very comfortable with the snow-hole, was very understanding. It was dark now and we struggled against the wind to erect the tent. After 15 minutes we sat in the flapping fabric together. The hastily stamped out snow platform was ludicrously uneven and the outer edge overhung the slope.

'Sorry Mick. Can't sleep here.'

And so, much as it might seem laughable, Chris ended up in the snow-hole and me outside in the tent. Fortunately the wind seemed to have dropped slightly, lessening my initial concerns about being blown away without Chris's weight.

There was one section of the tent ledge that was shaped like a small volcano and I curled myself around this in as comfortable a manner as possible. For a few hours all was well. Then, when I must have been half asleep, I had the awful sensation of my small volcano erupting and taking me into the air. All hell was let loose and my face was planted firmly into something hard and cold. This was a new experience for me. Fortunately I had a small torch around my neck, the light of which revealed that the tent was now upside down and the cold hard things against my face were the crossed poles that are normally at the top. My immediate urge was to escape from the claustrophobic fabric but there were a few things to be done first. For a start the wind was gusting wildly and jumping out only to watch the whole show blow away would not be clever. It was whilst I was putting my boots on that I came across Chris's inner boots. This was a worry. He must have put on only his outer boots to return to the snow-hole. But where was he now? Clearly the tent had been hit by a slide but what had happened to the snow-hole? If there was any problem he would certainly need his inner boots. Having located the entrance zip I stood on the tent fabric, cursed the phobias that had ended up with us sleeping apart and scoured the slope above me for signs of the hole. The narrow beam picked out nothing but flat, windswept snow. There was no sign at all of the two substantial entrances we had dug the evening before. Securing things as best I could I started to search for an entrance. I had only taken a few steps when a surprisingly loud and urgent shout stopped me in my tracks.

'Fowler! Fowler!'

And then, after contact had been renewed via a tiny hole:

'I'm stuck. Fucking well get me out of here.'

A section of the cave had collapsed leaving Chris disorientated and partially smothered. From outside it was easy to grab his extended hand and pull him to safety. But it turned my stomach just to look in at the partially collapsed low roof illuminated dimly by my headtorch beam. In the confusion Chris had been unable to find his headtorch. I could only imagine how terrifying it must have been milling around in the dark in such constricted circumstances, aware there could be further collapses and not knowing which direction the surface was in.

Together we retrieved items from the remains of the cave, dug out the tent, put it the right way up and squeezed inside. It was good to be together again. Checking everything took some time but, remarkably, nothing appeared to be lost or damaged. It was light by now and I was uncomfortably aware that the hours had slipped past quickly. The wind seemed stronger than ever, we were in the cloud and it was one of those situations where a negative decision could come all too easily. We decided to contemplate over a hot drink and half a chocolate bar. In the end we decided two drinks would be worthwhile but were unanimous from the start in recognising that there was nothing really wrong apart from frayed nerves and the weather. Onwards it would be.

The north (lee) side of the ridge was frighteningly steep, bottomless powder that appeared to defy gravity. This meant that we were forced onto a rocky crest that was technically challenging and outrageously windy. Nevertheless clearings in the cloud showed we were making progress. By mid-afternoon nearby Manamcho was below us. Some maps show Kajaqiao as 6447m and others as 6525m. Either way we knew we couldn't be too far off. At about 6300m my camera ran out of film. The wind and spindrift were such that changing the roll was out of the question. Fortunately, for the first time ever, I had packed a cheap, lightweight spare.

The final section to the base of the summit snow proved memorable. A shallow gully came up to the crest from the right-hand side and the far side of this was steep and technical mixed ground blasted by the full force of the

8. Chris Watts leading pitch four, day four, beset by the usual spindrift. (*Mick Fowler*)

wind-driven snow. It was with some relief that I completed this section and hung from a small but secure nut belay. Above me a snow overhang protected the summit snow/ice slope. We were nearly there.

'Your nose!' I screamed.

Chris had arrived at the belay and what I could see of him looked mystified at my concern. Goggles fully covered the top part of his face and his balaclava the bottom part. In between, though, his nose was fully exposed and sported a white patch the size of a small coin. Being engrossed in technical climbing in wild conditions, he had no idea that his nose had started to freeze. I had never seen anything like it before and could hardly believe it had happened so quickly. Dangerous combination this wind and cold. And with a fully exposed open slope above I feared that continuing could make matters worse. The thought of going down was even mentioned. But bodies are remarkable things. A protective layer, a few deep breaths through the nose and a healthily pink glow returned. Lesson learned. These conditions demanded great respect.

Our altimeter read 6500m as the slope started to ease off. The highest point was still six or seven metres above us but huge cornices were visible on the other side and we had that uncomfortable feeling that we were pretty close to the break point. It was 6.30pm. The skies had cleared a little on the final section and I had been looking forward to a glorious panoramic view. In fact, the views east and north were obscured by the cornice and those to north and west hampered by inconvenient clouds. And the wind still howled incessantly. My hopes for indulging in a photographic frenzy were dashed as I fought bravely to hold the camera still whilst taking shots I instinctively knew were destined to be blurred and unremarkable. After not very long at all we retreated to our last ice screw and abseiled into the gathering gloom.

It took an exciting bivouac followed by three days of abseiling, avalanche dodging and serious wading to rejoin Adam and Phil at base camp. They had reached about 5800m on Manamcho but had been stopped by the wild weather and low temperatures. But they were still smiling. Exciting mountains have that affect on people.

As for Chris and me; we felt great. Excess blubber had been used up and Kajaqiao, our objective of two years, was climbed. And with the cornice tip untouched we slept comfortably, content in the knowledge that the old lady in Tatse need not fear it would snow forever.

Summary: An account of the first ascent of Kajaqiao (6447m) in the Nyainqentanglha East range, Tibet, by Mick Fowler and Chris Watts in October/November 2005. The ascent took six days via the west face/north-west ridge and the descent three days by the same route.

ACKNOWLEDGEMENTS

Fowler and Watts would like to thank the Mount Everest Foundation, UK Sport, British Mountaineering Council, W L Gore Associates (Shipton/ Tilman Grant), The North Face, Black Diamond, Scarpa, MSR and Cascade Designs.

VICTOR SAUNDERS & JO CLEERE

Tsha Tung

And a lesson in trash clearance

I first saw Tsha Tung in December 2003. It was all Andy Parkin's fault. We had spent the previous winter, or at least several weeks of it, struggling up the Langtang glacier to Hagan's Col, where we completed a winter ascent of a minor summit while wondering at the vast and beautiful south face of Shisha Pangma. There was almost no wind and no clouds and though it was mid winter we thought that in these near perfect conditions Shisha Pangma looked inviting. The reality in the winter of 2003 was very different.

The summer base camp at 5400m (advance base camp of the 1982 south-east face expedition led by Doug Scott) was traversed by constant gale force winds, which destroyed our kitchen tent. We had to move the entire camp to the lee slope of the long ridge leading up to the mountain. Andy and I ground to a halt on the south face, crampons barely biting the bullet-proof ice, buffeted by the winds, teetering under the huge rucksack that alpine-style climbing in winter forces on you. We thought the chances of a fall had become greater than the chances of success in that season.

Before leaving we cleared away our base campsite; we have always made a point of leaving our campsites as clean as we found them. Waiting for the yaks to come we spent two days collecting tins and bottles from the summer campsites, and paid for the extra yaks to remove the rubbish. It seemed a pity to have to do that.

On the walk out I could not help noticing a peak that Nick Prescott's map in the 1984 edition of Doug Scott' *The Shishapangma Expedition* named as Gyaltsen Peak. The 2000 edition was revised to show the peak we were looking at as an outlier of Gyaltsen. Our Tibetan yak herder and camp assistant, Kesang Tsering, told us it was called Tsha Tung and, as far as anyone locally knew, unclimbed. It looked like a perfect objective for a short, semi-commercial trip (I believe the correct phrase is 'not-for-profit').

Later that winter I was guiding in Chamonix, when my client, Philip, said he would be interested in a trying something new but not too difficult in the Himalaya, and so the seed of the idea was formed. The group that eventually coalesced consisted of Philip, a human resources director for an engineering company; Vernon, a sociology lecturer at Stirling University; John, an urban regeneration consultant; and Josephine, a translator.

It was June 2005. Jo takes up the story:

'Our plan had been to trek from Shisha Pangma north-side base camp to the south-side base camp. The average altitude of our trek would have been around 5000m and we would have been sufficiently acclimatized to make an attempt on Tsha Tung, which is a fraction under 6000m. In the event, we were unable to hire yaks at the last village before the north-side base camp. We were told that the lack of rain in the spring had been hard for the yaks and the villagers and the herders didn't want to exhaust their animals on another expedition. The plateau in this part of Tibet is a barren and desolate place and the villagers rely on their yaks for food and transport. In addition, they are an important source of income during the climbing seasons on Shisha Pangma when they are used to carry loads.

So, after an exciting, and at times white-knuckle, three-day drive from Lhasa to the north-side base camp, we were in the 4x4 again on our way to Nyalam where we met Kesang Tsering. In 2003, when he and Victor had discussed the possibility of trekking from the north-side BC to the south-side BC, Kesang had described a way through used by yak herders. Moreover, there are great views of Tsha Tung from the top of the moraine above the Nyanang Phu Chu valley, which goes from Nyalam to the south face of Shisha Pangma.

In Nyalam there was an atmosphere of excitement and anticipation as we shared a hotel with a group of pilgrims on their way to Mount Kailash. The following morning we used yaks to carry loads up to our base camp at Drak Po Che (Smaug's Lair in *The Shishapangma Expedition*).

From our base the most logical route was the wide, snowy east ridge. We used a couple of donkeys to carry loads up to Camp 1, located in a beautiful hanging valley fed by a couple of streams. The following day we scrambled up loose boulders and rock for about 400m and then followed the rocky shelf and established Camp 2 at the snout of the glacier at 5135m. 19 June was to be summit day and involved climbing a broad glacial shelf, a short 100m ice-wall, a 700m glacial traverse and a fine summit pyramid. As the clouds drifted in and out we had the occasional glimpse of the fearsome-looking north face of Phurbi Chachi and a set of towers on its eastern end ('The Coolin Towers').

The descent was straightforward, retracing our ascent route. There was even some judicious glissading to ease tired legs. On 21 June we cleaned and tidied up around our base camp, bagged up our tins to be carried down by yak and took care to leave the camp as we found it.

We finished off our expedition with a trek up to the base camp below Shisha Pangma's south side where we were shocked to find huge amounts of rubbish left by recent winter expeditions. The piles of rubbish and debris were quite recent (winter 2004) and even included car batteries, which had been dumped next to the lake in the middle of the camp, together with large piles of plastic, unwanted gear and gas canisters. In our opinion, it is unacceptable to leave camps in such a state.'

9. and 10. Expedition calling cards. The rubbish which so disgusted Victor Saunders and his companions on their arrival at Shisha Pangma base camp. (*Victor Saunders*)

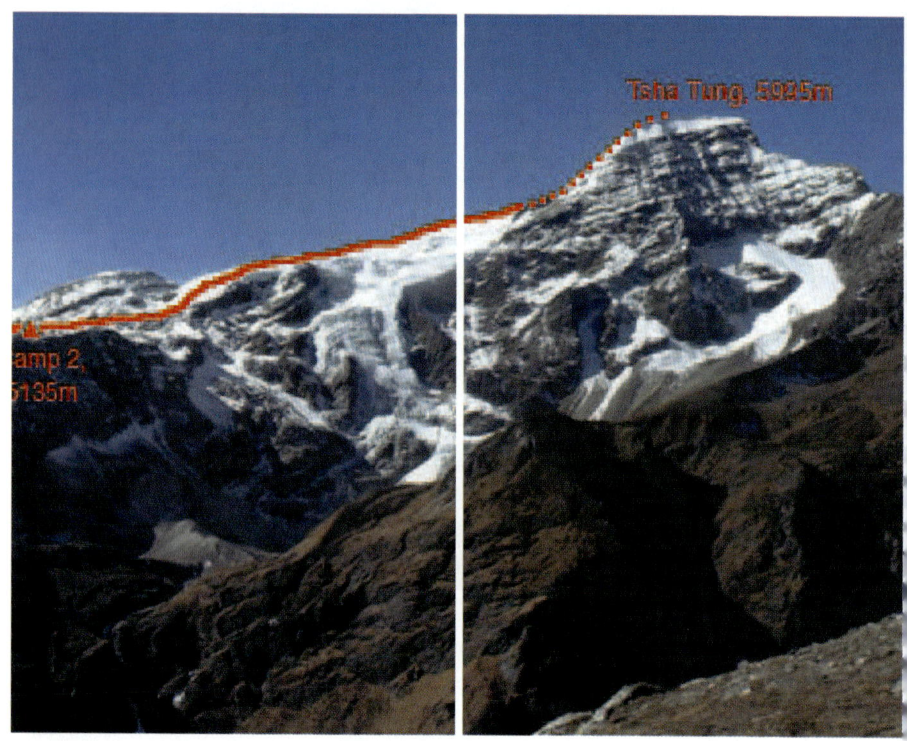

11. and 12. The east ridge of Tsha Tung (5995m), Shisha Pangma region. (*Victor Saunders*)

Jo is undoubtedly right. It is quite unacceptable. There has been a lot of informal discussion as to who is to blame for this execrable behaviour. American and Nordic expeditions are often contrasted (favourably) with other nationalities. Sometimes the blame is laid at the door of the growing commercial expedition industry but the more I visit the Himalaya the more I come to the opposite conclusion; that amateur expeditions often leave much more rubbish behind than commercial trips, possibly because commercial ventures have a vested interest in keeping their sites clean for future clients. On this campsite the most recent offenders left a calling card, a bleached yak skull set overlooking their midden. Theirs was not a commercial trip.

returned to Tangmai. Villagers told them of landslides in the Tralung valley on the left bank and the formation of the lake, as Bailey recounted in *No Passport to Tibet* (London 1957):

> Twelve year before, Tralung formed a dam higher up the valley and for three days ceased to flow. ... Those living in the valley below were frightened, because they knew that the water was building up behind the dam and the time would come when it would break through, and they went into hills to wait for it.
>
> On the third day in the afternoon the dam broke and rushed down the Tralung valley in a great avalanche of water, earth and rocks, which continued for one hour. Earth and stones were carried right across the Yigrong valley in a fan some two miles wide on the right bank of the river and 350 feet thick ... (On the left bank of Yigrong three villages and on the right bank two villages were buried.)
>
> Trouble did not end there. The mass of the avalanche lay across the Yigrong river and dammed it; and now the Yigrong river was stopped and began to form a lake which rose and covered many houses of Dre village and drowned many cattle and horses.
>
> For a month and three days the lake rose and then the top of the dam broke and the level of the lake fell. But even when we came there, the lake was still large, running up the valley for five or six miles, and at the point that we crossed it in the ferry it was 600 yards in width.
>
> This disaster must have been the one which Bentinck noted when in 1901 there were big floods in Abor Country and the bodies of strange people were found. ... Some of the people from the lake village had gone down to the Mishimi hills trying to make a new life there, but they had been forced to leave by the Mishimis.

In the rainy season of 2000, a large flood of water rushed down the river from Lake Yi'ong to the Po (and Yarlung) Tsangpo sweeping away both banks and destroying bridges. The water level of the Tsangpo Gorge suddenly rose about 60m and the disaster reached as far as Arunachal Pradesh (Assam) in India. The Sichuan-Tibet Highway was closed for a couple of months.

After Bailey and Morshead, came Kingdon-Ward in 1935. He was the first foreigner to complete the entire trek from Lake Yi'ong to Niwu. We were the second foreigners to have gone up the river from the lake. Kingdon-Ward reached Lake Yi'ong not via Tangmai, but by crossing a high pass, Sobhe La (4980m) from Dongjug. In those days there were only footpaths between Lake Yi'ong and Niwu, no horses could go up the trail and the journey took Kingdon-Ward two weeks on foot. He wrote in *Assam Adventure*: 'The gorge of Yigrong impressed me more even than that of the Tsangpo had done, perhaps because I had not expected such violent scenery.' (London 1942)

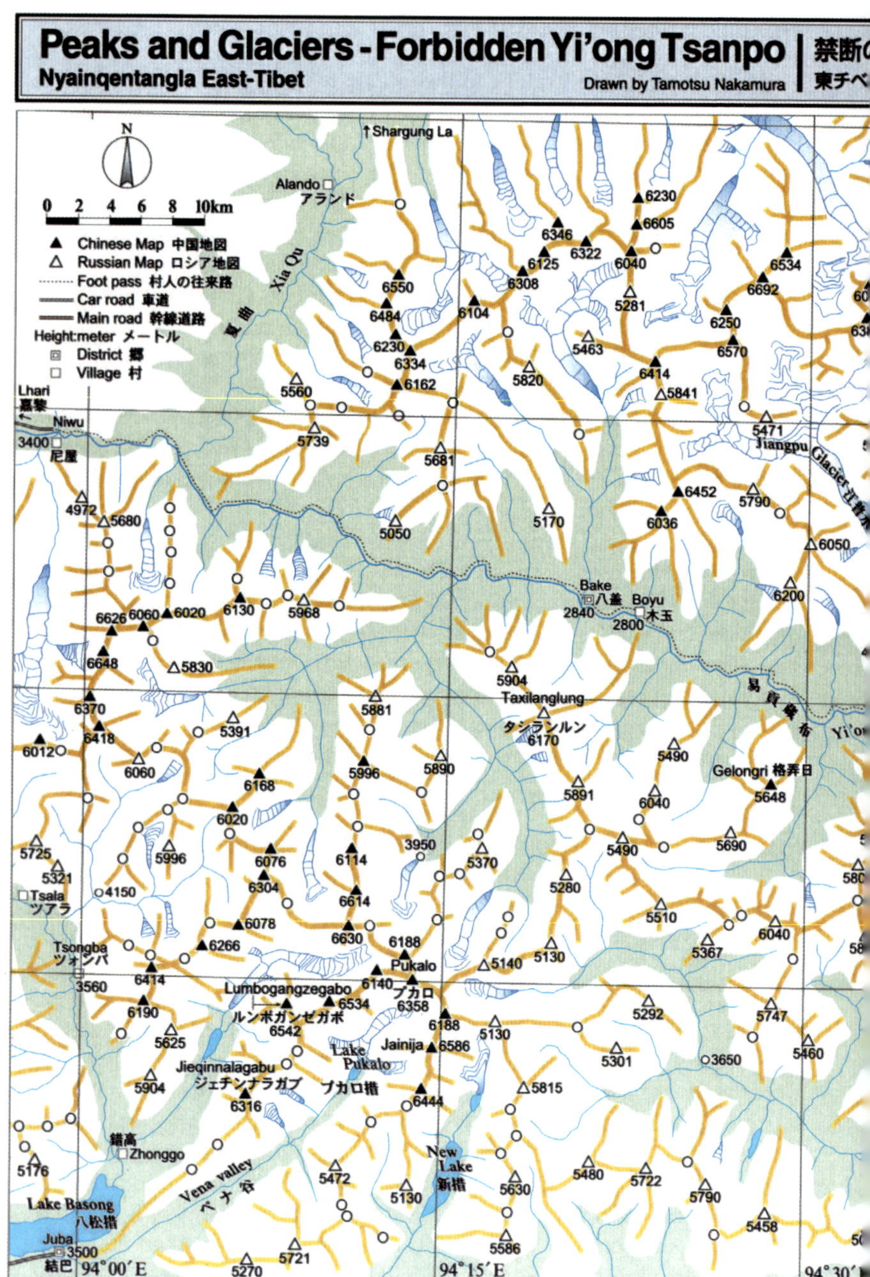
Peaks and Glaciers - Forbidden Yi'ong Tsanpo
Nyainqentangla East-Tibet
Drawn by Tamotsu Nakamura
N
0 2 4 6 8 10km
Chinese Map 中国地図
Russian Map ロシア地図
Foot pass 村人の往来路
Car road 車道
Main road 幹線道路
Height:meter メートル
District 郷
Village 村
Shargung La
Alando
アランド
Xia Qu
夏曲
Lhari
嘉黎
Niwu
3400
尼屋
6230
6605
6346
6322
6040
6125
6308
6534
6550
6484
6104
5281
6692
6250
6230
6334
5463
6570
6162
5820
6414
5560
5841
5739
5471
5681
Jiangpu
Glacier
4972
5680
6452
5790
5050
5170
6036
6050
Bake
八盖
2840
Boyu
木玉
2800
6200
6626
6060
6020
6130
5968
6648
5830
5904
Taxilanglung
タシランルン
6170
6370
5881
6418
5391
5490
易貢藏布
Yi'o
6012
6060
6168
5996
5890
Gelongri 格弄日
5648
5891
6040
6020
5725
5996
6076
6114
3950
5370
5490
5690
5321
6304
6614
5280
Tsala
ツアラ
4150
5510
6078
6630
6188
6040
Tsongba
ツォンバ
6266
Pukalo
5140
5130
5367
3560
6414
6140
Lumbogangzegabo
6534
ブカロ
6358
6190
ルンボガンゼガボ
6542
6188
5130
5292
5747
5625
Lake
Pukalo
Jainija
6586
5301
3650
5460
Jieqinnalagabu
ジェチンナラガブ
ブカロ措
5904
6316
6444
5815
错高
Zhonggo
New
Lake
新措
5176
Vena valley
ベナ谷
5472
5130
5630
5480
5722
5790
Lake Basong
八松措
5458
Juba
3500
結巴
5721
5270
5586
94°00′E
94°15′E
94°30′

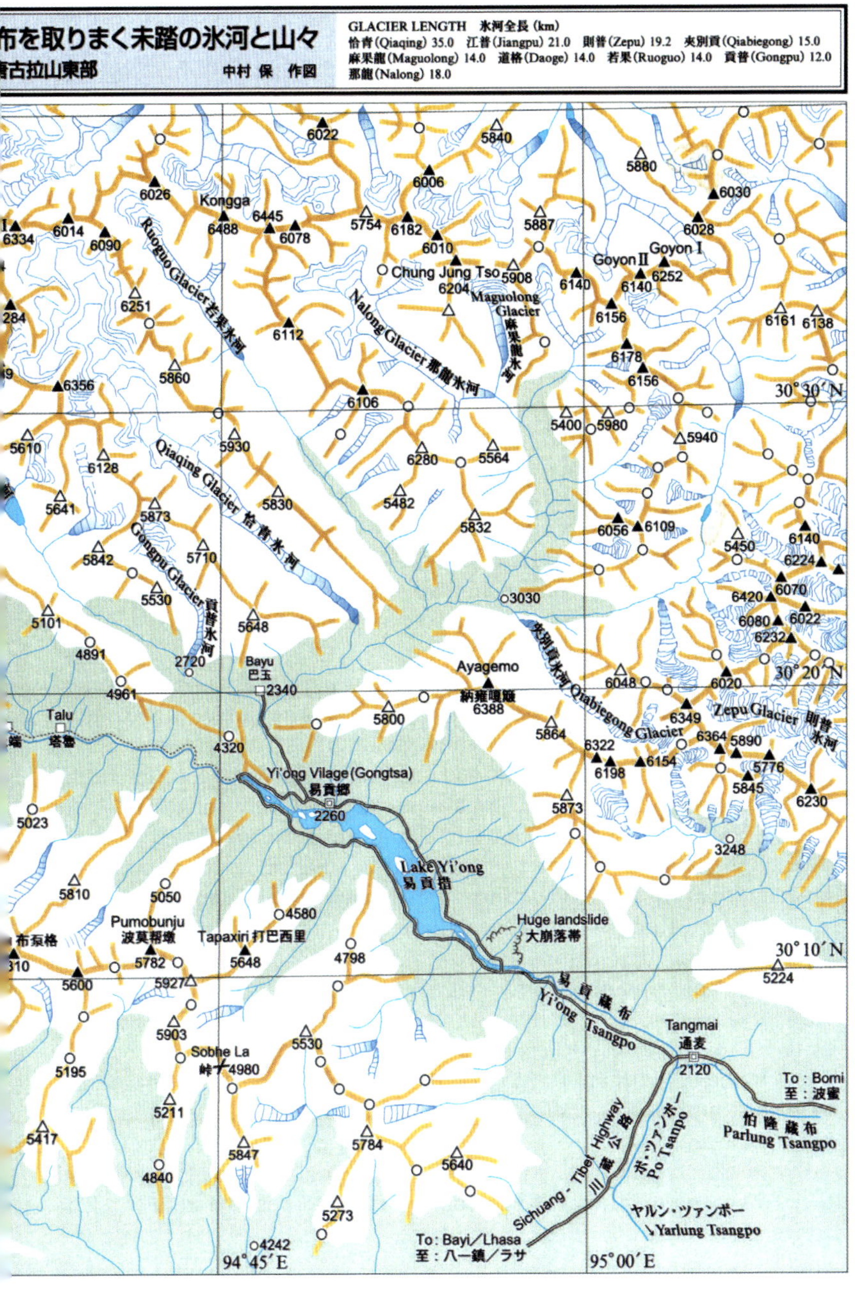
布を取りまく未踏の氷河と山々
古拉山東部
中村 保 作図
GLACIER LENGTH 氷河全長 (km)
恰青(Qiaqing) 35.0 江普(Jiangpu) 21.0 則普(Zepu) 19.2 夾別貢(Qiabiegong) 15.0
麻果龍(Maguolong) 14.0 道格(Daoge) 14.0 若果(Ruoguo) 14.0 貢普(Gongpu) 12.0
那龍(Nalong) 18.0
Kongga
6488
6445
6078
6022
6006
5840
5880
6030
6028
Goyon I
Goyon II
6252
6140
6334
6014
6090
6026
5754
6182
6010
5887
Chung Jung Tso
6204
5908
6140
Maguolong Glacier 麻果龍氷河
Ruoguo Glacier 若果氷河
Nalong Glacier 那龍氷河
6251
6112
6156
6178
6156
6161
6138
6356
5860
6106
5400
5980
5940
30°30′N
5610
6128
5930
6280
5564
Qiaqing Glacier 恰青氷河
5641
5873
5830
5482
5832
6056
6109
6140
5450
6224
Gongpu Glacier 貢普氷河
5842
5710
5530
3030
6420
6070
6080
6022
6232
5101
4891
2720
5648
Bayu
巴玉
2340
Ayagemo
納雍嘎暇
6388
夾別貢氷河 Qiabiegong Glacier
6048
6020
30°20′N
4961
5800
5864
6349
Zepu Glacier 則普氷河
Talu
塔魯
4320
6322
6198
6154
6364
5890
5776
5845
6230
Yi'ong Vilage (Gongtsa)
易貢郷
2260
5023
5873
3248
Lake Yi'ong
易貢措
5810
5050
4580
Pumobunju
波莫帮墩
Tapaxiri 打巴西里
Huge landslide
大崩落帯
5782
5648
4798
30°10′N
5600
5927
5224
易貢藏布
Yi'ong Tsangpo
5903
Sobhe La
4980
5530
Tangmai
通麦
2120
To : Bomi
至 : 波蜜
5195
5211
帕隆藏布
Parlung Tsangpo
5417
5847
5784
5640
Sichuang - Tibet Highway
川藏公路
ポ・ツァンポー
Po Tsangpo
4840
5273
ヤルン・ツァンポー
Yarlung Tsangpo
4242
94°45′E
To: Bayi／Lhasa
至 : 八一鎮／ラサ
95°00′E

Kingdon-Ward did not continue up the main stream of the upper Yi'ong Tsangpo but chose a way up along the Niwu Qu to the Laqing La (5300m). This high pass leads to Punkar and to Nyangpu where the path joins Gya Lam (Old China road from Peking-Xian-Lhasa. At that time, due to lack of geographical information, Kingdon-Ward thought that the Niwu Qu was the main stream of the Yi'ong Tsangpo. A map attached to *Assam Adventure* does not show the true main stream, which actually goes up to Lhari, and the northern side of the Yi'ong Tsangpo is blank and glaciers not drawn. In the summer of 1947, Henry Elliot, who accompanied the plant hunter Frank Ludlow as a medical doctor, crossed the Laqing La and entered a village called Nyeto Sama in the middle stream of the Niwu Qu.

A Journey to the Forbidden Land

We set off from Lhasa heading eastwards on 26 October. The Sichuan-Tibet Highway is now paved up to near Tongjug, a one and a half day drive for us from the capital. We stayed overnight at Bayizhen (3070m), a modern city and the centre of the Nyinchi Prefecture, which administrates Kongbo, Bomi and Zayul regions. Early next afternoon we arrived at Tangmai where we gathered information about the road to Lake Yi'ong. East Tibet is developing very fast. When I first visited Tangmai in 1999 it was a deserted village with a couple of shabby houses. Now it is a hive of construction, changing to a modern town thanks to economic assistance from Guangdong Province.

Though fine weather had continued for three days in Lhasa, it had rained continuously for more than one week at Tangmai. The climate of the humid gorge country is more unstable and worse than the Tibetan high plateau. Last year the rainy season did not end until three weeks later than in normal years and caused frequent landslides across the road from Tangmai to Lake Yi'ong. We started from Tangmai at 2.30pm and drove on a bad road along the right bank of the Yi'ong Tsangpo. Our Land Cruiser was stopped by a landslide at 4pm. The road was partly buried under mud, stones and rocks and villagers were undertaking repairs. It was a really dreadful and dangerous point, but fortunately we managed to get past after a one and a half hour hold up and arrived at Gongtsa village (2260m) on the north bank of Lake Yi'ong, at about 7pm. It had taken more than four hours to drive 50km. Gongtsa is the centre of Yi'ong Xiang and became the base for our activities. Stationing ourselves at the hospital, we invited a village chief to supper in order to gather information and inquire about arranging for a horse caravan.

Our main objectives were to reach the largest glacier, the Qiaqing, and then to go up the lower Yi'ong Tsangpo as far as possible to Niwu. The conversation with the village chief went as follows:

Nakamura: Do you know if any foreigners have entered the Yi'ong Tsangpo? Are the trails easily passable?

Chief: Only one party of six Americans came and went to Ruoguo glacier, east of Qiaqing glacier, in 1922 or 1923 to recover the remains of an airplane which crashed into the glacier. Now it is difficult to go to Qiaqing glacier as all the bridges built for the Americans have fallen down and are not repaired yet and no horses can be used. But if you wish to approach the other large glacier, Daoge glacier, there is a mule path to a lake at the glacier end, which would take you three days by horse caravan. As for the path to Niwu, you may avail yourselves of horses to at least Bake, 70km away from here. It is better to ask the villagers for more details at Talu and Bake.

28 October, fine then cloudy. Rain stopped and blue sky appeared. To the south-west a gorgeous ice and snow peak was towering before us on the south bank. The villagers called it Tapaxiri (5648m). To its west was another beautiful snow peak, Pumobunju (5782m) or 'seven sisters', with a spiky rock and snow ridge descending sharply to the west. Behind these two mountains must be two nameless peaks of about 5900m, according to a Russian map.

A higher range of mountains rose close to the north-east shore of Lake Yi'ong. The most dominant peak was a holy mountain, Ayagemo (6388m), its challenging south face a sheer drop of rock and snow. The height gain from lake to summit is more than 4000m. South-east of Ayagemo was an outstanding pyramid of 6322m and peaks of 5864m and 6198m. Beyond lay further peaks and the Zepu glacier, feeding the Botoi Tsangpo north of Bomi town. On the north-east side of this range is the 15km-long Qiabiegong glacier.

Flowing into the western end of the lake from the north is a substantial tributary, formed by two streams that join near Bayu village, 10km from the lake. From here one valley runs north-west to the 14km-long Daoge glacier while eastwards lies the main valley, leading to an area where the largest glaciers, including the Qiaqing, are concentrated and many unknown 6000m peaks soar above the glacier heads.

Kingdon-Ward wrote: 'In fact the plain (of Lake Yi'ong) is fringed by ranges of snow mountains, the glaciers on the northern range being visible... Northwards I could see bare granite peaks, as well as a cluster of snow peaks. Towards the south-west was another group of stark peaks.'

29 October, fine then rain, 5°C at 8:30am. At 9am our caravan arrived, consisting of six horses and five muleteers. All the muleteers were Khambas, four young men and one old one. Each horse was owned by a farmer. The agreed hire price was RMB 80.00 per horse per day plus RMB 80.00 per muleteer per day. Compared with the other regions of East Tibet, Sichuan and Yunnan, the muleteers were of the worst nature – rude, greedy, lazy and vulgar. They were a source of annoyance to us during the entire caravan.

17. North face of breathtaking Tapaxiri (5648m) soaring south of Lake Yi'ong. (*Tamotsu Nakamura*)

18. South-west face of nameless peaks (c 5800m) north-west of Lake Yi'ong. (*Tamotsu Nakamura*)

19. South face of Ayagemo (6388m), highest peak in the area of Lake Yi'ong. (*Tamotsu Nakamura*)

20. North face of unidentified 5800m-6000m peaks south of Talu village. (*Tamotsu Nakamura*)

At 10am we left Gongtsa, bound for the Daoge glacier, arriving at noon at Bayu village, set amidst small pastures and barley fields. The main valley to the east of Bayu appeared wide and open, but the Daoge valley, which we followed, soon became narrow, a humid primeval forest, with dwarf prickly ivies, hardwood trees and conifers. We felt as if we were in a sub-tropical rain forest, where no sunlight reached the ground. Marshy trails were covered with moss on rocks and stones. Who could imagine that we were in Tibet? After camping in a narrow, damp, grassy place, we continued up the valley on the following day, but realized that the information gained from the village chief was incorrect. A muleteer told us that three days' trek was needed to reach the lake of Daoge glacier, and horses were unable to go further.

I twice fell from my horse when I became entwined in prickly ivies. These then stung me. It rained in the valley and snowed in the mountains. Constrained by time, we were forced to turn back midway between Bayu and the glacier, so as to prepare for the second stage of our journey. We had not even glimpsed the Daoge glacier. We arrived back at Gongtsa village on 31October. At the hospital a doctor measured our blood pressure and found no health problems at all.

Up the lower Yi'ong Tsangpo to Bake

1 November, rain, 8°C at 8.30am. At 10am we set forth on an eight-day journey with our caravan of seven horses and six muleteers. Soon after the west end of the plain, ahead of us was a high buttress. The trail along the left bank was not bad in general, but there were sections dangerous for horses so we had to take care. We had been ascending gradually ever since entering the gorge and marched now 100m above the river, which we could hardly see for bushes and trees. White water raged in rapids past the buttress. An officer at Bake village told us that over six years 20 horses had fallen down to the river and perished.

Regarding plants in the valley, it is appropriate to quote Kingdon-Ward's observations from *Assam Adventure*:

> Veteran trees were of great girth, but I could not distinguish what they were except a species of oak, and another beautiful tree with large compound leaves which may have been either Cedrela or Alianthus. The canopy was close, and the tangle of big vines, the wealth of moss and epiphytes, and the luxuriant undergrowth made identification, and even collecting, difficult. I think, however, that this semi-evergreen moist temperate forest was confined to a narrow belt lining the bottom of the gorge and that a few hundreds of feet up the cliff, one would come to more stereotyped forest with some dominant conifer, either hemlock or pine.

21. Caravan descending Yi'ong gorge near Talu. (*Tamotsu Nakamura*)

2. Local Tibetan people near Bake village (*Tamotsu Nakamura*)

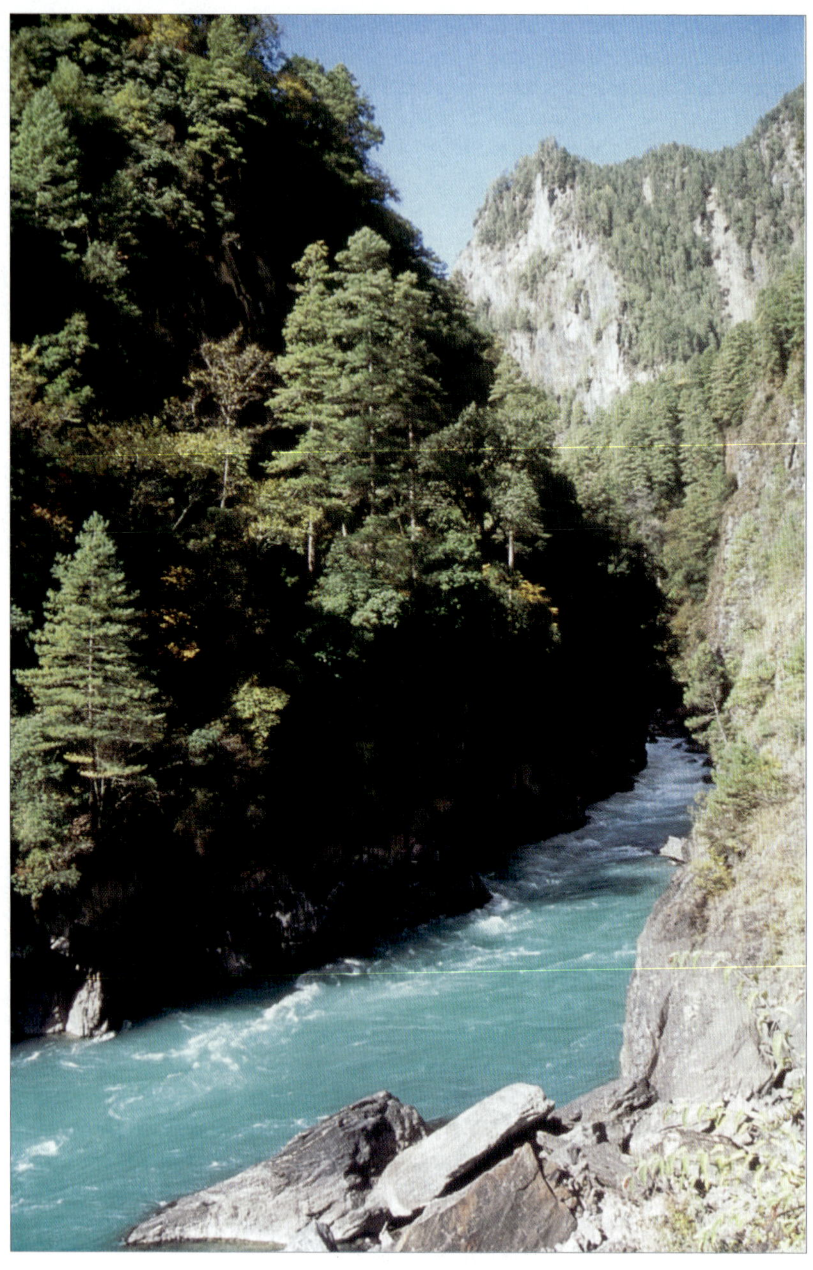

23. The beautiful Yi'ong Tsangpo flowing through a gorge near Talu village. (*Tamotsu Nakamura*)

It rained in the afternoon too. A short steep descent brought us close to the river, flowing here in a powerful torrent of stunning turquoise. At 6pm we arrived at Talu village (2575m) and stayed overnight in one room of a meetinghouse. It continued to rain until midnight. Talu is a village of medium size with a population of 200 in 31 families. Many villagers, adults and children, gathered at our room. We tried to collect information here too, particularly on the Jiangpu glacier, north-west of Talu. The river emanating from the Jiangpu flows into the Yi'ong Tsangpo close by the village. An aerial photo I have shows countless magnificent snow peaks at the head of the 21km-long glacier, the second largest in Nyainqentanglha East. However, our itinerary did not allow us to go to the glacier.

2 November, rain then cloudy, 6°C 8:30am. A guide with a horse joined our caravan from Talu. The trail became extremely muddy. All the villages are on the left bank of the river and no bridges to cross to the far bank were seen. The muleteers were lazy and wanted to take as much rest as possible and to march the minimum distance in a day. We took lunch at Ba village for two hours and camped at 2460m in late afternoon. Our guide Tashi got angry with the muleteers as the progress of the caravan was too slow. But they turned a deaf ear to his orders.

3 November, cloudy then fine, 5°C 8:30am. The trail remained muddy but the weather showed signs of improvement. Suddenly the west face of lofty peaks of 5700-5800m appeared beyond the right bank – nameless and challenging. The deep gorge ceased here and opened to a gentle stream flowing through pine and conifer forest. At 6pm we camped beneath large conifers at 2750m.

4 November, fine, 2°C at 8:30am. The Milky Way was seen very clearly in the night. As the sun rose, the east and north faces of Taxilanglung (6170m), south of Bake, were gradually unveiled. Pink changed to brilliant white. It was entrancing; a deeply satisfying moment for us old travellers. Soon after breaking camp at 9am, the north face of a shining peak (5891m), like a sugarloaf, came into sight on the right bank. We had lunch at Boyu village, where again many villagers gathered to see us. We were the first foreigners they had seen. At 4pm we arrived at Bake village (2840m), the destination of our 70km trek from Lake Yi'ong. I fell from my horse on the muddy trail and was injured.

Bake village is situated on a wide terrace above the Yi'ong Tsangpo at its confluence with a large tributary coming from the north. There is a sizeable glacier surrounded by 6000m peaks at the headwaters of the tributary. Farmers' houses are scattered in the fields and a lamasery stands at the southern end of the terrace. Almost all buildings along the lower Yi'ong Tsangpo are of wood construction.

Bake (population 192) is the centre of Bake Xiang District (total population 1,424) and has a local government office, hospital, primary school and some shops. We were the first foreigners seen in the village.

24. The north face of fascinating Taxilanglung (6170m) south of Bake village. (*Tamotsu Nakamura*)

Kingdon-Ward wrote very little about Bake village, which he called Shongy, but devoted more paragraphs to Ragoonka, west of Bake, as a centre of administration, agriculture and transportation.

There are plans to build a vehicle road from Lake Yi'ong to Bake. Construction is due to commence in a couple of years. Upriver, there are comings and goings of villagers between Bake village and Niwu. The journey takes four days on foot. Horses can go halfway from Bake, but cannot manage the trail along the formidable gorge near to the confluence with Xia Qu.

6 November, fine, 3°C at 8am. We set off from Bake and in three days arrived back at Gongtsa. The fine weather continued and on the way back to Lhasa we enjoyed a perfect view of Namcha Barwa (7782m) and the Gyala Peri massif from the Seti La (4500m). We also visited Lake Basong where the temperature recorded minus 6°C, a sign of winter to come.

ED DOUGLAS

Xiashe North Face

At the mess tent, Lenny is fussing around the stove, dressed in his bright red duvet. He looks up and smiles, his whole face crinkling with amusement.

'Hello, Eddy! Wan-som-teeee?' His voice rises with each superfluous vowel.

'Bless you, Lenny,' I say, and sit down at the table. Expedition life is *so* exhausting.

Lenny is a puckish figure, neat, energetic and full of surprises. As the sun dips from view, we cram into our mess tent to keep warm. The looming north face of Xiashe is zipped out of view for another evening and Lenny starts work on the evening meal. I ask him: 'What do you do in the winter, Lenny, when there are no expeditions?'

'I go swimming, in Chengdu. Is outdoor pool, yeah! I swim three kilometres every day. I do butterfly.' And his girlish laugh spills out, an octave higher.

'Butterfly?'

'Yeah, yeah, butterfly, I learn in a book.'

'You learned butterfly from a *book*?'

'Yeah, yeah, and I practise in my apart-a-ment, and then I go to pool, and I swim butterfly.'

'Show me.'

In front of us, Lenny transforms into a kind of vertical sea snake, writhing sinuously through imaginary green water. We applaud. (Later we make the mistake of teaching him our card game. He is expert at that rather quickly too.)

It was Lenny who brought Tamotsu Nakamura to the Zophu Pasture. They stayed at the old Nyingmapa monastery set above a turquoise lake filled with fat trout, beneath a series of granite towers. In the morning, Nakamura rose early and climbed a hill to view the mountains on the far side of the valley. Looking through his telephoto, he framed the north face of Xiashe, several miles distant, its bottom third lost behind an intervening ridge. Several weeks later, the image landed on my desk. I was editing the *Alpine Journal* at the time, and getting close to deadline. Most of Nakamura's shots were captivating, but this one was not. He simply hadn't got close enough. However, I had a half-page space to fill, and so Xiashe made the cut, tucked in at the last moment. After that, I completely forgot about it.

Towards the end of 2003 my friend Duncan Tunstall called me.

'Do you want to go to China?'

'Sure.'

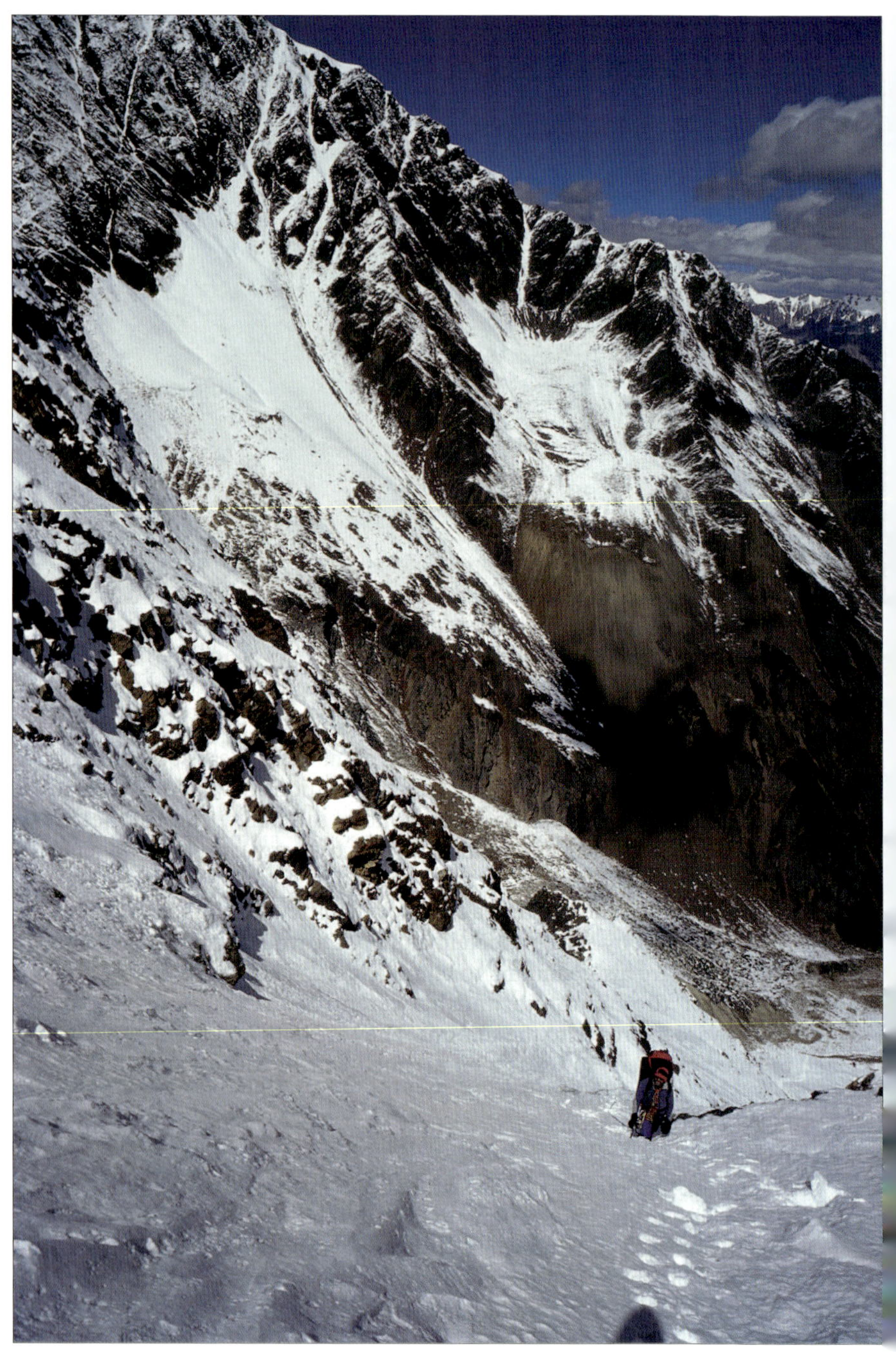

26. Day one, ascending the shallow gully on the face. (*Ed Douglas*)

But we'd come all this way, and so five minutes became ten, and the familiar landmarks started slipping behind us. Suddenly we'd turned right into the exquisite valley below the north face, forested with juniper and studded with flowers, even now, in late autumn.

By evening, we were putting up the tent on a precarious ridge of moraine beneath the long snow slope leading up to what we hoped was a straightforward gully. Then it was noodles, tea and wedging two farty old bodies into a very narrow single-skinned tent. Duncan set his alarm, and we fell asleep so successfully that its piercing beep was ignored utterly at five and we woke naturally at around 7am.

Luckily, the gully really was straightforward, rarely more than 50 degrees in fact, and for the rest of the day we made rapid progress on this expressway to the heart of the face. True, the snow was loose and often crappy, and the rubble beneath was often precariously close to the surface. But by 4pm we had turned the base of a spur that climbs towards the summit still 500m above our heads. On the other side of this spur was the steep continuation of our gully, and at its base we started hacking out a ledge for the tent.

It sounds impressive, writing it now, like something from a book, but then I remember getting out of breath and while moving a foot to improve my balance caught my front points on the tent fabric. I pitched forward, squashing the tent-poles almost flat. Hyperventilating wildly, I managed to save myself from plunging back down the gully. There was now a two-inch slit in the tent – Tom's tent, of course, who was, unknown to me, climbing along the ridge opposite Xiashe's north face, attempting a first ascent of his own. All night, spindrift hissed down the gully, slipping over and around the tent, squirting through the hole freshly made by my crampon points. Oh joy.

Still, we were optimistic in the morning. As the gully steepened, patches of ice and névé became more frequent. After a couple of hundred feet soloing on 60-degree ice, I took a belay and Duncan moved through into the lead. Close to the end of the rope he ground to a halt, and started rummaging around among the rocks on the left side of the gully. Duncan has developed an enthusiasm for difficult mixed climbing, so I found myself getting tetchy. Why couldn't he just keep ploughing up the white stuff?

When I follow, I understand why not. The snow and ice was now perilously thin and the rocks beneath worse than ever. I've never seen anything like it, some kind of red metamorphic crud that shattered and flaked at the slightest provocation. Duncan was hanging off a spike of this stuff, and suggested I continue up a short side gully that will bring us to the crest of the spur.

Almost immediately I find myself on desperate ground, scratching through the snow and fiddling in wires with shot nerves. The rucksack sags heavily as I thrash around, getting progressively more anxious and grumpy. I try to break back right into the main gully up the steep right bank, slotting my

27. Duncan Tunstall just above Camp 1. (*Ed Douglas*)

28. Duncan Tunstall leading on serious mixed ground on the evening of the second day. (*Ed Douglas*)

axe into a crack and torquing myself upwards, before talking myself down. This is insane. I lower off a wire tapped hard into a flaky crack with my fingers crossed. Duncan now launches straight up, and finds the going easier. Soon he has brushed clean a sequence of large holds to the spur's crest. I am required to follow the line of my original attempt to recover our precious and limited hardware. I find myself hooking blindly through the snow on ground more difficult than anything I've done for years. Oh God, I moan, I'm not sure I like this.

The crest proves reasonable for a pitch, but then I find myself torquing again on steepening, shattered rock, and this time without any solid gear. As far as I'm concerned, I want out and I say so. Duncan seems to have entered a world of beatific calm, however, and points out that as far as he's concerned it will be a lot easier to keep going than go back.

Suddenly, I realise, I've entered one of those stretched moments in time when you realise you are faced with a big and imminent decision that could affect you in ways that might be unexpected and painful. We are looking back at a closing door. I want to be on the other side of it, but I can see that Duncan doesn't. He really does want this climb more than I do, and for all kinds of reasons that I can fully understand. I guess he is just not seeing the world as I do right now.

29. Approaching the west ridge of Xiashe on the third day. (*Ed Douglas*)

30. Tunstall and Douglas relax in a thermal bath after the climb. (*Ed Douglas*)

31. Girls with a motorcycle, Xiashe base camp visitors. (*Ed Douglas*)

I realise that simply by not moving down I am now moving up again. I think very clearly about my family, and about being somewhere warm and safe, and then just shut them off. Duncan is stabbing his way across a steep, loose slope, and I am following, leading through, reaching a half-buried rognon of crumbling rock. I hack and chop away the loose stuff, and drape a sling over a flat spike. I can feel that rising bubble of fear in my chest, like heartburn.

'Just don't fall off,' I call down, but he just grunts and keeps slogging away. Two pitches later and we're climbing in the dark. And I am weeping with pain as frozen fingers suddenly recover sensation. It feels, I imagine, much like thrusting your hands into a tank of acid.

We are just three pitches short of the summit ridge, level with a huge sérac band that threatens the left-hand side of the face. Without discussion we start chopping a ledge in the cruddy snow and are rewarded by hard grey ice just below the surface. Feeling much happier, we bury every ice screw we have up to their hilts in the stuff and clip in. And then we sit, half on, half off the ledge, the stove propped between us, rubbing our knees and moaning occasionally in the cold.

Far below, leaving the mess tent for a piss, Lenny looks up and sees our headtorches. He smiles to himself and then shivers inside his duvet. Looks like they should make it. Climbers get up, or climbers don't get up – no matter, they still pay. But in the sunshine of early morning, I'm glad, for once, that it's me up there.

Summary: *Don't Cook Yak in Anger*, Xiashe north face (5833m). First ascent 13-17 October 2005 by Ed Douglas and Duncan Tunstall. Length: 1300m. Grade: TD+/75°/ Scottish IV/V.

Acknowledgements: Ed Douglas and Duncan Tunstall thank the Mount Everest Foundation and Berghaus for their support.

JULIE-ANN CLYMA & ROGER PAYNE

Chomolhari – One Perfect Day

The magnificent Chomolhari (7326m) was first climbed in 1937 by Freddy Spencer Chapman and Sherpa Pasang Dawa Lama. Chapman's team of five set off from Gangtok in Sikkim and in seven days walked to Phari on the plains of Tibet from where they carried out a reconnaissance of the south ridge. They found that the glacier and icefall that led to the ridge was impassable, so spent another four days making a detour into Bhutan and then continued on directly to make an alpine-style ascent of the mountain in just seven more days. The line of ascent started on the broad south-east spur and for the last few hundred metres merged with the exposed upper part of the south ridge.

Chomolhari received its second ascent in 1970 by a joint Bhutan-Indian military expedition led by Col 'Bull' Kumar. This team started in Bhutan and followed Chapman's route. The third ascent was in 1996 by a joint Japan-China expedition. This team climbed Chapman's impassable icefall to a col and then followed the south ridge to join the original route below the sharp crest of the summit ridge. The lack of activity on this notable summit is due to access restrictions on the Bhutanese side and the difficulty of access into Yadong County on the Tibetan side.

We first sought permission for an expedition to the north-west ridge of Chomolhari in 2002. After discussions with the Chinese Mountaineering Association, we got the necessary endorsement letter in 2003. However, at the last minute it was not possible to get the military permit to enter Yadong County. One year later, permission for the expedition was granted with the able assistance of Bikrum Pandey and Himalaya Expeditions in Nepal working with the China Tibet Mountaineering Association in Lhasa. Based on weather records and our experience of climbing in the east of Tibet the previous year, we decided to attempt the mountain in the spring when temperatures would be warmer, there would be more sun on the north-west ridge, and the winds (in theory) not so strong. We arrived in Lhasa on 6 April and spent three days there, meeting with CTMA staff, buying provisions, sightseeing, and waiting for local travel permits.

From Lhasa we travelled with Dawa Tsering, our Liaison Officer, by Land Cruiser to Gyantse (3950m) on 9 April. The route crossed the Kamba La (4794m), contoured around the massive Yamdrok Tso, and then crossed the Karo La (5045m) before dropping down to Gyantse. Much of the road was being improved, and the journey took nine hours. At Gyantse we met up with our cook Pemba who had travelled overland from Nepal, and the following day the whole team continued on to base camp.

32. Heading south from Gala you get a jaw-dropping view of the north face and north-west ridge of Chomolhari. The skyline ridge on the left marks the border with Bhutan. (*Roger Payne*)

On the map the distance from Gyantse to Chomolhari looked almost as long as the distance from Lhasa to Gyantse, but the time taken was much shorter (5 hours). From Gyantse it was only one hour to the town of Kangma (4175m), soon after which we passed through an army checkpoint without problems. The road continued past the small town of Gala to the Gala Tso from where we had our first sight of Chomolhari. After a photo stop we continued to the village of Tuna, finally turning off the highway near a road-workers' shelter, about two kilometres before the Tang La (c4760m). Exactly 100 years earlier, this was the route taken by Francis Younghusband during the 'Lhasa Mission'. We were surprised to hear that Tibetans were celebrating Younghusband's 'mission'. More than once, we heard Tibetans regret that Younghusband had not stayed in Lhasa and developed a stronger British presence as a counterbalance to 'other interests'.

Despite the relative comfort, excellent cooking and friendly company at base camp the almost constant strong wind was an incentive to go exploring. The first reconnaissance was made directly above base camp in a valley leading towards the west face of Chomolhari. In bad weather, but mercifully out of the wind, we spent three days under the west face looking for prospective lines of ascent. The west face is directly above the glacier basin and is an imposing rock wall, but any prospective routes are threatened by the large, continuous band of ice cliffs that girdles the top third of the wall.

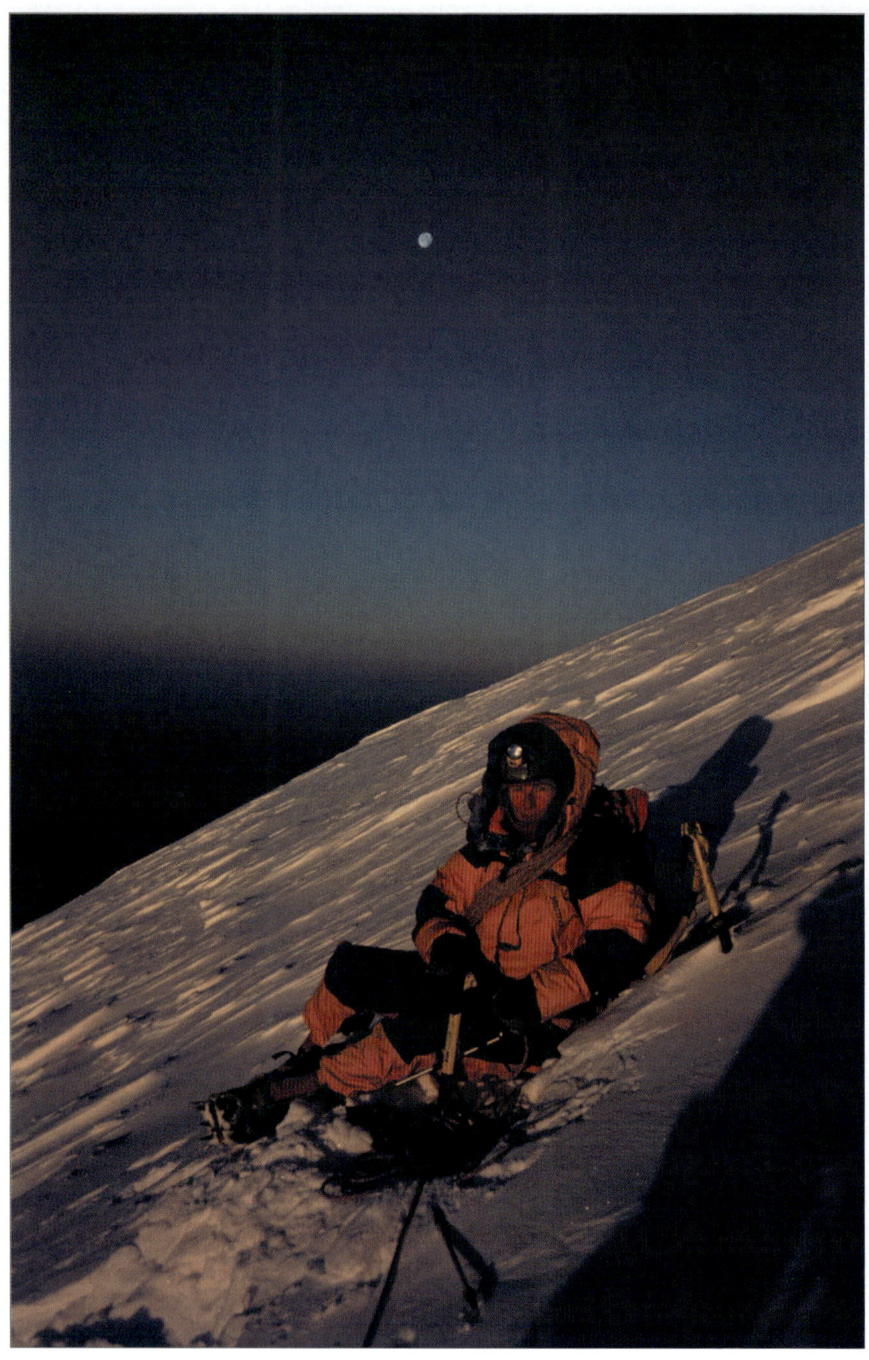

33. At the end of a long night of ascent Julie-Ann Clyma enjoys the first rays of a new day. The full moon above had lit the ascent of the south ridge. (*Roger Payne*)

On the right side of the face a ridge descends through the sérac band, and this would offer a feasible and challenging route to the summit. On the left side of the face is the north-west ridge, and from our vantage point a line of open gullies appeared to allow access onto the ridge at a distinctive boss of ice. However, closer inspection revealed that it was a series of stepped rock chimneys with a lot of very loose rock. We explored possible starts to the line, and concluded it would probably go, but it definitely would not be fun climbing the various wet and verglassed chockstones; and knocking rocks off would be inevitable.

Hoping that there might be more amenable access on the other side of the north-west ridge, we set out to explore the northern aspect of the mountain on 16 April. The face drops directly below the summit as a huge, slabby, granite wall covered in smears of ice. To the left are two spurs exiting onto the north ridge – either would give hard mixed climbs, but both have approaches threatened by séracs. One striking line is a huge ice couloir dropping from the summit beside the first spur. This is highly polished though, due to its being a major drainage line for spindrift whenever snow falls. On the main face the areas of ice are rather disjointed, but it is conceivable that the various ice smears and slabs could be linked together. Further left again and below the north ridge, the face is pure ice with many séracs, and any climbing there looked to be a combination of tedium and extreme danger.

Turning to the north-west ridge, our hopes of gaining the ice boss we had seen from the other side were dashed. Access to the boss was a steep hanging glacier covered in more impassable séracs. Scanning the bottom of the ridge through binoculars, a small fan of snow was seen at the base of the wall. Above was a slanting rock rib, which led to a snow basin that in turn led onto the north-west ridge. It seemed that there might be a hidden couloir that would give us access. Scrambling further up the ridge we were able to see into the bottom half of the couloir where there appeared to be good ice – but the middle section was blocked from view. We were encouraged that this looked much more feasible and appealing than the approach from the west side. Over the next two days we tried to climb a small peak (marked 5900m on the map) for acclimatisation, but were stopped by persistent snowfall and returned to base camp.

Having spent time looking at the north-west ridge from different vantage points (and assuming we could get onto it) it was clear that the crux of the route would be climbing a series of rock buttresses between 6500m and the summit. Once on this ground there looked to be little chance of tent platforms, and exposed bivouacs seemed likely. We estimated that the ridge would be likely to take 5-7 days to climb, and then there was a question of the descent. It would be possible to abseil back down the line of ascent, but an appealing alternative was to traverse the mountain and descend the south ridge by the route climbed in 1996. From a very brief description of this route by the Japan-China team, there was obviously a significant barrier in the form of the icefall near the start of the route. Having seen the ice conditions on the rest of the mountain we decided to go around to the south side to look at the descent and check whether the icefall was still passable.

We left base camp on 22 April and in three hours reached the valley where the Japan-China team had placed their base camp. We continued upward on moraine, and contoured around the left side of another enormous, frozen lake to reach the edge of the glacier and a camp at c5150m. The day had been cloudy and cold, and as we set up camp snow began to fall. It continued all night and through the next day, but we pressed on up the glacier until we could see the icefall. This was about 200m high, steep and very broken, and with very large séracs to either side. It was impossible to see a way through from our vantage point, but what was obvious was the threat posed by the séracs on both sides of the icefall and the frequent avalanches we were witnessing. Not wanting to proceed in such poor conditions and visibility we camped at c5300m, hoping for a better view the next day. Unfortunately the bad weather continued, so we left a small amount of food and returned to base camp.

Having looked at all the options we decided to try the north-west ridge from the north side, and set out from base camp on the 27 April. It was not an auspicious start as there had been snowfall overnight and the day remained cloudy and cold with the occasional snow flurry. We camped beside the holy lake at c5100m and hoped for an improvement. The following day we had a late start, first drying out the tent and sleeping bags before setting off at midday to traverse around the right side of the lake. From the lake we struck up a grassy ramp running under a rock wall, which took us easily into the moraine at the edge of the glacier. The first section of the glacier was straightforward, but by late afternoon we had reached a very broken section. With the sun now beating down we decided to stop and camp at c5430m.

Next morning we had expected to be starting the couloir, but waking at 4am we had more snow and no visibility, so went back to sleep. The bad weather continued, so we decided to finish the route across the glacier and camp again to the side of the start of the couloir. In the odd clearing and between spindrift avalanches we could see good névé leading into the first part of the couloir, although this seemed to run out among huge rock walls at the top.

The next day, 30 April, dawned clear and cold. We set off moving together in the first part of the couloir for around three rope lengths and then pitched another four rope lengths on good snow and ice, with occasional rock runners in the sidewalls. We were completely sheltered in the couloir, but strong winds were evidently blowing up high. We could see great plumes of spindrift streaming off the ridge and periodically great cascades would pour down the sidewalls and into the gully. The couloir petered out, and we were forced to traverse rightwards onto a mixed buttress. Two awkward

34. The north face and north-west ridge of Chomolhari. The crest of the ridge was very exposed to strong winds. (*Roger Payne*)

35. Roger Payne looks towards the 'impassable' icefall and the threatening séracs that have to be passed to reach the col at the start of the south ridge. (*Roger Payne*)

36. Julie-Ann Clyma crossing Spencer Chapman's knife-edge ridge. (*Roger Payne*)

pitches took us around the nose of the buttress, but then to our great relief we could see the route to the crest of the north-west ridge. Two more excellent pitches on easy mixed ground led to a shallow snow spur dropping from the ridge. This was the perfect campsite (c5900m) – flat enough to dig a platform for the tent and completely sheltered from the prevailing wind. Feeling really pleased with our route-finding, and amazed at the good climbing conditions, we settled in for the night.

May Day dawned clear and sunny, and, at our campsite, quite calm. Unfortunately, strong winds were still very evident above. We climbed onto the ridge and immediately felt its full force. From 6000m to around 6500m the ridge is a gradually steepening ice crest. The climbing initially was straightforward, but the ropes blew in a great arc and it was almost impossible to stay upright in the gusts. While the wind speed was strong at our altitude, it was clearly even stronger above. Faced with difficult climbing above, and the likelihood of an open bivouac, it did not seem wise to continue in such winds. After only about 100m we decided to return to our campsite. We woke on the 2nd to another perfectly clear day, but the same strong winds. Technical climbing on the ridge would simply be impossible and exposed bivouacs extremely perilous, so there was no point trying to go up. We had already lost time to bad weather and sitting out another day would mean that we were beyond the point of having enough food and fuel to complete the climb. Feeling very despondent we abseiled back down the buttress and returned to base camp where we took a rest day and considered our options. We had only five days left before our transport was due to collect us, so we did not have enough time for another attempt on the north-west ridge. However, the sun continued to shine, and finding it impossible to sit at base camp to wait for the jeeps to arrive, we decided to try another quick foray to the south side of the mountain to take a closer look at the icefall and séracs below the south ridge.

On 4 May we retraced our steps to the glacier under the icefall and on the 5th spent a fraught morning working our way up the centre of the icefall. We were forced out to the left to make a quick dash up the slopes under the smaller sérac barrier. This led to long but easy slopes to the south col at around 5800m. Our luck was no better here though, as the snow started to fall in the afternoon and a ferocious storm blew up in the night. In the early hours of the 6th we abandoned attempts to sleep and got fully dressed fearing that the tent could not withstand the constant battering. It did, thankfully, and a tedious day was spent until the storm abated in the late afternoon.

By now we were resigned to descending the icefall the next morning to arrive at base camp one day before the transport. But at nightfall a much-needed miracle occurred – the noise of the wind on the ridges died, at the col it was a gentle breeze, the skies had cleared, and the full moon was up illuminating our side of the mountain. This was not just our last chance for the summit, but also our last chance to do anything. We set off at 1.30am on 7 May.

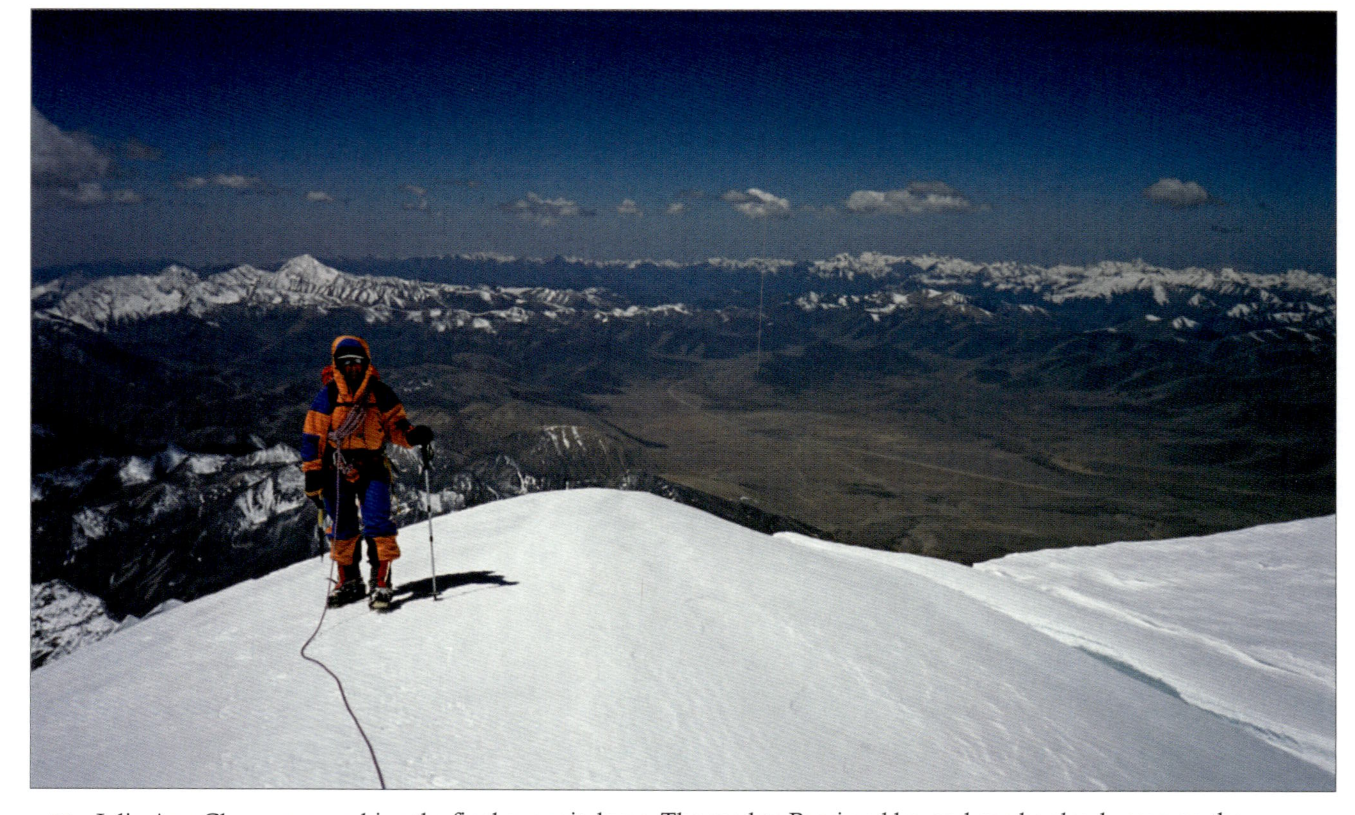

37. Julie-Ann Clyma approaching the final summit dome. The road to Pagri and beyond can be clearly seen on the distinct 'tongue' of the Tibetan plateau heading south; to the left is Bhutan, to the right Sikkim. (*Roger Payne*)

The sérac band above the col was the first obstacle. It was not particularly difficult, but finding a way through in the darkness was quite uncertain. However, once through we were on the ridge and the route above was obvious. Moving together we covered ground quickly. It was bitterly cold, and some large sections on the lower slopes were hollow windslab that echoed scarily under our feet. By sunrise we were on safer ground, the ridge narrowing to a most spectacular knife-edge (Chapman and Pasang Dawa had crossed this ridge without crampons). Looking down into Bhutan we could clearly see the line of the first ascent up a broad south-east spur. The knife-edge ran out into final gentler slopes where we took a good rest, then reached the summit just before midday. In contrast to all other days on the expedition, it was totally calm.

We spent half an hour on the top taking photos of peaks in Bhutan, Sikkim and Tibet, and left a small tribute with a prayer flag to honour the Buddhist faith and the mountain gods. Descending, we took an easier line in the upper section, following a large glacial shelf, then picked up our tracks to go back through the sérac barrier and down to the south col, reaching there at 5pm. Having been up and down the south ridge we now realised that our plan to make an on-sight descent after attempting the north-west ridge was extremely optimistic. Finding the route down to the south col was complex and we would have been likely to descend too low on the Bhutan side.

Next morning (8 April) we left the south col at 5am, bypassed most of the icefall by a nerve-racking descent of a large avalanche cone below the séracs and arrived back at base camp at 10.30 just after the Land Cruisers arrived. Everything was quickly thrown into duffels for an immediate departure and by early evening we found ourselves back in a hotel in Gyantse. The rapid transition in just over 24 hours from being on a summit at more than 7000m, to sitting in a restaurant drinking beer, was most bizarre but extremely satisfying. We had been very lucky.

Summary: An account of the exploration of the west and north aspects of Chomolhari, Yadong County, Tibet, and the first attempt on the north-west ridge by Julie-Ann Clyma and Roger Payne. The ridge was exposed to near constant strong winds, making technical climbing impossible and forcing a retreat from around 6000m. With a few days remaining, the pair moved around to the south ridge, which they climbed in one day from a camp at 5800m. The only previous ascent of the south ridge was by a China-Japan team in 1996 using fixed ropes and camps. At around 7000m the south ridge connects with the historic Spencer Chapman route of 1937.

Acknowledgements: Julie-Ann Clyma and Roger Payne would like to thank the Mount Everest Foundation, BMC and UK Sport for their support. Equipment was kindly provided by Lyon Equipment (Beal, Petzl-Charlet), Macpac, Oudoor Designs, Rab, HB and Kayland.

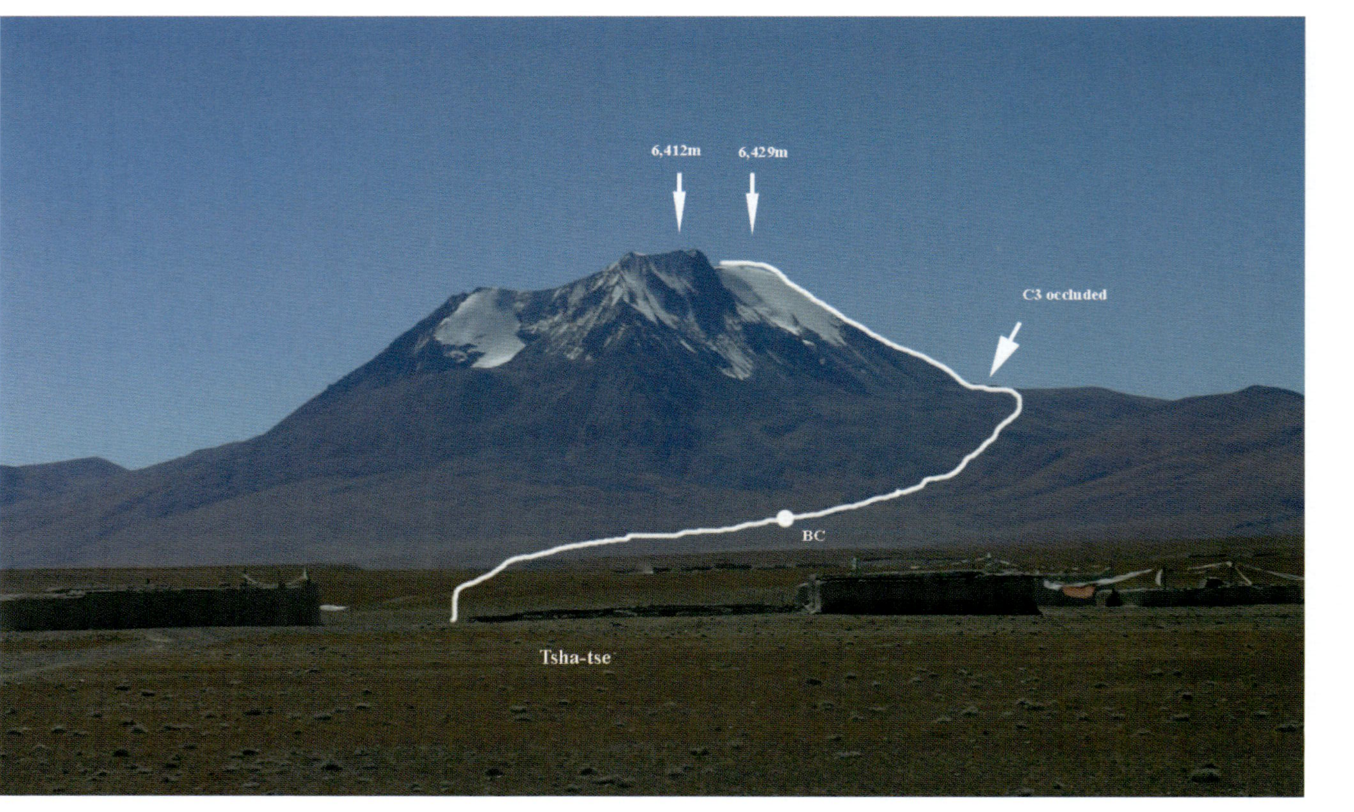

38. Dobzebo, north summit (*left*) and south summit (*right*) from Tsha-Tse, showing camps. (*Al Scott*)

MARTIN SCOTT & DEREK BUCKLE

Dobzebo and the Battle of the Mountains

Near the centre of the Transhimalaya are two mountains that once fought a battle. According to legend, Dobzebo fired an arrow striking Targo's knee, leaving a scar on the lower slopes still clearly visible today. In retaliation, Targo returned an arrow that struck Dobzebo in the stomach; though where the scar is on the mountain today is not obvious, unless perhaps it is the cirque that makes up the north face.

The central Transhimalaya of Tibet has many unclimbed peaks and after studying maps, satellite photos and books our team of four focused on an area south of lake Dangra Yutso that seemed to have been rarely visited. Further study and conversations with Julian Freeman-Attwood, who knows the area well (*AJ 108*, 103, 2003), led us to choose Dobzebo as our primary target with some peaks to the north, collectively called Lungmari, as a secondary objective. There was the additional attraction of visiting a Bon monastery shown on our map on the shores of Dangra Yutso.

Having entered Tibet via Kathmandu and the Friendship Highway on our last trip, we chose this time to fly to Lhasa via Beijing, mainly to save time and to avoid complications caused by the Maoist insurgency in Nepal. In Lhasa, as well as acclimatising, we again experienced the mysterious world of the Tibetan Mountaineering Association and the process of acquiring the necessary permits. We took this seriously as last year more than one party had been refused access at the last moment. We also stocked up on food, gas canisters and sundry items. Thanks to Mig Ma, our excellent support organiser, we left after two days with the required seven permits to get us past all bureaucratic and army check points.

The main road west being under reconstruction, we took the alternative dirt road to Shigatse, in fact a more attractive and interesting route. At Shigatse we met up with our Dong Feng truck, transferred our supplies and were at full complement with Lotta our truck driver, Dawa our interpreter, Kusang our cook, and our Land Cruiser driver, Quangming, a Tibetan despite his Chinese name (meaning 'the light'). Having arrived earlier than expected we were able to visit Tashilhunpo monastery, one of the very few to weather the storm of the Cultural Revolution, albeit with far fewer monks. The night was spent in unaccustomed comfort in a Chinese-style tourist hotel.

We next headed further west along a dirt road to the small town of Sangsang where, by contrast, we slept in a very un-Chinese traditional Tibetan guesthouse. Despite its attractiveness, the yak dung stove was unlit and our room was very cold. Characteristically, the yard functioned as the toilet, but the view was memorable.

39. Dobzebo north from Dobzebo south-west with lake Zuru Tso and the Targo range in the distance. (*Al Scott*)

Next morning we turned north off the main east-west road along tracks leading to Dobzebo. It was here that our earlier research, particularly with satellite photos available from the internet, and Julian's advice, paid off. We were now in typical Tibetan countryside with nomads in yak skin tents tending large herds of sheep. As we went higher and the land became more arid, sheep gave way to yaks and increasingly we saw kyang (wild asses), gazelles and other wild animals.

The weather continued fine with generally cloudless skies. We jostled in the Land Cruiser for the best photo opportunities, particularly of wild animals and the mountains. From the first major col at 5300m we could see south as far as the Nepalese frontier and were even able to identify Everest in the distance. Travelling further north, then west over a higher col at 5540m, we caught our first glimpse of Dobzebo in the distance before continuing down to Tsha-tse, the village just under its north face.

From Tsha-tse we headed back south past the old village and some hot springs, which we noted for a possible bath later. Beyond a small monastery we entered a valley immediately south-east of Dobzebo. Here the track petered out, forcing us to drive either up the riverbed or over a boulder field. Lotta seemed oblivious to the problems while Quangming was more cautious with the Land Cruiser. Unfortunately even his caution could not prevent the inevitable and eventually, at 5120m, we ground to an ignominious halt with ominous noises emanating from the rear axle. With the diagnosis a broken rear half-shaft, things were not looking too good. While the non-mechanically minded camped, the ever inventive Quangming and Lotta devised a number of plans, one of which was to hoist the stricken Land Cruiser onto the lorry. However by disconnecting the rear axle it proved possible to limp along on front wheel drive alone. Nonetheless this was base camp, as far as normal vehicles were likely to get, and further than most were likely to venture. We were close to the river, at a reasonable height, but unfortunately a long way from where we wanted to be.

The first thing that we noticed about Dobzebo, apart from how impressive it looked, was how much higher the snowline was than we had expected from earlier trips to Tibet. Indeed it was much higher than when we passed some 80km to the west at a similar time last year. Moreover, at first sight there seemed to be no water between BC and the snowline around 6000m.

A reconnaissance next day to the west of BC showed a possible route up the south glacier, but no easy route round to the south-west ridge, our preferred line of ascent. Further reconnaissance to the south the following day reinforced this initial impression and confirmed that the two major tops identified from maps and satellite pictures were of comparable height.

On 4 October we advanced to a sandy campsite nestling at 5690m in the complex moraine beneath the south face. Without animals, we were very fortunate that our support team volunteered to help with the loads since this allowed us to establish camp 1 in a single carry. Although this assistance was far more than we could reasonably expect, Kusang had similarly helped us in 2004 on Nganglong Kangri. This camp was ideal except for one small problem – water. We knew that there were several glacial pools nearby, but finding them among the undulations of the moraine was a challenge in itself. Moreover, it needed an ice-axe to get at and all our containers to bring sufficient volume back to camp.

The following day was spent identifying a viable route onto the glacier. Having found one more easily than anticipated, we made a partial carry before establishing Camp 2 high on the glacier at 6100m. Worryingly, Bill was suffering from incomplete acclimatisation and for a while it looked as though we might have to take him back down. Remarkably resilient, he rallied overnight but was not able to come with us as we set off for the north summit. Taking an impressive but relatively easy line above Camp 2 we climbed the south face on gradually steepening ground to a rock outcrop standing proud of the summit ridge. Moving westwards along a heavily corniced ridge we arrived at a steep wall immediately beneath the north summit. A short climb and we were there, at 6412m, just 2.5 hours after leaving camp.

The views were superb. To the north we could see across the plain, past Tsha-tse to the beautiful blue lake of Zuru Tso bordered by high mountains on the west. Further north was Dobzebo's enemy, Targo Ri, and the main Lungmari range. West and south, the crenellated ridge continued upwards

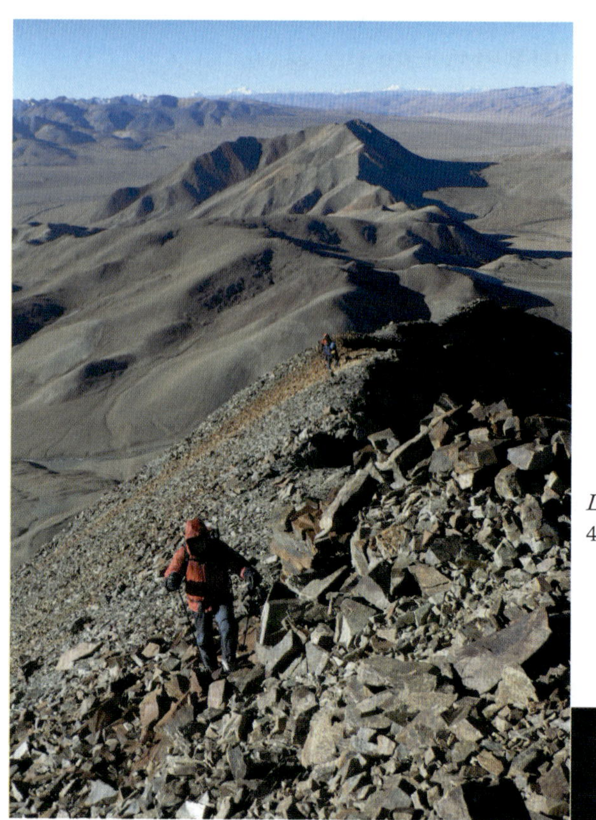

Left
40. Dobzebo, south ridge of south-west summit, with Cho Oyu, Everest and Makalu in the distance. (*Derek Buckle*)

Right
41. Al Scott on the headwall below the north summit of Dobzebo. (*Martin Scott*)

towards the dominant snow-covered south-west summit. A double cornice on this ridge leading to the main summit denied access from the north but, more importantly, meant that even climbing the snow couloir left of our ascent route would not provide easy access from camp 2. It was clear that we needed to relocate base camp nearer to the south-west ridge in order to have a realistic hope of reaching the main summit. Having dutifully photographed the Alpine Club banner that Peter Mallalieu requested we take with us, we rejoined a markedly enlivened Bill at camp 2 and the following day returned to BC.

Since the direct route from BC to the south-west ridge looked long, arduous and unpleasant we drove to Tsha-tse to seek advice. Here it was confirmed that no motorised access to the south of Dobzebo was possible, although a good footpath used by local yak herders led round from the north. On inquiring about horses we were taken to the headman's house where, perched on carpet-covered boxes around a standard issue yak dung stove, we sampled yak butter tea while discussions took place. The elderly headman was a memorable character, sitting cross-legged beneath a backdrop of former Dalai Lamas. His face, etched by the harsh Tibetan sun, resembled a gnarled ebony carving and he was simply clothed in traditional dress. Unhurriedly the negotiations proceeded as more tea was drunk. Eventually the hire of three horses was agreed, although we undoubtedly paid a generous price by local standards.

Having relocated BC to the valley north of Dobzebo, we set out next day following the horses and their minders, past the north summit and beneath spectacular steep granite cliffs that would make a fine objective for those more accomplished than ourselves. Further on we crossed a windy, cairned col before dropping to a lake at 5503m at the foot of the prominent south-west ridge where we located camp 3.

It was very clear and sunny, but the sun had little warmth. Camp 3 was a cold, dusty and windy place. Beyond here there appeared to be no water until the snowline, so we decided to make an early start and go for the top in one go; a height gain of more than 900m. Waking some four hours before dawn it was still very cold, but fortunately the wind had died down. We plodded up steep, boulder-strewn slopes in the dark, but apart from the effort at this altitude there was no technical difficulty. Shortly after daybreak we reached the crest of the broad ridge to be greeted by fantastic views south towards the Himalaya. It was minus 15°C, but felt a lot colder. Thankfully there was not much wind. As we walked and scrambled higher the broken ridge narrowed considerably before reaching the final icefield some 200m below the summit.

From here a heavily corniced arête led easily to the airy summit at 6429m. To the south Cho Oyu, Shisha Pangma and Everest were silhouetted on the horizon, while to the west was the prominent peak of Loimbo Kangri, and to the north the extensive Lungmari range. Closer to hand the complex ridge leading to the rocky middle top and then to the more distant north

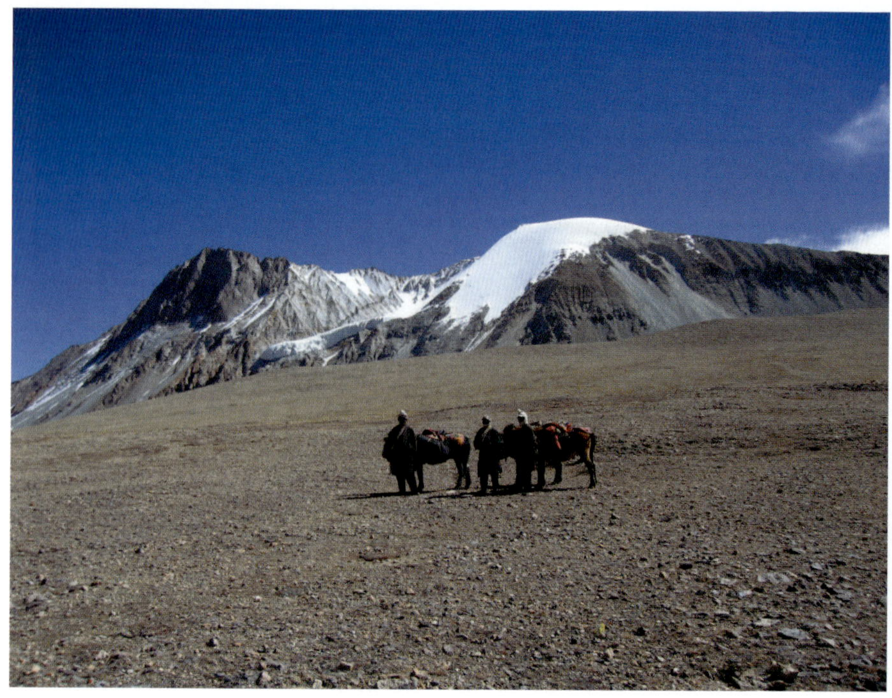

42. Hired horses moving our camp. In the background are Dobzebo north (*left*) and Dobzebo south-west summits. (*Martin Scott*)

summit that we had climbed earlier could be seen in detail. Prior analysis suggested that we were indeed at Dobzebo's highest point, but the middle top was certainly a close contender.

Since we had allowed ourselves more time than we had actually needed to reach the summit, we faced the prospect of another two days at the inhospitable camp 3 before our horses returned. Someone would have to return to BC to organise an earlier departure. Al and Derek, who were feeling fit, raced down ahead, exchanged their climbing gear for sleeping bags at the campsite and headed off in the late afternoon for BC. Bill and Martin (who was still recovering from a minor knee operation 10 weeks earlier) descended at a more leisurely pace. When the horses returned the next day they packed the camp and rejoined the others at BC.

With sufficient time still left to follow our plan to explore northwards, we drove past the village of Tsha-tse to Zuru Tso and took a good track on the east shore of the lake, passing under the impressive south face of Targo Ri with its famous scar. Continuing round to the east of the massif, it became possible to see the full extent of the Lungmari range running northwards. The map and satellite photos had led us to believe that these were relatively uninteresting, rounded peaks separated by a number of east-facing glaciers running down from intervening cols. In reality, the range was noticeably more impressive with varied climbing opportunities at a range of standards; all in all well worth another visit.

Our next objective was the Tershi Bon monastery, which was supposedly on the shores of Dangra Yutso. In fact it lies some 15km south of the lake on the west side of the valley nestling on the lower slopes of the principal peak of Lungmari.

Bon has its roots in the earliest religious beliefs of the Tibetan people. These centred on an animist and shamanistic faith shared by all central Asian people with an emphasis on the spirit world, exorcism and the cult of dead kings. This was supplanted by Buddhism in the 8th and 9th centuries, though Tibetan Buddhism is influenced by it rather as Christianity shows signs of Mithraism. A notable feature of Bon adherents is that they circumambulate lakes, monuments and mountains in an anticlockwise direction even today, in contrast to the clockwise circumambulation of Buddhists.

We camped at a pleasant, though cold, grassy campsite by a river on the broad valley floor and the next day made our way up to the Tershi monastery. As with most monasteries it is in a beautiful setting and we arrived to the chanting of praying monks. Rather surprisingly we were allowed to visit the monks during their devotions and, even more surprisingly, were permitted to take photos. The remoteness, poverty and location of Tershi conveyed a stronger spiritual air than that found at larger, more prosperous monasteries, and left us with fond memories of the area and its people.

In conversation with the abbot it transpired that despite its isolation even this monastery had been sacked during the Cultural Revolution. Encouragingly, it has now been fully renovated by the inhabitants and local nomads, although it has far fewer monks than previously. We were told that Tershi receives some visitors from other parts of Tibet but none from elsewhere.

Heading north again next day we arrived at the large lake of Dangra Yutso. It was more barren than we expected, with no visible monastery and almost no habitation until much further north. No track suitable for vehicles existed on either shore, but it was possible to continue on foot and with animals; a fact confirmed by two nomads that we met who were waiting to take some sheep given as payment for their summer labouring in Tsochen back to Shigatse.

On our return journey we had intended camping in the valley before Sangsang, but threatening clouds gathered overhead and the temperature dropped markedly. We therefore pushed on to Sangsang with its cold, but welcoming, guesthouse. Later we learned that this weather change was part of a prolonged depression covering much of the Himalaya, causing havoc and killing 18 people on Annapurna.

We kept to the main track east for our return, deviating only for a tourist trip to Everest base camp to photograph the north face, before travelling on to Lhasa, Beijing and home.

Summary: An account of the first ascent of Dobzebo North (6412m) by the south face on 8 October 2005 and of Dobzebo South-West (6429m) by the south-west ridge on 14 October. This was followed by a short exploration of the Lungmari range to the north that revealed a number of promising unclimbed 6000m peaks. Team: Alasdair Scott, Bill Thurston, Martin Scott and Derek Buckle.

Acknowledgements: The team wish to thank the British Mountaineering Council and the Mount Everest Foundation for their support.

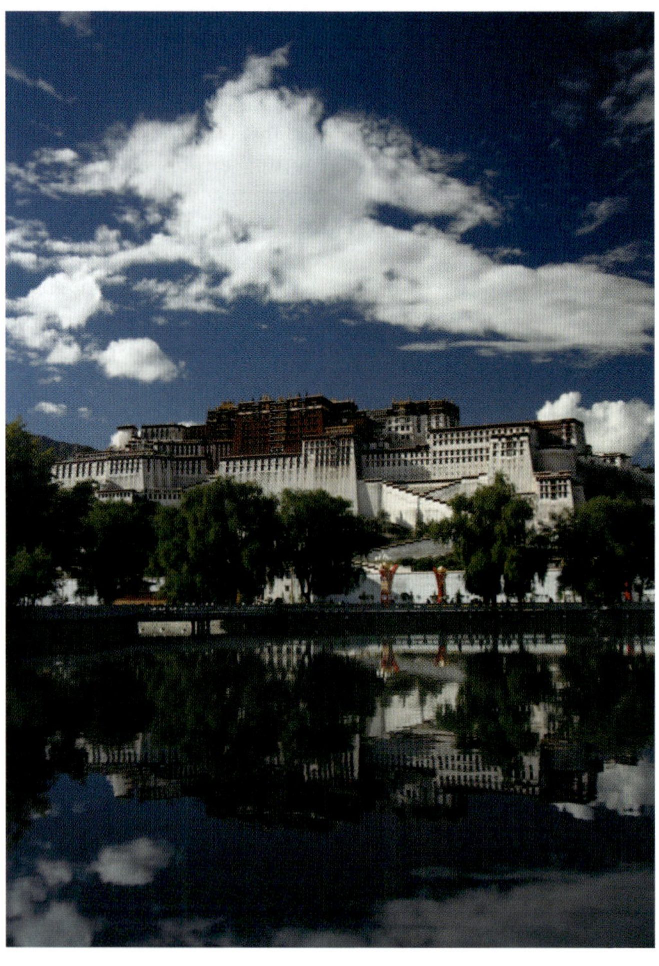

43. Potala Palace, Lhasa (*Al Scott*)

MARK JENKINS

Adventure is not Dead

We are moving through a mystery. Whiteness envelopes us, as if we were high inside the clouds. And, in fact, we are. We cannot see where we are going. We cannot see what lies to our left or right. Our only guide is ascent: we follow the fall line upward, our boots skittering on the ice-glazed talus.

We're in a cirque with no name in the Daxue Shan range on the far eastern edge of the Tibetan plateau. Other than perhaps a Tibetan boy tracking down a lost yak, the last visitors to penetrate the high reaches of this amphitheatre were two Harvard mountaineers back in 1932. Even though we can't see them, from the map we know there are four unclimbed 20,000ft summits looming above us. Ross Lynn and I have come to attempt just one: the east face of Nyambo Konka.

The slope steepens and scree changes to stove-size blocks teetering on black glacier ice at the angle of repose. We move cautiously, almost tiptoeing. A parsimonious expedition, our med kit consists of a few pills of oxycodone. There are no rescue choppers or Sherpas here; the nearest hospital is days away. We are on our own and without back-up.

'Can't see a damn thing,' shouts Ross, just a hint of his Louisiana boyhood in his speech. He stops to breathe. 'What's the elevation?' I peer at my altimeter through the murky gauze: '15,309. Two thousand feet above camp.'

Even in a whiteout, by cross-referencing our Russian 1:200,000 topo with altimeter readings and GPS satellite-beamed lat/longs, we can pinpoint where we are. But these are just numbers. They can establish positions, but not conditions – the rottenness or reliability of the rock, the hollowness or hardness of the ice, the depth and danger of the snow. (Let alone your own fatigue or fear.) All these, the actual exigencies of a mountain, can only be ascertained, thank God, the old-fashioned way: from the ground.

A squall swoops in, graupel rattling upon our helmets like gravel, then vanishes. We follow a spine of rock angling leftward up to a serpentine snow gully; clip on crampons, exchange trekking poles for ice axes, upward through layers of diminishing opacity. The higher we go the more light breaks through. Our depth of field expands from a mere ten feet to a hundred, to a thousand. In minutes the 4000ft east face of Nyambo is staring down on us.

The sinister visage stops us in our tracks. Not being able to see what was above us, we've managed to climb ourselves right up beneath a deeply fractured, quarter-mile-long hanging glacier, akin to wandering into a building that is about to be dynamited. Ross and I make an abrupt right-angled turn, nervously hightail it across a vast, telltale fan of hardened avalanche debris, drop our loads in a bergschrund and descend via a much safer route on the far right-hand side of the cirque.

'Let's not do that again,' says Ross on the way down.

'Scratch Plan A.'

In the morning we move camp up to the bergschrund. Plan B is to climb the central couloir. With the monocular, we discover it to be constantly running with avalanches. On to Plan C: ascend yet another couloir farther right. This is what happens when you enter terra incognita: you make it up as you go. There's no rule book. First-hand experience rather than second-hand advice dictates decisions. Improvisation is imperative.

Further along the base of the face, we dig out a tent platform inside a bergschrund we believe to be safe from the peril of avalanche. Erect the tent, eat cubes of yak gristle, drink Chinese tea; load our packs for the morning attempt, scooch into our sleeping bags. Ross is regaling me with an ascent of *Lurking Fear*, a notorious route in Yosemite, when the roar of an avalanche begins to drown out his voice. Usually the rumble fades, but in this case the volume increases. Suddenly our tent is being pummelled and bashed-in and Ross and I are screaming, tearing at the tent zippers and diving out into the darkness, clawing bare-handed and sock-footed along the sheer ice. After the avalanche passes we find our tent partially flattened, a softball-sized rock having sliced right down through the fly.

'Perhaps we should move,' says Ross in a calm Southern drawl. We spend the next two hours digging out a new tent platform by head lamp, only to have an avalanche sweep by on the opposite side the moment we're back in our bags.

'Busy place,' I say. The beam of Ross's headlamp responds by bobbing on the tent wall. Neither of us sleep. We listen, like infantry soldiers in a trench, ears straining to interpret the portent of each explosion. We don't talk much; we wait. We wait to see if we survive. We wait for dawn and Plan D.

In May 1932 four young men set sail for China from the docks of New York: Harvard students Arthur Emmons and Terris Moore, New York University student Jack Young, and Dick Burdsall, a graduate from Swarthmore. This exuberant, indefatigable team had ambitious goals. First, to measure the height of Minya Konka, an unexplored peak in western China rumoured to be higher than Everest; second, to climb it; third, to collect plants and animals from the region. They called their project the Sikong Expedition.

After a month at sea, the team arrived in Shanghai. They took a boat up the Yangtze River for 1500 miles, then went by car, rickshaw, horse and finally on foot to the base of the mountain, arriving early in August. They dedicated two months to reconnoitring the region, mapping and measuring not only Minya Konka, which turned out to be just shy of 25,000ft, but a dozen other peaks in the Daxue Shan, including Nyambo Konka.

Objective one completed, the mountaineers spent the month of October tackling Minya Konka. Entire camps were buried in snowstorms. They bivouacked on ridges, cramming three men into one sleeping bag while playing chess. And, almost unbelievably, they summited. Moore and Burdsall planted an American flag on Minya Konka on 28 October 1932. It was the highest mountain yet climbed by Americans, and the second highest mountain ever climbed by anyone, done without bottled oxygen or Sherpa support.The team even managed to fulfil their third aim, presenting the Metropolitan Museum of the Academia Sinica in Nanking with five blue sheep, three gorals, two wild boars, a grizzly bear, a black bear, a musk-deer ...and a partridge in a pear tree.

Moore, Young and Burdsall arrived back in the US after nine months on expedition. Unfortunately, Emmons had severe frostbite and was forced to stay behind in a small Chinese village. 'Yachow was destined to be my home for seven months while my feet underwent renovation and my toes were removed,' he wrote. 'One could have gone much farther and fared far worse in the matter of cheerful and sincere friendship than with these fine men and women.'

The Sikong Expedition was a bold success and the book Emmons and Burdsall subsequently wrote, *Men Against the Clouds*, is a cornerstone of American mountaineering literature. Here are lines from the last page: 'Ours had been some of the finest adventures imaginable. We had sweated and frozen, starved and feasted, faced hardship and danger, together.'

Of course that was three-quarters of century ago, back when the world was still fresh and real adventure could still be had. You could never do such an expedition today. Right?

Although he now lives in Livingston, Montana, Ross Lynn, 26, grew up on a farm in northern Louisiana barely above sea level. He's a fifth generation cotton farmer, returning every spring and fall to help his Dad with planting and harvesting. Sometime around 3am, clinging to the east face of Nyambo Konka, he began explaining modern tractors to me.

They're entirely computerized. The control panel is like the cockpit of an aeroplane, numbers and gauges everywhere. Seed count, seed spacing, planting depth – it's all measured and monitored. 'Thing is,' Ross paused for a moment listening to the foreboding whistle of a falling rock, 'in the end, you still have to know your dirt and your field. You still have to sit on the tractor and go up and down the rows. And you can still lose it all in one bad storm.'

Ross talked tractors and Louisiana cooking until a faint ribbon of orange appeared in the east. If we'd had any information about the east face, we would have started climbing in the dark. As it was, we had to wait until daybreak to determine which couloirs were safe.

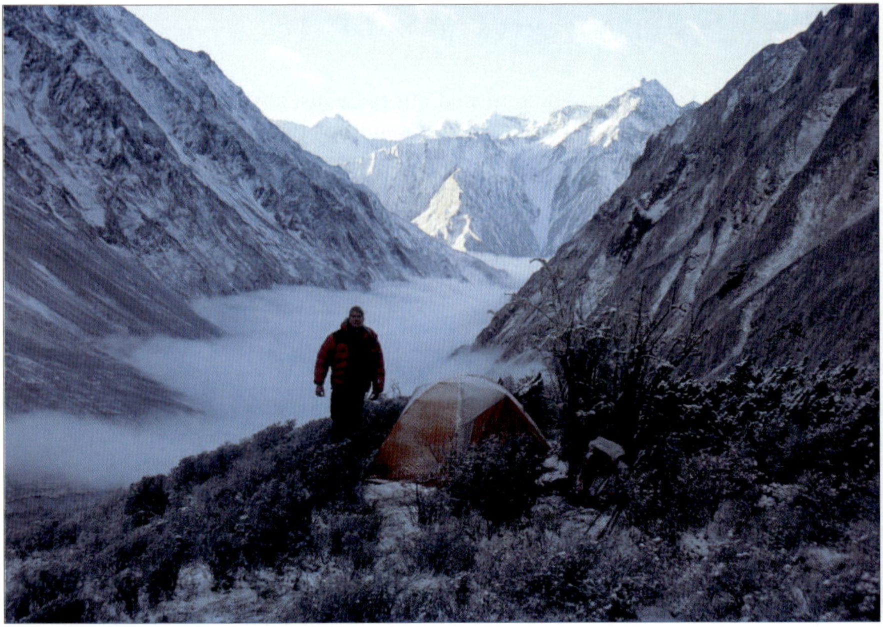

44. Ross Lynn at our 13,000ft cirque camp at the base of the east face of Nyambo Konka. (*Mark Jenkins*)

45. Ross Lynn soloing at 17,000ft on the east face of Nyambo Konka. (*Mark Jenkins*)

46. Ross Lynn at 18,000ft on the east face of Nyambo Konka. (*Mark Jenkins*)

7. Two Tibetan pilgrims circumambulating the stupa outside the Litang Monastery in Eastern Tibet. (*Mark Jenkins*)

'I'd say none,' said Ross handing me the monocular. 'Take a look.'

There was a 100ft-deep cornice hanging over the breadth of the face. Our best choice was to angle rightward, crossing avalanche chutes, trying to climb largely on the rock ribs. The first few hundred feet were a scamper, then the face steepened and we were confronted with the appalling insecurity of the rock – thousands of feet of sharp, irregular blocks stacked precariously one on top of the other. Only the mortar of ice held the wall together. Pulling out any one block might bring down a million tons of rock.

Plan E: Fuck the cornice. Climb a couloir.

Unroped, each kicking fanged feet and swinging ice tools, we gradually ascended a web of interconnected couloirs. It wasn't until we found ourselves on a 70° fin of ice that Ross laconically suggested we rope up. Both of us were ticklishly balanced on front-points with 2000ft of space between our legs. I pulled the rope from my pack while Ross dug out the ice screws. He seemed lethargic. I suspected altitude sickness, but said nothing. Removing the screws he accidentally dropped his harness. It bounced down the face catching on a ledge. We managed to retrieve it, but lost time and momentum. From then on we moved at a snail's pace.

It was afternoon sometime when we stopped at a ridiculously insecure belay. Spindrift was flying around our faces.

'We're moving too slow,' I shouted over the roar. Ross nodded. Yelling back and forth, we discussed our options. Continuing upward, whether we reached the summit or not, would guarantee an exposed, bagless bivouac. Hypothermia certain, frostbite probable. We had no idea of our descent route. We didn't have enough gear to rap what we'd come up.

Ross stabbed his finger downward, and we turned around.

We rapped off several disconcertingly small rock fragments frozen into the wall before finding a gully we could down-climb. It was a long haul back to the tent, where we both collapsed.

'Hardest day of my life,' Ross croaked. 'I've never been so exhausted.'

In the past decade, a *fin de siècle*, everything's-been-done jadedness has become trendy in certain outdoor circles. Everest has been climbed a thousand times, the Eiger a hundred times, Denali, Kili', Aconcagua, the other 8000ers, all have seen countless ascents. The world's mountains have been climbed, its rivers run, its ice caps crossed. Time to play Dragon Quest VIII. Even messianic Reinhold Messner, who should know better, declared in the *Guardian* last year: 'Mountaineering is over. Alpinism is dead. Maybe its spirit is still alive a little in Britain and America, but it will soon die out.'

Excuse me, but horseshit. I acknowledge that the age of geographical exploration, with the enormous exceptions of deep space and the deep sea, is over. There are no seas left unsailed and there will never be another Magellan. Every large village in Africa has the internet – Livingstone must be turning in his grave. For a price, you can fly to either pole and drink champagne on ice, blaspheming the achievements of Amundsen and Peary.

The Silk Road is an asphalt two-lane highway, the Inca Trail a tourist trap, the Oregon Trail an Interstate.

So grand exploration is over, but, the age of adventure, micro-exploration, I suggest, has only just begun. Take mountaineering: OK, all the biggies have been climbed – the fourteen 8000-metre peaks, the seven summits, Mont Blanc, Mount Cook etc. However, this list represents only a fraction of the world's tallest mountains. According to the International Union of Alpine Associations (UIAA) there are 146 unclimbed 7000-metre peaks! At the 2005 Alpine Club symposium at the Rheged Centre near Penrith, Tomatsu Nakamura, the leading authority on the mountains of eastern Tibet, estimated that there are 200 to 250 unclimbed 6000-metre (20,000ft) peaks in this region alone. Worldwide, there are thousands upon thousands of virgin 5000 and 6000-metre mountains.

As for cragging, there are unclimbed walls from Baffin Island to the Baltoro.

'As technical standards continue to grow, people look at things with different eyes and see new possibilities,' explains Kelly Cordes, assistant editor of the *American Alpine Journal*. 'Combine modern ice, rock and alpine skills with old-school vision and spirit, and lines previously believed to be utterly impossible go.' Cordes, 37, certainly walks the talk. He has put up unrepeated first ascents in Alaska, Peru and Pakistan, most recently ascending the south-west ridge of Great Trango Tower with Josh Wharton in a stunning four-day sufferfest. 'The potential for adventure is limited by your imagination, not by geography,' says Cordes.

The mere thought of all these unclimbed walls and peaks can send me to Google Earth (an internet mountain porn site) where I'll lose hours lasciviously zooming in and out on peaks photographed from space, but never touched. Sceptics quiz me about my passion for first ascents. There are so many proper classic lines, what's the point? Is it ego?

Yes. But here's the thing. Once a route has been climbed, you don't have to find your own way. If you get confused, check the guidebook. This is like looking at the answers to a crossword puzzle. You've missed the satisfying chance of figuring it out on your own. Well then, you say, don't take the guidebook. Fair enough, if contrived, and yet, if somebody's climbed it, you already know something elemental. You know it can be done, and therefore some of the magnetism of the mystery is lost.

If you know no one has been there, the mystery seduces you. Can it be done? No one knows. The reason to go is to find out. The reason to go is to find out whether *you* can do it; whether you have the nerve and craft, resilience and resourcefulness to overcome whatever the mystery might be. It is, if you like, to think on your feet and dance on your fears.

Ross and I back off all the way to base camp. While he rests, I recon' the south side of Nyambo Konka, finding four enormous south-facing ridges. They each begin along the Basong River and rise a staggering 10,000ft to the summit – more vertical than the north face of Everest. Because they start at such a low elevation, the first 2000ft consist of an almost impenetrable barrier of thorn bushes and brambles.

Ross and I choose the central south ridge for our second go and are practically skinned alive trying to breach the 'briar patch'. Imagine Jack's beanstalk spiked with thorns or a jungle gym of cactus reaching into the sky, then imagine climbing up it with a 50lb pack on your back. When we finally emerge onto the grassy alpine slopes above, we're so scratched and bloodied we will be pulling spines out of our hands for the next month. We dig camp into the rocks at 15,000ft. The wind is so fierce we resort to lining the inside of the tent with brick-sized stones to keep it, and us, from being blown into the sky like the house in the Wizard of Oz.

On our second summit bid we encounter a series of intricate, thoroughly unsafe gendarmes – castle-like towers of friable rock guarding the snowy ridge to the top. We are often cliffed-out and forced to find another route. We knock off boulders that careen frightfully through space. We climb sideways and down and over and sometimes, when we were lucky, up. The arête is a spectacular rock maze that no one before us has ever entered. I am thoroughly entranced. The weather is splendid, despite a spectacular wind. I think we have it made.

Unpropitiously, Ross is again moving slowly. It has nothing to do with his technical skills; he climbs hard rock and even harder ice, notably a 10-hour ascent of 2000ft Losar in Nepal, the highest frozen waterfall in the world. Altitude is just a frustratingly fickle fellow.

Somewhere above 17,000ft, Ross's legs simply refuse to go any further. And there's nothing he can do about it. 'This makes climbing in Yosemite seem like child's play,' he whispers. It's the end of our expedition. But we'll be back.

It took the 1932 Sikong Expedition three months to get to the Daxue Shan from the US. It took Ross and I less than a week. The Sikong Expedition exchanged formal letters with the government of China for over a year to obtain permits; I simply emailed my contact in Chengdu.

It may seem counter-intuitive, but 21st century communication and transportation have increased, rather than decreased, opportunities for micro-exploration. Aeroplanes and the internet have democratised adventure. You no longer need special contacts, huge sponsors or stacks of money to pull off a world-class trip. You need only a good partner, a few weeks, an airline ticket and a fistful of desire.

DICK ISHERWOOD

A Cautionary Tale

We all like Tibetans. They are generally friendly and smiling people, and even drink chang while they are praying, which I have always thought a very civilized habit. We think of them as deeply religious and very pacific people. Some of us associate their behaviour with great and inscrutable wisdom. Some of us even contribute to movements such as Free Tibet, though it is not too obvious how they propose to get the Chinese out. The story that follows is not meant to change this admirable view of things, just to show that it is not always quite like this.

In spring 2004 I was a member of a four-man party that attempted Haizi Shan (5833m) in the Daxue Shan mountains of western Sichuan. At the end of our trip we travelled north as far as Garze where my attention was caught by the twin peaks of the Gongkala group (5992m and 5928m) to the east of the town. Enquiries seemed to indicate there had been only one reconnaissance of these mountains, by a Japanese group in the 1990s, and no real climbing attempts. The only photos we could obtain (from Tom Nakamura) were all taken from on or close to the Sichuan Tibet Highway, which crosses a pass just north of the peaks.

It seemed almost too good to be true that here were two good-looking, unattempted peaks with a base camp within a day's journey of the road. I did not think such things still existed. I had no trouble recruiting three companions for a trip in the autumn of 2005. I knew Toto Gronlund and Dave Wynne-Jones from Steve Town's trip to Pokharkan in Nepal in 2002, while Peter Rowat and I had a climbing association going back to an ascent of Cenotaph Corner in 1965. Peter's wife, Nona, accompanied us to our base camps and also acted as trip doctor.

In two days' travel by road from Chengdu we reached Garze, and spent three interesting days reconnoitring the north and south sides of the Gongkala peaks. There were possible but not easy routes from the north, including a 1000m 'grand course' direct to the summit of Kawarani I, but we decided the south side offered better prospects for us.

A good grazing trail led from the village of Khur Chong, in the gorge of the Yalung Jiang river, around the hillside to a hanging valley directly below the southern glaciers of Kawarani I and II. From this it appeared possible to reach the col at about 5500m between the two summits. From the col there seemed to be routes to both.

Below the village were two or three apparently rather inactive monasteries. We stopped at the principal one but found literally no one to talk to, so we continued to the village where the people were very friendly and cooperative.

48. The south face of the Gongkala peaks. Kawarani I (5992m) is on the right. (*Dick Isherwood*)

One young man spoke good Mandarin, which helped as our interpreter had little or no Tibetan. He also told us he was the nephew of the Rinpoche, which made him seem even more useful. We explained our plans and they were very happy to assist us by making horses available to carry to the base camp. On the afternoon of our first visit there was a thunderstorm with lots of large hail; this was not unusual as it seemed that the monsoon was not yet over.

Two days later we returned with all our gear and had an uneventful journey to a base camp at 4200m. The monastery showed its goodwill by providing a monk leading a very large white yak at the head of our column. We were told he had been sent to bless our climb. It was like being led into battle by a knight on a white charger. We could hardly have got off to a more auspicious start. There was no evidence that any climbers had been in this area before.

We set to work and four days later had just completed carrying to a second camp at 4800m when we heard a commotion in the valley below. Eight young monks came running up the moraines in red robes and plastic shoes at an impressive speed. We did not have a word in common with them but it was immediately clear that this was not a social call. They wanted us off the mountain right away. As we argued in sign language, reinforcements appeared from below and we concluded that resistance was hopeless.

We returned to our base camp and found that the total delegation was around 40 assorted monks and villagers. The monks were from the same monastery that had assisted and blessed us four days earlier. When we pointed this out they simply said that they had changed their minds as a result of two thunderstorms that they believed we had caused. One mature and corpulent gentleman was introduced as their leader and for a few minutes I thought he might prove reasonable to deal with, but he was soon pushed aside by a younger and much more aggressive individual who said that *he* was in charge. As our meeting progressed it became apparent that this was a mob with no one in charge. They had no respect at all for our permit from the Sichuan Mountaineering Association. They were very confrontational and thoroughly unpleasant to deal with. After a long and unproductive discussion, during which distinctly unpacifist attitudes were repeatedly displayed, we decided we had no alternative but to go down. Toto began to swear in Finnish, which I have come to recognize as a bad sign.

By now it was past 5pm and there was not nearly enough horse and yak transport to clear the base camp that night. The mob was, however, adamant that as many of us and as much gear as possible should go down right away. Dave and I stayed up, with a posse of monks to keep an eye on us, while the others suffered a chaotic descent, largely in the dark. The gear that went down with them was taken to the monastery and we spent much of the following day retrieving it, not without cost. They claimed money for injury to the horses in the dark, which if it happened at all was entirely their own fault. Once this was handed over every one, even the most aggressive of them, became all sweetness and light. They waved us farewell like lifelong friends. While all this was going on we were told that the helpful young man and his family were being banished from the village for assisting us.

A telephone protest by our outfitter, Sichuan Adventure Travel, to the civil administrator of the Garze Tibetan Ethnic Group Autonomous Prefecture, which governs this area from Kangding, drew only the comment that these monasteries can be difficult to deal with. (This gentleman himself is apparently a reincarnate Lama.) As it was now 6pm on a Friday and the following week was one long national holiday we gave up on any further protest through the government, but I cannot believe it would have done any good for our immediate situation.

We were able to get our permit switched, with amazing speed, to Haizi Shan and spent our last ten days attempting to complete the route which Geoff Cohen, Martin Scott, Bill Thurston and I had tried on the north face in spring 2004. Unfortunately the weather was poor and we expended a lot of energy getting nowhere. We retreated from the bottom of the northern glaciers at 4800m in a foot of new snow on 10 October.

So what does one make of all this? Firstly, if we had been a bit faster up the hill rather than allowing time for acclimatisation, rest days, etc, we would have been in the snow and ice and well out of plastic shoe country before the monastery took umbrage. The eventual consequences might not have been pleasant, but we might have climbed the mountain.

Secondly, we are not the only climbing party to have run into this sort of problem in recent years. See, for instance, the *American Alpine Journal* 2001, p408, and 2003, p410. The latter, though in Yunnan rather than Sichuan, describes a very similar experience in that the villagers welcomed the climbers, but the monks told them not to co-operate and threatened punishment if they did.

Third, the Chinese Government seems to have a 'hands off' approach to this area, in striking contrast to what goes on in Tibet proper. The Garze Autonomous Prefecture was established in November 1950 within a few months of the invasion of Tibet. This is perhaps more than coincidence. The Khampas of Sikong, as this western slice of Sichuan was formerly known, have clearly been given freedom of religion, and also considerable economic assistance, just possibly in return for making no trouble. Their communities certainly look prosperous today. How this squares with the well-known Khampa resistance to the Chinese occupation of Tibet in later years I do not know. In trying to find out a bit more about this I got as far as a Khampa website which seemed to be dominated by different tribal sub-groups trading insults. I guess there are Khampas and Khampas.

The monastery's stated reasons for their actions have little credibility, since thunderstorms and hail were regular events in the area. Perhaps the simple fact that we were the first outsiders to go onto the mountains was enough to spook them, but it seems more likely that we got into the middle of a feud between monastery and village, which we could hardly have foreseen.

There is also, as ever, the question of money. It is possible that a sufficiently large donation to the monastery up front might have averted what happened, but on our arrival there seemed to be no one suitable to give it to, even if we had thought it necessary. Certainly a number of previously hostile monks became remarkably friendly once we had paid $250 for the return of our gear.

We did not have a liaison officer. It did not seem to be a requirement in this area and was not a condition of our permit. Possibly if we had had one of suitable stature the outcome might have been different, but I suspect that even if we had asked for one we would have been given someone too junior to be effective in this situation. You would have needed a general in the PLA to make an impression on these people. Besides, who would want to go down in history as the first expedition to have *insisted* on having a liaison officer? Our interpreter was a pleasant but very young Han Chinese lady from Chengdu who was clearly and understandably intimidated by the situation and not very effective as a negotiator. Perhaps a different individual in this role could have achieved a better outcome, but I doubt it.

I guess it is a matter of opinion how much of this really relates to religion, or superstition, or local politics, or plain greed. I do not have any answers – it is just a cautionary tale.

Climbs

Jim Curran *Trango Tower* 2005
Oil on canvas
Private collection

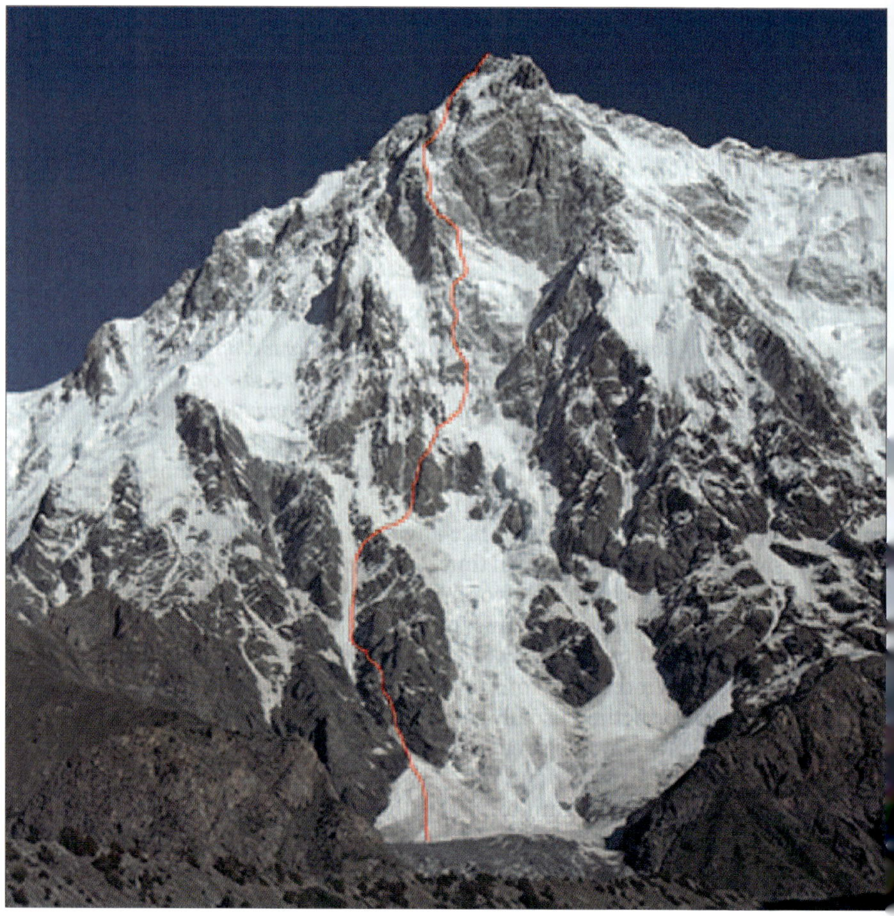

50. Nanga Parbat's Rupal Face showing the House-Anderson route and bivvi sites. (*Steve House*)

The wall is great, but it is not steep; at least not on the first day. The ropes stay in the pack and we climb more than a thousand metres to a rimaye below the first major difficulties. The sun is strong and snow avalanches continue all afternoon. Several times we have to cross their paths, pretending to time them as we race across.

The second day starts early. Well before dawn we cross another rimaye and front-point up the first gully, which turns out to be the wrong one. Down-climbing, we return almost to our starting point before locating the correct goulotte. I'm in the lead, unroped. But icy conditions force me to stop, build an anchor, and take out the rope.

Vince leads out. Steady and solid. He carries the light 10kg pack and I follow with the heavier 18 kg rucksack. We climb five pitches to the crux headwall. First light is breaking over Vince as he heads up into the crux pitch. Thirty minutes later he finally finds a good piece of protection, just below the crux moves, and lowers back to me. It is too difficult and too steep to climb with the rucksack at this altitude. Energized, I rush up, fresh and without any extra weight. The pitch is steep and the protection very minimal; it is physically and psychologically demanding.

The rest of the day goes quickly and easily. We make our bivouac in a safe place with several hours of light remaining.

It is dark when we awake and start off. Today promises to be a long one. The wall is steep now and places to bivouac are difficult to find. Our worries are temporarily suspended in the grandeur of a sunrise that neither of us will ever forget. K2, Broad Peak, the Gasherbrums, Masherbrum, K7, and K6 are all visible on the horizon as another perfect cloudless day dawns. We climb for hours on the 50-degree névé. Conditions here, at nearly 6000m, are close to perfect.

After four hours of soloing I place a screw in an ice-filled crack, take off my pack, and flake out the rope. Vince racks, ties in, and leads off. From here our route deviates from my 2004 attempt. Now we will head up the central pillar on the face. This climbing is fun. Good quality rock, secure gear, and delicate veins of ice lead to the icy prow of the pillar.

Now we switch tactics. We climb with running belays, one screw on the rope between us. Conditions continue to be excellent. Every five rope-lengths we take the packs off, eat, drink, and change the lead. Morning turns to afternoon. Clouds boil up and the sun disappears behind the peak. In the shadow we climb on and on.

When darkness comes we are forced to belay individual pitches. The ice is steeper and harder now. Our muscles are tired and our picks seem dull. I lost count of the pitches we climbed today at around 30. Now I lead off, heading up and right, looking for a spot to bivouac. I'm tired and know that now I must focus. I must be at my best. Mental energy drives each kick, each swing is directed with care.

Picks are twisted into cracks. Pitons are hammered home. Front-points mount rough edges. I have to pull and pull hard. The climbing is steep and mixed. I traverse past a bulging block, around into a corner, and stem my way to the top. With weak arms but a determined mind I swing my tools into the 60-degree ice at the end of the pitch. I set up the belay, yell for Vince to start climbing, and slumped in my harness I dry heave (vomit) for five minutes.

Eighty metres of traversing later and I'm in a perfect bivvi cave. Vince crawls in. We're both stupid with exhaustion. He starts the stove and I begin to dig a place for the tent. Midnight finds us in our sleeping bags and eating the daily meal of dried potatoes and soup.

Sunshine fills the tent with warmth and the night's frost is soon melted and dripping into our faces. I start the stove, already thinking about the day ahead. Above us is a section of the wall that might be unclimbable. Our photos do not reveal a solution to this section. Through the binoculars it appears steep and impenetrable. If we can't climb this section it will be impossible, or at the very least epic, to descend the 3000m of wall below us with our small rack of gear. I worry that the climbing could be difficult and slow here at 7000m. A few hard pitches could take all day. One bad bivouac could drain us completely.

We are committed. We are beyond the reach of any help, necks firmly positioned in the noose. But I have a feeling, an intuitive notion that we will find a way through, a raw confidence that we can climb whatever we come across. Maybe it is just a hope. Some would call it vain recklessness. But uncertainty is a crucial ingredient to our journey. Without uncertainty we have no adventure. If not for true adventure we wouldn't have come here. But now we must simply climb. We ascend easy névé towards the start of the rocky wall. I am in a hurry to see the terrain that will determine our fate. All I see above is steep, snow-covered rock. There must be something else, a weakness in the citadel. I rush, but the altitude checks me to a slow pace. Patience, I say to myself, patience. At the base of steep rock I hack out a ledge and remove my pack. There is only one more possibility; one small section of the wall that we haven't been able to see. Now we have to rest, drink, and eat. The tension is tight and we hardly speak.

As soon as I can, I shoulder my pack and head off, traversing straight to my right. Slowly my eyes gain access to a hidden corner. The most beautiful ice rolls upward in a frozen cascade. I holler back to Vince and start up the ice. Fifty metres later I'm smoked, having just soloed ice to 90 degrees with a backpack. My enthusiasm might have been the end of me, and Vince. But now I place two ice screws and lower the rope to my patient, understanding partner.

Pitches of excellent ice follow one after the other as we race darkness, looking for a place to spend the night. Just before dusk I belay Vince up and warily float an idea. 'What about up there?' I point to the corniced crest of the pillar. 'I could lead a pitch to the crest and maybe we could find a spot to chop a ledge. It'd be easier than trying to dig into this.' I kick the steep, ancient ice at our feet. We can't see any better options.

'Alright. I'll belay,' says Vince. And I'm off; climbing quickly, focused on not making any mistakes. 15m above my last ice screw I plant my right tool firmly in the ice and start chopping at the cornice on my left. 'If I can just get on top of this thing,' I think, 'maybe we can find a good place to bivvi.'

Finally, with a notch chopped into the cornice, I swing my leg up and start to pull myself over. The cornice breaks and I swing back, falling onto my right tool. The cornice crushes Vince.

'Fuck. Shit. Ohhhhhhhhh,' he cries.

I get my left tool in again and swing up onto the ridge crest, standing in the place where the cornice broke.

'Are you okay?' I yell down.

'I'll be fine,' Vince replies, but his voice does not sound fine. But what else can we do? I continue along the ridge for 20m where I find a solid bit of rock and build an anchor by the light of my headlamp.

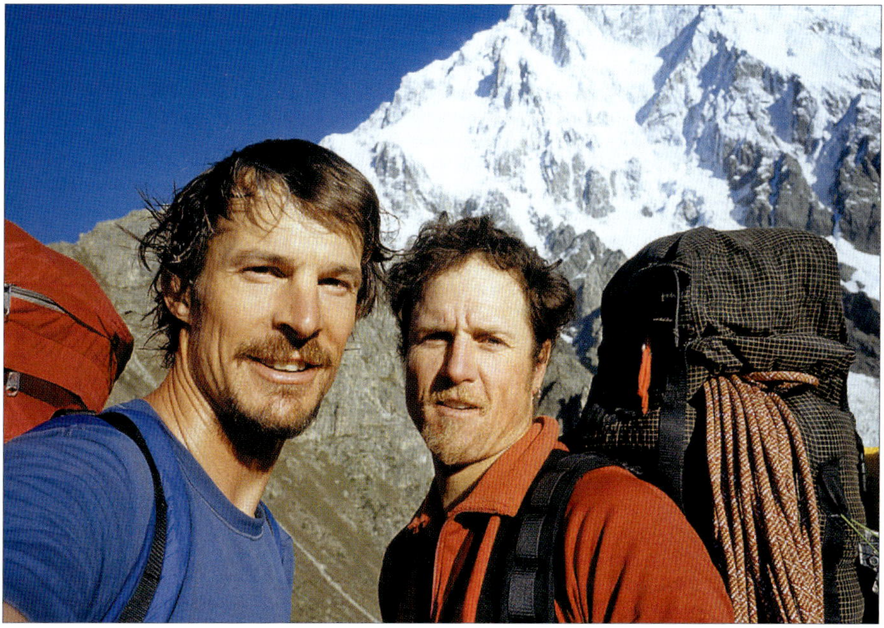

51. Steve House and Vince Anderson at the base of the Rupal Face on the first morning of their climb. (*Steve House*)

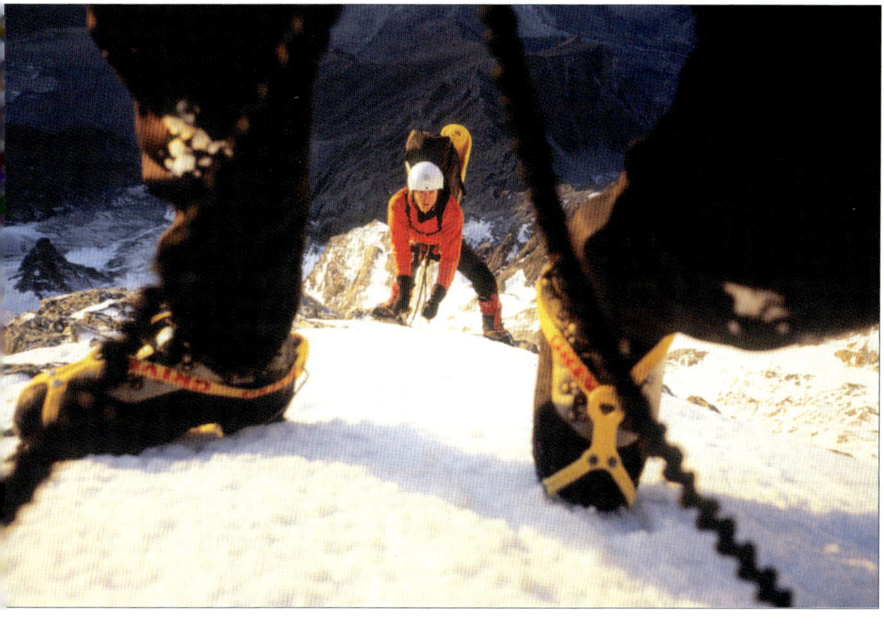

2. Looking down the Rupal Face on the morning of Day 3. (*Steve House*)

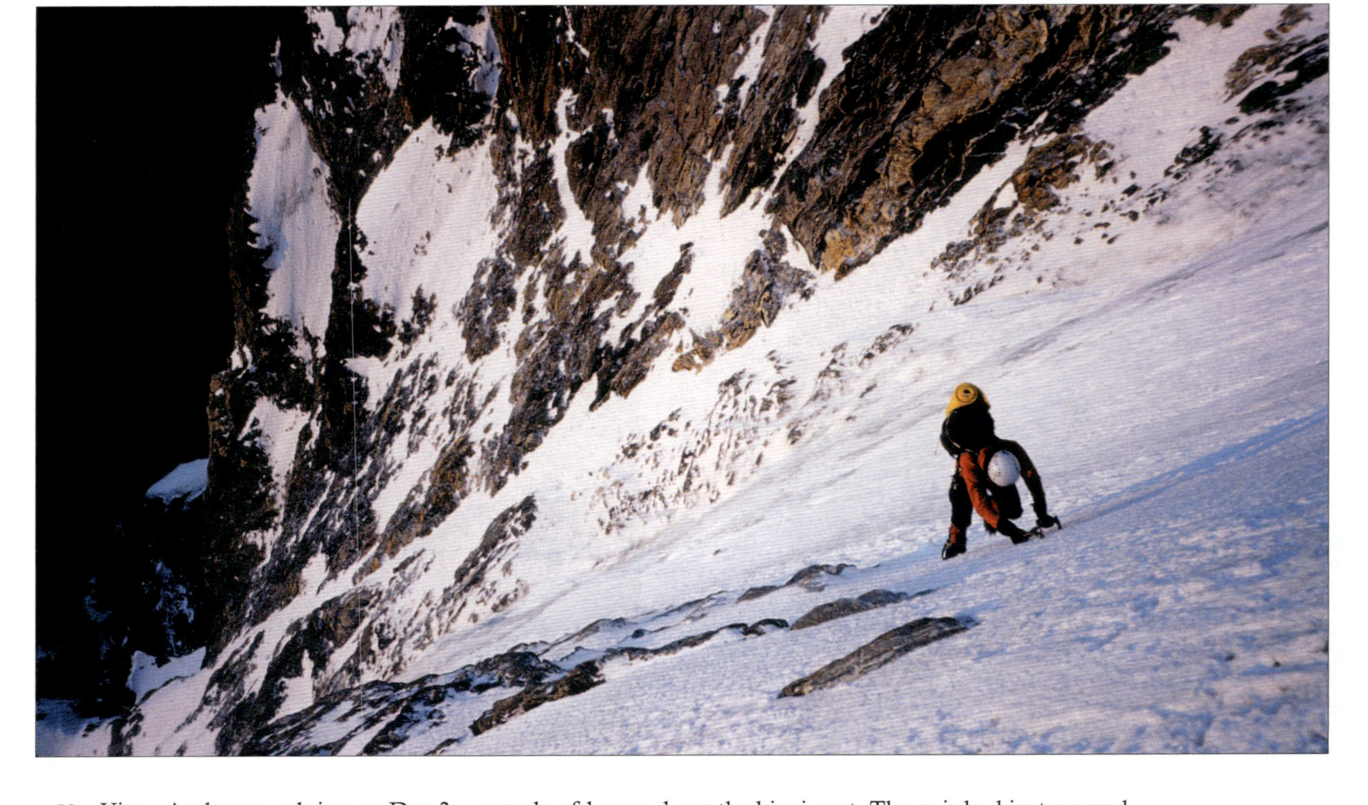

53. Vince Anderson soloing on Day 3, a couple of hours above the bivvi spot. The pair had just crossed an area threatened by séracs – note the scoured ice behind Anderson. (*Steve House*)

4. Anderson climbing one of the first pitches of the central pillar proper on Day 3. For most of the day the pair climbed on running belays, switching to full belaying after dark and climbing on until midnight. (*Steve House*)

5. Anderson higher up on the pillar on Day 3. 'We've been simul-climbing and I'm out of gear so I'm belaying Vince to me to make the transfer.' (*Steve House*)

Left

56. 'We worked really hard to get good bivvis each night where we could lay flat and have a proper sleep. This shows the extent to which we went to accomplish that goal. It was exposed, but without any wind or weather it was quite a comfortable night's sleep. Good view too.' (*Steve House*)

Vince is bruised. The biggest piece of the cornice missed him, but a smaller piece hit him squarely in the shoulder. We carefully arrange the anchor and begin the task of preparing the bivouac. It is a small perch and we are glad not to have to weather any storms here. Its precariousness really hits home next morning as we prepare to rappel back to the main line of the route. Yet it was plainly the only place to set up the tent and it was fortunate we followed our instincts to its sanctuary.

It is day five and we're above 7000m now, climbing slowly. Our intention is to have an easier day and find a good bivvi as early as possible so that we can eat, drink, and rest before the summit attempt tomorrow. At around 7400m we find a snow arête. I recognize the place as we have now rejoined my 2004 attempt with Bruce. We quickly excavate a tent platform and begin the job of taking care of ourselves.

At half past midnight the alarm goes off. Vince immediately starts the stove and we begin the wait. I stare at the flame, willing it to burn hotter. Ironic how the more you need things to work well, the less well they work. The altitude takes its toll on the mechanical as well as the human.

At 3am we are tying into the climbing rope and I am leading off. One hundred metres of mixed climbing starts our day, pitches that would be enjoyable at a lower altitude but here it is difficult to make even the easiest moves. At the top of the rock we tie the climbing rope and most of the gear to a big boulder, continuing with one rucksack and a 5mm static rope for rappelling. We also carry food, water, and clothes. The one without the pack breaks trail.

The couloir we are following steepens and the snow starts to get deeper. Soon we are wallowing like buffalo in the deep, loose snow. I am worried about the stability of the slope. Vince says that he wonders how long we can work this hard at such an altitude. I feel my hope of a few hours ago slipping away. The dream of completing the route and standing on the summit of Nanga Parbat seems so distant now, and we're so close.

We both go quiet. Some mutual signal of determination passes between us, unspoken. I push the snow down with my ice tools, push it down again with my knees, then stomp it with a foot until I can raise myself up a few centimetres. Sometimes I fall back, but slowly I make progress. After five minutes, I step aside and Vince has his go. For over two hours we work like that, one behind the other.

Eventually the sun starts to colour our rarified world. I look down and see that two and a half hours have gained us only 60 metres. Impossibly slow. But we work on. Maybe because we know the day is young; maybe

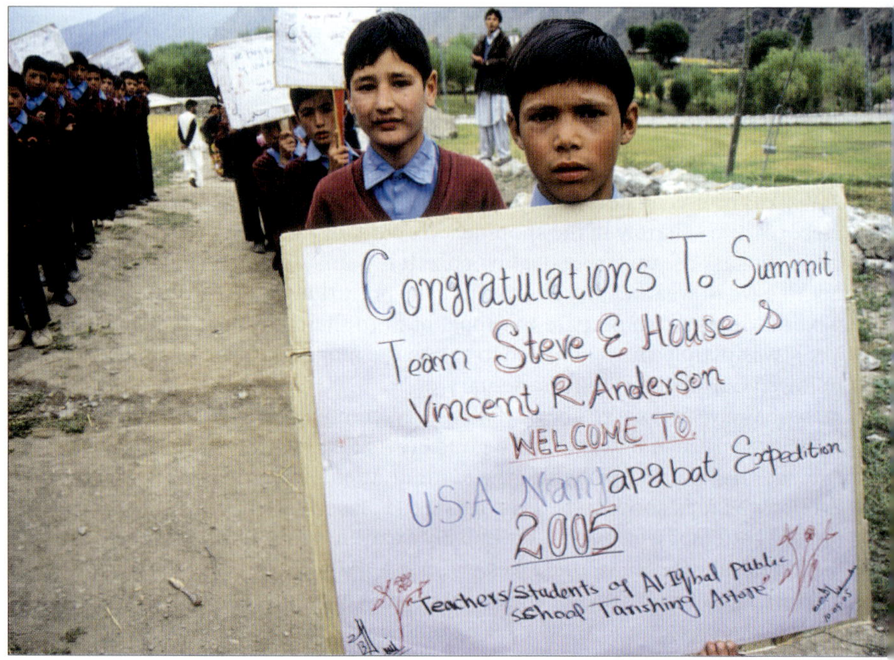

57. The welcome at Tarshing, the village at the roadhead. Several hundred schoolchildren lined the path. (*Steve House*)

because we have come too far, worked too hard, been too lucky to throw it all away now. I'm comforted by our determination but see the summit as something well beyond the line of impossible.

With the sunlight I notice a different texture in the snow near the rock wall on my left and move towards it. With one crampon scratching for edges on the rock and one in the snow, I start to make faster progress. Soon we have gained another 60m and the snow supports our steps. We are happy, however any confidence we had that we would easily reach the summit has been shaken. With few words we continue trading the work of breaking trail toward the top of the Rupal face.

At 7600m plus I'm stripped to my shirt and sweating. I'm not wearing gloves or a hat as I work steadily up toward the top of the wall. I can smell the summit now but it still seems impossibly far. We're both tired and Vince especially is sleepy. But there is no place to sit or rest. The wall drops away below us for almost 4000m. We are surprised to be able to look directly down on base camp, another world away.

The wall breaks like a four kilometre-high wave of stone and ice. The transition is indescribably sudden. I step from the steep snow couloir over a ridge and I can see down across the top of the Merkl gully. My gaze travels over to Nanga Parbat's Diamir side and the mountains beyond her northern flank. I am washed by a sense of relief. It is as if I've been kept in a small room for many days and suddenly I've stepped outside. I'm in a place with planes other than the vertical.

Above us is a complicated array of gullies, pinnacles, and false summits. We scrape out a place to rest. To take advantage of the break I remove my socks and hang them on the rucksack. It has been very warm and my sweat has soaked my socks; I am worried about the cold afternoon and night ahead.

When I ask how he's doing, Vince just holds his fingers like a pistol and points it to his head. I laugh. If he still has his sense of humour then he is still in good enough shape to climb. I, though, am feeling good. I've eaten and had water and my strength is still holding out. When we start again we notice that our pace is slow and our altimeter is reading only 7700m. Hopefully it is wrong. We want to be on the summit by 2pm and now I realize how much the deep snow set us back. But the weather is good; clear skies, no wind.

At 4pm we crest a false summit and see, finally, the true summit. We both sit on a big flat rock. It is the first place we are able to sit and relax without a belay in six days. Vince lays back and soon starts sleeping. I put my dry socks back on. That finished, I shake Vince awake and follow him as he starts off up the last 50m of our dream mountain.

Never have my last steps to the summit of a mountain been so emotional. The light is low and the massive shadow of Nanga Parbat is cast far out into the valleys to the east. My crampons crunch into the summit névé, Vince follows just a few paces behind. I kneel in the snow just a metre below the top. After all I've gone through to reach this point: the lifetime of devotion to alpinism, the physical work to make myself strong enough, the psychological journey to discover if I am courageous enough, the will to see it all through. Now it seems almost sacrilegious to step onto the summit.

A few moments later Vince arrives. I stand to face him. As he approaches I take one step backwards onto the summit of Nanga Parbat; Vince joins me in an embrace. Tears well up in the corners of my eyes. They freeze and fall to the snow at my feet, becoming part of Nanga Parbat, as it became part of me so many years ago.

Summary: An account of the first ascent of the central pillar of Nanga Parbat's Rupal face in pure alpine style by Steve House and Vince Anderson, 1-8 September 2005 (VII, 5.9, M5X, WI 4, 4100m). The two Americans were awarded the 2005 'Piolet d'Or' for this exemplary climb.

NICK BULLOCK

The Emotional Tightrope

A stooped 6ft 4in frame; gaunt, rangy like a newborn foal, and surrounded by large duffel bags; unmistakably Powell, waiting patiently by the National Express drop-off at Luton Airport. I've been looking forward to meeting him again. It's his attitude, his 'no bullshit' yet modest demeanour. But will it all be the same? Al Powell has just qualified as a mountain guide, started a business and become a father, with a baby son, Adam, and another child on the way. I wonder if having so much to think about will affect him, will affect the climb. Will affect me!

'Hey up Mr Powell, how's it going?' I call from the window of my Berlingo van – my transport, my office, my home. I drive the wrong way around the car park to pull up as close as possible, on double yellows, to the pile of bags. We load them quickly as a dark-suited, peaked-capped, gold braided private security guard heads purposefully in our direction.

Making our escape, we chug along toward my sister's house, deep in conversation, catching up. Powell is mumbling, another one of his traits. I nod, frown, shake my head and add 'oh' and 'ah' and hope they are in the right place; not that it would matter as Al is so engrossed in stories of fatherhood, business strategy and work he wouldn't notice.

'So when exactly are you flying home?' I ask nervously.

'Oh, it's...err...hang on let's check.'

'My god,' I think, 'he doesn't even know when he returns.'

Powell pulls a small notebook from his pocket and flicks the pages.

'Yes, here it is,' a note of triumph at having found something in this topsy-turvy filing system. 'The 23rd.'

I narrowly avoid driving the van off the dual-carriageway; then, composing myself, attempt to answer neutrally. 'Oh, that doesn't give us long to nail Chac', does it? What was wrong with the flight on the 31st I secured for you?' I know the answer before it is spoken but have to let my disgruntlement be known, if only quietly.

'Under a little pressure from home.'

It's hardly surprising really. Al is never at home and with a growing young family his climbing would strain the most settled of relationships. His partner has been very understanding, but of late the reins were being shortened and with him away with work so often, this was understandable. But why does it have to affect *me* and impinge on *my* obsession?

We are heading south together once again, to the Peruvian Andes and another big, unclimbed face. This time I really hope the story of 'safe and secure' I have been telling my family and friends, is not untrue. Neither of us want a repeat of the Jirishanca death lob of 2002 or the very scary, though successful, ascent of *Fear and Loathing* on the same mountain in 2003.

The familiar journey went well: hours of flight, dossing on the floor of Lima airport, taxis, a whole day crushed and sweltering in a bus, and finally meeting friends as we disembarked in the middle of the bustling town of Hauraz. We rushed the acclimatisation. Time was of the essence. I secretly cursed Powell and his limited time affecting my chances of climbing a new route on the pointed east face of Chacraraju Este. But I said nothing, reasoning that even with limited time I would rather climb with Al than anyone else.

Returning to Hauraz, on a visit to the dark interior of Mount Climb, the local gear shop, we were dealt a hammer blow. All the area's new routes and topos are collated at the shop, and it emerged that two Slovenians had climbed our line in 2000. Both had been killed later that year in Nepal, leaving news of their Chacraraju ascent unreported beyond Hauraz.

We decided to go anyway. They had used aid to climb the line. Maybe we could free it?...Maybe another unclimbed line would present itself?...Maybe we fooled ourselves?...Crazy?...Maybe?

With a full rack of climbing equipment and full of dreams and aspirations, we followed the donkeys, carrying 10 days' worth of food, into the deep valley, richly covered with quenal trees, dark green leaves, flaking bark like burnt skin, into loneliness, into solitude, into the unknown. This is what I live for – my chosen route, a first and only ascent. Above, broad open slopes of pampas, glaciated slabs and stunted trees promised a lung-busting time ahead. I hoped I could fully acclimatise while stocking a high bivvi beneath the icefall and the awesome east face. Time would tell, but there wasn't much of it.

Two days of bad, snowy, rainy weather have made our route decision for us. No longer the steep direct line following a shallow runnel, following the Slovenians. Snow dusting the faces has made technical rock climbing impossible. I'm glad. Since the discovery that 'our' line had already been climbed it has lost some of the aura that surrounds an unclimbed route.

We sit together close to the campfire; silent, immersed in our own personal thoughts, watching the mackerel-shimmering embers glow and spark as the wind catches the growing mound of hot charcoal. The wild and windy west coast of Scotland comes to mind; hand-line fishing, Dad, my sister and me; Mum sat in the car listening to the Radio 4 play, protected against the cold and wet north wind. Feathers of bright blue, red and green disguise the barbed points of the fishhooks; hit the mackerel shoal and drag them in, all blue and silver and shimmering.

Tomorrow we go, our ambitions now set on Chacraraju's south-east ridge. It has had one ascent but only from the final headwall by a Japanese team in 1976 who used aid over many days. Condemned men, we sit in quiet contemplation. Powell breaks the spell.

'It's a fine line you know, the direct one; if we were in the Alps people would throw themselves at it. Why should it matter if the Slovenians beat us to it?' He continues in a whisper, wondering what motivates climbers.

58. Chacraraju, showing east face and south-east ridge. (*Nick Bullock*)

'Why does it have to be a new line? Why do some climbers choose the partners they do? Guaranteed article, guaranteed publicity, pleased sponsors, more work with a successful summit?' Powell is getting louder and angrier.

'Is this why some climb in a style which almost guarantees success? Alpine style, bollocks! Anyone starting a route with a portaledge and jumars who then calls it alpine style should have a serious look at their motivation. They should be truthful in their reasons. They should be truthful in their reporting. They should leave the climb until someone better comes along, someone who can do it in good style. Start at the bottom carrying what you can in a rucksack and go to the top. At times aid is needed but you don't go expecting to aid it, jug it, sit it out on your ledge, abseil back to the valley for a break, restock, de-stress, start again, rested, fresh.'

Powell is really animated, his face lit by the red glow of the fire. The freezing temperature outside the ring of the fire does nothing to cool his rant.

'What is really motivating these people? Piolet d'Or awards? I don't know, but one thing I do know for sure – it isn't alpinism, and as long as this type of ascent goes on we are going back, not forward.'

I sit quiet, digesting, assessing my own motivation. Being sponsored does not sit comfortably with me. I feel the need to give back so I feel the need to perform, but I will always climb for me, and at times fail; the line and the style are paramount, nothing else matters. Powell has spoken for the two of us.

The following night we begin our climb, a methodical kick and pick, head torches illuminating the snow and ice, until we reach the lowest point in the ridge and turn right. A mile of Peruvian, fluted, mushroomed, overhanging uncertainty awaits us, but the way to this scary stuff is barred by a red and grey crumbling granite step. I lead; it's difficult climbing, out of balance and unprotected. I take my gloves off to feel the grey stuff, but it doesn't help. Nor does taking off my rucksack. The impasse remains. I have a nagging feeling of being a let-down. Have I lost it since breaking my ankle?

'This is desperate, I'm coming back down, I've broken one ankle this year and that's enough.' I feel justified in my decision when Powell doesn't even contemplate leading the pitch. He scuttles off, following a gangplank out right, secures himself at the foot of another difficult-looking rock pitch and informs me it will be easy.

'Look at all the holds,' he says.

'So why don't you lead it?' I think.

Fortunately it goes, with gear and a little technique. Powell follows on a top-rope.

'How did you do the move right?' he shouts, quite loud for once.

'I did it by using all those holds you helpfully pointed out,' I answer with smug satisfaction, thinking, 'Yes, you bastard, now you try, you see, use all those big holds.'

Powell completes the pitch then leads up very loose but easy ground

59. Al Powell climbing the south-east ridge of Chacraraju. (*Nick Bullock*)

50. 'A spine of unconsolidated Gothic formations.' (*Nick Bullock*)

until we are stood on the knife-edged ridge. Moving together is the only option. There is nothing to belay to. The snow feels solid; overhanging at times and corniced, but OK, though the sun is shining with a worrying intensity.

We continue moving together, balancing, tiptoeing, a circus performance. Large gargoyles of snow push into the blue and settled sky, barriers for easy progression, barriers in time. All this tightrope-walking is tenuous, thought provoking, attention grabbing. Large snow formations grow at right angles to the ridge; they remind me of the peak of the cap worn by the security guard at Luton Airport. Over, under, around to the left, the right, tunnel, cut, move together, no belay, ropes hang in a great arc across a knife-edge of mushy-white. Powell confidently stands. I crawl. A BELAY!

We sit and talk. 'This is a fine spot for a bivvi isn't it, Mr P?'

'It is, Mr B, and I think we should take it.'

Powell enlarges a tent/sleeping spot. He's keen to try his new toy. Powell-designed, it's super-light and tent-like. He plays and studies, adjusts while I sit on a perfect crescent-moon-shaped scoop beneath an overhanging roof of condensed rotten snow and watch. Adam, the son he talks of so often, will surely be a designer, a scientist, a thinker and a doer, constantly on the move, constantly planning, working, competing. All day we have been on the edge, walking the tightrope. Defying the inevitable.

I think of a paragraph in the book I was reading before the climb started.

> In a world of insecurity and ambition and ego, its easy to be drawn in, to take chances with our lives, to believe what we do and what people say about us is enough reason to gamble with death. Now looking at your sleeping face, inches away from me, I wonder how I could ever have thought glory and prizes and fame were sweeter than life.
>
> Fergal Keane, *Letter to Daniel*

The writing had nothing to do with climbing but as I read the words it struck me that it had everything to do with climbing. The previous year, on Jirishanca, we were involved in a search for two Austrian climbers who were buried and killed in an avalanche. I witnessed the heartache and trauma felt by friends left behind. It was then I started to understand. I have no wife or partner or children, but my parents are still living and I have a sister and many close friends. I have lived away from Britain for long periods since becoming a full-time climber. My mother grows old without her son near. Each time I return to Britain she is older, she has more grey hair, she is thin. She worries. I feel guilt at this life I have chosen. Is it fair to inflict this on my parents?

Powell talks of his son; his hair, his smile, the way he moves, plays, cries. I cannot begin to comprehend the feelings of being a father. I watch Powell's face light up when he talks to me about Adam. The fact that he takes the time to talk to me, the world's most cynical bachelor, is telling in itself.

51. 'Large gargoyles of snow push into the blue.' (*Nick Bullock*)

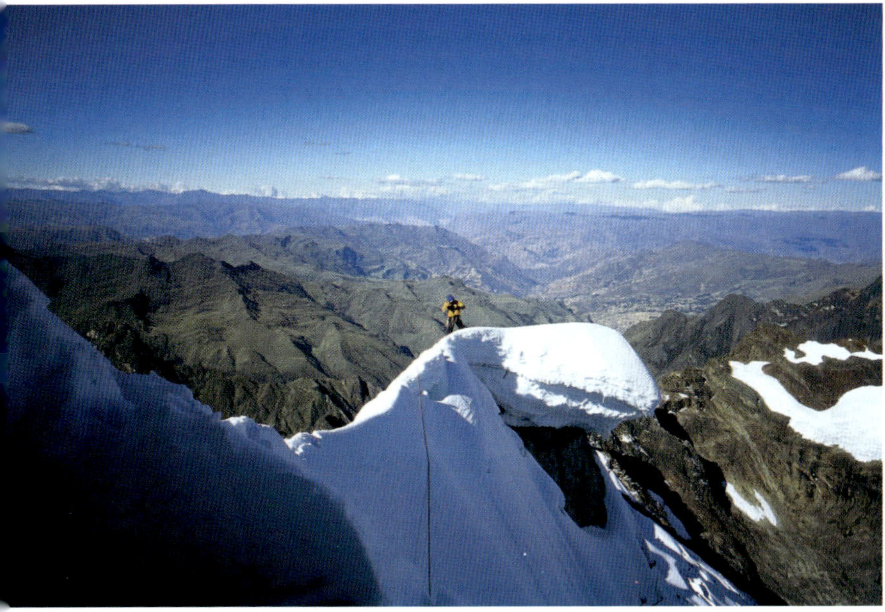

52. 'Snow formations grow at right angles ... a reminder of the security guard's peaked cap.' (*Nick Bullock*)

The night passes and the sun hits the ridge. Immediately the temperature increases from deathly cold to just cold, even warm on the north side. I grow concerned. The ridge ahead is becoming more serrated, a spine of unconsolidated Gothic formations that will be weakening, sagging and melting. The rock ribs we climb, to bypass the snow-overhangs, are loose and moving. I pull on freezer-sized blocks of granite and watch, horrified, as they rip from the face and fly past the ropes – ropes attached to my waist and nothing else, hanging in arcs across gullies, over fins of ice, around bulges of snow and back to Powell who is out of sight, out of hearing and unable to fathom what is happening.

More blocks pull away, crumble and tumble towards the glacier hundreds of feet below. The ropes come tight at my waist. Without shouting I wait for the tell-tale release. When it comes I know Powell has stripped the belay and is moving over the same unstable, uncertain ground. I try to remember what gear I placed. Was it good, would it hold if both of us should fall or one of the fins we balanced across collapse? I decide to forget.

The norm now is 90-metre pitches. The only time I feel safe is when Powell is on one side of the ridge and I'm on the other. I plan what I could do if he fell when belayed 40 metres away on the opposite side of the ridge, beneath an overhang of snow. How long would I wait before it becomes apparent he has fallen and is hanging, injured, or unconscious?

He has been over an hour now on this pitch. Is he OK? What is happening? The ropes have remained stationary for ages. I hear tumbling, rock-blocks crashing down rubble-strewn gullies, as slowly the ropes inches out.

'Al, are you OK?' I shout as loudly as my dry throat will allow, but there's no reply. I'm under an overhang of ice, the wind whipping spindrift into my face, and longing for the sun. Fingers are numb, feet and toes cold. I want it to be just a bad dream and to wake up back in England, make a coffee in my kitchen, sit in front of my fire, eat fresh toast and read a book. I don't want to be scared anymore.

The ropes pull me out of my dream world. Following Powell's trench it becomes apparent why he has taken so long. Balancing on the crest the ropes run away, down the opposite side of the ridge, across loose crumbling blocks held in place by rotten, sun-bleached ice and aerated snow. He has placed a wire low, the rope's pulled it up, an ice-screw into crud, and a wire into crumbling rock, and then his best piece – one of his tools smashed into ice. I don't fancy my chances should I fall. A downward traverse, following a four-inch ledge of gravel, onto a flake system of loose granite ears, onto rotten ice; then the *pièce de resistance*, a vertical down-climb of a loose corner.

Powell cheers me up by shouting from his hanging position: 'I call this the Paul Daniels pitch.'

'Why's that then?' I call back, glad of the wait, glad to delay the oncoming horror show.

Powell grins, then yawps: 'You're going to like this ... But not a lot!'

'Ha, you don't know how right your are, Mr P.'

I can delay the inevitable no longer and begin the traverse; it reminds me of entering the headmaster's office years ago. Fifteen intense minutes later I am down-climbing the corner and enjoying the looseness of the pitch.

'Jesus, you wouldn't want to be climbing this at the top of your grade would you?'

'No. This would really freak some folk out, you definitely need grades in hand for this stuff.'

'Yes, about 10 of them,' I think, scrabbling to Powell's position.

Exchanging gear, I wonder about the worth of what we are doing. Are we ever going to reach the steep stuff at the end of this horror-show ridge? The next pitch is as tenuous and desperate-looking as everything before. I don't want to lead it. I want to descend the rotten, deadly rubble-strewn gully to escape. I want an end to the insecurity.

'We're never going to reach that headwall, you know, let's just bail out now while we can. Did you see the ridge further on? It looks more dangerous than anything we've done yet. Two days' worth of climbing, I reckon?'

'Aye, I think you're right, but lead this pitch and then we'll have a better idea back on top of the ridge.'

'OK, I'll give it a go.' It is said without conviction or confidence. An hour later I feel pleased that I had the balls to lead the pitch. Vertical, air-pocketed, a warped and twisted wall of layered ice, wood grain without the strength, and only three pieces of protection within 60 metres, a crumbling ice bollard, one loose ice-screw and one which had a chance of holding. Tucked beneath another overhang of rotting ice, waiting for Powell, I look at what is to come. It looks horrific. Our two days of climbing have just been the warm-up. Buoyed up by my lead of the last pitch, I am inspired to continue yet simultaneously feel it would be pointless.

A feeling of worthlessness threatens to overpower me. It is useless to feel these conflicting emotions. I crave safety and security but also want to push on. Why would it be pointless to continue, even if we only reach the end of the ridge, then have to escape? Would it be because it would be just another failed attempt, not newsworthy, not worth the space for a picture or words in a magazine? Here I am having an adventure, pushing myself to the limit, doing what I set out to do 11 years earlier, so it shouldn't matter if we don't reach the headwall, it shouldn't matter if we run away and escape ... but it does.

Powell comes over the crest and down-climbs to my shivering form beneath the ice-roof.

'Have you seen the ridge? Jesus, it looks impossible. Two days' worth of climbing, at least, and that's only if we live that long.'

I'm glad he has come to a similar assessment. It helps when one so driven as Al has decided the situation is getting out of hand. I still feel a let-down though. I still feel a fraud and a lightweight. Would the alpinists of the past have retreated now the going was getting a little difficult? I don't think so. They didn't have all this new technology, light gear, synthetic, breathable,

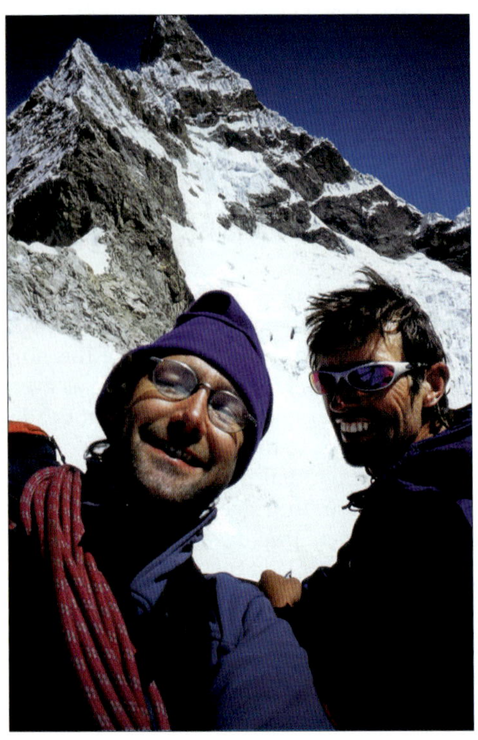

63. Nick Bullock (*left, with rope*) and Al Powell beneath the south-east ridge of Chacraraju. (*Nick Bullock*)

quick-drying, as warm as you like clothing, but look at what they climbed and in what style. They were the real pioneers, the real alpinists.

For once we still have plenty of food, gas and equipment to continue; we still have energy for climbing and the weather remains settled. But enough is enough. It is time to descend, time to escape and continue life with less uncertainty, to lick wounds and plan the next adventure.

Summary: An attempt on the south-east ridge of Chacraraju Este, Cordillera Blanca, Peru, in 2004 by Nick Bullock and Al Powell. After two days' climbing on the ridge with sections of Scottish V/6 (though this gives little idea of the seriousness) the pair abseiled down the south side of the ridge. Bullock later joined Swede Adam Kovacs to climb a new direct finish to the *Jaeger Route* on the mountain's south face, with two pitches of Scottish VI and one of V.

Nick Bullock and Al Powell would like to thank the MEF, the BMC and the Sports Council for the grants, which made this trip possible, and also Mammut, DMM, RAB, and Outdoor Designs for gear.

ERMANNO SALVATERRA

El Arca de los Vientos

A true first ascent of Cerro Torre's north face

Thirteen long years have passed since I first tried to climb Cerro Torre from the north. It was in 1992 with Guido Bonvicini and Adriano Cavallaro. We made our first attempt during October, and managed to reach the base of the so-called 'English Dihedral', climbed in 1981 by Phil Burke and Tom Proctor. We had climbed 550m to that point but turned back because the face was covered in snow. While we waited for better conditions, we climbed the *Franco-Argentina* on Fitz Roy and the *Compressor* on Cerro Torre. In November we made a second attempt and slept at the base of the dihedral inside the English box portaledge, left by Brian Wyvill and Ben Campbell Kelly. The following day the weather was terrible and my partners wanted to descend, but I asked them to give me at least a couple more hours to climb a little higher. I wanted to get to the Col of Conquest, and this we managed to do. I was simply curious to see it. There the storm forced us to retreat.

In 1994 I made another attempt on the same route with the Austrian Tommy Bonapace. He had already tried this line half a dozen times. In the morning we left base camp and by afternoon had reached the base of the triangular snowfield, some 300m above the glacier. We were faced with a series of unfortunate events, and after an awful bivouac Tommy told me, 'Finish, Ermanno, never more.' I knew then that his relationship with this line had come to an end.

The years passed and yet every now and then I was seized by the memory of the face. For a long time I had defended Cesare Maestri, Toni Egger and Cesarino Fava.* I had done so in public debates and bar conversations, and I had argued tooth and nail with Maestri's most persistent doubter, Ken Wilson, then editor of the English climbing magazine, *Mountain.* Nevertheless, little by little my mind was changing. As I re-read and studied everything that had been said and written in defence of Maestri, I started to have some serious doubts. There was no doubt, however, about my desire to climb this supposed route of Maestri's. This dream of mine never died.

In November 2004 I returned home from Patagonia, after completing a new route on the east face of Cerro Torre and two months later celebrated my 50th birthday. For the first time I realized that time was passing, and in

* Maestri claimed that he and Egger made the first ascent of Cerro Torre in 1959 via the north face. Egger fell to his death during the descent, taking with him their only camera, according to Maestri.

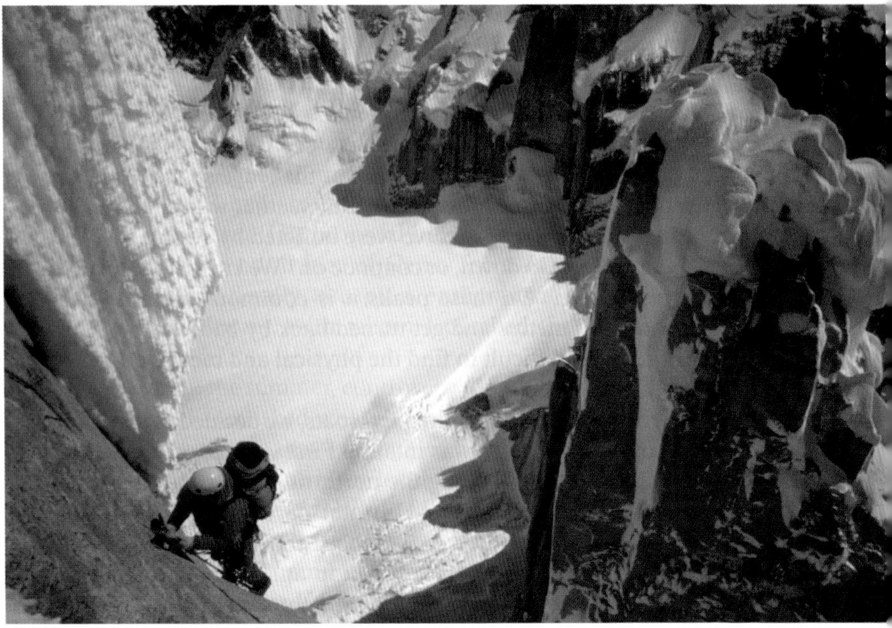

64. Rolando Garibotti on the last pitch of the north face, just shy of the west ridge, where they joined the *Ragni di Lecco* route along which they climbed three pitches to reach the summit. (*Ermanno Salvaterra*)

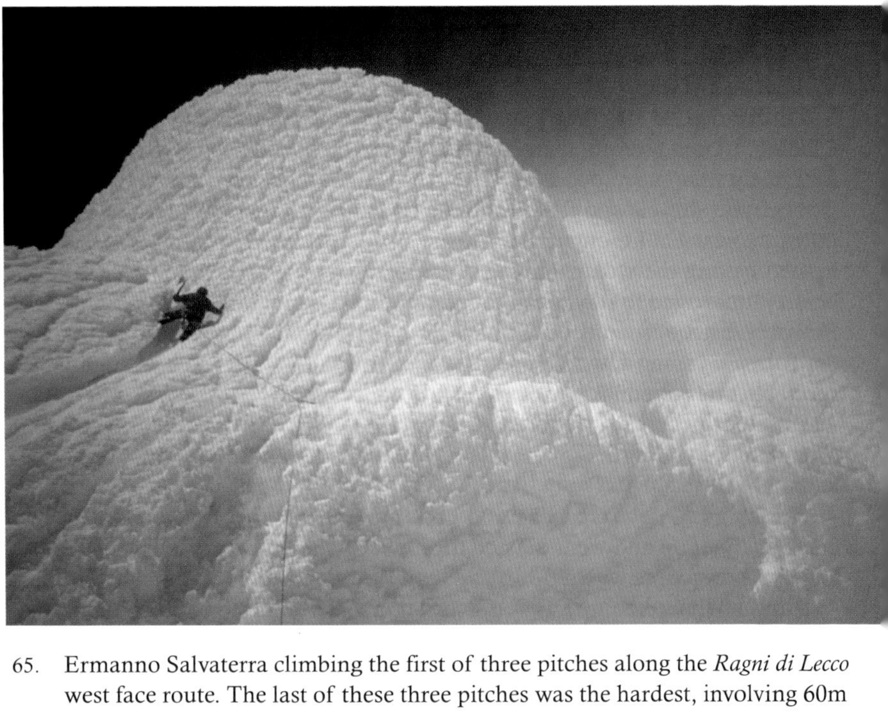

65. Ermanno Salvaterra climbing the first of three pitches along the *Ragni di Lecco* west face route. The last of these three pitches was the hardest, involving 60m of vertical and inconsistent frost. (*Rolando Garibotti*)

It was snowing as we hiked back to El Chaltén, planning our next attempt as we descended. We would travel as light as possible, leaving behind absolutely everything that seemed superfluous. We were quite tired and knew that we would need a few days' rest. Bad weather the next day left little choice. On the 11th the sky seemed to be clearing, and although we had wanted to rest a couple more days, practically against our will we decided to go back up. We didn't talk much during the walk-in, but our legs felt good and in less than six hours we arrived at the snow-cave. We quickly prepared to climb and Rolo and I started up the wall, climbing the first four pitches, as before fixing our three climbing ropes. Ale stayed behind to work on a new snow-cave that for safety sake we had moved underneath Torre Egger. In little more than two hours Rolo and I returned 'home', and helped Ale with the finishing touches. Our new cave was quite lovely and much more secure than the previous one. The weather was turning out to be fantastic, without even the tiniest breeze, and our enthusiasm was empowering us.

The alarm went off at 3.45am. Breakfast was ridiculously hurried. The weather was perfect and there wasn't a second to lose. At 4.45am, with headlamps on our helmets, we began jumaring the three ropes. We climbed another two pitches and soon arrived at the triangular snowfield. At six the sun began to warm us up.

Retracing our line of just a few days' ago, we moved fast. Rolo used a technique he had learned in Yosemite called 'short-fixing', where at the belay the remaining rope is pulled up, anchored, and then the leader continues up a few more metres. In this way we were able to climb between 10 and 20 metres in each pitch. The slabs above the snowfield are fairly difficult but knowing exactly where to go enabled us to maintain momentum. The snow covering the ramp up to the pillar above the Col of Conquest was in better condition than before, and again we were able to save a lot of time. It was barely noon when we got to the pillar, 50m above the col.

With the cracks on the north-west face still clear of snow from our previous attempt, we were able to get to the small terrace on the edge of the north ridge at around 4.30pm. On our first attempt it had taken us two days to reach this point. We decided it would be a good place to bivouac, but as a few hours of daylight remained we opted to fix a couple of pitches on the north face. After a pause I set out on a short traverse, following a thin crack, and then made a couple of hard moves on a slab, to another traverse. The wall was now in shade and the cold was biting our hands. After this first pitch Rolo and Ale climbed one more, also fairly hard. While we were busy on the north face, the north-west face began to release huge pieces from the frozen mushrooms above, but luckily on the ridge we were safe.

The bivouac spot was phenomenal; in front of us Torre Egger, to the right Fitz Roy, and to the left, the immense Continental Icecap and its mountains. The cold was penetrating and the sky filled with stars. Night passed quickly and we even managed to sleep a bit.

66. Ermanno Salvaterra jumaring on the last pitch of the initial dihedral, just below the triangular snowfield. (*Rolando Garibotti*)

67. Rolando Garibotti and Ermanno Salvaterra on the summit of Cerro Torre. (*Ermanno Salvaterra*)

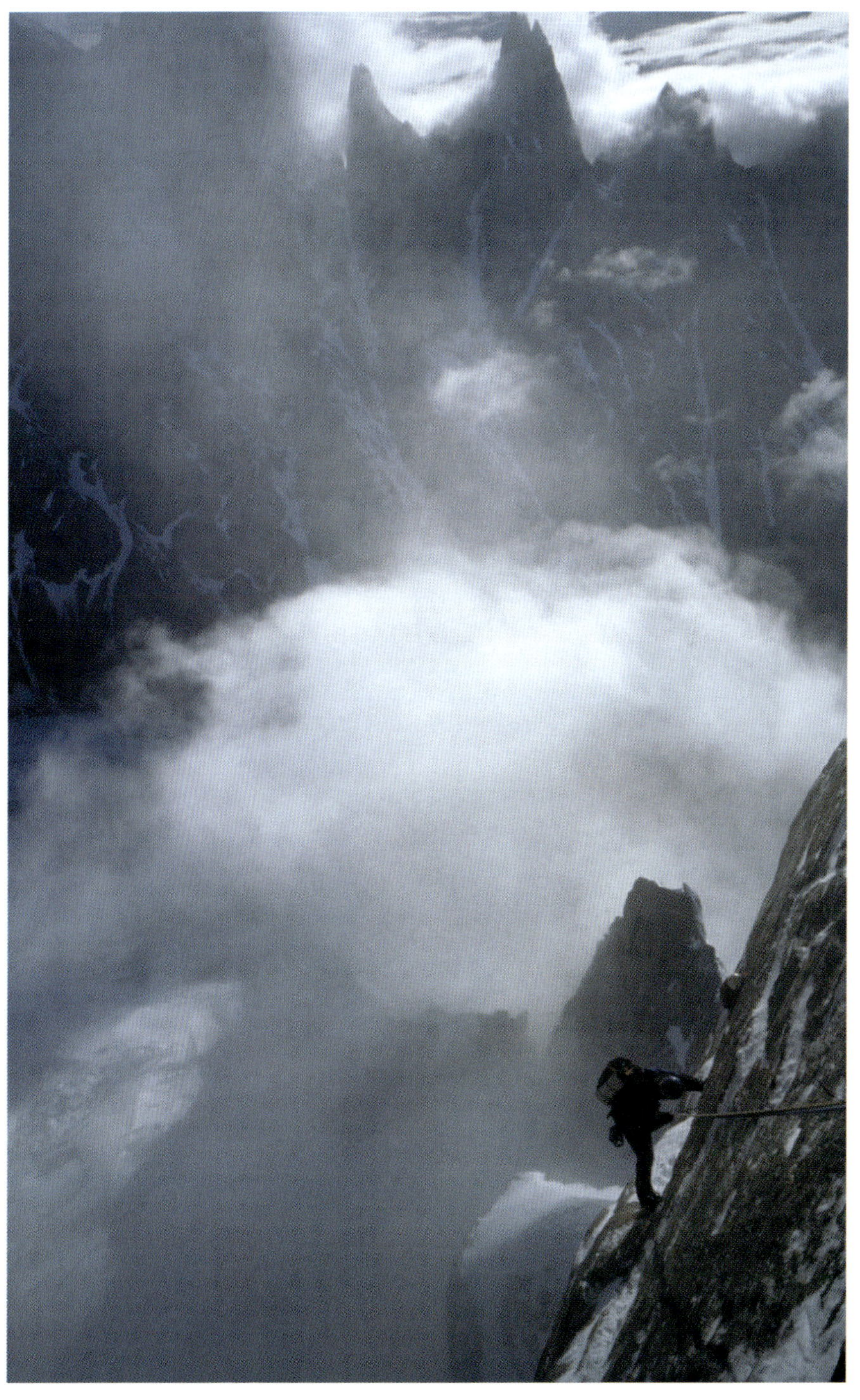

68. Alessandro Beltrami rappelling along the SE ridge of Cerro Torre after the ascent of *El Arca de los Vientos*. (*Rolando Garibotti*)

Cerro Torre
East face
fot. R. Garibotti

Cerro Torre
North-west face
fot. R. Garibotti

Cerro Torre
North face
fot. R. Garibotti

Left
69. Cerro Torre route lines. (*Rolando Garibotti*)

1 American route on Torre Egger by John Bragg, Jim Donini and Jay Wilson, 1976. (First ascent of the peak)
2 Highest point reached by Toni Egger, Cesarino Fava and Cesare Maestri in 1959.
3 *Arca de los Vientos*, Alessandro Beltrami, Rolando Garibotti and Ermanno Salvaterra, 2005 (1200m, ABO). "(a)" marks the first bivouac site. The second bivvi was right under the summit mushroom, before descending via the *Compressor* route the following day.
4 *Compressor* route by Jim Bridwell and Steve Brewer in 1979 to the summit. In 1970 Enzio Alimonta, Carlo Claus and Cesare Maestri reached a point 30 metres below the summit.
5 *Ragni di Lecco* route, Daniele Chiappa, Mario Conti, Casimiro Ferrari and Pino Negri, 1974. Theirs was, it is now generally believed, the first ascent of the mountain.

Next morning, 13 November, I felt as if I was in a movie or in a dream. Though we started getting ready at 6am, it was two hours later before we began climbing. Luckily, soon after, the sun began to warm our frozen bodies. The wall was nearly vertical and quite difficult. From the top of the ropes we had fixed the day before, Rolo climbed another two pitches, zig-zagging between ice mushrooms to arrive at the top of the north face. When I got up to him at the last belay we hugged each other with emotion. We spoke breathlessly. Now below us, the north face was no longer a problem. With another pitch on perfect ice we joined the *Ragni de Lecco* route, climbed in 1974 by Daniele Chiappa, Mariolino Conti, Casimiro Ferrari and Pino Negri.

It was around 1pm and above us huge unconsolidated ice formations promised to make progress quite difficult. The summit of Torre Egger was now far below us, but we still couldn't see Cerro Torre's summit. The next series of pitches took a lot of effort. The ice wasn't solid or consistent and sometimes we had to dig more than 50cm deep before finding ice or snow solid enough to climb on. We only had two snow pickets and since ice screws were useless, protection was nearly non-existent. But we weren't about to surrender. We were ready to do whatever it took. The sky had clouded over and it began to snow and blow a bit. The last pitch we did in sections, each of us going up a little. Once again the cold became penetrating. Finally, three quarters of an hour before midnight, we reached the highest point on Cerro Torre. Ale reminded me that exactly one year before we had arrived on this same summit after climbing a new route on the east face. It was a profoundly emotional moment. After taking a few pictures we descended the mushroom and sat under a snow overhang to wait for night to pass. Next morning we descended via the *Compressor* route on the south-east ridge.

70. West face of Mount Alverstone in the Wrangell St Elias range. Yates-Schweizer route follows the couloir left of the central glacier cwm. (*Simon Yates*)

71. Base camp on the Alverstone glacier. (*Simon Yates*)

72. Paul Schweizer climbing the 50 degree couloir on day one, Mount Alverstone's west face. (*Simon Yates*)

We set up base camp in the lee of a rognon and the following day made a reconnaissance. The foot of Alverstone's west face turned out to be a mere hour and a half walk away. The prominent west buttress on the left side of the face had been climbed by Pilling and Diedrich in 1995, and the broad gully to its right by Blanchard and Wilford in 1998. On the right hand boundary of the main face we spied a fine unclimbed couloir line that led almost to the top of the mountain.

On the evening of 7 May we left base camp with four days' worth of food and gas and camped beneath the face. Early the following morning we began solo climbing up reasonably angled slopes of hard névé. As the sun came up and warmed the upper part of the face rocks started to fall. At one point, about 750m up, the couloir narrowed. As we hurried through the dangerous bottleneck two rocks hit me almost simultaneously on the forearm and shoulder. My arm immediately swelled and stiffened, but did not appear to be broken. With the sun now out, the névé turning to bare ice and a fatal drop below, we decided to dig out the ropes and start pitching. It was a wise move. The climbing steepened to 50 degree ice, with short steeper sections and the hot intense sunshine ensured sporadic rock-fall continued for the rest of the climb. In the evening we found a snow bank above a small icefall and excavated a tent platform 1200m up the face. It had been a long day.

Due to tiredness and the need to rehydrate we did not start early the following morning. Seven rope lengths of good 55-60 degree ice eventually led to a flat col on the summit ridge. We dumped our rucksacks and wandered up to the top, marvelling at the mountains and glaciers spread out before us in perfect weather. After savouring the views we returned to our rucksacks and put up the tent. The sky became hazy as the evening drew on and a strong smell of wood smoke hung in the air. Somewhere, a long way off, a huge forest fire was blazing. The night was still, but bitterly cold.

Next morning, our hopes for a fast descent were soon quashed. After some easy down-climbing of Alverstone's north flank to the Great Shelf we failed to find a good route down to the Alverstone glacier. Instead we crossed a watershed and dropped down on to the Dusty glacier to the north. With no prior knowledge of the sérac- studded face we found ourselves descending, route finding was soon a little nerve-racking. Finally, we made a nasty abseil from a snow bollard down a sérac, kicking off at its base to clear a huge crevasse, before sprinting down the lower part of the face until clear of the avalanche debris on the glacier below. Hours of trudging up the Dusty glacier followed until we called it a day.

Our last remaining gas canister provided breakfast and then expired. We set off for a col that we knew would access the upper Alverstone glacier, but then just below it we convinced ourselves that a lower col further to the west would be the better option. It was not. Our fit of collective optimism forced a further unpleasant descent on to a fork of the Hubbard glacier.

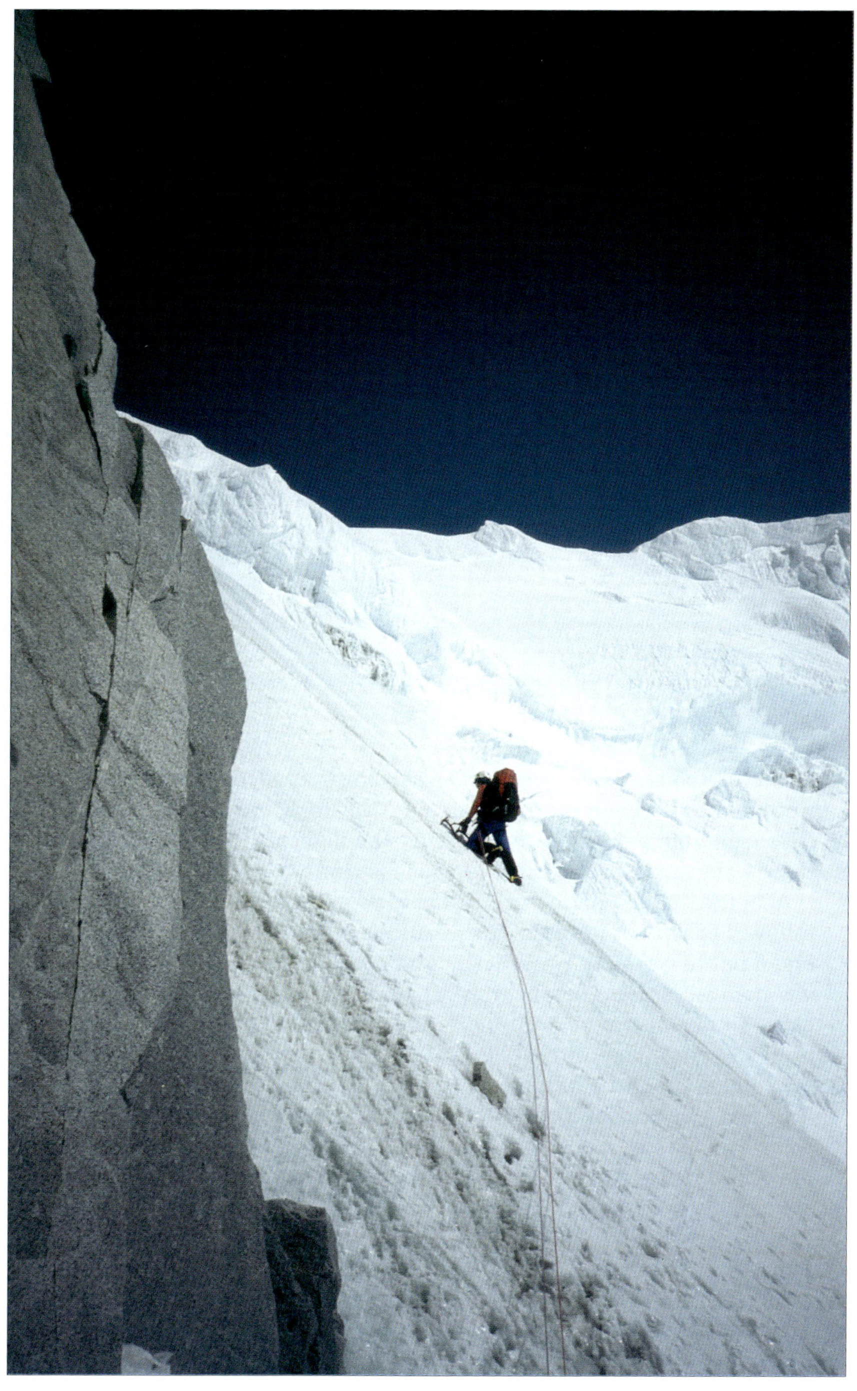

73. Day two on the west face, Paul Schweizer heading for the col on the summit ridge. (*Simon Yates*)

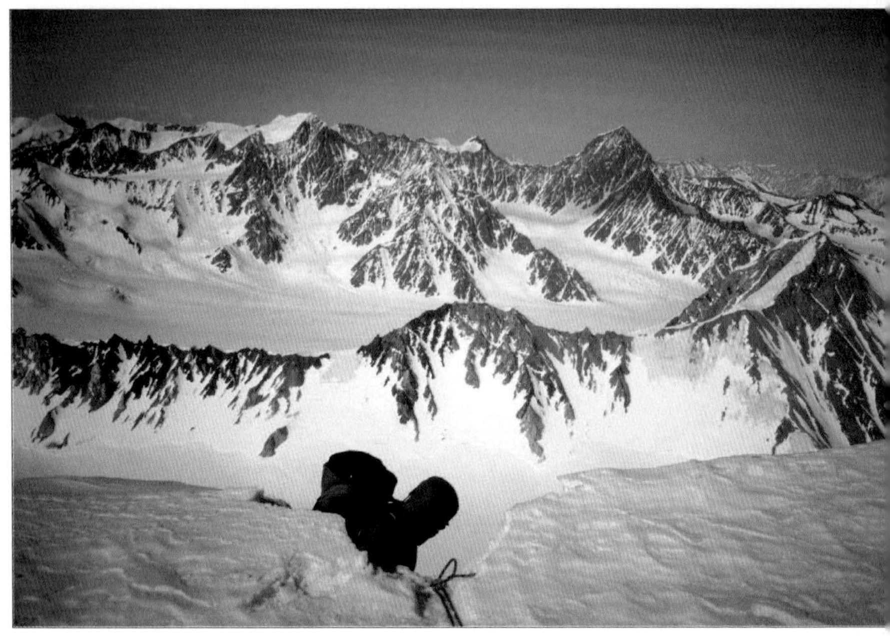

74. Paul Schweizer begins the descent from Mount Alverstone to the Dusty glacier. (*Simon Yates*)

However, the real penalty for our mistake was a hideous climb up a long ridge in the afternoon sun to regain the Alverstone. We finally reached our base camp tents in the early evening. The descent, with the crossing of three watersheds, had taken as long as the climb.

A quick satellite phone call to the airstrip arranged a pick-up for the following day. Alas it was not to be. A storm moved in. It snowed for three and a half days. With two weeks' food and fuel remaining, our situation was hardly desperate, but the whisky had run out. After a further two phone calls Andy empathised with the serious nature of our position and in a brief clearing flew in to effect a well-timed exit. We had been in the mountains a mere 11 days.

Back at the Kluane Lake airstrip we celebrated our good fortune with some Yukon Gold Ale. The bottles carried the slogan 'Melt the snow. Brew the beer. Life is good'. We drank to that simple but fine philosophy.

Summary: The first full ascent of Mount Alverstone's 1800m west face in the Wrangell St Elias range from 8 -11 May 2005 by Paul Schweizer and Simon Yates. The route is Alpine IV+, TD+.

Acknowledgements: Paul Schweizer and Simon Yates would like to thank Sport UK and The British Mountaineering Council for their financial support of the expedition.

ADE MILLER & SIMEON WARNER

Good Times on Good Neighbor

On a clear day you can see Good Neighbor Peak – the south summit of Mt Vancouver – from the end of the runway in Yakutat, Alaska. The south rib appears to rise directly from the sea to the summit, just asking to be climbed. In May 1993, Ade had met Bill Pilling and Carl Diedrich outside one of the airport hangers; Bill was hardly a welcoming advertisement for the south rib. The pair had just completed the first ascent of Good Neighbor but Bill had smashed his leg in a crevasse fall near the summit. He and Carl then spent several days descending the mountain, Bill crawling most of the way.

Twelve years later we were camped below the initial couloir on the south rib at 2517m. The previous afternoon we had skied from our base camp and descended a couloir to the glacier below Good Neighbor's south-west face. Our plan: climb the route in three to four days and descend the south spur of the south-east ridge in one day. We packed food for four days and fuel for six.

The following morning, after a short wait for the weather to clear, we set off up the initial couloir. Simeon got the ball rolling by kicking steps up the already soft snow to the top of the couloir at around 2790m. The rock was rumoured to be of dubious quality in places and so it proved. We climbed the entire day trying to stick with the crest wherever possible as the rock there was slightly better. At just over 3050m the ridge became icy. Traversing the final section to 'bivvi nirvana' provided some excitement when one of Ade's crampons detached. This gave us a few moments pondering the possibility of an exciting, if brief, top-down inspection of the south face. Ade managed to hop to a better stance and reattach his crampon whereupon we found a good tent site behind an ice block at 3240m.

Day 2: A colder and windy dawn. The inevitable wait for the sun on the tent ensued. We aren't the best practitioners of the prompt alpine start and this route didn't look like it was going to change things. Above, the route takes the west side of the ridge and climbs a couloir system for 600 metres. We could see this from our tent, although getting into the base of the couloir from the ridge seemed tricky. We started up the ridge but were forced to rappel into the couloir at about 3350m. Simeon set off up the couloir and disappeared into a narrow section about 30m above. It soon became apparent that things were not going quite as planned. Swearing and curses started to float down from above – generally a bad sign in Simeon's case. Above, the gully had turned to a mixture of wet gravel, slush and poorly bonded wet ice; the shale sidewalls offering no opportunity for protection.

75. The route from the south-west. The south rib is the obvious ridge in the foreground. The descent follows the ridge in the background. (*Ade Miller*)

We were forced to simul-climb until Simeon found something approximating to an anchor. Ade adopted a 'don't ask, don't tell' policy on the anchor as he continued up, finally finding better rock to the right as the couloir widened.

We climbed a mix of couloir and rock ridge all day. With no flat spots in sight, we pushed on, eventually reaching a snow rib at 3870m. There was a stiff wind blowing as we chopped out an ice ledge below the crest. By the time we got bored with chipping, our ledge supported about a third of the Bibler tent's floor space. If you've ever wondered what could be more claustrophobic than the Bibler, and what could be more foolish than using a gasoline stove inside it: spend a night melting snow with the stove balanced on your knees and then take turns to snatch a little sleep in the usable corner of the tent. You'll have answers to both questions – 'very little'.

Day 3: A predictably early start. We stuck to the ridge, skipping the next snow couloir for fear of a repeat of the previous day. The rock on the ridge improved but the climbing became harder, eventually defeating us at a steep wall. We rapped into another couloir and, this time, luck was with us. We climbed the couloir for some 150m-200m on *névé*, getting good gear most of the way and only finding a short section without snow.

The route description mentioned a knife-edged ridge, but as we pulled over the final rock section it was still a surprise. It wasn't as corniced as

76. View from the first bivvi showing a couloir that splits the rock band. (*Ade Miller*)

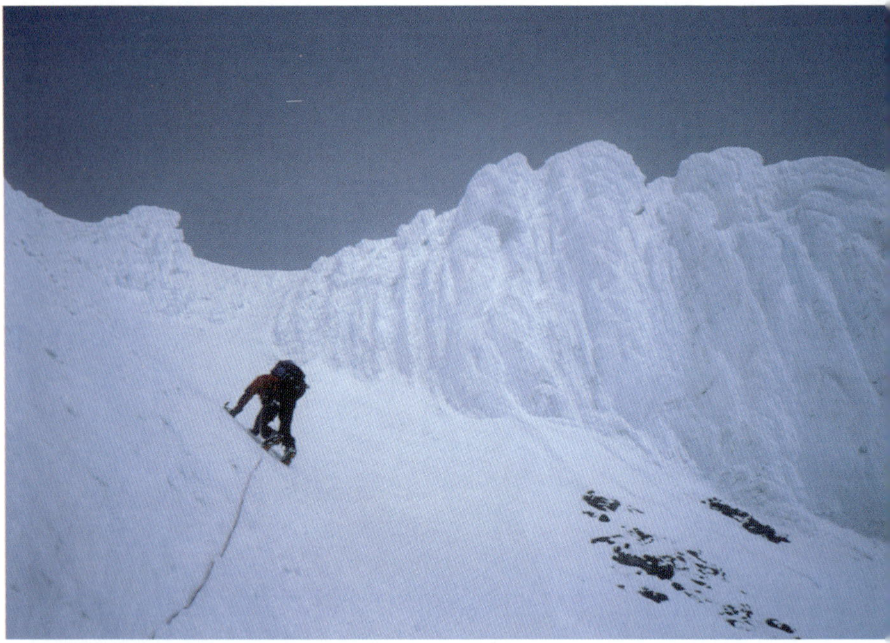

77. Ade early on the morning of day 6, after the storm cleared. (*Simeon Warner*)

78. Simeon descending the south spur of the south-east ridge. (*Ade Miller*)

reported on the first ascent but was nonetheless thought provoking, with big drops into the cloud on either side. Our three screws were enough to make the ascent reasonably sensible by leapfrogging each other's leads; sometimes balancing on the crest, sometimes shuffling astride it or traversing on the icier east side. The last rope length on the ridge reached the base of a sérac below the summit slopes. Another pitch brought us to a flat bivvi spot on top of the sérac band at 4360m.

We were a little concerned that cloud had been moving in and out throughout the day. Should it cloud in on the summit, navigation would be difficult. From the tent we could see the rimed séracs that guarded the south side of the summit plateau. The ground below them looked straightforward though we failed to factor in the altitude, which had finally caught up with us.

Day 4: We kicked steps to a large crevasse 100m above the bivvi; above that, the slope turned to hard ice. We simul-climbed some of it but for the most part were reduced to swinging rope lengths as it was just too tiring to move any faster and falling off seemed inadvisable. We each pushed out our leads ten steps at a time before resting and then going on again. Eventually we reached a runnel in the rime leading to the top of the final ice cliffs guarding the summit, and – we hoped – flat ground. The final runnel proved steep but short and we topped out at 2pm, five and a half hours after leaving the bivvi.

The terrain abruptly became horizontal. Gaps in the cloud gave us views along the ridge to Vancouver itself but that was about it. We ditched packs and postholed to the highest point on the lumpy summit crest. After a few photos and congratulations on a job half done we trudged back to our gear, ready to descend.

We dropped down onto the north side of the south-east ridge to avoid some séracs and were immediately in thigh-deep unconsolidated powder. This seemed like very bad news but we hoped it was localized to north-facing slopes. For most of the descent to the col we were able to stick to the ridge crest where conditions were better. We pitched the tent at the col on a nice site dug into the ridge.

It took us two days to descend the south-east ridge, the first spent sitting out bad weather near the top. The following day treated us to a spectacular dawn as the storm cleared and we set off early before the newly loaded slopes warmed up. We down-climbed most of the broad ridge, rappelling from a huge snow bollard to negotiate a large sérac that split the entire slope at about 3350m. The remainder of the descent was relatively straightforward with the exception of a near miss with a small avalanche as the sun started to loosen the new snow.

Another hour brought us back to our cache at the base of the route. And thanks to our pilot, Paul Swanstrom, we were back in Haines the following afternoon to engage in some 'social drinking' with the locals.

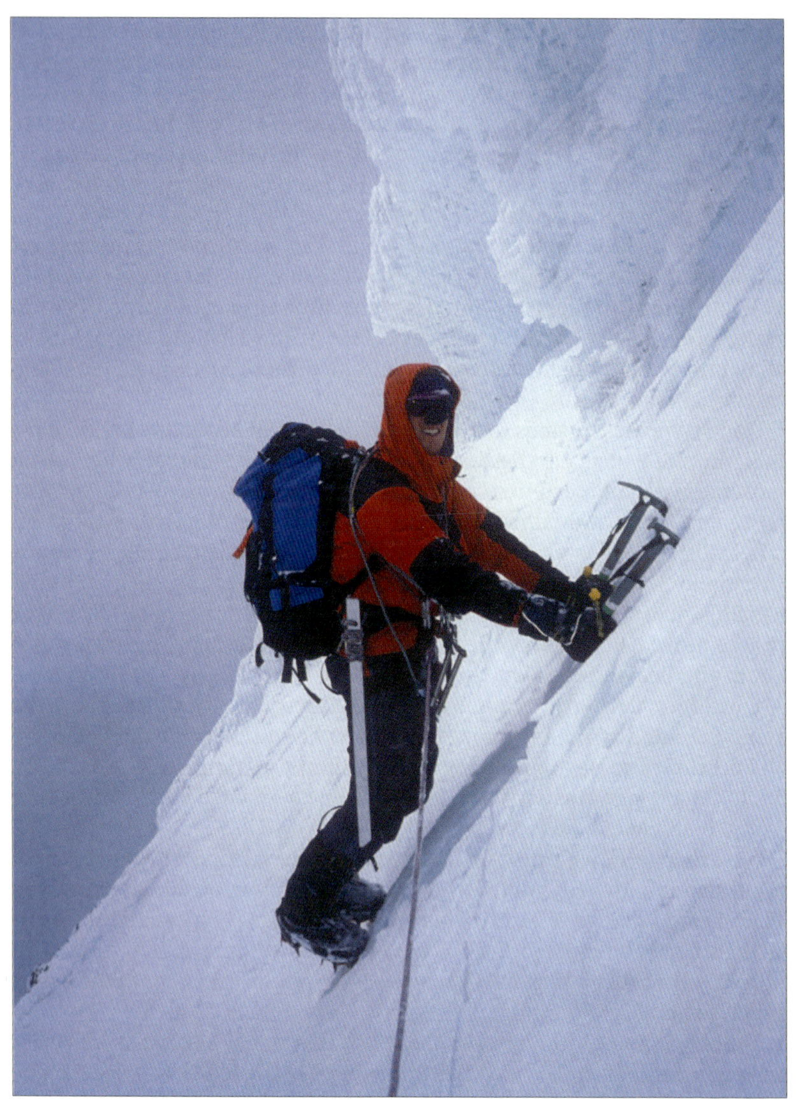

79. Simeon climbing below the summit ice cliffs. (*Ade Miller*)

Summary: Ade Miller and Simeon Warner climbed the south rib of Good Neighbor Peak (4724m, AK 4+, Pilling-Diedrich, 1993). The route was completed in six days starting on 17 May 2005 and summiting on the 20th. It was the third ascent of the route and first ascent of Good Neighbor by a British team. Further details of this and other climbing activity can be found on: http://www.bivouac.com

JOHN ARRAN

Rainbow Jambaia

A first free ascent of Angel Falls face

Climbing is not about dreams, not usually. It's about tangible things: challenge, strength, guile, camaraderie, judgement, fun. The stuff of everyday life without the dull bits. But as I walked from the edge of one of the highest overhanging cliffs in the world, finally leaving behind a thousand metres and 19 days of free-climbing adventure, I knew this dream had been as real as any of our marginal placements. As real as the burning pump that had seared though our forearms like the hot-aches. As real as the very rock we had sought to climb, had been thwarted by, and had finally overcome by all manner of devious and sometimes desperate measures these last three weeks.

And suddenly it was over. Silently exploded into a thousand cherished memories; each a smile or a warm glow, but together as rich a resource of satisfaction as I could ever have imagined possible from such a simple act as starting at the bottom of a rock wall and finishing at the top.

The view from the top of a mountain, so they say, is much finer after a long and difficult ascent. And our irrepressible glow of satisfaction that afternoon on the summit plateau was all the more radiant for the years of trial, heartbreak and finally success that eventually brought us there.

Little could we have imagined, as we sat watching television on a cold and dark evening in the year 2000, that the course of much of our energy and emotion for the following five years was quite literally passing before our eyes. The programme was a documentary about BASE jumping and the hero of the piece – the venerable Eric Jones no less – was becoming the oldest person ever to launch himself from the top of the highest waterfall in the world, Venezuela's remote and magnificent Angel Falls. As the plunging photographer locked his helmet camera on the free-falling alpinist, the immaculate orange cliff behind him was disappearing out of frame at an alarming rate. Anne and I sat mesmerised, wondering how such a huge, staggeringly beautiful and quite possibly climbable face could have escaped the attention of the world's climbers, and the very next day I determined to find out more.

Five years later our team of seven internationally accomplished climbers had finally discovered what it would take to free climb this incomprehensibly high and relentlessly overhanging edifice. In doing so we had all pushed our physical and psychological limits, particularly as we had been determined not to protect the climbing with bolts or other fixed gear.

80. A very happy Alfredo Rangél jumaring the final 80m rope to the summit. (*Anne Arran*)

So wonderfully remote and pristine was the objective, it would have been a crime to have bludgeoned our way up the wall rather than to have met the challenge in all of its natural glory. We had been scared. Exhausted. Baffled. Sometimes all three at once. The terrain had been sustained and unpredictable, every day bringing new and unique challenges with a constant threat of coming up against a free-climbing impasse. So much so that it wasn't until the nineteenth and final day of climbing that we could admit to and enjoy any certainty of success.

For Anne and I, and for our good Venezuelan friend Ivan Calderón, it was our third attempt on the face. Hindsight tells us that the first, in 2002, was a triumph of determined optimism over reasoning. 'Some routes have been climbed from the jungly shoulder on the left,' explained Ivan as we excitedly approached our rainforest base camp for the first time. 'Maybe we should repeat the American free route, or try to free the Japanese line, which traverses across closer to the falls at the top. That would be very hard.' But Anne and I were insistent. We had come to free climb the main challenge of the wall direct – an unrepeated line up which had been forced by Basque climbers at A4 twelve years earlier – and we weren't to be talked out of it, however daunting a prospect it was now we were there, gazing up at its *impossible magnitude*.

With little prior knowledge to go on we had arrived under-prepared. Despite our best endeavours, our optimistically lightweight ropes were no match for the super-abrasive rock, and one by one we had to knot out sections that were no longer safe to use. One time the sheath of a fixed line ruptured while our other Venezuelan team-mate, Andre, was nearing the top of a free-hanging 85m jumar, plummeting him five metres or more before the tattered remains of the sheath rucked up enough to catch him on the bare rope core. At 300m, having climbed enough of the route to convince us that maybe it could be climbed but if so it would be hard, very loose and extremely hard to protect, we realised we soon would not have enough good rope to descend. Retreat was sad but inevitable.

Much sadder was retreating the following year. Venezuela was in the grip of political turmoil and the General Strike almost prevented us from getting there at all. As it was we made scant progress up the wall before Henry – our replacement for the absent Andre – had to retreat with a fever. When Ivan slipped and cracked a wrist bone soon afterwards, we knew our chance had gone. Clearly a bigger team would help, and we had many a day to ponder our mistakes as we waited by the dried-up river for it to rain again so that a dugout boat would be able to navigate up the river to fetch us.

Fast forward to 2005 to see seven excited climbers crammed into a tiny basecamp clearing. 'We're gonna beast it', declared Miles Gibson, his positive enthusiasm at once capturing the mood of the team and banishing any lingering doubts. Miles was our secret strongman; when the going got fingery and steep we were sure that he would see us through. Ben Heason was with us too; he was our secret death-defier – when the protection dried up completely and we needed someone to solo huge sections we were sure he would come up with the goods. I was our loose rock aficionado; when the holds became disposable I felt sure of being able to levitate up whatever was still perched without dislodging too much of it. And if all of these options failed we still had our ultimate secret weapon. Alex Klenov was Russian and therefore hard as nails and able to cope with infinite amounts of adversity. He had more big-wall experience than the rest of us put together, most of it on aid but much of it in seriously hardcore Russian competitions in which the winner seems to be the one who endures the most hardship en route to topping out on a blank wall in hail and snowstorms. Yes, we were indeed 'gonna beast it'!

Anne was keen to get in on the action too, as were the Venezuelans Ivan and Alfredo, so it quickly became a challenge to give everyone enough time at the front to keep them happy. Complications worsened when we started running into cruxes, often on consecutive pitches, which threatened to stop us all, and certainly put pressure on whoever's turn it happened to be. But we loved it, and somehow everyone found challenge enough to thoroughly scare themselves. Secretly we wanted it to be hard, to live up to our expectations and to leave us with an experience we truly couldn't forget. But too hard and all of our hopes would be dashed. Just a single point of aid or one bolt for protection and the dream would disappear just as quickly and as surely as it had sprung into being those years ago in front of the telly.

It was close too, maybe a little too often for our liking. Ben repeated my crux scare pitch of 2002, which I had thought to be nudging E7 and which had so little gear a fall was utterly out of the question. The very next day he went on to lead another, even scarier pitch, with just as little protection and with harder moves thrown in too. When we met up with him later that day he was still shaking! Miles on-sighted an E7 pitch too, although not the line he intended to climb; there was an obvious weakness through a 60m bulge and I was privately glad for it to be his lead as it looked so loose, so steep and so holdless as to be almost suicidal. The first four metres straight off the belay was some of the hardest and scariest climbing I've ever belayed, and the subsequent steepening clearly would be much harder still. He followed the only path available, improvising leftwards ever further from our intended line, one by one dismissing each of the possible options for regaining the route. All except one. Miles appeared from beyond a protruding fin where he'd arranged a cramped, hanging belay in a small corner. 'I think it'll go,' he declared, optimistically as ever.

He was right as well: it went, but not without a fight. I tried onsighting and fell onto Alex's head. He tried aiding and snapped a wire in the resulting whipper. Finally, after two days and two headpointed E7's, we found ourselves once again in E5 terrain. Surely we'd cracked it now. Plain sailing to the top.

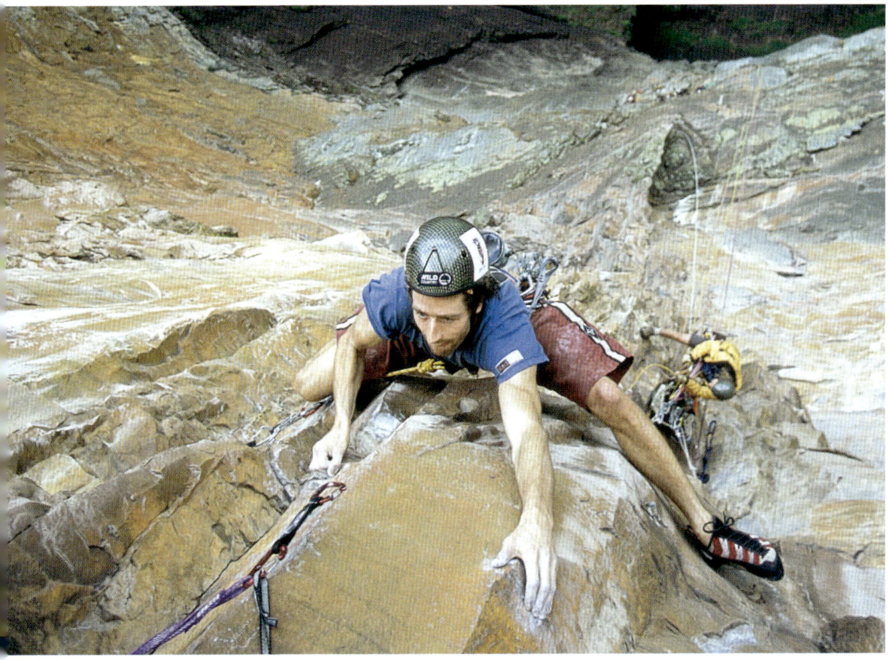

31. Ben Heason eyeing up the final dyno on his successful headpoint of pitch 17 (E7 6b). (*John Arran*)

32. What a life! Anne, Miles and Ben wake up in one of the most spectacular locations on earth. (*John Arran*)

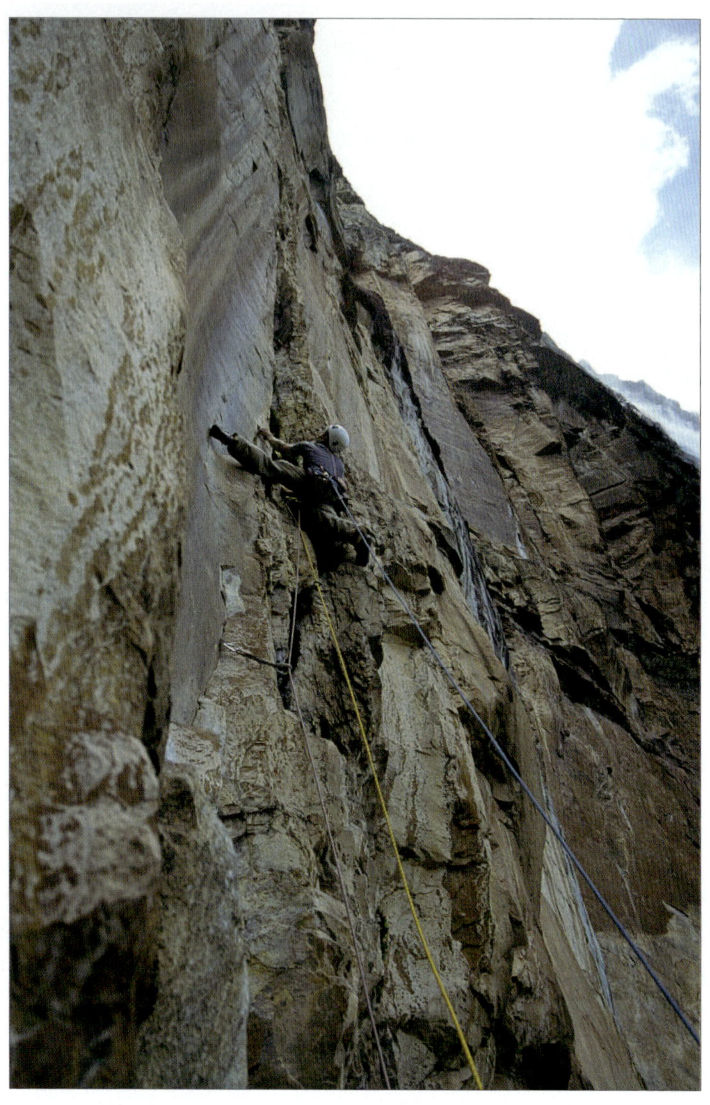

83. John Arran onsighting the last of the crux (E7) pitches, 900m up and still not sure of success. (*Ben Heason*)

Or maybe not. Relief lasted only two pitches then we were back into crux terrain; a Gogarth-like flaky weakness but with the smoothest of walls all around. Certainly it was this way or no way. Two more E7s, one of which I managed to flash but only after Ivan had impressively aided through it first. And then another hint of relief. Anne pounced on the rare chance of a lead and determinedly teetered up a loose, RP-protected wall to an exposed ledge and welcome belay.

While the lead team rotated duties at the front, the others were kept busy in supporting roles. We needed nearly 300 litres of water between us, even with a fairly severe 2-litres a day rationing, which meant hauling 300kg – the weight of four people – in water alone. And before this water, our food, fuel, ledges and sleeping equipment could be hauled we needed to make sure the jumar and haul lines were in the best possible places, which seemed to require constant reorganisation of belays and ropes. Many of our 'rest days' from climbing didn't feel too restful.

Once again our sharp-end reprieve was short-lived, and within another pitch the wall reared up above us again, neither holds nor protection evident in any quantity. With options severely limited, we picked our way up thin walls, along breaks and through bulges, now within a couple of hundred metres of the top but still far from certain our line wouldn't disappear into even blanker unclimbability. Miles impressed us all with another scary E7 onsight, all on Avon-like sloping holds, and just before even he confessed to serious fatigue he pulled off another crux headpoint – well enough protected but seriously sustained and with fantastic technical moves.

Back on a narrow, snaking ledge – our most comfortable accommodation since we'd left the ground seemingly eons ago – we finally had time to relax. Not that we had much choice because steadily we were becoming incapable of hard work; the incessant toil, heat and discomfort having worn us down to shadows of our former energetic selves. We were reduced to one day at a time at the front, the pattern of two days on having been abandoned in favour of more frequent and increasingly necessary rest. We played backgammon, slumped against packs and ropes, and at times felt barely strong enough to roll the dice.

I recovered just enough to finally get an E7 onsight, which was just as well as that pitch was unavoidable and would have been enormously difficult to climb on aid. Ben followed, gashing his leg when he pulled a huge block off, but managed to lead on through up a rising traverse at E6, taking us to within spitting distance of the falls' spout. Once again we were on a roll. Surely we couldn't be stopped now?

Sure enough, the next afternoon Alex and Miles topped out, upon which our whoops and hollers could almost have been heard back in Caracas. It's fair to say we were happy, even though the rest of us wouldn't endure the arduous series of jumars until the following day, one by one inching up the four 60m rope sections with aching muscles but with a euphoric anticipation we wouldn't have swapped for the world.

I arrived on the summit mid-morning, alone. My first feeling was relief, mixed with fascination about the curious landscape that now presented itself – the wind-sculpted boulders, deep rocky ravines and curious, unique-looking plants I'd never seen the like of before. I untied. What a wonderfully liberating feeling, after two full weeks of tethered living, eating and sleeping. Then as I walked from the edge into a horizontal world I was overcome by a well of emotion I never could have predicted. It was over. The dream hadn't ended; rather it had become reality. Finally we would inhabit a world we had imagined so vividly and so often. Finally we, and the climb, were free.

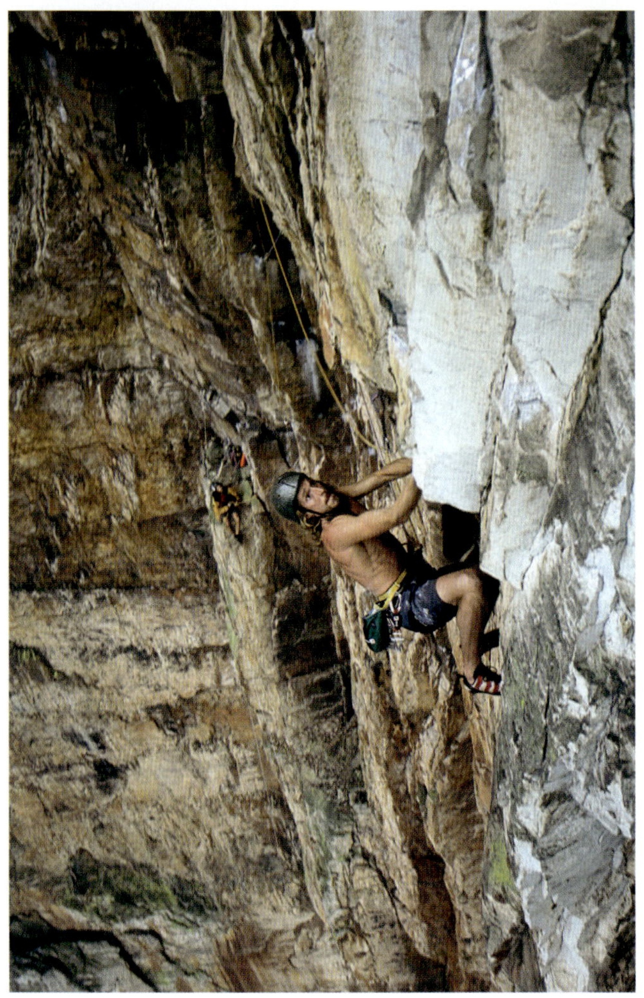

84. A weary Miles Gibson rose to the challenge of headpointing pitch 27 (E7 6b) at the end of day 16. (*John Arran*)

Summary: The first ascent of *Rainbow Jambaia*, Auyan Tepui, Venezuela, in 2005. The route takes a direct line up the face behind Angel Falls, the highest waterfall in the world, and there are other superlatives. The face is 1000m high and overhangs some 60m in total, making *Rainbow Jambaia* the biggest overhanging free climb in the world. The 31-pitch route took 19 days to climb with the nine hardest pitches rated E7. The team comprised: John and Anne Arran, Miles Gibson, Ben Heason, Alex Klenov (Russia), Ivan Calderón (Venezuela) and Alfredo Rangél (Venezuela).

Acknowledgements: The team would like to thank the Mount Everest Foundation, UK Sport and the Alison Chadwick Memorial Fund for their support.

PAT LITTLEJOHN

Adventure Guaranteed

From Ethiopia to a little-known corner of Kyrgyzstan

THE TOWERS OF TIGRAY

In the far north of Ethiopia, near the troubled border with Eritrea, lies the fabled province of Tigray. Much of the land is close to being desert, but its altitude means that it is never unbearably hot. Even in the sun it is possible to climb. The landscape is mountainous, having broad flat valleys lined with sandstone cliffs, many of which hold amazing secrets. Throughout Tigray, often in the most unlikely and inaccessible places, are rock-carved churches unique in the world. Whether Ethiopia could ever be a mainstream climbing destination is doubtful, but anyone seeking a truly adventurous rock-climbing destination in the middle of winter will find something special here which could not be further away from the bland bolt-clipping we often settle for on our 'Sun Rock' holidays.

Culturally and historically Ethiopia is fascinating. Known as the 'Cradle of Humanity', its human history stretches back 4.5 million years, the famous skeleton of the hominid 'Lucy' being displayed in the National Museum. As one of the oldest Christian cultures it has an amazing heritage of rock-hewn churches that in places like Lalibela are reminiscent of Petra. The story of Ethiopia's ruling dynasty begins with the legendary liaison of King Solomon and the Queen of Sheba. Their son, the ruler Menelik, is said to have brought the Ark of the Covenant to Ethiopia, where it has supposedly remained for the past 3000 years, guarded day and night. Ethiopians are knowledgeable and proud of their culture, which remains strong partly because they are the only Africans never to have been colonised.

From a climbing point of view, Tigray was like being pitched back into the early days of climbing the desert towers of Utah and Arizona – a golden age if ever there was one. We explored a fairly limited area, climbing three big towers during an eight-day stay. Our style of climbing was beautifully simple – start at the bottom with a rack of nuts and cams, climb everything free, and be prepared to fail. Adventure guaranteed.

Internal flights are the way to get around this vast country, being cheap and good fun. We flew in a small propeller plane to Mekele, the regional capital of Tigray, then hunted around for a vehicle and driver to take us to Hawzien, a one-hotel village which we hoped would be in the thick of all the climbing potential.

Abune Yemata Guh

This group of towers is the site of one of the most remarkable rock-hewn churches in Tigray, carved into the base of a great castle of rock seemingly impregnable on every side. Beside it is a slender tower with an enticing crack line running down its north face – but not quite reaching the base. This was our first venture on to Tigray sandstone, the point where dreams meet reality…

At the base, Steve Sustad takes one look and announces that it's my lead – he's like that in the mornings. I manage about 10 metres, thrash around for 20 minutes then give up, put off by the rock, the runners and the deceptive steepness. Plan B is to climb the right edge of the face for a pitch then traverse in to the crack. This keeps us busy for the next couple of hours but fails too, for the same reasons. So it's on to plan C, following cracks and chimneys to gain the dreaded south face, the sunny side. We'd planned to climb as much as possible in the shade, fearing that to climb in full sun in Ethiopia would be unbearable, but Steve had a theory that the rock would be better on the south side, baked hard in the sun or something, so off he went into a chimney system heading in the right direction. My lead is a horrid off-width but above this it looks beautiful, a perfect hand crack leading to a promising weakness going all the way to the summit.

Steve makes short work of the crack, putting to use his misspent youth climbing the cracks of Squamish Chief, then I get another nice pitch to a point where the top looks within reach if it weren't for two intervening off-widths, both overhanging and rounded. I should say at this point that our rack was all wrong for climbing in Tigray. Our biggest cam was a Camelot 3 – a grave mistake we would pay for time and time again – that made any off-width look even more frightening than it usually would. Ah well, Americans are off-width experts, I thought as I snuggled into my overhang-protected stance and passed over the lead.

Steve went up for a bit, then to my surprise didn't go up any further, he went *inwards*. Muffled cries of 'You're gonna love this' followed by 'F…ing Hell!' played havoc with the imagination till after what seemed a long, long time it was my turn to follow. I climbed 10 metres then looked into the crag and saw daylight. A narrow slot, and I mean narrow, went straight through to the north face. Skinny Steve had just about made it, but being more muscular around the midriff I had to exhale and wriggle like a snake before popping out into a position of stomach-churning exposure, 150m off the ground with overhanging rock above and below us. Steve was tied to a cluster of dodgy belays out to the left, trying to look cheerful.

For the next two hours I tried everything but the obvious, traversing out left, then right, then back into the tower to squeeze through to the upper of the rounded off-widths. In the end there was nothing for it but to attack the overhang directly. With just one runner between me and Steve I had visions of stripping both of us off the face if I fell, but eventually I passed the first

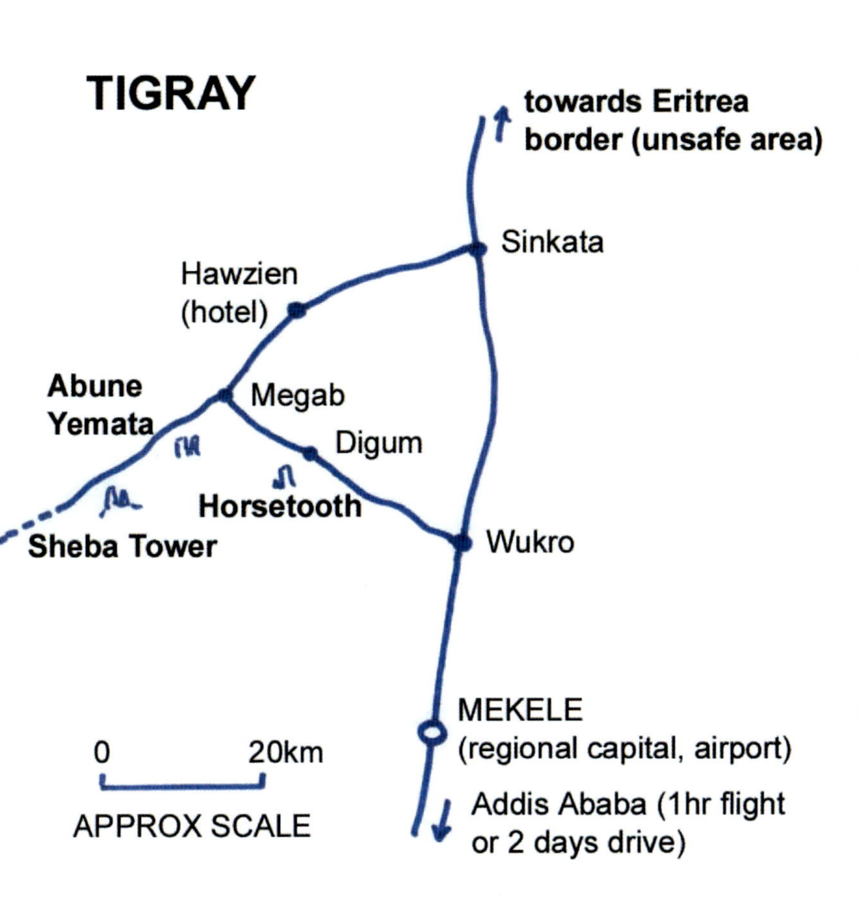

bulge, only to be confronted by another. With time and energy exhausted we abseiled off and walked back as the sun set.

After a day to recover we were back, and with Steve belayed more securely in the middle of the tower I had the confidence to push on up the final crack and get us to our first virgin summit in Tigray. If pressed to give the route a conventional grade, I'd take a stab at E4. 'XS' seems more fitting.

Sheba Tower

Queen of the towers discovered so far, a 150m monolith of beautifully sculpted sandstone in the Nevelet group of towers, just 15 minutes drive along the track from Abune Yemata. The fissures in the north side looked

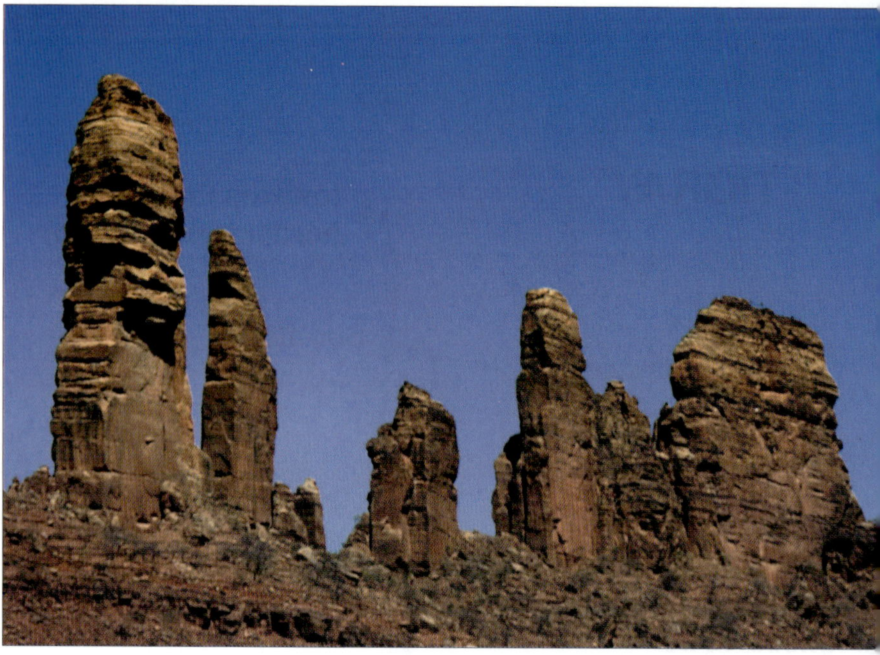

86. Nevelet Towers. Sheba is the biggest tower on the left. (*Pat Littlejohn*)

87. Horsetooth Tower, where the odd foothold snapped 'for that extra buzz'. (*Pat Littlejohn*)

smooth and scary so again we chose the south where a more featured chimney led to a massive bulge that looked like it might be a bit of a problem.

Four pitches of enjoyable and very atmospheric climbing led to a great chamber in the heart of the tower. The only way onwards was an unprotected section of wide bridging. It was either commit to it or give up, and I hesitated for a long time before I was mentally ready to go for it. Now we were on a huge jammed block at the level of the bulge, and Steve's lead. He went upwards and outwards in a bottomless slot that cut through the giant overhang. When I asked how it was he replied 'F…ing mind-blowing!' so I decided to keep quiet. There were scrapings, there were expletives, but the rope inched out steadily and eventually the shout of 'Safe!' echoed down to me.

On following I discovered he had done 20m of unprotected squeeze chimney in an incredibly exposed position, truly the Sustad Slot. 'Your mate's lead,' as they say. From here a relatively normal pitch featuring a 5c bulge at the end led to the summit, a fantastic spot with the whole of Tigray province spread below us, and some very interesting-looking rock peaks shimmering in the distance. A fantastic climb but another XS I'm afraid.

Horsetooth Tower

This was the first tower we investigated and it hadn't excited us as much as the others, being a bit smaller (120m) and at first glance less impressive. So we left it till the end for an 'easier' day.

Horsetooth is in a slightly more populous area than the other two towers and as the only whites in the area we got a lot of attention. To the children we were the mad *farangi* (foreigners) who had come to climb the towers they had scrambled around all their lives. They ran to greet us everywhere we climbed, wanting to carry bags, show us the path, guard our sacks. With the usual group of a dozen children in tow we slogged up to the base and chose our line - again, unfortunately, on the sunny side. Steve took the first pitch, that looked straightforward but had a mean bulge, and then I took over and enjoyed some great climbing up grooves in the crest of the tower.

We were following an intermittent crack that Steve took for another 5c pitch to a hanging belay. The crack steepened and gave some 6a climbing to pass a bulge and so reach a long narrow shelf. I thought I'd cracked it till I looked at the face ahead, which was lower angled but essentially devoid of cracks. Traversing back and forth didn't reveal anything easier or any protection. It was one of those situations where the runners are distant and you have to commit yourself into unknown hostile territory, risking a big fall if it doesn't pay off. 'Why always on my pitch?' I thought, till I remembered the Sustad Slot.

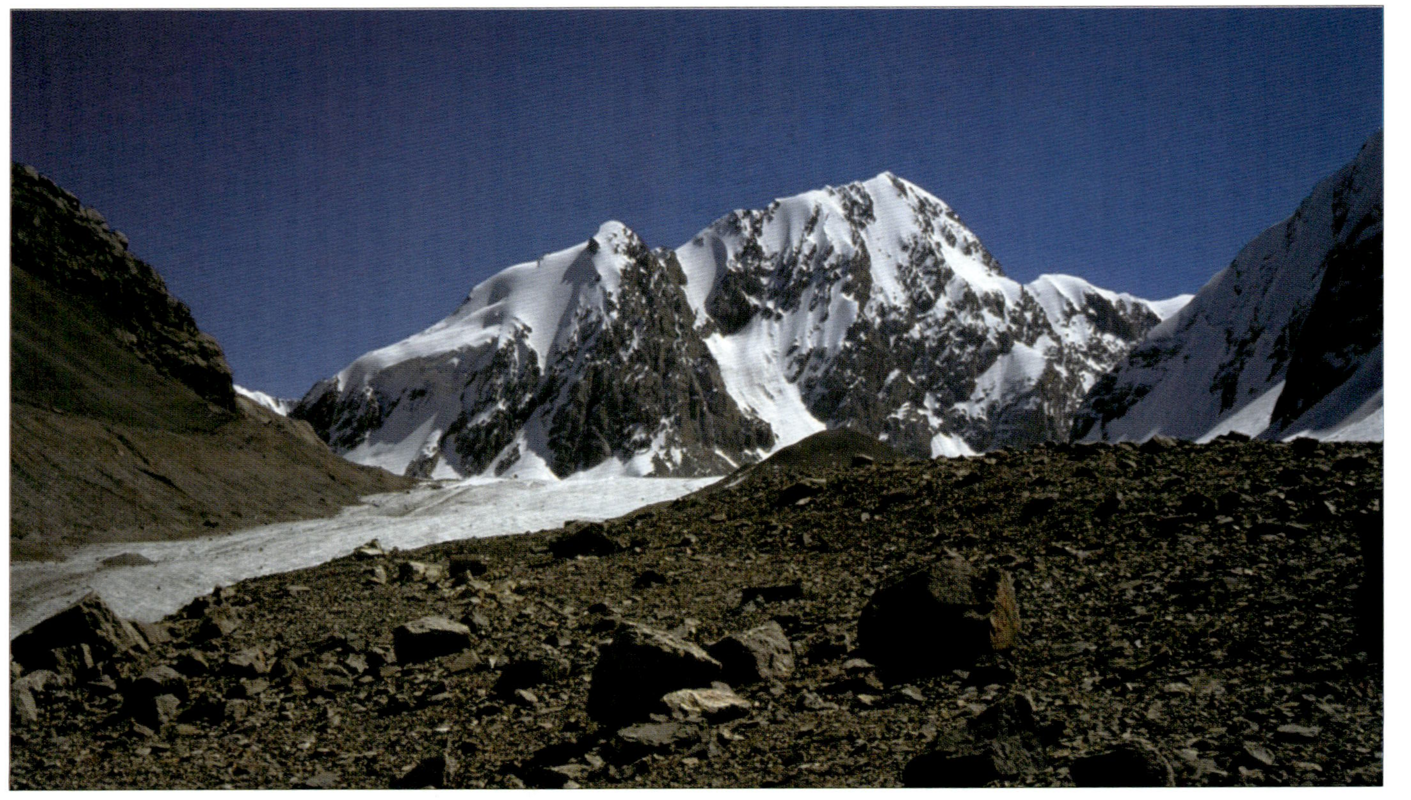

89. 'Pik Borkoldoy' (5171m), highest peak in the group. The first ascent was made by Pat Littlejohn and companions in September 2005. *(Pat Littlejohn)*

The forepeak of Pk 5171m gave a pleasant excursion to 4915m (named Sakchi-Sentry) then a serious attempt was made on Pk 5171m via a couloir on the west flank and north ridge. At c5000m the ridge became seriously knife-edged and corniced and the attempt was abandoned. Three smaller summits on the opposite side of the glacier gave easier days before the expedition decamped. All in all a very enjoyable trip to the most remote mountains any of the team had visited.

2004 team: Pat Littlejohn, Adrian Nelhams, Vladimir Komissarov (guides); Ben Box, Steve Brown, James Bruton, Tom Fox, Phil Naybour, George Ormerod, John Porter and Nick Wheatley.

Twelve months later I led another ISM group to the Borkoldoy group and was pleased to find our repair work of 2004 intact, enabling us quickly to reach the river delta and motor to our former base camp at 3570m.

An advance base was set up at 4240m on Ilbirs glacier west. Adrian Nelhams, Bill Thompson and Mark Samuels climbed the north ridge of the big peak on the left side of the glacier, Pik Tansovsitsa (4911m, AD), while higher up the glacier, myself, Jane Whitmore, Ben Box and James Bruton made several attempts and finally succeeded on the west ridge of Alpinistka (4959m, D). After a spell of rock climbing on the 150m limestone crag above base camp, the Nelhams' team, along with Vladimir Komissarov and Peter Kemble, turned their attention to the previously untouched 'Hidden' glacier north of base camp. Over the following days they climbed four fine peaks, the highest and most difficult being Pik Koldunia (4895m) by the south ridge at AD+.

The main objective for my team was Pk 5171m, where Bruton, Box and I had been turned back at 5000m on the east ridge in 2004. This time, in better snow conditions, we were able to try the snowy north-east flank, picking the safest line through big séracs. The south ridge was gained at 5000m and followed on perfect névé to the summit. Though very arduous the route was technically straightforward at PD+. As the highest peak in the range it was given the name of Pik Borkoldoy. Clear weather on the summit gave stunning views of the West Kokshaal-Too and the unexplored peaks in the eastern sector of the Borkoldoy, some of which look very inviting.

The trip was rounded off with a brief stay at Lake Issyk-Kul, where the swimming was still found to be pleasant in late September and our stone-built hotel gave good training for keen rock climbers in the team!

2005 team: Pat Littlejohn, Adrian Nelhams, Vladimir Komissarov (guides); Ben Box, James Bruton, Jane Whitmore, Peter Kemble, Bill Thompson and Mark Samuels.

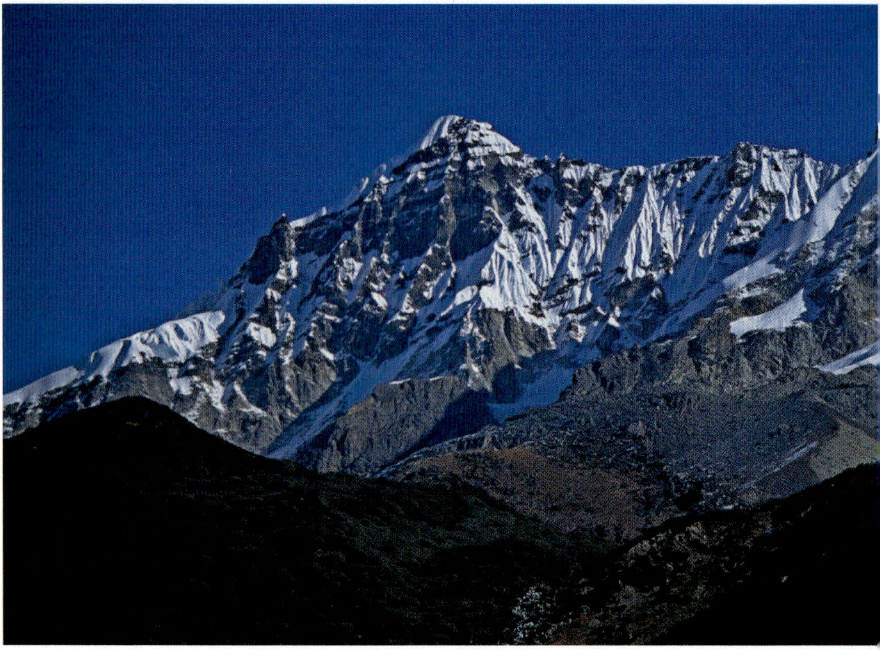

90. Mt Tichenkang seen from the popular trekking route to Guicha La. The route of ascent follows the left-hand skyline. (*Roger Payne*)

91. Unclimbed sub-6000m peaks in West Sikkim. The Sikkim Government is considering opening more peaks for alpine-style climbing trips. (*Roger Payne*)

JULIE-ANN CLYMA & ROGER PAYNE

Early Season Alpine Summits in West Sikkim

In 2004 we had been very lucky to meet Kunzang Bhutia, the young President of the Sikkim Amateur Mountaineering Association. Bhutia was leading our group of four, made up of Ian and Loreto McNaught-Davis and ourselves, trekking in the Thangsing Valley of West Sikkim. We were interested in attempting some of the peaks, and Bhutia suggested a joint trip the following year. So, in 2005 we returned, and in a 20-day round trip from Gangtok between 15 March and 3 April we made three excursions on peaks in the Thangsing Valley. We were joined by Bhutia's climbing partner Sagar Rai; Bhutia and Rai are both experienced young mountaineers active in providing training for local trek guides and opportunities for school children in Sikkim.

After the usual trek from Yuksum to Thangsing, on 20 March we started a reconnaissance and acclimatisation trip on Mount Tinchenkang (6010m). We followed what we believed to be the original route of ascent, climbed with fixed ropes and camps by an Indo-British military expedition in 1998. Deep fresh snow made progress on the rocky wall below the north-west ridge very slow and precarious. Having reached around 5100m on 21 March, we decided to return to our valley base on the 22nd.

After a rest and delay for bad weather, we then set off on 25 March to make a reconnaissance of the unclimbed Lama Lamani group of peaks. On the 26th we traversed from the north-west side of the group to the south ridge to look for a possible line of ascent. There were very strong winds on the ridges and fresh snow underfoot. On the 27th we moved up to a position under the north-west flank of the mountain, which seemed to offer the best ascent route. Next day we made a pre-dawn start and by 10am had made the first ascent of the north summit of Lama Lamani (c5650m). The climbing on the north-west flank and west ridge was around UIAA grade III+ (or AD+) and mostly on snow with rock steps and a good icy ridge. It was very windy and cold on the ridge, but the views were exceptional. Descent was by the same route and involved some abseiling. We reached our valley base the same evening.

After one day's rest, just the two of us set off for an attempt on Mount Tinchenkang. Because of cloudy conditions it had not been possible to get a good view of the glacier on the north-west side of Tinchenkang. Despite previous glimpses of threatening looking sérac barriers, we decided to try this approach, which we understood had been climbed the previous autumn by a Himalayan Club group. Strong winds limited progress on the first day and we stopped to camp at c4850m near the start of the glacier slopes. Next day, in cold and windy conditions and very deep snow, we reached the crest of the north-west ridge (junction with the 1998 route) and camped just below it at c5400m. Despite appearances, the glacier route is not threatened by séracs.

Next day, 1 April, we made a pre-dawn start. Once again, there was deep snow and cold conditions, but no wind. Getting onto the bottom of the rock wall was delicate (around UIAA grade IV – but probably easier when clear of snow). The wall had two fixed ropes in place that led towards, then through, a short chimney (some loose rock), then onto the crest formed by the top of the wall. Above this there is an ice wall and couloir (on a previous trip this point had been reached by Bhutia and Rai, but they had to turn back because of lack of good ice climbing equipment). We followed the couloir, which was in good condition, for about 150m, then exited onto the upper snowfields. Straightforward snow slopes led to the final summit pyramid, which was climbed on the west side to avoid a wide bergshrund. The summit was reached just before 2pm. Alas, warm air and clouds blew in from the south-west to obscure the view. On the summit were two snow stakes and the top of a line of rope, which was otherwise buried. We removed one of the snow stakes as a souvenir for our friends back at the valley base.

The weather improved during the descent with excellent views. Some down-climbing and three abseils were needed to descend the rock wall. The previous night's camp was reached by 6pm, but with the walk-out due to start next morning, we continued down to the base at Thangsing, arriving just before 11pm. Bhutia and Rai were waiting.

These two climbs, each made in three-day round trips from a base at Thangsing, demonstrate the potential for alpine-style climbs in West Sikkim.

Summary: An account of the first ascent of Lama Lamini by Kunzang Bhutia, Julie-Ann Clyma, Roger Payne and Sagar Rai; and the first alpine-style ascent of Tinchenkang, Thangsing Valley, West Sikkim.

Acknowledgements: Julie-Ann Clyma and Roger Payne would like to thank the Government of Sikkim and the Sikkim Amateur Mountaineering Association for making this trip possible, and to the Mount Everest Foundation, British Mountaineering Council and UK Sport for their support. Equipment was kindly provided by Lyon Equipment (Beal, Petzl-Charlet), Macpac, Outdoor Designs, Rab and Vaude.

Journeys

Jim Curran *Karakol Lakes from Kongur* 2005
Oil on canvas

SKIP NOVAK

Strictly for Aficionados

A South Georgia journey

Our kit was secure in the pulks and the pulks, in turn, were anchored by our firmly planted skis. It was high time to break down the tent. The katabatic wind was hitting the wind scoop with punishing gusts from all directions. Out on the col it was impossible to stand and it must have been blowing a sustained 70 knots. We collapsed the tent on to the snow and withdrew the poles, then rolled up the flysheet, always being careful to have body weight holding the whole mess down. But it only took a second's lack of concentration for the inner to inflate like a giant beach ball and levitate itself out of our grip with a frightening force. Julian was dragged partly up the slope and I had a split second hysterical thought that I would see my mate launched in full flight down the Spenceley glacier and out to sea. We looked at each other, incredulous, both of us no doubt remembering how we always laughed in an 'I told them so' manner when we heard about expeditions losing tents on the island. It would never happen to us experienced hands of course, but we had been hoist by our own petard. Luckily Crag and Richard had the adjacent snow cave just about hollowed out to fit the four of us in . . .

Adrift like a ship far offshore in the South Atlantic, the sub-Antarctic island of South Georgia is arguably one of the least travelled destinations for mountaineers, despite its manifest attractions. The island has prolific wildlife, a whaling past, and a savage alpine terrain historically underpinned by the Shackleton saga. Climbers ruminate over it often, but seldom embrace its challenge. Significant expeditions can be counted on two hands since George Sutton's private survey party in the 1950s climbed the easier peaks. With the exception of the highest and dominant massif of Mt Paget (9625ft), which rises right out of the sea, the principal summits have had only single ascents, and there are many unclimbed and unnamed peaks in waiting.

South Georgia's remoteness makes access a costly business, but the real reason the island has seen little mountaineering activity is that its reputation has preceded it. On the receiving end of the storm tracks that funnel through the Drake Passage below Cape Horn, the weather is generally so ferocious there is only a slim chance of getting up anything. A typical 35 or 42-day expedition includes the likely scenario of spending 10 of those days retching into a plastic bucket on the sea passages, the only way of getting there being by private sailing yacht from the Falkland Islands. And then there is the sojourn at base camp, if you can get one established, waiting for windows of opportunity that are measured in hours instead of days. If there is trouble on the mountain, self-rescue down to the coast is clearly understood. Frankly it is an area for aficionados.

Enter Julian Freeman-Attwood, Crag Jones, Richard Haworth and myself, all veterans of many trips to the island by sea in search of a view. The plan, had we been together in one place, could have been sketched, *a la* Shipton and Tilman, on the back of the proverbial envelope. Instead, via email from four points on the globe, we agreed simply on a rendezvous in Ushuaia in late December 2004 to join my 54-foot steel sloop *Pelagic* that had a convenient gap in the charter season; bring own tents, skis, pulks and gear. And we decided at the outset: no sponsors, no films, and no trekker/punters along to help pay the bills.

Our aim was to complete a ski traverse along the length of the Salvesen range that dominates the southern half of the island. Rather than the inevitability of getting bogged down under a single summit target while waiting for the weather to break, we would keep moving with all our gear on pulks, following the relatively easy, undulating terrain characteristic of this more heavily glaciated end of the island. We could cherry pick any unclimbed summits along the way if we happened to be in the right place at the right time. The journey – 15 to 20 days off the boat – would be the main focus and if we managed to get up something it would be a bonus.

Expeditioning implies difficulties along the way, even before the big ones of the mountains themselves are encountered. For the Himalaya, the tummy bugs in Delhi have first to be negotiated, or maybe your paperwork is somehow not quite in order. When 'sailing to climb', the bugbear is the boat and the sea voyage. To get to the island we had to sail over 1000 nautical miles. It only takes one rigging pin to shear and the mast will go, or a serious engine problem could render the boat incapable of navigating inshore. So we always labour under a certain anxiety when under sail, with our climbing project hanging in the balance. The trip could be literally scuppered.

Julian, Crag and I, along with a French couple Jeromine and Laurent who volunteered as crew, left Ushuaia in the Argentine section of Tierra del Fuego on 31 December bound for Port Stanley. Arriving after two uneventful days of mainly motor sailing, we picked up Richard to complete our gang of four and also Dion Poncet who would skipper the boat while I was on the mountain. Dion grew up in the Falkland Islands and has been visiting South Georgia all his life. His knowledge of the coastline is second to none. We knew he would be a strong addition to the team as the drop off was critical. Nor, as it turned out, was the recovery an easy operation.

Although not necessary, it is advisable always to begin a trip to South Georgia from Stanley. As a consequence of the Falklands conflict in 1982, South Georgia was separated from the Falkland Islands Dependencies and is technically a stand-alone overseas territory called the Government of South Georgia and the South Sandwich Islands. This makes the Foreign

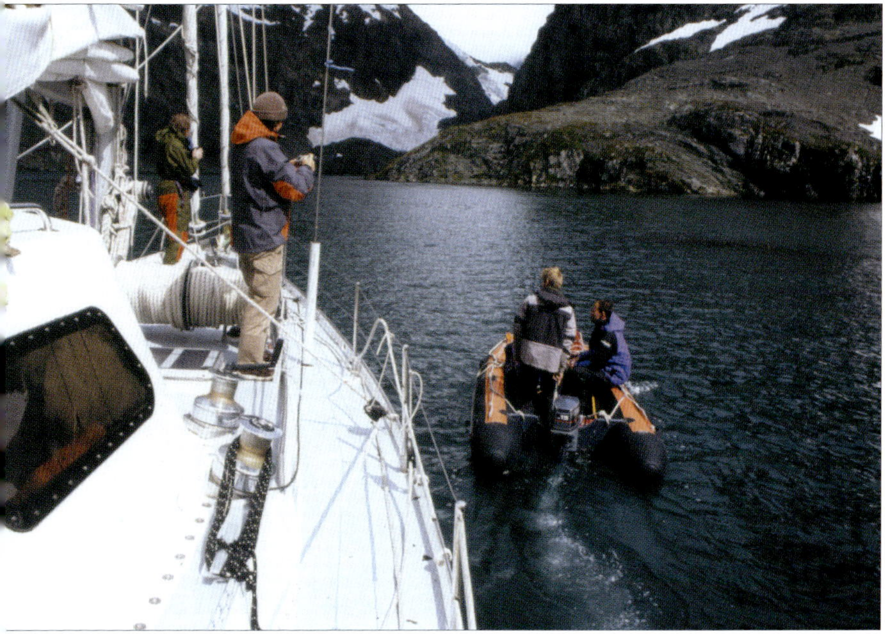

3. *Pelagic* at anchor in Larsen Harbour. Rich and Dion ferry the first load of gear to the snout of the Philippi glacier. (*Skip Novak*)

4. Crag Jones and Rich Haworth carrying heavy loads on the beach in Larsen Harbour. (*Skip Novak*)

95. Camp Six on the Spenceley Col below the summit of Mt Baume (6272ft), the day after the failed attempt. The buttress climbed is lower right. (*Skip Novak*)

96. Crag looks out from the snow cave, with Mt Baume (6272ft) on the left and Mt Pelagic (5680ft) on the right. (*Skip Novak*)

Office in London the official overseer, but the bulk of the day-to-day administration continues to be by a commissioner from Stanley. With the pressure of cruise ship tourism on the island increasing, the government recently began a permit procedure for land-based adventurers requiring yacht support. If you spend one night ashore you fall into the category of an 'expedition' which means an application must be filed. A committee (consisting of Crag Jones, Jerome and Sally Poncet, Stephen Venables, myself and others) vets the applications and makes recommendations regarding the primary issues of environmental impact and ability to carry out the expedition safely and have the ability to self-rescue. Needless to say, we were successful in the application process!

Pub crawling is *de rigueur* in this town of 2000 odd inhabitants, but our socializing was limited to one night to crawl and one night to recover. After buying a few steel garden spades at the greenhouse in Stanley, along with sacks of potatoes, carrots and boxes of fruit imported from Chile, we lashed our regulation mutton carcasses to the backstays and set sail. It rarely blows from the east and a downwind 'sleigh ride' is almost guaranteed.

Idleness is a large part of voyaging under sail, especially if you have a good autopilot. Cooking, eating, reading and occasionally taking in or shaking out a reef is usually all there is to do when on watch. Of course the map of South Georgia was stared at endlessly, like a crystal ball, and when speculation on the mountain route was exhausted we tested each other on Tilman and Tintin trivia of which Julian is the mastermind. On day four we made out Cape Disappointment through the mist at the south end of the island. The headland was named by Captain James Cook who landed on the island in 1775 and took 'possession' of it on behalf of his king. Cook sailed south along the north-east coast, convinced he had discovered the Antarctic continent until he rounded the cape and was surprised to find only open ocean.

Larsen Harbour, our start point at the southern end of the island, is more fjord than harbour, culminating in a narrow, shallow section at its head between steep rocky walls. From a recce in the dinghy I saw that the snout of the Philippi glacier had receded considerably. When I was last on it in 1988 we could walk up easy snow slopes right from the shore. Now it began with a gravelly moraine overlaying steep blue ice which meant a short relay to get our gear on pulk-pulling ground. Satisfied with the plan, we returned to *Pelagic* and continued sorting the equipment ('If you take the round of cheese, I'll take the salami, OK?'). The four of us would be in two tents and each be pulling a Snowsled pulk and carrying a small rucksack.

Next morning we made the first haul up to level ground at 1000ft, stashing our load in a rock gully and scuttling back down. It began to snow and blow a bit, and even though it took less than three hours to gain this position, knowing the weather here you could not help but wonder if we would ever see the gear again. We had one more slap-up dinner on the boat, then on 13 January waved Dion, Jeromine and Laurent 'au revoir' and made the second and final pull to establish ourselves on the Philippi snowfield. The weather looked threatening and we decided to use a wind scoop as the obvious place for Camp One. This filled quickly with spindrift during the night and we took turns digging out, though with the wind blowing a good 40 to 50 knots a half buried tent is no bad thing. We spent the next day tent-bound wondering if we would ever get started.

Early on the 15th the wind abated and after four hours of extracting ourselves and our gear from enormous snow drifts we were up and running, shuffling rather, across the head of the Philippi and Graae glaciers, more or less undulating level ground. We were very clear about being roped up four in a line at all times other then when skiing downhill. If one of a party of two had gone down a slot, the combined weight of man and heavy pulk would probably drag the other down. With a three-man deadweight we felt very secure. We also attached prussic loops from the back of our pulks to the rope, so in the event of a fall, the weight of the pulk would hopefully be off the climber. We were even smart enough, when we remembered, to have the medical kit in the caboose.

The next four days – two days on the move and two tent-bound – were accomplished in whiteout conditions. Pulling on the damp surface was hard work. Wind was light but visibility nigh on zero so we navigated purely by compass and GPS position overlaid on the old Bomford/Carse map. Swapping the lead, the first man at times could barely see the ground in front of his skis in the soup. If the second could see him, he would steer the leader on a compass course, shouting him left or right. Only a rare glimpse of higher ground would reinforce our assumption that we were in fact heading up the right glacier.

Camp Four was on a plateau underneath Mt Starbuck, one of our unclimbed targets – but we never saw it until days later from afar. Unclimbed peaks score one, climbers zero. Tent-bound days were spent chewing down the salami and the cheese while arguing about the correction we should be applying to our GPS positions so they would agree with the map. Staying dry and comfortable is the key to surviving, let alone operating in the generally damp maritime conditions. Meticulous camp protocols must be observed and it usually took several hours to dig in and become established, and not much less to pack up. Thus our effective hours on the march were never more than six or seven which was enough for our mature party.

Finally on the 19th we had better visibility, at least below us to the coast, and we slid, still roped, down to, across and up the other side of the Novosilski glacier, which alarmingly is marked on the map as a wind venturi. It was a strong pull up a gritty surface to Camp Five, not far from Spenceley Col from where we hoped to have a go at Mt Baume, an unclimbed summit marked as 6272ft on the map. Next morning, after a short pull we were beneath its north-east ridge, under calm sunny skies.

Camp Six was established in the middle of the col at 4120ft, operating on the theory that it is better to be in an open area in high winds rather than up against any features suffering katabatics (down draughts). A short recce to the base of the ridge revealed a mixed section of snow and ice gullies on the lower buttress, which looked do-able, and after that it appeared to be plain sailing on snow to the summit rocks. The true summit was not evident from our perspective though.

A late start, combined with deep snow on the snow fan, meant it was mid-morning before we were established on the buttress. Soft snow and thin ice cover over slabby, ice-shattered rocks made it slow going and digging out belay positions also took time. After nine pitches, some of Scottish grade IV, with a lot of fussing about we exited on to a precarious position at the top of the buttress. The day was gone and it was clear that continuing would mean a bivouac near the top without bivvi gear and with water bottles empty. Only Crag was willing to risk a night in the open – at the top of a mountain, on the island of South Georgia, with no fluid. Adding all that together, we voted to retreat in spite of perfect weather conditions. It took four hours of abseiling in the dark to reach our skis and we slid back to the tent under a beautiful starlit sky, each with his own thoughts of what might have been.

Even worse, the next morning we awoke to sunny, stable conditions with the south coast of the island spread out below us. But we were knackered. So a perfect climbing day was spent drying out and milling around when, as it turned out, we should have been digging a snow cave. Peak 5680 on the map, just to the north of Baume and also unclimbed, was a must target – if the weather would hold fine for just one more day. So at midnight, with Julian opting to stay behind, the three of us skied down to its base and strolled up the mountain's corniced north-east ridge. It was an easy plod up a fine ridge, requiring a belay only when crossing a bridge over a deep crevasse that split the crest near the top. But by first light the weather had turned and the Martians had arrived. Pastel coloured, saucer-shaped lenticular clouds sailed over Paget and all the big peaks in the Allardyce and Salvesen ranges. The beginnings of a breeze were felt as we reached the summit at 6am and agreed to name it (unofficially) Mt Pelagic. The GPS height was recorded at 5960ft. We lingered for half an hour watching the clouds eerily evolve, then high-tailed it down, skiing into camp just as the big wind hit.

The next five hours was a struggle for survival, breaking down the tents, by then somewhat flattened, and moving everything over to the wind scoop where we would later lose the tent inner. At times it was impossible to stand and looking back on our track in the snow from the campsite it was that of a drunken man, taking three steps and then falling over. It took 24 man-hours to dig a cave, mainly in snow but also through bands of hard ice. (Remember those steel garden spades? Don't go to South Georgia without them.)

The cave was to be our comfortable home for the next four days while a real South Georgia hooly blew itself out.

97. *From left* Crag Jones, Dion Poncet, Skip Novak, Rich Haworth and Julian Freeman-Attwood at the beach camp at Royal Bay, South Georgia. (*Skip Novak*)

98. Dion and Laurent land on the beach at Little Moltke Harbour, Royal Bay to recover the first load. (*Skip Novak*)

On day 16, with gas and food getting low, we made our move and packed before first light in very cold conditions. The intention was to slide down the length of the Spenceley, hook into the Ross glacier and continue down it to the coast, in one long day. The 2000ft Ross Pass cleaves the island in two between the Salvesen and the Allardyce ranges and consequently is recognized as the windiest place on South Georgia. So our day's run was made with some trepidation. After an enjoyable unroped ski down the Spenceley in warm sunshine, we climbed a small ridge and dropped down on to the Ross, wasting no time given the rare, windless conditions. On the pass we saw the wind scoop used by Julian, Stephen Venables, Lindsay Griffin and others on the British Southern Ocean Mountaineering Expedition in 1990, when they spent 19 days in their famous snow cave. Julian admitted it was a silly place to have put it in the first place!

The skiable ice ended at about 1000ft above sea level, forcing us to cache the pulks and skis in a crevasse and continue on foot – or sometimes on our knees as it was blowing another gale and boiling black above us on the pass. Negotiating a convoluted lateral moraine, we made the beach by early evening and, after some searching using clues 'text messaged' to us on the Iridium phone by Dion, found the emergency blue 60 litre barrel he had cached amid rocks near a stream. Later that evening we had a major feed, the four of us cramped into a tent for three, surrounded by the usual throng of bellowing fur seals. Next day, in very windy conditions, we recovered the gear left up on the glacier, then returned in the Zodiac to the comfort of Base Camp *Pelagic*, following a tricky surf recovery operation that left us soaked to the skin. Everything had gone like clockwork. I can only describe this extraordinary adventure with good friends as an elegant example of 'sailing to climb'.

Summary: An account of a six-week 'sailing to climb' expedition to the sub-Antarctic island of South Georgia in search of unclimbed summits. The sailing vessel *Pelagic* was the expedition's mobile base camp.

rise the five highest in the entire range: Jachacunocollo (c5820m), the 'Grand Ice Peak' of the Aimaras, Huaynacunocollo (c5750m), Gigante Grande (5748m), erroneously stated in guidebooks as the highest in this cordillera, León Jihuata (5680m) and San Luis (5620m), the latter forming a showy background to the frigid Huallatani lake.

The third district lies further east of León Jihuata and is Amazonian. It is called the Choquetanga group (Aimara: 'Golden Comets'). Since access to them is somewhat complicated, its peaks are not well known. Its easternmost points, over 5200m, rise above the warm hills of Quime, a subtropical area.

The Quimsa Cruz comes to its southern end with an undistinguished cluster of dark brown rock peaks, unglaciated, some of which are fairly rugged. Its main point may be Santa Fe (5210m). On the wide pass of Tres Cruces is located the hamlet of Huañascota (4080m).

Glaciers occupying high valleys occur mostly in the main or central district. Particularly extensive are the Laramcota, Atoroma and Chococota glaciers. Hanging ice can be seen on many south and east faces of the first three districts. Local ice is unbelievably firm and hard, so that often my greatest fear when visiting this range was whether my crampons would bite into that granite-hard ice. The exceptional hardness of the ice results from the low temperatures typical of the Bolivian Andes. An average of –15C to –20C can be expected in June and July, the coldest months of the year. The rock is good to excellent. Most peaks offer a brown, solid granite and only the group around Gigante Grande has slate walls and ridges.

There are numerous small lakes and some big ones, including the Huallatani, well seen from the western vehicular roads, and the Chatamarca, located between the main district and the Choquetanga group. Water is found everywhere on the western slopes, but in some lower valleys it is mildly polluted by llamas and, in a few places, polluted more seriously by mining. Water is likely to be scarce on the eastern or Amazonian slopes, since it is absorbed by the porous ground.

The natural environment of the Quimsa Cruz is desolate and the human population scarce. There are only two important settlements, one in Viloco (between the Araca and the main massifs) and another in Pongo at the south-east end of the range. But resources are limited and these settlements have difficulty in offering anything more than basic necessities. Even fresh bread is rarely found here. Human encounters are not a problem in the Quimsa Cruz region. Miners are usually friendly, but the few Aimara highlanders one may come across are rather aloof. On the trail, if a hiker meets one of the local people, a friendly hand raised in salute with a 'Buenos dìas' or 'Buenas tardes' (evening) will suffice; then continue the march unconcernedly. Good Spanish is a necessity in this region.

00. Cordillera Quimsa Cruz, Bolivia. The two highest peaks in the range, Jachacunocollo (c5820m) and Huaynacunocollo (c5750m), from the south-west. (*Evelio Echevarría*)

1. Abandoned mining constructions and the northern flanks of unclimbed Cerro El Aguilar (c5450m) and Nevado Vilacollo (c5400m), ascended in 1911 by Dr T Herzog. (*Evelio Echevarría*)

Mountaineering

Mountaineering/climbing in Bolivia is better done between May and September, the country's cold but generally dry winter. After October, precipitation, with higher temperatures, begins.

Access into the Quimsa Cruz is by the two existing gravel roads that remain open all year. At the La Paz bus terminal there are two *flotas* (rural bus companies) that use them on a daily basis. One runs to Viloco and the other to Pongo-Quime. The latter provides access to the eastern (Amazonian) side, but at Pongo it is necessary to enlist a ride with a passing mineral-loading vehicle in order to reach the high-mining hamlets, almost abandoned, of Caracoles, La Argentina and Carmen Rosa (c 4700m). All forms of transportation will drop visitors off somewhere high, always above 4000m – a definite advantage. Valleys are short and camps can be placed where water is at hand. Very cold nights – about 13 hours long in the high tropics – must be anticipated.

The mountaineering history of this range began in an unknown time when hillmen ascended some lesser, unglaciated peaks. They were followed by mining and military surveyors who left their ascents, if any, unrecorded, but who did leave local sketch maps and charts. Between the years 1968 and 1981 the Instituto Geográfico Militar de Bolivia, the main geographical authority in the country, produced its Carta Nacional on sheets on a scale of 1:50 000. These are quite acceptable, one feels, since the heights are accurate, even if a good many mountain names are not.

Sport Climbing per se began there with Henry Hoek, a Freiburg geologist, who, in 1903, visited the Viloco mining district. Along with a very young Aimaran 'with cat feet', he climbed the 5260m Chancapiña (in Aimara: 'rough and savage'). Dr Theodor Herzog, a botanist-skier-climber of the University of Jena, followed in 1911. He and a companion reclimbed Chancapiña and made the ascent of several other peaks, although with much discomfort due to a snowy November at the time of their visit. Herzog produced two excellent books (in German) and the first map of the Quimsa Cruz, scale 1:200 000.

Twenty years later Dr Federico Ahlfeld (1892-1982), who was to become a much honoured citizen of Bolivia, also climbed there and produced another good monograph and a sketch map. His contemporaries, all German residents in Bolivia, also climbed a number of peaks, among which are the two highest in the Quimsa Cruz, Jachacunocollo and Huaynacunocollo (c5820m and c5750m).

Two interesting cases pertaining to the earlier Quimsa Cruz climbing remain in need of investigation. We do not know exactly what several enterprising German residents in Bolivia climbed between, say, 1915 to the early 1930s. El Yunque (c5400m, Spanish: 'Anvil'), of the challenging Araca towers, was certainly scaled by Overlack and Schulze. But what else did those enterprising pioneers perform in the region? And then there was the mysterious case of T Ifor Rees, chief British diplomat in Bolivia during the

2. Cerro León Jihuata, also called Torre Jihuata (5680m), west side. (*Evelio Echevarría*)

3. The Salvadora massif (c5400m) seen from the Salvadora apachita (pass). Typical unclimbed south flanks in the Viloco group. (*Evelio Echevarría*)

104. The Nevado de Atoroma (c5550m), with typical west-slope glaciers. (*Evelio Echevarría*)

105. The Huallatani lake basin: Nevados Piroja (5440m), San Luis (5620m) and a spur of Huaynacunocollo showing in the centre. (*Evelio Echevarría*)

Second World War and after. One of his companions, Alpine Club member E de la Motte, and a Bolivian climbed the sharp ice pyramid of Ninacollo Grande (5352m) in or before 1946. But what else did Rees and companions do? In his book *Sajama* (1960), a copy of which I was once able to hold in my hands, he apparently showed that he knew much about local climbing and about regional mountain lore. But this work was published in Welsh. So far we do not have a clear evaluation of the Rees performance in the Andes.

In March of 1946, six Bolivians, led by the ever-present Federico Ahlfeld (founding member of the Club Andino Boliviano), skied on the Laramcota glacier and made the first ascent of Gigante Grande (5748m), third highest point in the range. Bolivian participation there was at its best. Strong German parties climbed here in 1969 (Bayerische Naturfreunde, Möhldorf) and 1987 (Bayreuth). Their impressive accomplishments were recorded in text, sketch maps, and black-and-white photography.

As well as mystery there has been confusion. Without proper maps in earlier times, confusion was probably inevitable. But at present, we are unable satisfactorily to identify several peaks ascended, such as those by the Mexican expedition of 1964 and the Japanese expedition of 1968. The first of these claimed three first ascents, 5850m to 6000m high, and bestowed upon the mountains inappropriate names. In my researches in La Paz I ascertained that this party had indeed made two second ascents and the first of a *nevado* still unlocated. Was it Princesa Blanca, c5600m, in the Gigante Grande group? The same confusion can be expressed about the large 1968 Japanese expedition. This party climbed seven peaks, six of which were probably first ascents, and proposed unsuitable names for Bolivian and Andean peaks, such as 'Shimotsuke', 'Tochigi','Nikko', etc. However, credit must be given to this expedition for having been the first to be active in the Choquetanga group and to have included a sketch map and good accompanying photographs.

It is also pleasant to record several expeditions we could describe as exemplary. In August 1974 the Italian Bergamo expedition, led by the accomplished alpinist and explorer Santino Calegari, entered the Laramcota and Mallachuma valleys and glaciers and ascended six peaks. One great mountain in that area had undergone a name change, which caused an involuntary mistake: León Jihuata (5680m) had been won by two La Paz climbers in 1952. By 1974 its name had been locally changed into Torre Jihuata, which led the Calegari expedition to believe that this was a different peak. But, even so, leader Calegari bestowed upon the newly-climbed mountains names that fully respected local traditions and furthermore produced a report exemplary in both its text and illustrations.

The same could be said of the smaller and very recent Spanish expedition (1998), led by Javier Sanchez (Madrid). His group of four friends entered the Chococota valley and ascended three *nevados*. In his fine reports, Sanchez described well the mountain area, the peaks won and the new names the group imposed (in the vernacular Aimara). The main objective had been Nevado de las Vírgenes (c5600m). A previous party, led by the American Dakin Cook, had already climbed it, but the reports this group produced twice misidentified the peak, so it was natural for the Spaniards to have been misled. Only when Yossi Brain published a photo of the mountain could everything be explained.

Another expedition deserves mention: Anton Putz (Regensburg), like Bergamo's Santino Calegari a constant visitor to the Andes, could not have missed the Quimsa Cruz. His party, which included his wife Ria, traversed the entire ridge of ice peaks, descending south from Jachacunocollo, and accomplished other ascents in 1982. Putz simply listed the peaks won as 'RAV' plus numbers. His efficient report proved that he correctly interpreted all the local heights.

With such diversity in the field of expeditionary activity, there remains the question: what is left for future visitors? Plenty, in my opinion, provided visitors do not seek the rewards of glory or profit. These mountains are not famous. The answer to the question lies in making a choice between rock and ice. For rock, Quimsa Cruz candidates will have two fields: one would be the search for new routes and even new peaks and needles in the Araca district. The other would be to tackle the higher east faces, nearly all rock, in the main and Choquetanga massifs. To my knowledge, none of these has been reported as climbed.

Ice is also found on the south faces of the southern Araca peaks but, above all, in the main or central area and in the Choquetanga massifs. As for exploratory mountaineering, all four areas seem to have a number of unascended summits. An entire ridge of unknown ice peaks (c5200-5300m) are visible at the north-east end of the Choquetanga district, above the Bengala mine.

And there is yet another side to Quimsa Cruz mountaineering: simple travelling, hiking, learning, adventuring, climbing. To me, these activities reveal the Quimsa Cruz at its best.

Appendix A: Quimsa Cruz journeys by the author

I have visited this range in nine different seasons because it offered the unique advantage of comfortably reaching over 4500m by means of rural buses or other vehicles. I always climbed alone since in those days this range attracted very few parties, but excellent (and inexpensive) Aimara porters sometimes carried my pack to high camps.

Dec 1983 Ascent of Cerro Colorado (5280m) and Don Luis (5360m), north-west and south, respectively, of Lake Huallatani. A cairn on the latter.

April 1985 Laramcota Chico (5380m), a surveyor's cairn on top; Cerro Don Luis (5360m), third ascent.

July 1989 Curicampana del Sur (5200m) and the pure white Nevado Anco Collo (5460m), first ascents; Cerro Nuñucollo (5215m), second ascent.

July 1990 Chamacani (c5200m), first ascent; Cerro Mamani (c5400m) second ascent.

July 1991 Nevado San Luis (5620m) and Cerro Santa Rosa (5540m), first ascents; Nevado San Juan or Altarani (5540m) and Cerro Chamac Collo (5350m), second ascents. On the summit of the latter, a cairn erected by Britons Angus Andrew and Neil Howell, who later distinguished themselves in the Nepal Himalaya. A comment about Nevado San Luis: it is the handsome background of Lake Huallatani. It is always recognised as a mountain but it is actually only a long ridge, running east from Putz's RAV 7 (5680m). I climbed San Luis, a long corniced ridge, by its north side.

July 1992 Cerro Chancapiña (5260m), third ascent after the pioneers Hoek and Herzog (a ridge with numerous pinnacles); Cerro 5300m to the east, which I christened Curumiña ('precipice'), first ascent.

July 1993 Nuñucollo (5215m) again; its vassal Cerro Chumpi (c5100m), a first, and Laramcota Grande (5400m), second ascent.

July 1994 Pusicota (5220m), a well trodden peak; Cerro Huilucu (5200m), first ascent; Chiar Huyo (5500m), second ascent.

July 1995 Nevado Imantata (5380m) and Cerro Copagira (5300m), second ascents.

Appendix B: Climbs and Expeditions

For recorded ascents between 1903 and 1970, refer to Evelio Echevarrìa, 'A survey of Andean ascents', *AAJ* 36 (1962), p191, 'A survey of Andean ascents, 1961-1970', *AAJ* 87 (1974), p87, and 'Ascents in the Quimsa Cruz', *AAJ* 44 (1970), pp55-57. The two surveys include bibliographic sources. The last entry was a summarised list.

The present editor and former editors of the *American Alpine Journal* have taken special care to publish short but useful notes on international climbing. For the Quimsa Cruz area the following have appeared:

Vol 14 (1965), 455-6
Vol 16 (1969), 444-5
vol 20 (1975), 180
vol 21 (1978), 579
vol 24 (1982), 190
vol 25 (1983), 205
vol 26 (1984), 213
vol 28 (1986), 195-6
vol 30 (1988), 176-9
vol 32 (1990), 200

vol 33 (1991), 193
vol 34 (1992), 157-60
vol 35 (1993), 174
vol 36 (1994), 169-70
vol 37 (1995), 199-201
vol 38 (1996), 218-9
vol 40 (1998), 263-4
vol 42 (2000), 258
vol 44 (2002), 312-13
vol 45 (2003), 315-17

Appendix C: Bibliography. Publications after 1969:

Evelio Echevarría, 'Cordillera Quimsa Cruz, Bolivia', *Pyrenaica 162* , 211-215, Bilbao, 1991.

Hoy, 'La Cordillera Quimsa Cruz fue exitosamenta explorada', *La Paz*, November 16, 12, 1971.

Ekkehard Jordan, *Die gletscher der Bolivianischen Anden*. Stuttgart: Franz Steiner Verlag, 1991.

Rudi Knott, *Anden Expedition 1969*. Altmuhler: Bayerische Naturfreunde, 1969.

La Razón, 'Miembros del Club Andino Boliviano realizaron una travesìa por la Cordillera de Tres Cruces', *La Paz*, March 8, 1946.

Alain Messili, *Los Andes de Bolivia. Guía de escaladas*. La Paz: Producciones Cima, 1996.

T Ifor Rees, *Sajama*. Aberystwyth: C L Ceredigion, 1960.

Javier Sánchez, 'Quimsa Cruz. Los nevados de Choco Cota'. *Desnivel 151*, 32-37, 1999.

Hermann Wolf, *Cordillera Quimsa Cruz, Bolivien*. Bayreuth: Druckerei Lorenz Ellwanger, 1987.

Yossi Brain, *Bolivia. A Climbing Guide*. Seattle: The Mountaineers, 1999.

Santino Calegari, et al, 'Ande boliviane-Cordillera Quimsa Cruz', *Anuario 1974*, 122-141, Bergamo: Club Alpino Italiano, 1974.

Appendix D: Cartography

The Jordan work entered above includes a separate carpet of glaciological maps. 'Karte 16' corresponds to the Quimsa Cruz, scale circa 1:70 000, executed by personnel of diverse German and Bolivian scientific institutions. Height and location of major peaks should be regarded cautiously. Glaciological and photographic detail is remarkable.

Sketch maps: Calegari, op cit, for the Laramcota area; Knott, Messili and Wolf, op cit, and *AAJ* 30 (1988), p167, and 37 (1995), p200, for the Araca area.

Maps: Instituto Geográfico Militar de Bolivia, 'Carta Nacional', hojas (sheets) 6043-I, 6142-IV, 6143-III and 6143-IV, scale 1:50 000, La Paz, 1981.

MICHAEL BINNIE

The Yak King of Lashkergaaz

In the far north-east of Chitral, in a remote country of grasslands below the Borogil Pass, and a stone's throw from the Wakhan Corridor of Afghanistan, lived, or so people said, the richest man in all Chitral. He was Mirza Rafi, yak herder, sheep grazier, horse dealer, power-broker, drug smuggler and clan chief.

It was late June 1995. My wife Carol and I had been living for two and a half years in the village of Garam Chashma, in the west of Chitral District, where we had established a school via the agency of Voluntary Services Overseas. Carol had already returned home and in two months I was to hand over Pamir Public School to two incoming VSOs. One last adventure beckoned. I declared the three week summer holiday, packed a rucksack and set off to meet the legendary Yak King of Lashkergaaz.

My trek began after a morning's jeep ride from Chitral Town. I walked along a gravel flood plain, through avenues of poplar trees and beneath the ice peaks of the Hindu Raj. Always there was the rumble of the nearby Yarkhun river and, occasionally, I heard the evocative four note fluting of the golden oreole. In four hours I reached the village of Paur where I stayed with an extended family of 27 adults and children. Young men and boys took it in turn to sit with me in the guest room as we waited for the evening meal. Politely they asked me the standard questions: Did I have a wife and family? Was I a Moslem? Did I say daily prayers? At bedtime they helped me undress, carefully tucked me into bed and left a lamp burning beside me on the floor.

'You can turn that off,' I said.

'No', they said, 'it is better. In case you are afraid.'

Next day the valley narrowed to a series of gorges between which were little fields of cultivated land. As soon as I was seen, men and boys, even women rushed down to the path to shake my hand and then kiss the backs of their own in return. They were Ismaelis whose spiritual leader is the Aga Khan. 'Where was I going?' they asked. 'Borogil.' 'Why?' 'To meet Mirza Rafi.' 'Ah!' they said, 'Mirza Rafi.'

Occasionally I met Afghans, on their way home across the Borogil Pass, carrying enormous loads. I caught up with one man sitting on the grass nursing the stump of his truncated leg. His artificial foot and boot lay beside him.

'What happened?' I asked.

'Rooskies,' he said and made exploding sorts of noises and gestures.

'A mine?'

'Yes, a mine.'

On the third day I passed through the hamlet of Lasht where the cliffs fell back and I walked in bright sunlight through a grassy plain with horses grazing. I was reminded of Oxford's Port Meadow. Dotted about were little woods and lanes lined with wild roses dividing fields of ripening wheat. Herd boys were galloping about playing bare-back polo and young girls squatted in groups combing each other's hair. Skylarks were rocketing into the air claiming their spaces and in the background rolled the rhythmic drum-beat of the river.

Halfway across Port Meadow I fell in with a young man on a horse. His mount was no more than a pony, very dainty and neat, the colour of lightly done toast. It minced along beside me on delicate hooves, reminding me of a rocking horse. After a while the man asked me if I was a doctor.

'I'm afraid not,' I said.

'But perhaps you've got some medicines? You see, I get these pains in my back.'

I fished around in my sack and gave him four Paracetamols. He put them into a pocket and was about to ride off when he said, 'Look, I'm not going far but I'll take your bag for you.' He strapped my rucksack onto his saddle and for half an hour I walked blissfully unencumbered as he trotted along beside me. Eventually he stopped and gave me my sack before cantering off into a wood, twisting and turning through the trees like a cossack in a scene from Doctor Zhivago.

I was tired and hungry and lay down beside a stream. I fell asleep. I woke to find three small boys with catapults crouched on the grass a few feet away, staring into my face.

'Where are you going?' they asked, predictably.

'Borogil,' I said.

'Why?'

'To see Mirza Rafi.'

'Ah,' they said like everyone along the way, 'Mirza Rafi.'

Port Meadow narrowed to yet another gorge and my path wound its way up a steep, loose cliff. A rope length below me the river slid by like wet cement. A fall here was unthinkable. Twenty minutes later the gorge opened out into the narrowest of valleys where I sank down onto a patch of grass. Beside me stood a grove of poplars and behind was a field of ripened wheat, no bigger than a tennis court , completely taken over by cornflowers. Across the river a vast, inverted cone of scree, looking as smooth as brown sugar spilling from a bag, ended only at the water's edge. Little fishes darted about the stream beside which I was lying in the last hour of sunlight. I switched on my radio. It was the first Saturday of Wimbledon and Agassi was knocking hell out of someone.

Early next morning I surprised some playing children who ran away from me screaming in terror. It was definitely getting wild. 'Tea?' asked a man who emerged from a hut and, as I sat drinking it in the sunlight, his children crept back to examine me, like wary kittens. I walked all day quite

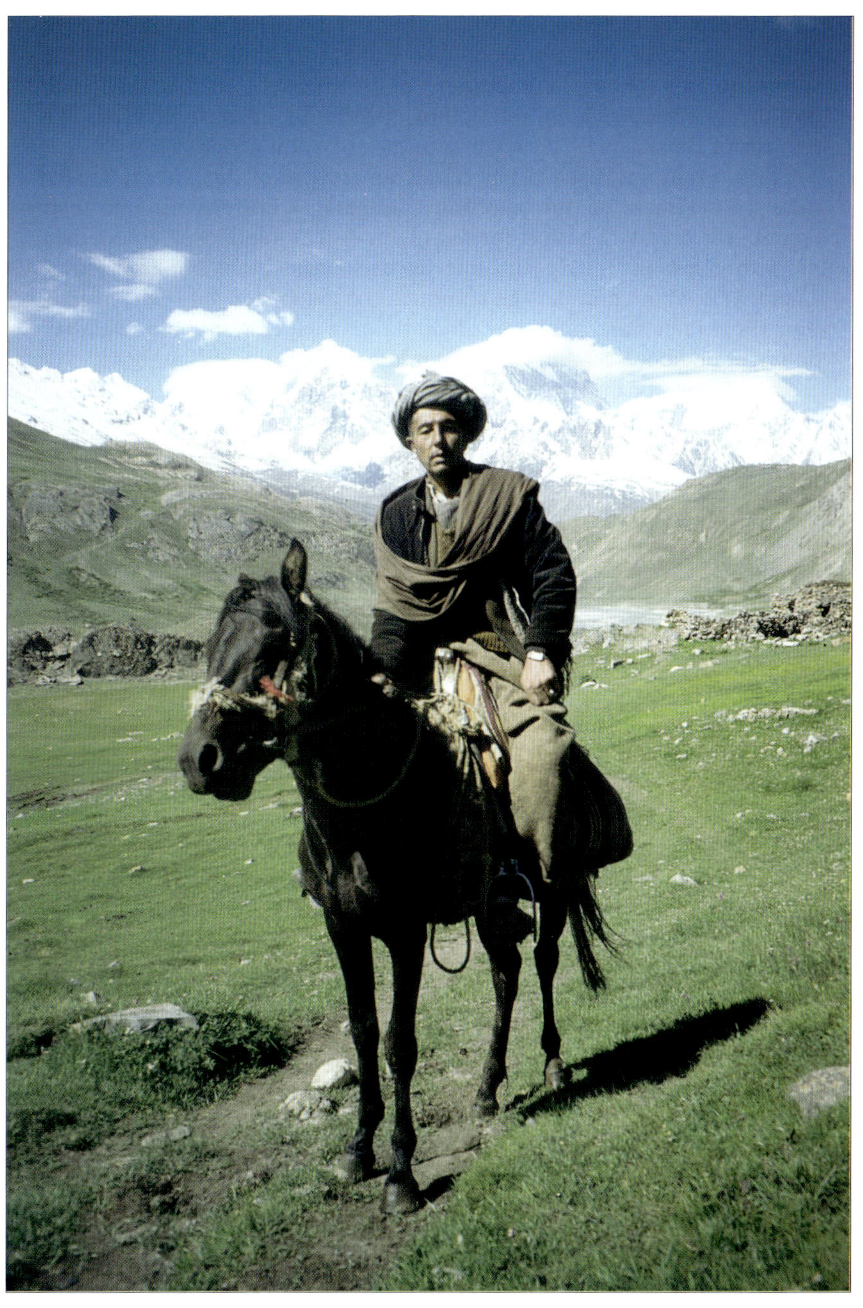

106. An Afgan horseman who carried Binnie's pack for a while after receiving a gift of Paracetamol. (*Michael Binnie*)

alone except for the company of hundreds of marmots whistling to each other to warn of my approach. Above me, intermittently, circled the silhouette of a solitary lammergeier. In the afternoon of this, the fourth day, the gorges opened out into rolling grassy hills. The country was like the fells of Eskdale with a backdrop of distant, snowy tops.

In the evening I reached Ishkerwaz, an outpost of the Chitral Scouts, once the regiment of our own Tony Streather, who took me into their crenulated, mud-walled fort for the night. After supper they entertained me with folk songs and dancing then lay back on cushions and lit up joints. There were 11 men under the command of a subadar. I wondered how they spent their time. Did they go on training expeditions? No. Did they do target practice? No. Patrol the borders? Not really. What then?

'Well,' they said dreamily from beneath clouds of smoke, 'nothing much.'

The height of the fort was 3000m. Next morning it was chilly out of the sun and the Scouts squatted in the compound huddled in their blankets waiting for their breakfasts. They looked like vultures. I wondered about their winter days and nights doing nothing much.Today I would reach Mirza Rafi's. There was some debate as to how long it would take me to get there.

'A day,' said one of the Scouts.

'No, half a day,' said another who was supported by a third.

The first man thought better of his advice. 'Yes, half a day.' Then he said (the ghost of Eric Newby, you have to believe me!), 'It's only *a short walk*.'

I walked for two hours through the undulating grasslands of Lashkergaaz, the territory of Mirza Rafi, before reaching a junction of two paths. Straight on was Mirza Rafi. To the left lay the Borogil Pass, an historic and strategic vantage point crossed by the young George Curzon, future Viceroy of India, in 1894 during an exploration of the Pamir and Hindu Kush mountains. Of it he wrote:

'...realizing its great importance owing to its geographical position in the scheme of frontier defence of the Indian Empire, the Government was convinced of the necessity of closing this small chink in the mountain palisade, which at that time Russia showed a persistent desire to penetrate at whatever point she could find an entrance.'

She never did penetrate it, the Great Game soon petered out into a stalemate and the importance of the Borogil Pass was consigned to a back-burner of history. I examined my map. I could nip up to the pass and still reach Mirza Rafi's that day.

Forty minutes later I was standing on an inconspicuous col. Ahead the ground fell away to a huge, empty valley. Afghanistan. The Pamir mountains in Tajikistan filled the distant skyline. Far away the valley made a dog-leg beyond which, I knew, flowed the fabled Oxus river, scene of Matthew Arnold's 'Sohrab and Rustum' to which I had thrilled as a boy. I sat down and ate a few raisins. The Scouts were back at the fort rolling their spliffs. Nobody would know. With a frisson of devil-may-care I strode down the slope into the Wakhan Corridor.

07. Descending from the Borogil Pass into the Wakhan Corridor. In the distance are the Pamirs. (*Michael Binnie*)

The path was a zig-zag donkey track, easy enough for a column of Russian mountain troops to have rushed, and soon I reached the stony bed of the Ab-I-Warsing, a tributary of the Oxus, which here is called the Ab-I-Wakhan. The landscape was dry and bare. There were no irrigation channels or signs of agriculture. A few huts had long since been abandoned. I passed some grazing camels but there seemed to be nobody around to herd them. I was alone in an enormous, empty landscape.

Or so I thought. I had been walking for some time when in the distance I made out a man sitting on a boulder. I reached him and we shook hands. He was about my height, strongly built, with coarse, thick hands and I understood he was returning home to Afghanistan after working on one of the jeep roads in Chitral. It was taken as read we would go on together, he hoisted a heavy sack onto his back and off we went.

We walked for what seemed like hours along the gravel beds of the Ab-I-Warsing, frequently crossing and re-crossing the stream. Sometimes we were thigh deep in swamps. Swarms of fishes and tadpoles fled before us. On and on we plodded across this desert of gravel with the Oxus seemingly getting no nearer. I had no particular plan. I knew that by now I would never get back across the Borogil by nightfall. Eventually I heard the continuous muffled sound of a huge volume of running water and suddenly we were there and, dazed and exhausted, I flopped down beside the banks of the Oxus. A hot strong wind blew downstream.

108. Binnie's Afghan fellow traveller 'Wakhi' wades into the Oxus river, returning home. (*Michael Binnie*)

Wakhi began to make preparations to cross the river. The far bank seemed to be about a mile away. He now asked me if I would come with him to his home.

'Where is it?' I croaked.

He gestured towards a distant landscape across the river. It might have been two miles or 20. Supposing the river rose in the night? I would never get back. I was due to re-open the school in just over a week. I had made an illegal crossing of the border. No one knew where I was.

'I would love to, but…'

'Please,' he implored.

'Sorry, old chum. No can do.'

He then crouched down by the river side and started to pray. 'Al-lah, Al-lah, Al-lah,' he intoned, perhaps as many as 20 times ,then stepped gingerly into the swirling water and, balancing with his stick, inched his way 40 yards across the channel to an island.

I watched him through my binoculars as he crossed islands, waded more channels, until he finally disappeared in a wobble of heat haze. I focused my binoculars on the far bank and made out tantalizing green meadows and herds of horses and yaks grazing. I thought – I should have gone.

After some time, perhaps half an hour, I collected myself together and walked slowly back towards the Borogil Pass in the late evening sun and found a patch of grass beyond the swamp where I slept. In the morning I passed the camels again, their double humps hanging beside their ribs like empty, flaccid breasts, and crossed the Darwaza An (the Doorway Pass) back into Chitral. I had been in Afghanistan for 24 hours.

By late afternoon I reached a house. A man appeared. 'Mirza Rafi?' No, he was his brother. Mirza Rafi was a few hours away on some higher grazing grounds. It would be better if I spent the night with him, he said. He went back into the house and returned with a rug which he flicked onto the grass. A few minutes later he reappeared with a bowl of yoghurt and a hunk of bread. Soon an extremely dirty little girl came out of the house with a baby on her hip and sat down beside me, fastening her eyes unwaveringly onto my face. Twice I tried to give the baby a smile but each time its face contorted in terror so I gave up. A friendly, shaggy puppy squirmed guiltily onto the rug beside us. I was sitting in a shallow bowl of grassland almost at the point where the ranges of the Hindu Kush and Hindu Raj converge. Three cows, two horses and a bull yak were grazing nearby. I could hardly have been happier. I fell asleep.

Next morning I set off for Mirza Rafi's summer encampment on grass as crisp as a golf links. Streams were cutting through the grassland and the air was filled with the rhapsody of skylarks. About two hours later I crossed a shallow col and, momentarily unseen, looked down on a scene of intense colour and activity. Inside a stone corral a number of women, dressed in reds and yellows and wearing Gilgiti pill-box hats, were milking sheep and goats. Children were rushing about playing. Scattered about were a number of low, stone huts. Almost immediately somebody saw me, gave a shout, and the ensuing silence was like the crash of a slamming door. I walked down into the settlement.

A tall, sunburnt man with Mongol features approached from one of the huts. He was wearing a Russian army bush hat, faded jeans and a garment straight from the pages of *Country Life* – a Barbour jacket.

'Welcome,' he said in English.

He took me to another hut and spread a felt rug on the mud floor. A crowd of children stood gazing in at us. A bowl of curds and another of cream were passed inside.

'I was waiting for you to arrive,' said the man.

He was Mirza Rafi.

We ate together sharing a single spoon and conversed in Urdu. He also spoke, or said he spoke, Chitrali, Pushtu, Farsi, Turki, Uzbek and a dialect of Chinese. The men, women and children of the settlement were all members of one family of which he was the head. He had been born in a Western province of China from which he had escaped as a boy with his family at the onset of communism. He spoke slowly, leaving long pauses between sentences. His courtesy and magnetism were almost overwhelming.

After eating, Mirza Rafi took me on a tour of his establishment. Milking was over and the flocks, accompanied by wolf-hounds, were heading for the pastures. Further up the valley were his yak herds. Ponies, donkeys, hens, pigeons and a solitary camel made up the livestock. My host was a man of few words to whom everyone in the camp genuflected at the start of the day, and to whom he extended the back of his right hand to be kissed. His sphere of influence, I was told, extended into the Wakhan Corridor and as far as the passes above Gilgit. I didn't doubt that the Chitral Scouts kept well out of his way. Well was he known as the Yak King of Lashkergaaz.

We sat down on a rock and he told me about his life. He owned 200 yaks and 700 sheep and goats. Every autumn the passes from Gilgit were crossed by buyers to whom he sold 40 yaks and a third of his flocks. I calculated that this amounted to around £20,000, a spectacular figure by local standards, yet his summer house was no more then a pile of stones and his winter residence only marginally more solid.

He was keen to know about my life. What was the language of England? Ah! English. And were yaks grazed in England? He took an enormous shine to my binoculars. Could I possibly sell them to him? These days he didn't actually have any cash but would I accept a yak? He had to be joking. No, he said, he would give me one of his best animals which I could drive to Chitral and there sell for a profit. I foresaw a number of difficulties to this arrangement. I extricated myself from the impasse only by explaining that the binoculars were a gift from my son. Ah, well, he said, in that case…

Again that night we shared a meal entirely of milk products and, a little after night fall, the entire company went to bed, I in my own little bothy. I left the next morning though he pressed me to extend.

'Next time, please, you bring your wife and children,' he said as he walked half a mile with me at my leave taking. His final words, like his first, were in English.

'Forget me not,' he said.

I turned and started out on my journey home.

Summary: A fortnight's solo journey on foot in the Hindu Kush, straying into Afghanistan, in summer 1995.

Alps

Jim Curran *Looking up the Verdon Gorge* 2005
Oil on canvas
Private collection

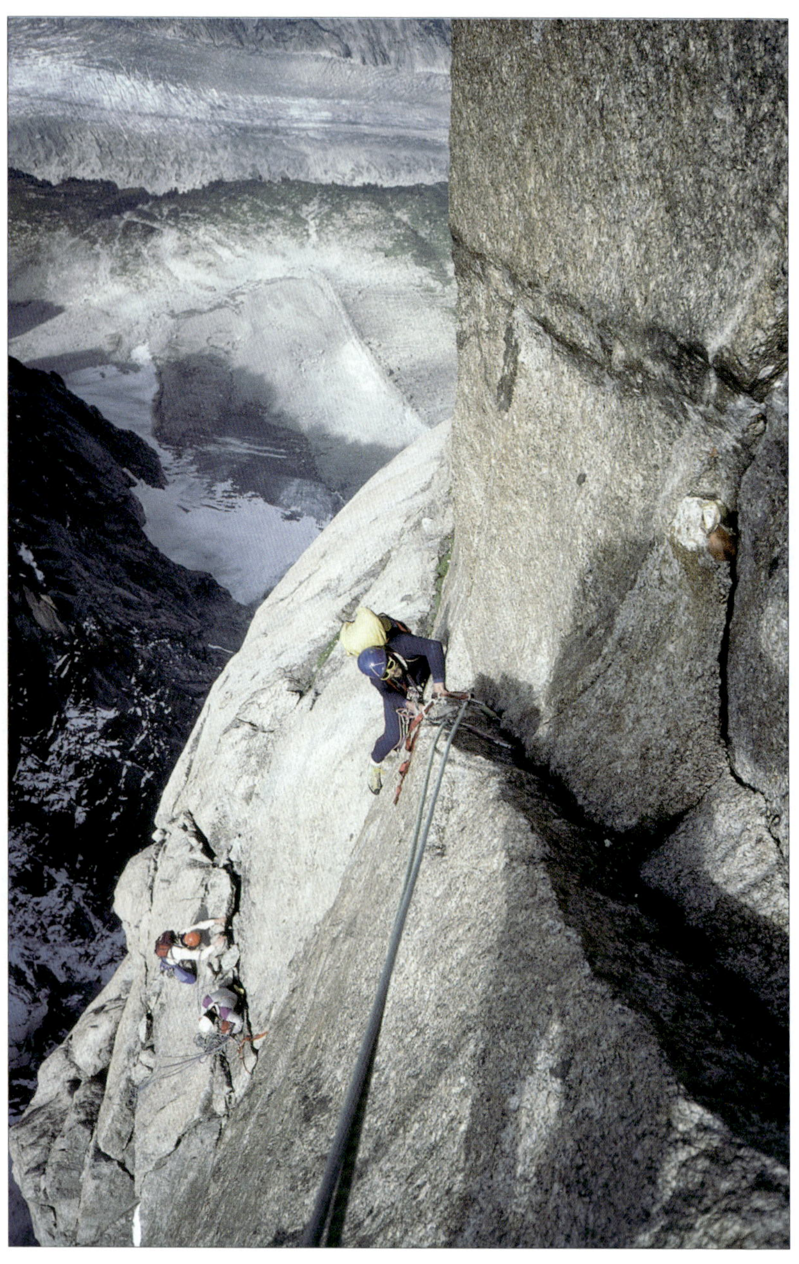

110. Guy Muhlemann on the Bonatti Pillar, Petit Dru, July 1991. (*Simon Richardson Collection*)

VICTOR SAUNDERS

The Bonatti Pillar 1955-2005

So farewell then
The Bonatti Pillar
(forty nine and three quarters)

Walter took five days
to put you up

nature
took five years
to take you

down
to the Torrent
des Drus

And now I find
your holds and ledges
by those troubled waters

So hello then
The Bonatti Pillar
(forty nine and three quarters)

Victor Saunders
with apologies to EJ Thribb

A brief biography of the Bonatti Pillar and adjacent routes

1955	Bonatti Pillar, solo: Walter Bonatti
1957	West face of the Dru, winter: Jean Cousy, Réné Desmaison
1961	Bonatti Pillar, winter: R Guillaume & A Vieille
1962	American Direct: G Hemmings, R Robbins
1963	West Face, solo: Réné Desmaison
1965	American Direttissima: J Harlin, R Robbins
1969	Bonatti Pillar, British Solo: Eric Jones
1976	American Direttissima, winter: P Malinowski, M Piekutowski, Z Wach, J Wolf
1976	American Direct, winter: A Bellica, I Koller
1979	"C'est arrivé demain": Patrick Bérault, Claude Rémy, Yves Rémy
1982	American Direct, solo: Christophe Profit
1982	Geneva Route: N Schenkel, B Wiestlbach
1982	French Direttissima: Hervé Sachetat, Hubert Giot
1983	The American Direct free: T Renault, P Etienne, C Profit, E Escoffier
1986	Absolu: P Camison, P Grenier
1987	French Direttissima, winter: S Long and J Silvester
1989	Bonatti Pillar, winter solo: Alain Ghersen
1991	Destivelle Route: Catherine Destivelle
1992	French Direct, solo: François Marsigny
1997	First rock falls affecting the Bonatti Pillar area
1998	February 10 to 16: Russian Route. V Babanov et al
2005	Final devastating collapse of Bonatti Pillar the day after George Bush rejects the Kyoto Accord on Global Warming.

JOHANNA MERZ

Prayers in Stone

The rock engravings of the Vallée des Merveilles

A yellowing cutting from *The Times* of March 1983 describes a week-long circular walk, starting and ending in Nice, and stretching as far north as the foothills of the Maritime Alps and the Italian frontier. When I re-read it twenty years later I realised that there had been something about the article that had made me cut out and keep it, thinking that one day I myself might explore these mountains above the sparkling coast of the French Riviera. Richard Wilson, the author, had stayed briefly at the Refuge des Merveilles, though he and his wife had pressed on with their circular journey and had not penetrated the rugged heart of the valley where the famous engravings that gave the valley its name are to be found.

The first person to write about this area in the *Alpine Journal* was Douglas Freshfield in an article entitled 'The Maritime Alps'. In the winter of 1877, from the hills around Cannes, he had observed and been excited by 'the snowy chain'. On the morning of 6 April 1877, when the country was in its 'fullest spring outburst', he set out to reach them with a local guide from the village of San Martino di Latosca. Not without difficulty and some stiff rock climbing, they reached the summit of the Cima della Rovina in the Mercantour valley. From this viewpoint they were unable to see Mont Blanc nor Monte Viso since their view was cut off by the Roca dell'Argentera, the highest peak in the Maritime Alps, and its two satellites, the Cima di Nasta and Cima di Culatta; but to the north-east they could trace the broad plains of Piedmont shining in the morning sunshine and stretching away to the base of the Pennine Alps.

Freshfield had come up from the coast to an area west of the Vallée des Merveilles. In his account he mentions a pamphlet describing a visit to 'the rude designs ... found at a height of 7,800 feet, on rocks smoothed by glacier action, at the head of a glen which opens into the Roya valley at San Dalmazzo di Tenda'. But his guide had never been there and could tell him nothing of the prehistoric carvings. Freshfield returned to the area the following year with François Dévouassoud, when they climbed the Cima di Nasta, but so far as is known he never visited the Merveilles itself.

In 1879 W A B Coolidge came to the Laghi delle Meraviglie during an expedition with the two Almers (his regular guides) 'in order to examine the mysterious rock drawings'. However, they cannot have spent much time there since, by the next day, 25 August, they had managed to reach the inn on the Col de Tende, a prodigious distance to cover on foot in a single day.

In September 2004 I determined to try to explore the rock engravings in the Vallée des Merveilles and, having flown to Nice, I took the train that winds slowly up the Roya valley through limestone gorges to the ancient village of La Brigue a few miles from the Italian frontier. I had no idea how I would get from there to the Vallée des Merveilles other than on foot but I was extremely lucky to join a party of German-Swiss who had a spare place in their two 4x4 vehicles. The walk to the refuge from the nearest village, St Dalmas de Tende, would have taken at least four hours, whereas in our two jeeps it took about an hour and a half to negotiate the twisting, precipitous, unmade road that winds its way through beautiful larch forests to the remote valley where the prehistoric engravings are to be found. This road was originally completed in the late 1920s, only to be destroyed during the Second World War. It was recreated again after the war but now, as part of the Parc National du Mercantour, it has been allowed to revert to its natural state in an attempt to preserve the beauty of the area and, with little success, deter tourists. This explains why reaching the valley involved such a bumpy, boulder-strewn ride.

Eventually our party of German-Swiss, together with our French guide, disembarked at the furthest point accessible to stalwart vehicles. Here we found the Refuge des Merveilles, at about 2300m, and beyond it the desolate slopes of Mont Bégo which are under snow from November to June. The refuge was sited on the edge of Lac Long, the cerulean blue of which made a striking contrast against the barren landscape surrounding it.

Passing this sparkling lake, the first of several higher up, we followed a rough path winding its way through a chaotic jumble of huge rocks, many bearing a surface patina of green or orange, which had been worn to a smooth polish by glacial action. We slogged on steeply upwards for a further hour or so until the guide pointed out to us the first of the carvings. These are widely scattered and not easy to find. Most are located away from the footpath or tucked behind rocks as if they were not intended to be found by casual passers by. The images were simply drawn but were easily recognisable as the animals, farming implements and weapons that were part of the daily lives of the Bronze Age nomads (circa 2000 BC) to whom the engravings are most often attributed. We saw various horned animals, ox-drawn ploughs and many odd geometrical shapes.

Our guide recounted the history of the engravings and of the people connected with their discovery but since he spoke very quickly in heavily accented French I was unable to understand much of what he was saying. However, the name Clarence Bicknell attracted my attention, since Bicknell is a name familiar to many Alpine Club members. I was sufficiently fascinated by what I had seen to try to find out more. A visitors' guide later told me that Clarence Bicknell had been the first person to make a serious study of the engravings. In the short time available to me it had only been possible to see and try to photograph a tiny selection of the thousands of carvings which survive in this extraordinary valley.

Back in London I discovered that Clarence Bicknell came from a family of mountain lovers. His brother, Raymond, a keen mountaineer, was Vice-President of the Alpine Club from 1926 until his death in a climbing accident the following year. Some of us will remember Raymond Bicknell's son Peter, whose application for AC membership was backed by famous names like Claude Elliott and E L Strutt. Peter and his brother Claud were taken on holiday to Grindelwald by their father in 1924 and both became prominent mountaineers. Peter wrote several articles for the *Alpine Journal*, such as 'Wordsworth and the Alps' with Janet Adam Smith in the 1992 volume.

112. Sparkling Lac Long, one of the string of glacial lakes at over 2000m near the Refuge des Merveilles. (*Johanna Merz*)

113. Close-up of an inscribed rock, showing a horned animal. (*Johanna Merz*)

There is in the Alpine Club Library a copy of Clarence Bicknell's first book on *The Prehistoric Rock-engravings in the Italian Maritime Alps* (1902) which tells the story of his extensive research carried out between 1897 and 1902. I was intrigued to discover, too, that one of his detailed descriptions, made more than 100 years ago, of that 'wild desolate region' echoed almost exactly my memory of the path taken by our own party. The area had evidently changed little since his time. In Bicknell's day the Vallée des Merveilles and Mont Bégo were in Italy which accounts for his use of 'Meraviglie' rather than the French 'Merveilles'.

> The valley ... opens out into a wild desolate region with huge masses of glaciated schist rocks, and others fallen from the surrounding mountains, and containing numerous small lakes. We cross the stream and pass the two largest of these lakes, the "Laghi Lunghi". On reaching the farthest of these, the scenery is extremely grand ... The mountains are of fine forms, and the rocks of a wonderful variety of colour, purple, green and yellow. In many parts low down they have been rounded by the action of the ice, and in others higher up where they are of a more slaty nature, they are shattered into pinnacles ... On both sides of the stream in the Vallone delle Meraviglie, on the hillside above its right bank, and round and above the lake, are the figures cut on the glaciated rocks, which are known as the "Meraviglie" or "Wonders".

Clarence Bicknell's interest in botany had taken him naturally to mountain regions. In about 1870 he settled in Bordighera, on private means, in order to study the unique flora of the Maritime Alps. In 1885 he published *Flowering Plants and Ferns of the Riviera*, illustrated with many of his own paintings, but after visiting the Merveilles in 1881 his sphere of interest changed to archaeology and he became obsessed with the rock engravings. In 1906 he built a Colonial-style bungalow, Casa Fontanalba, in the Val Casterino. For the next 12 summers he moved up here from his home in Bordighera in order to pursue his studies further, identifying more than 15,000 figures many of which he described in the more comprehensive *Guide to the Prehistoric Rock Engravings of the Maritime Alps* published in 1913. He continued with this work until his death in 1918.

Many theories have been put forward about the people who covered these rocks with their marks and what their engravings signified. It has been suggested, for instance, that Hannibal's soldiers were the sculptors but this unlikely theory can be discounted. It is probable that the engravings are very much older than that, as the forms of the weapons would indicate.

As Bicknell points out, the figures have nearly all been made by the repeated blow of some blunt implement, probably of flint or other hard stone, and not by metal of which no trace has been found. It is also likely, he thought, that the figures were not all made at the same time and may have continued at distant intervals through many centuries.

116. The village of Tende where Clarence Bicknell is buried and where there is now a museum for the study and display of the area's archæological heritage. (*Johanna Merz*)

abundant grass on the lower slopes. Moreover, Bicknell was told that shepherds would have been deterred by the wolves which used to abound in the area

It has been suggested that the markings may have acted as a kind of archive to preserve the records of memorable events such as victories, truces or peace treaties, alliances, marriages, rights of pasture or judicial decisions. Bicknell tried to find traces of old encampments but without success. He and Luigi Pollini, his Italian servant and friend, went to the trouble of making trenches in several different directions starting from a large stone shelter formed by immense blocks where goatherds had recently built a wall at the entrance. But they found no traces of human habitation, such as pieces of flint or quartz, nor traces of the tools which are depicted in the engravings.

Clarence Bicknell continued his researches until he died in 1918 at the age of 76. He was buried in the village of Tende. During the years that followed little systematic study of the rock engravings was carried out until teams of researchers led by Professor Henry de Lumley started working on them in 1967. Largely as a result of their efforts, upwards of 36,000 engravings were subsequently discovered.

In 1996 the Musée des Merveilles was established at Tende for the study and display of the archæological heritage of the Vallée des Merveilles, Mont Bégo and the surrounding area. Although it has now been established that the engravings date back to the Chalcolithic (Copper) and early Bronze Ages (2900 to 1800 BC), no consensus seems to have been reached as to their original purpose. Visitors to the museum are told that the rock engravings 'lend themselves to different interpretations'. One of the more imaginative of these was proposed in 1997 by a French researcher, Chantal Wolkiewitz, in an article which appeared in the magazine *La Recherche*. She attempted to compare the position of some engravings to the constellations of the bronze age sky and the visible paths of the moon and the sun.

Clarence Bicknell's conclusions were more realistic. After much thought and study, he summarized what he and Pollini believed to be the habits and motivation of these primitive people:

> We ourselves have a half belief that the imposing pyramid of Monte Bego did mean something special to them, as it does to us, who have watched its cliffs crimsoned by the first rays of sunrise, or at midday covered with racing storm clouds, and in the evening black against the western sky ... We therefore consider these innumerable rock engravings to have been a sort of votive offering, reminders to unseen powers good or malignant, of the peoples' needs or fears, the expression of their desires for the well-being of their beasts, the safety of their settlements, the increase of their property and general prosperity and good luck in agriculture or in hunting. These enduring prayers in stone would have been a witness not only for a moment but for ages to come.

BIBLIOGRAPHY

Clarence Bicknell, *The Prehistoric Rock Engravings in the Italian Maritime Alps*. Bordighera, 1902.

Christopher Chippindale, 'Clarence Bicknell: archaeology and science in the 19th century' in *Antiquity, LVIII*, 1984.

W A B Coolidge, 'New Expeditions in 1879' in *AJIX*, November 1879.

Claude Elliott, 'Raymond Bicknell (1875-1927)'. Obituary in *AJ39*, 303, 1927.

Douglas Freshfield, 'The Maritime Alps' in *AJ9*, February 1880.

Desmond Hawkins, 'Labour of Twelve Summers. Clarence Bicknell and the Mount Bego Engravings' in *Country Life*, 28 April 1983.

Richard Wilson, 'Walking back to Alpine happiness' in *The Times*, 11 March 1983.

I would like to thank Yvonne Sibbald, librarian of the Alpine Club Library, for her help in preparing this article.

STEPHEN GOODWIN

Echoes from 'Headquarters'

The AC's record above Zermatt

What on earth has happened to the Church of England? Doing my homework for next year's 150th anniversary gathering of the AC in Zermatt, which I have been subtly manœuvred into organising, it struck me how many of the great peaks of the Zermatt skyline were first climbed by clergymen. Muscular Christianity indeed.

Of the 19 first ascents involving Alpine Club members (including ascents by 'members to-be' prior to the club's formation), no less than 10 had Anglican ministers in the party. When did you last hear of a first ascent by a man or woman of the cloth? I thought not. Climbing kit, it seems, has been consigned to the rectory shelf along with the King James Bible and the old Prayer Book.

With the Zermatt jamboree coming up, this brief article is intended to whet appetites for a return to the resort the AC virtually put on the map with a peak-by-peak reminder of how much our forebears achieved there. It is merely a sketch. Fine detail abounds elsewhere, mainly in old *AJ*s, with Alan Lyall's compendious *The First Descent of the Matterhorn* (Gomer 1997) standing as the definitive work on the single epic that sealed Zermatt's reputation.

What I was unable to find, however, was a general summary of significant ascents associated with AC members. (I don't say such a summary doesn't exist and I expect one will now be pointed out to me.) Cicely Williams' *Zermatt Saga* (Brig 1964) includes a useful chapter on 'peaks and passes' but like the various guide books, including Whymper's own, there is no distinction made between peaks ascended by AC members and the minority that were not. And why should there be, save for our own particular curiosity? It is, however, rather easier to spot the clergymen, dog-collared by their titles, though inconsistently. (The latest AC Valais guides – the ones you'll need for Zermatt – sensibly omit all titles for men, then chivalrously include them for women.)

The Zermatt of the 'Golden Age' no longer exists. From a village with just three guest beds in 1839 it has grown to an upmarket resort with 6,800 beds in 116 hotels and another 8000 beds in 1800 holiday apartments. A plaque on the wall of the Monte Rosa Hotel, still mercifully without too much ostentation, recalls AC president Charles Mathews' description of the hotel as 'the mountaineer's true home', but the days when its high table was reserved for club members are long gone. Active mountaineers today are far more likely to be found down the high street cooking pasta in the kitchen of the Bahnhof Hotel or at the campsite in Randa.

Above the tree-line, though, Zermatt's attractions remain much the same, if better documented – the greatest concentration of the highest peaks in the Alps, arranged in a vast pear outline above the Mattertal. Tackle any of the peaks listed below and you are treading in the footsteps of AC pioneers. Each one of these first ascent parties included someone who was, or would become a member of the Alpine Club, with peaks listed clockwise from the north (St Nicklaus) end of the valley. How many of these routes can members repeat during the AC's 150th summer?

Lenzspitze (4294m) August 1870, Clinton Thomas Dent (AC president 1887) with Alexander and Franz Burgener by the north-west ridge (PD). Dent recalled that the elderly Franz chivvied him on 'with a stick after the fashion of an old Smithfield drover persuading a refactory beast to enter a pen'.

Dom (4545m) 11 September 1858, Rev John Llewellyn-Davis with Johann Zumtaugwald, Johann Krönig and Hieronymus Brantschen by the north-west ridge (Festigrat) (PD+).

Täschhorn (4490m) 31 July 1862, Rev John Llewellyn-Davis and Rev J W Hayward with Johann and Stephan Zumtaugwald by the north-west (Kin) face (PD+). In 1906, Geoffrey Winthrop Young was involved in an epic first ascent of the south-west face (TD+), penduluming crazily off the final rock pitch that had been superbly led by Franz Lochmatter. Part way up the face Young had estimated the odds of their escape at 'five to one'.

Alphubel (4206m) 9 August 1860, Rev Leslie Stephen (Pres 1866) and Thomas Hinchliff (Pres 1875) with Melchior Anderegg and Peter Perren by the south-east ridge (PD).

Allalinhorn (4027m) 28 July 1856, Edward Levi Ames and clergyman Johann Imseng from Saas Grund with J Imboden and Franz Andenmatten by the south-west ridge (PD). Ames, a barrister and country gentleman, was an original member of the AC.

Rimpfischhorn (4199m) 9 September 1859, Rev Leslie Stephen and Dr Robert Liveing with Melchior Anderegg and Johann Zumtaugwald by the west-south-west ridge (Rimpfischwänge) (PD+).

Strahlhorn (4190m) 15 August 1854, the Smyth brothers (reverends James Grenville and Christopher and Indian Army officer Edmund) with Franz Andenmatten and Ulrich Lauener by the west-north-west flank (PD). Though this ascent was before the formation of the AC, both James and Christopher Smyth became members.

117. Matterhorn: looking up the Hörnli ridge, east face catching the sun, north face in shadow to the right, April 2006. Not a day for climbing, with high winds even at the Schwarzsee. (*Stephen Goodwin*)

Monte Rosa (Nordend) (4609m) 26 August 1861, Edward and T F Buxton and John Cowell with Michel Payot and Binder by the south-west ridge (PD).

Monte Rosa (Dufourspitze) (4634m) 1 August 1885, the Rev Charles Hudson, reverends James and Christopher Smyth, John Birkbeck and Rev E J Stevenson with Johann and Matthais Zumtaugwald and Ulrich Lauener by the north-west flank and west ridge (PD). This clerical quartet, plus Birkbeck, a Quaker and original AC member, packed a wealth of experience and cajoled the guides to the west ridge, away from the trodden route to failure at the Silbersattel.

Liskamm (4527m) 19 August 1861, W Hall, J Hardy, C Pilkington (Pres 1896), A Ramsay, T Rennison, F Sibson and R Stephenson with J Cachet, F Lochmatter, K Herr, J & P Perren and S Zumtaugwald by the east ridge (PD).

Castor (4226m) 23 August 1861, William Mathews (Pres 1869) and F W Jacomb with Michel Croz by the south-east ridge (F).

Matterhorn (4477m) 14 July 1865, Edward Whymper, Rev Charles Hudson, Lord Francis Douglas and Douglas Hadow with Michel Croz and the Peter Taugwalders (father and son) by the north-east (Hörnli) ridge (AD). For all the printers' ink consumed by the 1865 ascent and tragic descent, the finest route on the mountain is perhaps that climbed for the first time on 3 September 1879 by another AC legend – Alfred Mummery with guides Alexander Burgener, Johann Petrus and Augustin Gentinetta on the Zmutt ridge (D).

Dent d'Hérens (4171m) 12 August 1863, Florence Craufurd Grove (Pres 1884), William Hall, Reginald Macdonald and Montagu Woodmass with Melchior Anderegg, Jean Pierre Cachat and Peter Perren by the south-west flank and west ridge (PD+). Hall recalled that Anderegg led all day, hewing steps 'the shape and size of Glastonbury chairs' and that Woodmass danced a Highland Fling on the summit, everyone drunk with delight.

Dent Blanche (4356m) 18 July 1862, Thomas Stuart Kennedy and Rev William Wigram with Jean Baptiste Croz and Johann Krönig by the south ridge. In wild weather Wigram's hair became a 'a mass of white icicles'. Twenty years later, the guide Ulrich Almer coined the phrase that stuck as the name of ENE ridge (D) after a difficult first ascent with fellow guide Aloys Pollinger and 'Herrs' John Stafford Anderson and George Percival Baker.

Anderson recalled the summit moment in *AJ* XI:

> Our first proceeding was to shake hands all round, then Almer, grasping the situation in its entirety, exclaimed in a loud and solemn manner, 'Wir sind vier Esel,' (*We are four asses*) a sort of concentrated summary of the day's proceedings, which, it has since been suggested to me by a friend, who I need hardly say is *not* a member of the AC, might be appropriately worked up into a motto for our club.

Ober Gabelhorn (4063m) 6 July 1865, Adolphus Moore and Horace Walker with Jakob Anderegg by the east face. Lord Francis Douglas arrived at the summit just a day later via the NNW ridge or *Couergrat* (AD). It was his third attempt on the mountain that season, but much worse luck was about to befall him.

Zinal Rothorn (4221m) 22 August 1864, Rev Leslie Stephen and Florence Craufurd Grove with Melchior and Jakob Anderegg by the north ridge (AD). Stephen found it a tough one, observing that, 'the last rocks of the Rothorn will always count among the decidedly *mauvais pas* of the Alps'.

Schalihorn (3974m) 20 July 1873, Thomas Middlemore with Christian and Johann Jann Lauener from Moming pass. 'Thomas Middlemore always lived strenuously,' recorded his *AJ* obituary.

Weisshorn (4506m) 19 August 1861, John Tyndall with Johann Josef Bennen and Ulrich Wenger by the east ridge (AD). However, the Weisshorn is more readily associated with Geoffrey Winthrop Young who made four first ascents on it, notably, on 7 September 1900, the west face rib, or *Younggrat* (D–).

Bishorn (4153m) 18 August 1884, George Barnes and Rev R Chessyre-Walker with Josef Imboden and J M Chanton by the north-west flank (F). Three years earlier Mrs Aubrey Le Blond (as Mrs Fred Burnaby), who would go on to found the Ladies Alpine Club, reached the Bishorn east peak (4134m) with guides Josef Imboden and Peter Sarbach yet unaccountably did not continue up the easy-angled ridge to the summit.

EDWARD PECK

If Matterhorn, Why Cervin?

The derivation of 'Matterhorn' is straightforward. There is this great Horn rising out of the Matten (meadows) on the Zermatt side. Indeed, it was known to the locals as simply 'das Horn'. From the south side, the mountain is less domineering and looks like a hunchback crone, some distance beyond the last habitation of Breuil in the upper Valtournanche. Although the locals referred to it casually as 'le grand Becca', no one felt the need for a more formal name.

From the local point of view the nearby pass of 3317 metres was much more important. It was the only way across the main range from Aosta to the Valais between Monte Mosso and the Simplon to the east and the Great St Bernard to the west, and could be crossed in summer on foot or on horseback despite the wide expanse of everlasting snow on the Zermatt side. (For people in mediæval times a 'mont' was not the top of a mountain but simply the summit of a pass, as with Mont Cenis and Mont Genèvre). Before the small chapel dedicated to the local patron saint St Théodule was erected in 1688, this pass enjoyed a variety of names: Mons Silvius, Mont Servin, or simply 'der Gletscher' in German, or, in the local patois, 'le Roise' (or 'Rosa') denoting a large area of snow. (The 'Rosa' of Monte Rosa or of the Rosa Blanche did not relate to the colour of the west face at sunset, but to the vast expanse of snow.)

This pass had been in use since Roman times, but it was only in the 16th century that the name Mons Silvius was first recorded – when Aegidius Tschudi made the crossing in 1528, and again in 1554 when Josias Simler, who was disabled and presumably did not cross the pass himself, drew attention to the 'great mass of snow and some abrupt rocky peaks nerby'. Mons Silvius gave rise to some dubious derivations, such as a mythical Roman general believed to have travelled in these parts, or the German 'silbern' (or 'silvery'), which might apply to the expanse of snow on the pass but scarcely to the rocky slopes of a peak of 4477m. The simple metathesis of 'l' to 'r' – a mistake often made by Japanese and others – and the change of S to C, thus converting 'Selva' to 'Cervin' – misled Coolidge into deriving it from the French 'cerf' for 'stag', thereby justifying Voltaire's cynical view that 'l'étymologie est une science où les consonnes comptent pour peu de choses et les voyelles pour rien du tout'. It took a map-maker for the Duke of Savoy to apply the name 'Servin' (still spelt with an S) to some indefinite peak west of the Théodule, and for de Saussure, who crossed the pass in 1786, to use the initial C and relate it to our peak, when he admired the 'proud summit of Mont Cervin – a triangular obelisk in living rock which might have been cut out by scissors'.

According to Jules Guex, author of *La Montagne et ses Noms*, to whom I am indebted for much of the above information, we must look elsewhere for a description based on locality. 'Silva' or 'Selva' (used in modern Spanish for 'wood' or 'forest') is suitably used for hills with forests in their lower reaches. This applies to three other Mont Servins (one in Savoy, two in Piedmont). Those are humble mountains of no more than 2000m and deserve an appellation of 'woody' or 'forested', which hardly applies to the steep rocky slopes of our mountain of 4477m. The name of Servin or Cervin might be suitable if our peak is viewed through the forests of the upper Valtournanche, but it was not generally applied to our peak until about 1855 when, 10 years before it first ascent, mountaineers made their early attempts from the Italian side.

And so we end up with the anomaly that the name of our spectacular, high rocky peak, with little snow on its flanks and certainly no forests, should have been derived from 'silvery' or 'forested'!

BIBLIOGRAPHY

Jules Guex, *La Montagne et ses Noms*
W A B Coolidge, *Alpine Sketches*
Landeskarte der Schweiz: Arolla sheet No 283 (for heights) 1:50 000

Art & Literature

Jim Curran *Rackwick Bay, Orkney* 2005
Oil on canvas

Jim Curran *Goredale Scar (after James Ward)* 2005
Oil on canvas

JIM CURRAN

Nothing Lasts Forever

Returning across Tibet from the 1998 Sepu Kangri expedition with Chris Bonington, I was aware that the journey marked the end of an era. For Chris it would probably be his last high profile media extravaganza; for me, 20 years of expedition film-making had lost much of its allure, though I remain grateful and privileged to have climbed, travelled and filmed in many of the world's great mountain ranges. But nothing lasts forever.

I had come to film-making late. I had studied fine art in the heady days of the early sixties, and throughout my twenties and until my mid-thirties painting had been my raison d'etre. Then in 1974 a year's secondment to the (then) Sheffield Polytechnic had dramatically changed my life. The multi-disciplines of film-making had, almost overnight, superseded the world of brushes, easels and canvas.

Superseded but not totally erased. My job lecturing on the Foundation Course at the University of the West of England kept me in touch, particularly as I taught life drawing one day a week throughout most of my career. So when I started using pencil drawings to illustrate my biography of Chris Bonington and then my travels in *The Middle-Aged Mountaineer*, I was back on familiar territory.

Starting to paint again was not so easy and it wasn't until 2001 that I summoned up the courage to take the plunge. The problem was not how or what, but why? Was there any compelling reason in the 21st century to start smearing oily pigments onto bits of canvas and abandoning the high-tech world of digital videos and computer-generated images?

It would have been all too easy to have talked myself out of doing anything at all, particularly as I still consider myself deeply lazy, and have always used the motto 'don't do anything today that you can put off until next week'. Eventually I got bored with soul-searching and decided on a straightforward course of action; to paint mountain landscapes based on some of the highlights of the last 20 years, and leave the theorising to others. A professional career in art education had to be (at least temporarily) forgotten: not so easy, for it is impossible to be consciously naïve. Knowledge of landscape painters past and present still haunted me – Turner, Constable and Cezanne couldn't be ignored and I had come to think of the work of Julian Cooper as the last word on the subject of mountain painting.

Anything I produced would inevitably be compared with him (if only by me), and how could I compete with his marvellous Kangchenjunga or Eiger series? But, nothing ventured nothing gained, and I made the first tentative marks on a blank canvas.

120. Jim Curran, *Rising Mist on Hoy*, 2004, oil on canvas.

121. Jim Curran, *Looking down the Verdon Gorge*, 2005, oil on canvas, *Private Collection.*

I would like to have been able to say that, like riding a bicycle, the old skills instantly came flooding back. Not so, and the first few paintings were technical nightmares. The only bonus was that while simply trying to resolve practical problems, I couldn't worry much about anything else.

Slowly, big paintings of K2, the Trango Towers, Chogolisa and Gasherbrum 4 took shape. They were based on memory, experience and, inevitably, photography, which many people still view with some suspicion, if not regard as downright cheating. But there is a world of difference in simply copying a photograph, which is not a particularly difficult thing to do. (If you don't believe me, take the evidence of my quarter of a century spent interviewing prospective art students whose folders all too frequently contained lovingly detailed copies of photographs of Jimi Hendrix – they all looked exactly the same.) But for generations, painters have found that using photography to glean information is something quite different. Vermeer used the camera obscura, Degas' paintings of race horses and ballet dancers relied heavily on photography – Walter Sickert frequently used newspaper photos and, more recently, David Hockney made endless experiments with photo-collages.

Hockney in particular intrigued me. In the mid-seventies and early eighties he made dozens, if not hundreds of what he called 'joiners', using a comprehensive documentation of landscapes to present strangely compelling images that in their almost Cubist complexity seemed to recreate the way we scan and understand reality. In particular, a series based on his visits to the Grand Canyon were later translated into vast paintings. But his supposed innovations weren't exactly new. Photographers had long used the technique of jointing prints together. Memorably, Vittorio Sella had produced his famous panoramas of the Karakoram and the Caucasus. One in particular, of K2, Broad Peak, the Gasherbrums and almost the whole length of the Baltoro glacier had stuck in my mind. One of my last paintings before my conversion to film had in fact been based on several old black and white prints stuck together showing Paul Nunn climbing in Cheddar Gorge. I had treated the image almost as a still life and lovingly painted, *trompe-l'oeil* fashion, the strips of grimy sellotape and brown sticky paper holding the prints together. The painting was one of only a few to survive and for many years hung at the top of my stairs to remind me of my roots.

Whilst on the subject of photography, I have never considered myself any more than a competent amateur (despite, or maybe because of, squillions of undocumented slides). Like Julian Cooper I have a rather perverse penchant for 'bad' photographs. Snaps, out of focus, over or under exposed images, can and do spark ideas for painting. The 'perfect' photograph doesn't do this for me, and in truth I have invariably found that viewing my best photographs for the first time has been accompanied by a twinge of disappointment.

The first exhibition I felt able to mount was during the 2002 Kendal Mountain Film Festival at the Brewery Arts Centre. It was, in retrospect, a bit of a hotch-potch of paintings, drawings and watercolours old and new, along with photos, videos and books. It was more successful than I dared hope, and two years later I showed in the hallowed portals of our Club. I felt much happier with the exhibition and it seemed to me to be more focused.

By now I had (almost) got the ambitious Himalayan paintings out of the way and was concentrating on material nearer home, including the Old Man of Hoy. While the Alpine Club show was still on, I went back to Hoy with Terry Gifford for a few days of intensive drawing and painting of the wonderful decaying sandstone cliffs of Rackwick Bay. Their horizontal strata, towering arêtes and hanging 'grassfields' had fascinated me since my first visit to Hoy in 1983. The Old Man itself had previously given me four memorable outings, including filming Catherine Destivelle in 1997. But Rackwick Bay became an obsession and I spent most of 2005 producing drawings, watercolours and paintings. One measuring nearly ten feet by four was probably the most successful. These formed the basis of my third exhibition, this time back at the Brewery Arts Centre. This time I felt I had really hit my stride and many possibilities seemed to open out.

However, my pleasure was definitely tempered by the unwelcome diagnosis in the middle of 2005 of prostate cancer. Hopefully a wake-up call and not a go-to-sleep one, it certainly focused my mind on the remaining time I have left. During and since my treatment I narrowed my interest right down to my own Sheffield home, drawing mundane, everyday objects; bookshelves, lamps, towels draped over radiators, even flowers and a couple of self-portraits. There was certainly a therapeutic element in doing them but I discovered many of the same elements on a much smaller scale of the themes I had tackled in the mountains.

At the time of writing, I don't know where the next paintings will lead me or even what the subject matter may be. Mountains have always been central to my life and always will be, but it may well be that in order to develop my work I will have to move on to something else. Nothing lasts forever.

ACKNOWLEDGEMENT

Jim Curran would like to thank Andy Curtis of the Sharp Edge Gallery, Keswick for photographing the paintings shown on pages 1, 75, 141, 191, 192, 194, 195,

JOHN DUGGER

'And I made a rural pen'

The Story of Mountain Banners

In the early 1970s I began drawing landscapes; then after acquiring some basic climbing skills, I drew mountainscapes as well. I always carried a small portfolio on my climbs, sketching on the run, learning to capture the profiles and defiles with a stroke of my pen, recording the concourses of rock, snow and sky. I found my true drawing school in the open fields, climbing and rambling the hills of Snowdonia, the Lake District and the Scottish Highlands. My first Mountain Banner, the *South Cluanie Ridge 1985*, depicts five Munros in Glen Shiel, traversed with some friends on New Year's Day, and was based on three original drawings sketched during our approach and climb. It was made using the cut-fabric appliqué style of my early strip-banners but it was especially fabricated in Nylon Cordura – complete with climbing rope and prussic-knot rigging. While initially pleased with the result, I felt the need for a technique capable of a sharper rendering – something more akin to the mountainscapes I was drawing in the field.

A significant advance came in 1988 while I was working with discharge-dye techniques, trying to achieve what was then my 'holy grail' – a cheap, simple and low-tech method for making permanent original drawings on fabric. My method, which uses an oxidizing agent to burn out the image on canvas, has the added advantage of being a two-stage process – so work on-site in the out-of-doors is dry and only requires the liquid discharge to develop the field drawings once back in the studio. From 1988 to 1991 I did a first set of new-style Mountain Banners, using canvases carried into the mountains on several climbing trips to the Swiss and Italian Alps, and finished in my strip-banner format. The initial success of these early works suggested the correct tools and techniques were at hand – all that was needed was that rare gift of free time to build upon these discoveries.

In 1991, during the International Year of Tibet, I was asked to make a large-scale banner artwork for the public address that His Holiness the Dalai Lama would make at the Cathedral of St John the Divine in New York as part of the *Kalachakra for World Peace*. The Sanskrit word *Kalachakra* means 'wheel of time' and it is a teaching that originated in India, spread throughout Central Asia and is considered a jewel in the crown of Tibetan Buddhism. The *Kalachakra* ceremony includes beautiful rituals such as the 'earth pacification dance' and the construction of a great multi-coloured sand *mandala* depicting three levels of temporal existence. Related to these themes of earth and time is the *Kalachakra* legend of *Shambhala*, a legendary city of the Central Asian plateau hidden in the great mountains, where the population is blessed with good crops, good health and good governance. In ancient texts the flag of *Shambhala* was described as a 'plaque of snowy mountains surrounded by peacock feathers'. So it was this that I set out to make.

I selected as two 'snowy mountains' the Himalayan peaks of Mount Everest and Mount Kailas, both of which attract human participation in a distinctive way. Mount Everest is the target of repeated attempts on its summit, in a motion of up and down, whereas Mount Kailas is the centre of an ancient pilgrim's *kora* (or circling) of this sacred mountain, moving round and round. Mount Everest is the 'summit of achievement' whereas Mount Kailas is a 'centre of being'; together they represent the balanced whole that fulfills our potential as human beings. This serendipitous project provided me with the perfect opportunity to try out my newly developed fabric technique on a major artwork, creating a great mountainscape of Tibet and banner of *Shambhala* in modern form. The Cathedral event was a great success and looking back I can see that it achieved something beyond my ability to measure.

The year after making the *Shambhala* banner I was invited to meet the Dalai Lama at the Namgyal Monastery in Dharamsala, India. Before the meeting his Private Aide advised me that it was customary to have a question to pose to His Holiness. This stumped me and became a source of some discomfort for several days before the interview as I could think of very little he didn't know about most subjects as compared to the very little I knew about anything. After much soul searching I decided to ask what was an intriguing question to me: considering the complexities of Tibetan Buddhist iconography in the context of the ever-increasing interest taken by Westerners in Tibetan Buddhism, had His Holiness had any thoughts on what a modern Buddhist art would look like? 'What a fine question!' exclaimed the Aide on the day of the interview as I waited anxiously in the anteroom, but it was still with some trepidation that I was escorted into the Dalai Lama's private study. After the formal introductions and some small talk, his Aide said, 'Holiness, John-la has a special question for you.' So I repeated my question again; considering the complexities of Tibetan Buddhist iconography in the context of ever-increasing interest by Westerners in Tibetan Buddhism, had His Holiness had any thoughts on what a modern Buddhist art would look like? A deep, extended and anticipatory silence was followed by His Holiness slowly looking at me with a smile, and saying most matter-of-factly, 'No'. In the profound emptiness that followed, I was caught for words and embarrassed beyond belief and wished only that this honour would be over quickly so that I might run back and hide in my lodgings. Soon enough the interview was wound-up; the Dalai Lama personally took my hand and walked me to the door of his study where he spoke quietly to his Aide.

22. *South Cluanie Ridge 1985.* Appliqué strip banner, from an original on-site drawing in Scotland, made of nylon with prusik knot rigging. 72 sq.ft. (*John Dugger*)

123. HH the XIVth Dalai Lama speaking at the Cathedral of St John the Divine in New York, in front of the *Shambhala Banner 1991*. 324 sq. ft. (*John Dugger*)

the tradition of Chinese mountainscape painting, the Western Classical tradition and more recently, the Alpinist legacy of field sketches and mountainscapes.

The most ancient mountainscape tradition directly available to us is that of China. Great painters such as the 'Four Wangs', Mi Fei, Ni Tsan and Ma Yuan are all fertile sources for understanding the language of mountainscapes and the 'way of the brush'. What is significant about Chinese painting style is the systematic codification of brush-strokes, the 'idea-writing', which is related to the Han calligraphic character. This codification has both an *interpretive* aspect and a *placement* aspect. The *interpretive* element shapes the brush-stroke so as to represent a rock, a ridge, and a tree in a gully or a mountain beck. The *placement* element enables the artist to write a kind of geographic-shorthand of the actual mountain. It is this codification of brush strokes that speeds the hand of the master painter forward, allowing the timely completion of a painting while paying attention to every detail and achieving a freshness of style that allows the artwork always to live in the present. There is also the striking phenomenon that most Chinese mountainscapes have shared the same scroll-format for more than a thousand years – thus there is a continuum of form that all, even the most contemporary landscape painters, share. This gives a sense of antiquity to the artwork that contrasts effectively with the spontaneity of the brush work. This quite accurately corresponds to the feeling we have in the mountains – of walking in an ancient landscape, through 'geological eras' – where nevertheless everything lives in a total freshness in the here and now.

When visiting China in 1972 (I believe as the first American artist since the 1949 revolution), I made a small study of the manner in which traditional landscape painting had been influenced by the cultural changes of that turbulent era. I interviewed traditional painting master Sung Wen Chih in Nanjing. He explained that whereas the traditional landscape painters of the old society rarely, if ever, left their studios, in the new post-revolutionary society the artists were encouraged to make a close-up study of their subject, for instance by climbing on the mountain or walking the length of a valley landscape, but that on-site sketches were seldom made. Rather the artist would return to the studio and create the landscape or mountainscape from a memory of first-hand observations. Master Sung said that they didn't paint like Western painters – from a viewpoint in the field – but rather made what we would call *synthetic* landscapes. Asked how the Cultural Revolution had affected his work, he said painters added red flags to their mountainscapes and painted historical sites or used their painting skills to visualize the outcome of major construction projects. This is an example of mountainscape painting serving the ends of the *scenic* and the *prosaic*.

However, Chinese landscape painting has traditionally also served the ends of the *symbolic* and the *poetic*. By this mode Ching Dynasty artist Pa-Ta Shen-Jen (literally, 'Eight Great Mountain Man') created his *political* mountainscapes – paintings of impossibly balanced, precariously up-ended boulders symbolic of the top-heavy imperial court – and Sung Dynasty artist-scholar Mi Fei created his *psychological* mountainscapes that challenge us to see the Tao in great rock faces floating amidst the clouds. As a metaphor of the mind itself – the cranial shape and local topology of the mountains recall the convolutions of the brain surface – the clinging trees are like the synaptic connections outlining habitual energies, and the rushing waterfall suggests the ceaseless flow of thoughts and desires. The 'moods' of mountain weather reflect fluctuations similar to our own changeable emotions and feelings, especially at high altitudes and under physical stress. In these areas, Chinese mountainscape and landscape paintings are unparalleled and their cultural influence was significant in the national artistic styles and traditions of Korea and Japan.

In our Western Classical tradition I have been fascinated by the 'little blue mountainscapes' that appear in the background of many Renaissance religious paintings by such masters as Leonardo da Vinci and Bellini. In these paintings, the foreground figures represent allegorical or religious figures of social convention, whereas the 'little blue mountainscapes' seem to reveal a perception of the world of objective reality, the fertile seed of Western natural philosophy, in the process of shedding its mythological husk. Over time, these background mountainscapes moved into the foreground and became the central theme of the painting, forming the basis for our Western landscape traditions. John Ruskin's remarkable study in Volume Four of *Modern Painters (1843)*, concerning the formation of the mountains by the very *forces of nature* (then a novel concept), had an important influence in promoting an increasingly scientific observation of the mountains, as it were elevating the *objective viewpoint*. Moreover Ruskin was a true scientific observer and despite his deeply held Christian world-view (he suggested that God put the best mountains in the best countries - rather the reverse of what most climbers would think today!) he was a revolutionary modernist when he identified the mountain as 'giving motion to water, giving motion to air and giving motion to earth'. We can see his influence not only in the English landscape tradition of his time, but likewise in the very competent artworks made by climbers and explorers most often on-site – what we call 'expeditionary drawing' – as seen in the Alpine Club's own noteworthy collection of drawings and paintings. With the Modernist movement in painting, in the late nineteenth and early twentieth centuries, two trends developed, each of which represented an elevation of the *subjective viewpoint* in the painting of mountainscapes. The first trend could be characterized as the *proto-cubist* style, seen first in the paintings of Paul Cezanne in his *Mont Sainte Victoire* series, and later, for example, in the work of climber-artist T H Somervell. The second trend corresponds to the *symbolist* style – such as the paintings of Nicholas Roerich, who travelled widely in mountainous regions and led a major expedition to Central Asia in the 1930s.

A contemporary practice from which I have drawn inspiration, shared both by alpinists and trekkers, is that of sketching rudimentary pictographs of mountains and passes (often on-site using the back of an envelope or a scrap of found paper) to use as a navigational aid when one is too close to the rock face to get perspective on the path up or around the mountain. These are different from 'expeditionary drawings', being instead field diagrams used to describe the routes, footpaths, markers, cairns and obstacles (such as waterfalls or glacial crevasses) that the climbers will encounter. In a sense, these loosely made charts are more like a 'musical score' of the mountain than a picture or a map. Even the terminology reflects this melodic quality – pitch, run, bridge, scale, ascent and descent, high and low. I find this *'first-hand, free-hand'* notation of the mountain and its jazz-like nomenclature a kind of post-modernist document blending the 'romantic and the pragmatic', not unlike a kid's treasure map complete with cautionary skulls and a beaconing 'X' marking the goal.

Over time, I have been moved to assimilate some of the ideas from all these traditions into my own artwork. When creating a Mountain Banner, I will hike into the field to make an original *'first-hand, free-hand'* drawing directly onto canvas – rendering it in what Robert Macfarlane refers to as the mountain's 'austere, Manichean colour scheme of black and white'. While making the drawing I will seek to capture for myself, as much as for the viewer, that sense of expanded proportion and exalted awareness we often feel as we experience the freedom of the hills – to touch what John Hunt called 'the realm of lasting values'. At that point I always search about for a local stick or twig – to carve into what William Blake calls 'a rural pen'– that I will use back in the studio to apply the 'holy grail' mixture to my canvas. This process permanently fixes the original drawing in the exact moment of freshness, investing the artwork with an authenticity that I think is present in all the best mountainscapes – the dual qualities of *being fresh* and of *being there*. I have tried to differentiate the Mountain Banners from my 'expeditionary drawings' by creating a more concentrated, visually striking form and working on a larger scale. Finishing the artwork with a fabric-frame that I learned from Dorjee Wangdue, but using the most modern heavy Nylon Cordura fabric (similar to my first Mountain Banner) makes for an artwork that more accurately reflects our own technology and mode of production. This gives rise to the apparently contradictory image of the dark, sometimes brooding mountain within the bright framing – a quality that makes the Mountain Banners so modernist in form – serving as a contemplative device as much as a dazzling banner celebrating the mountaineer's ideal. (*Excelsior!*)

I think the success of a good mountainscape in artistic terms, its function if you will, is to challenge and provoke the imagination, initiating a moment when the mind of the observer pauses between the *scenic* and the *contextual* – between what Descartes referred to as the difference of *situation* (place) and of *magnitude* (space). Schopenhauer wrote that the sight of a mountain range rising before our eyes suddenly 'puts us into a serious, even sublime mood', and indeed it is this sombre quality, provoked by the stark and often terrifying beauty of great mountains, that awakens us to our planetary reality – to what Robert Macfarlane calls 'deep time', to what the Tibetans call *Kalachakra*, 'the wheel of time'. It is true that there is something of the mountains that appeals to both the realist and the mystic. Drawn up to altitude by different paths, into that geometric apex, they nevertheless share the same awe, the same sense of 'deep time'. This awareness acts to caution us on the fragility of our existence and the ultimate, infinitely precious nature of life on earth – as it yet beckons us to reach for the physical, as well as an intellectual and spiritual, summit. Perhaps when we, in our culture and by our actions, appreciate the mountains sufficiently to preserve their natural content as well as their scenic beauty, and honour their symbolic function as much as we seek to gain from our sporting or scientific knowledge of them – when we have allowed them, as Chris Smith writes, to 'speak to the heart' – only then will we have touched the snowy peak with our art and succeeded in our long climb.

The development of my Mountain Banners series has been encouraged by the American Himalayan Foundation for more than a dozen years by its Chairman Richard Blum and President Erica Stone. As well, the Alpine Club presented the first one-man show of these works in 2004 at their London Gallery, to be followed by exhibitions at the Mountain Festivals of Kendal (2004), Banff, Canada (2005) and Telluride, Colorado (2006). I owe a great debt to all of these institutions for their support. For the wonderful opportunity of staying at the Namgyal Monastery, and its profound influence on my art, I shall always be grateful for the great kindness shown to me on that day in 1992 by His Holiness the Dalai Lama. Did I get my question answered? 'Yes'.

BILIOGRAPHY

William Blake, *Songs of Innocence,* New York, Dover Publications, 1789 ed.1971. (The essay title is also taken from this work.)
Rene Descartes, *Discourse on Method.* New York, Barnes & Nobel, 1637 ed.2004.
Sir John Hunt, *The Alpine Journal, Vol. LXII.* London, The Alpine Club, 1957.
James Joyce, *Portrait of the Artist as a Young Man.* New York, The Modern Library (1916/ed.1996).
Robert Macfarlane, *Mountains of the Mind.* New York, Vintage Books, 2003.
John Ruskin, *Modern Painters, Vol. IV.* Boston, Dana Estes & Co, 1843.
Arthur Schopenhauer, *The World as Will and Idea.* London, Routledge & Kegan Paul Ltd. 1883, ed.1998.
Chris Smith, *The Alpine Journal, Vol. CX.* London, The Alpine Club, 2005.

SIMON RICHARDSON

Evolution of the Scottish Mountaineering Club Climbers' Guides

When I first moved to Scotland more than 20 years ago there was no comprehensive climbing guidebook coverage. The wonderfully idiosyncratic MacInnes guides, with their own unique grading system, provided the best overview of selected climbs, whilst the SMC guidebook series was incomplete and hopelessly out of date. I quickly resorted to a do-it-yourself approach and bought as many back copies of the *Scottish Mountaineering Club Journal* that I could find and with the help of a photocopier, scissors and paste, compiled my own mini guidebooks to the areas that most intrigued me.

The early 1980s saw a surge of activity across the Northern Highlands, and it soon became clear that just keeping up with activity there was becoming a monumental task. Other changes in the climbing scene were afoot too. E grades for rock climbs had been introduced in the late 1970s, and were slowly being introduced across Scotland, but even in the mid eighties there were still some E3 routes masquerading as VS climbs ready to trap the unwary! The biggest change however was the development of mixed climbing through the 1980s that led to a leap in winter climbing standards. Scottish Grade V could cover anything from a well-known classic such as *Zero Gully* to a modern day Grade VIII, so in the early 1990s active Scottish winter climbers started experimenting with a two-tier open-ended winter grading system. After publication of a list of provisional two-tier grades in the 1992 SMC Journal, the new grading system began to catch on, and guidebooks began to look even more out of date.

Fortunately the SMC is a club that is willing to embrace change and the Publications Sub Committee, under the strong business leadership of Graham Tiso, was determined to bring the climbing guides up to date. After publication of new guides to *The Cairngorms* and *Central and Southern Scotland* in the mid 1980s it was decided to launch a comprehensive guidebooks series that would cover all climbing across Scotland whether it be in the mountains, on outcrops or on sea cliffs. This was a bold step, because until then, only one or two SMC climbing guides had ever broken even. Fortunately the financial backing for the new series was made possible due to the runaway success of *The Munros*, an illustrated guidebook to the 3000ft peaks in Scotland. This attractively produced hardback walking guide sold in the tens of thousands, which in turn provided a healthy cash flow to launch the new climbing guidebook programme.

The first key appointment was Roger Everett as Series Editor, and many of the activists of the day such as Rab Anderson, Cubby Cuthbertson, Kev Howett and Tom Prentice were invited to join old stalwarts such as Allen Fyffe, Ken Crocket and Andy Nisbet as guidebook authors. Soon after, I was invited to be one of the authors of the new Ben Nevis guide. Roger and I were regular climbing partners at the time, and in a matter of months we had moved from outsiders bemoaning the lack of guidebook progress, to being given the responsibility to do something about it!

Roger Everett took his role as Series Editor seriously and over a period of seven years he masterminded the writing of eleven guides to give Scotland's first-ever comprehensive guidebook coverage. Roger's input was a labour of love and evening after evening and wet weekend after wet weekend he added order and consistency to successive guidebook scripts, many of which were written from scratch. Roger was ideally suited to the role. His ability to focus on fine detail combined with his understanding of the bigger picture, coupled with an extensive knowledge and passion for Scottish mountains was all wrapped up with a dogged determination to see the task through. Roger once told me that he would only be satisfied once his bookshelf held a complete new series of guides.

Glen Coe (1992) was the first volume in the new series. 'The Publications Sub Committee was instrumental in determining the style and the look,' co-author Rab Anderson recalls. 'The active climbers on the committee were particularly involved and a working party moved things forwards. Those of us who were climbing south of the border at the time had seen Phil Gibson's excellent diagrams in *Yorkshire Limestone* (1985). We persuaded the SMC of the need to improve diagram quality and *Glen Coe* used Kev Howett's diagrams, which were seen as being some of the best around. *Glen Coe* kind of tested the water - new series, new editor, new writing team and so on. The writing team certainly had their moments with the Editor, especially me!'

Everett and Publications Manager Donald Bennet soon became a fine-tuned machine, and with the enthusiastic assistance of Niall Ritchie as Photo Editor a new volume was published every six months or so. With a clear layout, frequent diagrams and colour illustrations they were attractive books, but their major asset was that they provided full coverage of Scotland's climbs and spurred a new generation of Scottish climbers to develop and explore new areas. This led to a further explosion of activity fuelled by detailed descriptions and modern grades.

Soon after publication of *Arran, Arrochar and the Southern Highlands* in 1997, the last in the series, Everett handed over the reins as Series Editor to Brian Davison, and Tom Prentice took over from Donald Bennet as Publications Manager. Prentice's appointment was an inspired choice as he brought with him experience as a professional journalist coupled with a detailed knowledge of Scottish crags and mountains and an intense passion for climbing. His meticulous attention to detail, flair for design and a ruthless determination to see work done to a high standard and completed on time meant he was the ideal successor to fill Bennet's shoes.

Left
125. *Twilight* E1 5B, Polney Crag. Dunkeld. Climbers: Bill Wright and Ed Douglas. (*Grahame Nicol*)

Once again, a small working party was set up to consider the options for the next series. The underlying premise was that the SMC saw itself as the guardian of route information and would continue to publish comprehensive guidebooks covering the whole country. 'Guidebooks for climbers by climbers' was the watchword. The previous series had been criticised for its 'brick-like' handling qualities so a thinner more flexible book was required. The answer was to go for dimensions similar to a folded OS map - the size that many pockets in outdoor jackets are designed for. By using thinner paper, a smaller typeface and flexible covers the seemingly impossible trick of fitting 50% more climbs into a thinner volume was achieved.

But who would buy this new series given that the current one was comprehensive and reasonably up to date? The answer was to make the guides appear very different with a complete redesign. A design house was approached for suggestions, and the result was a neat and modern looking layout that is easy to read and conveys authority. The quality of writing of the existing series was very good, but it was realised that the illustrations and diagrams needed further improvement, especially as these can sway a purchase when someone is idly thumbing a guide in a shop. Niall Ritchie and Grahame Nicoll embarked on an extensive search and review of new photographs and greater effort was put into the creation of more detailed crag diagrams. For example, Mark Hudson was contracted to re-draw the Ben Nevis diagrams, and the resulting superbly detailed artwork added a touch of class to the book.

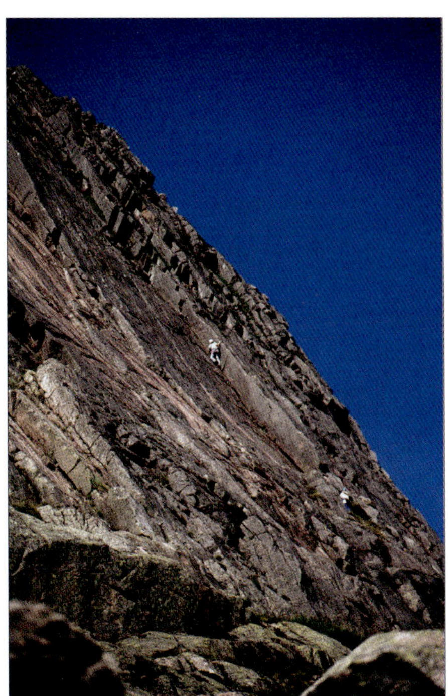

Right
126. *The Dagger* VS 4c.
Creagan a' Choire Etchachan.
(*Niall Ritchie*)

The first volumes in the new series, *Glen Coe* and *Ben Nevis* published in 2001 and 2002, were enthusiastically received and with the publication of *Northeast Outcrops*, *Lowland Outcrops* and *Northern Highlands North* we are now a third of the way through the new series. New titles will include sports, bouldering and scrambling guides. The latest volume is *Scottish Rock Climbs*, a selected guide to summer routes, which represents a further development as it uses photo diagrams instead of traditional line art. It has received rave reviews and re-awakened many climbers across the UK to the breadth and quality of Scottish rock climbing. Compiling the text and collecting the crag photographs was masterminded by the ever-enthusiastic Andy Nisbet and the book was superbly produced by Tom Prentice who made a very complex production appear vibrant and clear.

'In my opinion, SMC guides have now caught up and overtaken many of the club publishers,' Tom told me recently. 'This is largely thanks to the solid foundations of the last series, but also because we have embraced the digital age and are making as much as possible of modern printing and costs, desk top publishing and graphics packages. Maps aren't hand drawn anymore. We are modern, fully digital and now fully colour. It's a colour, digital, Internet world out there and our guides feel part of it rather than lagging a few steps behind.'

Prentice went on to highlight several other factors that are unique to SMC guides. 'Firstly, our books are run by our own commercial company with 30 titles,' he told me. 'This must make us not only the largest club publisher, but also one of the largest publishers of climbing guidebooks in

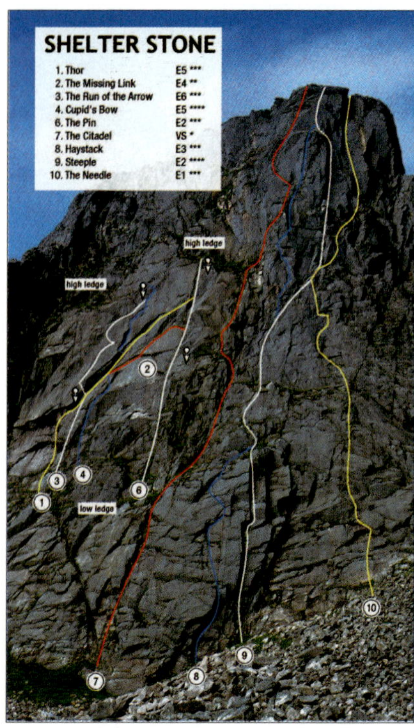

Left
127. Colour photo diagram of Shelter Stone in the northern Cairngorms, typical of the clarity of the SMC's new guides. (*Andy Nisbet*)

the UK. One commercial legacy from Tiso is that we are all aware of the need to generate revenue to stand still, let alone create more titles. Cash cows like *The Munros* do not usually last forever.' Another key factor is that guidebook contributors get paid. 'This must focus people more on what they are doing,' Tom explained. 'The voluntary system is under increasing pressure. Yes, we still rely on volunteers, but paying contributors is another indication of a professional, commercial organisation.'

The SMC is already looking ahead and thinking through options for the next series. 'We have an eye on the future,' Prentice insists. 'We already sell from the SMC website by Paypal and we offer Internet books. We have discussed website routes, pdf guides, downloads etc. Where will guidebooks go, now that the digital world is bringing film, TV, radio and photos to our mobiles and ipods? It's all changing so fast that you and I don't know what the future will bring, but I think we'll be well placed, whatever it is.'

The greatest strength of the SMC is its continual ability to attract many of the most active climbers and mountaineers in Scotland to its ranks. As a result, the SMC as a whole has unrivalled knowledge of Scottish climbing and Scottish mountains. Throw in a committed group of authors and an experienced production team and the future of Scottish climbing guidebook production looks to be in safe hands.

Scottish Rock Climbs, published 2005, retails at £21. SMC books due for publication in 2006 include a new climbing guide *Northern Highlands Central* (£20) and a full revision of the ever-popular *The Munros* (£20).

History

Jim Curran *Old May of Hoy, evening* 2005
Oil on canvas
Private collection

129. Peter Aufschnaiter and Tessala (Tsering Yangzom) on an excursion to Tra Yerpa, the cave of Padmasambhava who brought Buddhism to Tibet. (*Heinrich Harrer, Ethnographic Museum of the University of Zurich*)

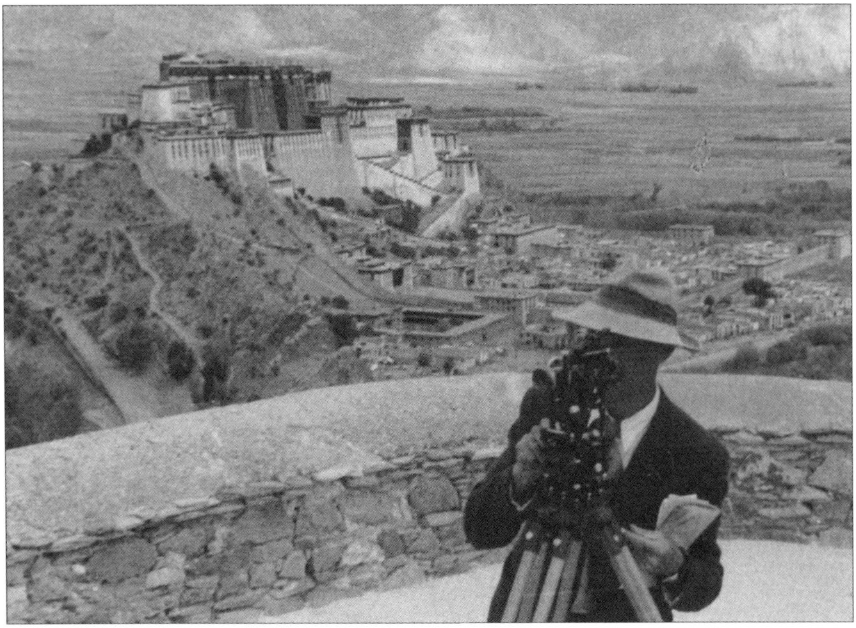

130. Peter Aufschnaiter and theodolite with Potala Palace. Surveying Lhasa from the Chakpori (College of Medicine) for a city map, with 60-year-old theodolite found in the house of Tsarong, the wealthy host of Aufschnaiter and Harrer. (*Heinrich Harrer, Ethnographic Museum of the University of Zurich*)

131. Heinrich Harrer skating in Lhasa with the Chakpori Medical College in the background. (*Heinrich Harrer, Ethnographic Museum of the University of Zurich*)

Epilogue

Harrer and Aufschnaiter resided in Lhasa until 1950 when China invaded and annexed Tibet. Aufschnaiter later worked for the governments of Nepal and India plus the Food and Agriculture Organisation of the U.N. in Kathmandu. At his life's end he returned to Austria, dying aged 73 in Innsbruck in October 1973. Harrer wrote his famous book and in 1953 lectured at the Royal Festival Hall, London, where he received a letter from his former Camp Commandant, Colonel Williams, which Harrer read out: 'As commander of your prison camp in India I had to take the blame for your successful escape, from headquarters in New Delhi. Not only that, but adding insult to injury, tonight I even had to pay to listen to you as to how you did it.' Harrer devoted much energy campaigning for the Tibetan cause.

All internees were repatriated, most landing in Hamburg in January 1946 wearing tropical kit. In 2004, Treipl recollected how they were cruelly forced to stand outdoors for hours in extreme cold by a Czech division of the British army – it was months before he could walk properly again. Kopp, an engineer, returned to India in 1948 to work on a dam project at Bhakra and again met Aufschnaiter in New Delhi. He went trekking in Tibet in 1954, a land that fascinated him. He moved to Ontario, Canada, to run a motor business and died there in the mid 1980s. Sattler was also transferred to Deoli where the Maharaja of Bundi was building a summer palace - he employed Sattler in his profession as an architect. He was repatriated to Germany and returned to work in Jakarta in 1949; he died in Germany in 1985. Treipl returned to Austria where he ran hotels with his wife and sold agricultural machinery. In 2006, aged 89, he was living in his native Salzburg where his father had been one-time Castle Commander. Magener and von Have, re-interned in Japan by the Americans, were returned to Germany 18 months after the war to be interned yet again. Magener joked how he would have got home much earlier had he stayed in camp. He later built up the export business of the German multinational BASF, becoming their Chief Financial Officer. An anglophile, he lived in London in the 1950s and died in Heidelberg in 2000, just short of 90. Heins von Have returned to Hamburg in 1948, where his family had been for generations, to join 'Johs. Rieckermann' a trading company set up for him in his absence by his father. In 1949 he established 'Panobra' to trade with Brazil and Japan, plus 'Heins von Have Co.' in 1967 to trade with Indonesia. All three companies still exist. He frequently travelled to Japan and Indonesia, was a member of many German institutions and became president of the East Asiatic Association of Hamburg. He died in 1985 aged 78. Dr Ludwig 'Lutz' Chicken returned to South Tyrol, Italy, where for many years he ran his own medical practice; he published his autobiography in 2003 (*see Book Reviews, p367*). In 2006 aged 90, he was happily retired. Finally, Bruno Treipl put the author in contact with fellow internee Peter Schümmer, aged 94. He had been working in India for Klöckner Humboldt Deutz on diesel engines. He had escaped with Schmaderer in May 1943. Their first plan had been to do a 'wire job' using a homemade ladder but their plans were betrayed. One day they were delegated to clean up the cemetery at a far end of the camp where they told the sentry that they needed to urinate in the bushes – it was not noticed until evening that they had absconded. For the next two days they hid in a cave in a nearby gorge where they had cached supplies, before heading north. After three weeks they were recaptured near Badrinath, one march short of the Tibetan border.

For a second joint escape attempt Schümmer had planned to run into the jungle with Schmaderer when the group of 22 persistent escapers were due to be transported to Deoli. However, a Colonel Hunt, while searching his baggage found a book on Central India, which much interested him and he struck up a conversation with Schümmer. Meanwhile, fearing excess delay, Schmaderer ran for it. Schümmer was prevented from following as he was suddenly surrounded by six soldiers pointing guns at his sides. He made no further escape attempts. He later worked in India, East Pakistan and Iraq before retiring to his native Cologne, where in 2004 he concluded that it was 'far better for us all to have been interned than to die a pointless death in a stupid war'. He died in autumn 2005.

It would be September 1947 before all Dehra Dun's internees were repatriated.

BIBLIOGRAPHY

Published in London unless stated:

Peter Aufschnaiter, 'Diamir Side of Nanga Parbat, Reconnaissance 1939', *Himalayan Journal* 14, 110-115, 1947.

– 'Escape to Lhasa 1944-1945', *Himalayan Journal* 14, 116-120, 1947.

Martin Brauen (ed), *Peter Aufschnaiter's Eight Years in Tibet*, Orchid Press, Bangkok, Thailand, 2002.

Lutz Chicken, 'Nanga Parbat Reconnaissance 1939', *Himalayan Journal* 14, 53-58,1947.

– *Durchs Jahrhundert. Mein Leben als Arzt und Bergsteiger*, Edition Raetia, Bozen, Italy, 2003.

Ernst Grob, Ludwig Schmaderer and Herbert Paidar, *Zwischen Kantsch und Tibet*. F Bruckmann, Munich, Germany, 1940.

Heinrich Harrer, *Seven Years in Tibet*, Rupert Hart-Davis, 1953.

– *Mein Leben*. Ullstein, Munich, Germany, 2002.

Anderl Heckmair, *My Life, Eiger North Face, Grandes Jorasses, and other adventures*. Baton Wicks, 2002

Hans Kopp, *Himalayan Shuttlecock*. Hutchinson, 1957.

Rolf Magener, *Our Chances Were Zero*. Leo Cooper / Pen & Sword Books, Barnsley, 2001. (Originally *Prisoners' Bluff*. Rupert Hart-Davis, 1954.)

Peter Mierau, *Die Deutsche Himalaja-Stiftung. Ihre Geschichte und Ihre Expeditionen*. Bergverlag Rudolf Rother, Munich, Germany, 1999.
– *Nationalsozialistische Expeditionspolitik. Deutsche Asien-Expeditionen 1933-1945.* Herbert Utz, Munich, Germany, 2002.
Herbert Paidar, 'Destiny Himalaya', *Himalayan Journal* 15, 69-74, 1948.
Friedel Sattler, *Flucht durch den Himalaja. Und Erlebtes beim Maharadscha von Bundi.* Das Bergland-Buch, Salzburg, Austria, 1956. Republished, Edition Dax, Hamburg, Germany, 1991.

Interviews:

Rolf Magener	Heidelberg, Germany. 23 June 1999.
Heinrich Harrer	Hüttenberg, Austria. 12 May 2003.
Bruno Treipl	Salzburg, Austria. 21 May and 30 August 2004.
Peter Schümmer	Cologne, Germany. 13 June and 27 August 2004.

ACKNOWLEDGEMENTS

The author is indebted to the former internees for their interviews and to Dr Lutz Chicken and Heins von Have for their correspondence. Frank Drauschke in Berlin, and Dr Isrun Engelhardt of Munich both generously provided information from their respective researches in the National Archives of India and the India Office Collections in the British Library. Finally, the author is grateful to Bettina von Reden of Hamburg for assistance with translation and in locating and interviewing former internees.

PETER BERG

From the Archives

One of the most evocative items in the Archives of the Alpine Club is a letter written in 1827 on the summit of Mont Blanc. The writer, John Auldjo, was a well-to-do young man who in the course of a conventional Grand Tour decided that he must climb to the top of the highest peak in Europe, and, with the help of a mere six guides, did just that.

A 1952 article in the *AJ* gives an account of Auldjo's life and achievements.[1] Suffice it to say here that he was born in Canada just 200 years ago, in 1805, to parents of Scottish descent and was educated in England. His Mont Blanc climb is counted as the 19th ascent, but his account[2] published the following year met with considerable interest and ran into three editions, not least attributable to the quality of the illustrations taken from his own sketches. He later lived in Naples, and his investigations of Vesuvius were subsequently rewarded with Fellowships of the Royal Society and the Royal Geographical Society. Auldjo ended his days in Geneva where he was British Consul until his death in 1886.

The letter from the summit of Mont Blanc was preserved in a presentation copy of Auldjo's *Narrative* and later presented to the AC. It is addressed to his sister and written in pencil in a rather shaky hand. Confusion over the date and odd spelling point to the effects of altitude and lack of acclimatisation.

Summit of Mont Blance [*sic*]
11 o'clock Thursday
9th August 1825 [*sic*]

My dear Annie

It may give you some pleasure to know that I am looking down upon you at this moment. You can judge of the gratification I have in being above the habitable world – a thing I'v [sic] much desired. I have just drank [sic] a bottle of wine to your health. My guides join me & we all wish you well while drinking – long life and happiness – & even this high I am not forgetful of the many times I have written & now write again the I am your

affectionate brother
John Auldjo

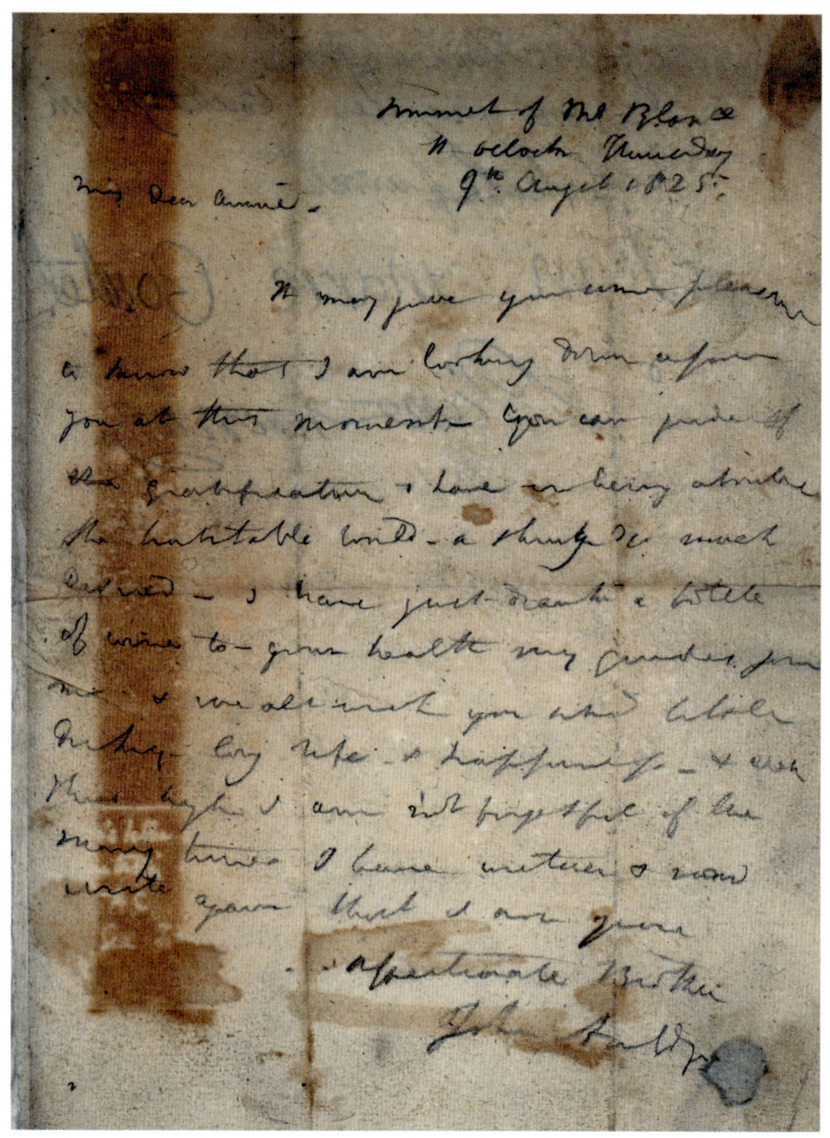

Summit of Mt Blanc
11 o'clock Thursday
9th August 1825.

My Dear Annie –

It may give you some pleasure to know that I am looking down upon you at this moment – You can judge of the gratification I have in being above the habitable world – a thing so much desired – I have just drank a bottle of wine to your health my guides join me & we all wish you [illegible] during long life & happiness – & even this high I am not forgetful of the many times I have written & now write again that I am your

affectionate Brother

John Auldjo

132. Letter from the AC archives written from the summit of Mont Blanc in 1827.

The letter is signed on the back of the single sheet: Julien Devouassoud, Simond Jacques, Couttet, Joseph, Michele Favret, Jean Marie Couttet, Pierre Tairraz. We have a number of other Auldjo documents in the AC archives and these have been of particular interest to researchers during this bicentennial year.

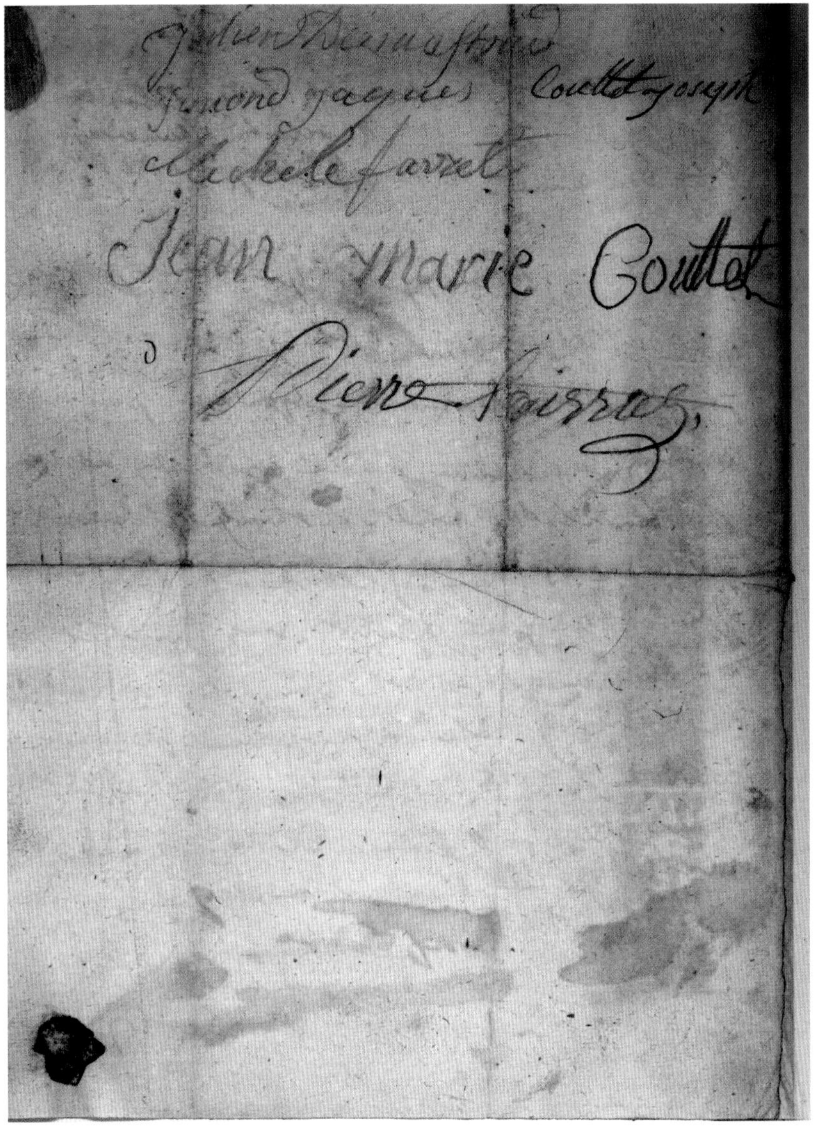

1 J Monroe Thorington, 'John Auldjo, Fortunate Traveller' in *AJ* LVIII 285 (November 1952).

2 John Auldjo, *Narrative of an ascent to the summit of Mont Blanc.* Longman 1828.

C A RUSSELL

One Hundred Years Ago

(with extracts from the *Alpine Journal*)

> The view was again magnificent – almost indescribable. We looked across the island from sea to sea, and, in addition to the views northward, eastward, and westward, we now beheld a glorious alpine panorama stretching to the S. as far as the eye could reach. The giant Tasman and all the lesser mountains were dwarfed, and the whole country was spread out like a map in relief at our feet.

The extensive views from the highest point in New Zealand were recalled by Malcolm Ross who with Samuel Turner, T C Fyfe and the guide Peter Graham reached the summit of Mount Cook (3764m)[1] on 10 January 1906 from a bivouac below the north-east, Zurbriggen ridge. After securing 'the first photograph of a party that had ever been taken on the summit' Ross and his companions descended to the Hooker glacier and the Hermitage Hotel by way of the north ridge and Green's Saddle.

This outstanding climb – the first traverse of the highest peak of Mount Cook – was one of several notable expeditions in the Southern Alps during the first two months of the year. On 1 February the Rev H E Newton, R S Low and Dr Ebenezer Teichelmann with Alex[2] Graham reached the summit of the unclimbed La Pérouse (3079m) and a few days later Newton, Low and Graham made the first ascent of Mount Hicks (3183m). Another visitor to this region was the Dutch climber Dr Hank Sillem who with Peter Graham completed a number of new routes including the first ascent of the Low Peak (3593m) of Mount Cook and, on 15 February, the ascent of another unclimbed peak, Mount Elie de Beaumont (3109m).

In the European Alps severe storms during the winter and early spring were followed by a long period of dry and sunny weather which continued for much of the climbing season. In the Mont Blanc range, where many peaks were in perfect condition, a number of outstanding routes was recorded in the Chamonix Aiguilles by some of the strongest parties of the day. On 20 June a classic climb was completed by V J E Ryan who with Franz and Josef Lochmatter made the first ascent of the east ridge of the Aiguille du Plan. In the following month, on 23 July, the summit of the unclimbed Aiguille du Peigne was reached by G Liégeard and Count Robert O'Gorman with Joseph[3] Ravanel and Joseph Couttet. A few days later two other ridges were ascended for the first time: the south-east, *Chapeau à Cornes* ridge of the Dent du Requin on 3 August by R C Mayor, C D Robertson and Geoffrey Winthrop Young accompanied by Josef Knubel and a porter; and, on 7 August, the north-east ridge to the north summit of the Aiguille de Blaitière by Henri Bregeault and T Thomas with Auguste and Pierre Blanc. On 22 August another successful climb was completed when Mme Berthelot and her guides Joseph and Edouard Ravanel made the first ascent of the south summit of the Aiguille des Ciseaux.

Other notable climbs in the range included the first ascent of Mont Brouillard by Karl Blodig and Oscar Eckenstein with Alexis Brocherel on 11 July and two ascents of the Brenva ridge route on Mont Blanc: by Ryan and the Lochmatter brothers on 10 July; and, on 19 July, by J Maunoury with Camille Ravanel, Jean Amiez and Alfred Ravanel as porter.

Following their successful expedition in the Mont Blanc range Young and Knubel moved to the Pennine Alps where on 11 August they joined forces with Ryan and the Lochmatters to complete an epic climb: the first ascent of the very dangerous south-west face of the Täschhorn. After forcing a way onto the south-east ridge 'some 60ft. only from the highest point' the two parties descended in darkness to the woods below the peak where Young found the path to Randa 'by falling headlong down a bank of pine-roots and alighting on the abrupt surprise of a horizontal surface.'

A week later, on 18 August Young, Robertson and Mayor with Knubel and Moritz Ruppen completed another classic climb: the first ascent of the Klein Triftji ridge, now known as the Younggrat, below the east summit of the Breithorn. In the same district Ryan and the Lochmatters, one of the fastest parties of their day, undertook other outstanding expeditions including the first ascent[4] of the north-east ridge or *Cresta di Santa Caterina* on the Nordend of Monte Rosa and, on 30 July, the first complete ascent of the long east ridge of the Dent d'Hérens. Another fine climb, on 10 and 11 August, was completed on the south face of the Matterhorn when Ugo De Amicis and Arrigo Frusta, without guides, made the first ascent of the south-south-west ridge or *Cresta De Amicis* of Pic Tyndall. On 1 September a daring solo ascent was undertaken by Hans Pfann who reached the summit of the Matterhorn after scaling the north-west, Zmutt ridge.

In the Bernese Alps on 7 August a successful climb on the Trugberg, the long rock spur between the Jungfraufirn and the Ewigschneefeld, was completed by Gustav Hasler and Miss Marie Hampson-Simpson, his future wife. Accompanied by Heinrich Fuhrer they reached the north summit by way of the unclimbed north-west ridge and continued to the central, highest summit before descending the east face. Later in the month, on 12-14 August, V A Fynn and H Brüderlin made the second ascent[5] of the north-east face of the Finsteraarhorn, a climb involving two bivouacs one of which the party spent sitting in rope slings.

To the east in the Dolomites S Bögle and M Niedermaier opened a new route on the Punta delle Cinque Dita – the Fünffingerspitze – by climbing the south-west ridge. In the Julian Alps on 9 and 10 July an outstanding expedition was completed by Felix König, Hans Reinl and Karl Doménigg who forced the first route up the great north wall of Triglav.

On 19 May ceremonies were held to mark the completion of a major engineering project.

> On Saturday King Victor Emmanuel passed through the Simplon Tunnel and formally opened to traffic that great work of the modern engineer. By a curious but quite undesigned coincidence, the formal opening has taken place in the centenary year of the opening to traffic of the magnificent road over the Simplon Pass, begun by Napoleon in 1800 and completed in 1806.
>
> The Royal train reached Brig at 11.30. It consisted of seven coaches drawn by two powerful steam locomotives, the electric traction installation not being completed. As King Victor Emmanuel alighted the President of the Confederation advanced and shook hands with his Majesty, and, after the usual exchange of greetings and introductions the King and the Swiss President, followed by their suites, inspected the guard of honour. ...
>
> The tunnel is a double one, the bore having been a twin from the start, but the work of completion has only been pushed on in the eastern tunnel, the western one being used for ventilating purposes, and its further development[6] is left for future consideration. If the volume of traffic is sufficient to call for a double route, the double tunnel will be finished.

On 7 May the Duke of the Abruzzi arrived at Entebbe in Uganda to commence his expedition to the Ruwenzori range. The Duke was accompanied by Comdr Umberto Cagni as surveyor, Dr Achille Cavalli Molinelli as medical attendant, the geologist Alessandro Roccati and Vittorio Sella. Four guides from Courmayeur – Joseph and Laurent Petigax, César Ollier and Joseph Brocherel – travelled with the party which was completed[7] by Erminio Botta, Sella's assistant, and the cook Igino Igini. Earlier in the year other parties had undertaken exploratory ascents in the range. On 18 January Rudolf Grauer accompanied by H E Maddox and the Rev H W Tegart of the Church Missionary Society climbed to the small peak now known as Grauer Rock (4484m) on the main, summit ridge of Mount Baker (4843m); and several high points on Mount Baker were reached by the naturalist A F R Wollaston and other members of a British Museum expedition led by R B Woosnam.

After engaging some one hundred and fifty porters the Duke and his companions approached the peaks from Fort Portal and on 7 June established a base camp at the head of the Mubuku valley. Three days later, after reaching the main ridge of Mount Baker

> ... in the clear hours of the dawn of June 10, the Duke had a complete view of the mountain range and was able to obtain a notion of their position in the main axis of the range and their relation to the valleys.

133. Simplon Tunnel, south portal during construction: *right* Tunnel 1, *left* entrance to parallel gallery. (*Gesellschaft für Ingenieurbaukunst, Zürich*)

134. Alexandra Peak and (*right background*) Albert Peak, Mount Stanley. (*Vittorio Sella, Ruwenzori, 1906*)

In South America the Swiss climber Robert Helbling and the German geologist Fritz Reichert mounted an expedition to Aconcagua (6959m). On 31 January Helbling reached the summit to complete the third recorded ascent of the peak and three days later Reichert repeated the climb to a height of some 6900m. Later in the year the American Miss Annie Smith Peck spent several months in Peru where she travelled extensively accompanied by a number of local men. Starting on 20 July Miss Peck made two determined attempts to climb the north peak (6655m) of Huascarán but on each occasion was forced to retreat after reaching a height of some 5350m.

In the Canadian Rockies a successful expedition was completed in August when I T Burr, Samuel Cabot junior, W R Peabody and Robert Walcott with the guides Gottfried Feuz and Christian Kaufmann became the first party to reach the south, higher summit (3328m) of Mount Mummery in the Freshfield group, one of the main peaks near the Continental Divide. Kaufmann also accompanied Miss Henrietta Tuzo during the first ascent of the peak now known as Mount Tuzo (3245m), one of the Ten Peaks near Moraine Lake.

In Britain many parties were able to take advantage of the fine weather experienced during the summer and autumn in all the principal regions and several outstanding new climbs were recorded. In Wales on 12 August H Mitchell, A E Barker, W J Drew and G T Atchison made the first ascent of *Schoolmasters' Gully* on Cyrn Läs, one of the steep cliffs above the Llanberis Pass. In the following month on Lliwedd J B Farmer accompanied by Mrs Farmer, A W Andrews and Oscar Eckenstein completed *Central Gully and East Peak*, reaching the summit ridge from the slabs of the Central Gully by way of the ledge known as the Bowling Green. In the Lake District on 8 June F W Botterill, leading L J Oppenheimer, Arthur Botterill and J H Taylor completed his second memorable route[12] in this region: the first unaided ascent of *North-West Climb* on Pillar Rock. On the Isle of Skye in July J N Collie and the guide John Mackenzie succeeded in reaching the Cioch, the rock pinnacle on the face of Sron na Ciche which Collie had discovered seven years earlier.

An important development during the year was the formation of several new climbing clubs. In Canada passes to travel on the Canadian Pacific Railway were donated by the Company to a group of enthusiasts who assembled at Winnipeg on 27 March to found the Alpine Club of Canada. The surveyor A O Wheeler was elected as President and in July the Club held the first of its annual camps, on this occasion at Yoho Pass in the Canadian Rockies. A welcome event in March was the publication of the first issue of *Sangaku*, the journal of another new club: the Japanese Alpine Club had been formed[13] with the encouragement of the Rev Walter Weston, one of the pioneers of mountaineering in Japan.

137. Fell and Rock Climbing Club group at Coniston, 1908. (*Alan Craig*)

At home a famous club, the Fell and Rock Climbing Club of the English Lake District, was formed after Alan Craig, E H P Scantlebury and three other climbers had held an informal meeting at the Sun Hotel, Coniston on 11 November. The first President of the Club was Ashley Abraham and by the end of December 'upwards of 40 members had been enrolled.' Other clubs founded during the year included the Wayfarers' Club in Liverpool and the Derbyshire Pennine Club.

An event of considerable note was the publication of *Rock-climbing in North Wales*, written and illustrated by George and Ashley Abraham. This companion work to the book[14] by O G Jones on the climbs of the Lake District was soon in demand and received a favourable review in the *Alpine Journal*.

> We may say at once that the book is a great success. The writers have for several years given close attention to the district, and they enjoy the very great advantage of combining in an unusual degree physical prowess as climbers with practical mastery of all the resources of the camera. The result is a beautiful and very instructive volume.

It is appropriate to conclude this account with a comment by D W Freshfield in his note 'The Conquest of Ruwenzori' which was published in the *Alpine Journal* during the following year.

It is not uncommon, even in unexpected quarters, to find it assumed that 'a mountaineering party' is incapable of rendering any return to geography and science. Mountaineers may point, in Ruwenzori, to an instance where they have succeeded, after many experienced travellers, who were not mountaineers, had failed, in lifting the veil of centuries and giving the world accurate knowledge of a most interesting and fascinating region – the Snows of the Nile.

REFERENCES

1. For details of a recent alteration to this height see *AJ99*, 221, 1994.
2. Graham was known to everyone as Alex.
3. The famous guide Ravanel, *le Rouge*.
4. The ridge had been descended by Walter Flender with Heinrich Burgener and Ferdinand Furrer on 5 September 1899.
5. The first ascent had been completed by Gustav Hasler with Fritz Amatter on 16 July 1904.
6. The enlargement of the parallel gallery, 'a rectangular opening one-fifth of the full size', was completed after the First World War, the tunnel being opened on 4 December 1921.
7. The other member of the party was Lt Edoardo Winspeare, Comdr Cagni's aide-de-camp, who contracted fever during the voyage to Africa and was obliged to depart for Europe on 12 May, shortly after his arrival at Mombasa.
8. Named by the Duke of the Abruzzi in honour of Queen Margherita, consort of King Umberto I of Italy.
9. Named by the Duke after Queen Alexandra, consort of King Edward VII.
10. The expedition to Mount St Elias (5489m) in 1897.
11. For details of this ascent see *AJ79*, 100-102, 1974.
12. On 3 June 1903 Botterill, leading H Williamson and J E Grant, had made the first ascent of *Botterill's Slab* on Scafell Crag.
13. A meeting to found the Club had been held on 14 October 1905.
14. Owen Glynne Jones, *Rock-Climbing in the English Lake District*. London, Longmans, Green, & Co, 1897.

Science

Jim Curran *Almscliffe Crag* 2005
Oil on canvas
Private collection

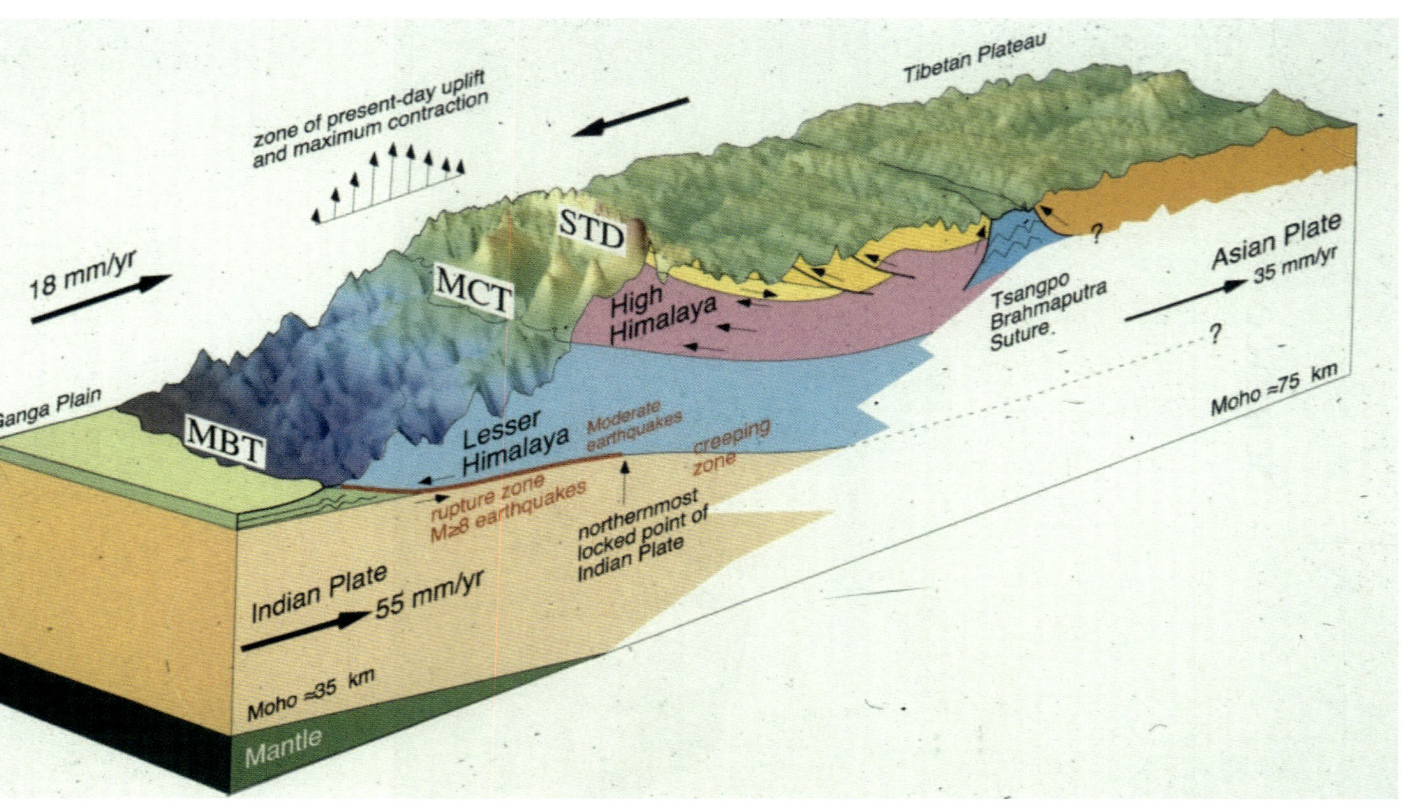

Tibetan Plateau
zone of present-day uplift
and maximum contraction
18 mm/yr
STD
MCT
MBT
Ganga Plain
High
Himalaya
Lesser
Himalaya
Moderate
earthquakes
creeping
zone
rupture zone
M≥8 earthquakes
northernmost
locked point of
Indian Plate
Tsangpo
Brahmaputra
Suture.
Asian Plate
35 mm/yr
?
?
Moho ≈75 km
Indian Plate
55 mm/yr
Moho ≈35 km
Mantle

MIKE SEARLE

Himalayan Granite

Of all the rocks that make mountains, granite has to be the most satisfying. Many of the most beautiful, spectacular, and awe-inspiring mountains are made of granite. Think of the elegant spires of the Trango Towers, the majestic shapely peaks of Shivling, Bhagirathi and Meru, the gleaming orangy granite of Makalu and Chomolonzo, the massive great fortresses of Kangchenjunga, Shisha Pangma and Manaslu, to name only a few. Further afield there are of course those iconic monoliths of granite: Cerro Torre, Fitzroy, El Capitan, Half Dome, Huascarán, Huandoy, the Aiguille de Dru. Granite is a rock that crystallized from a magma, or melt, and is composed of the minerals quartz, potassium feldspar and plagioclase. Himalayan granites may also contain red garnets, black tourmalines, glistening white muscovite mica and black biotite micas, as well a whole range of other minerals in minute quantity. Most useful of all these minerals are tiny uranium and thorium-bearing minerals, zircon, monazite, xenotime, allanite that we use for dating granites. Himalayan granites are some of the most intensely radioactive rocks on the planet.

The backbone of the Karakoram range is composed of magnificent pale coloured granite, the Baltoro granites that formed between about 24 and 15 million years ago. The peaks north of the Hispar glacier, the Ogre, the Latoks, Trango Towers, Biale, Masherbrum and the Charakusa and Hushe spires all are made of this young, solid Baltoro granite. Many of the highest peaks along the Himalaya are composed of granites that also formed around 20 million years, some 30 million years after the initial collision of India and Asia. Major episodes of crustal melting therefore occurred both along the southern part of the Asian plate (Karakoram) and along the northern part of the Indian plate (Himalaya). How then did these granite peaks along the Himalaya form?

Origins of the Himalaya

The Himalaya and the great plateau of Tibet were formed as a result of a collision between two continental plates, India and Asia, about 50 million years ago, the like of which the planet had not seen since Precambrian time, more than 480 million years ago. The Indian plate was attached to the East African continental margin and Antarctica until around 140 million

Left

Fig. 1 Block diagram showing the structure of the Himalaya. The active thrust along the southern boundary is the detachment along which India underthrusts the Himalaya and the fault along which active earthquakes occur.

Fig. 2 Himalaya viewed towards west from the space shuttle, with the Tibetan Plateau on the right. (*Photo courtesy of NASA*)

years ago when India and Madagascar rifted apart from Africa. Mid-ocean ridges in the Indian Ocean created new oceanic crust, and ocean floor spreading forced the continental plates apart. The Indian continent became an island and began its northward drift across the Indian Ocean at the enormously high plate tectonic velocity of around 5cm per year.

Roughly 50 million years ago, India collided with the southern margin of Asia somewhere near equatorial latitudes, closing the Tethyan Ocean that lay between them for some 200 million years (from Permian times to the Early Tertiary). The collision slowed India's northward flight down to about 2cm/year, but the spreading centres in the Indian Ocean continued to push India northward, relative to stable northern Eurasia, indenting into Asia as it went. GPS stations across Asia show that India continues to converge with Tibet and Asia and that the Himalaya are still rising today. Earthquakes in the historical record show that India is still underthrusting the Himalaya along the active Main Boundary Thrust, the southern margin of the Himalaya. The 8 October Kashmir earthquake of 2005 was one such event. The earthquake ruptured approximately 100km of the Himalayan frontal thrust, releasing a huge amount of energy, and the mountains north-east of Muzaffarabad actually rose about one metre during the earthquake. It was 50 million years of earthquakes like this that made the Himalaya.

One has only to look at a satellite image of Asia to see the mountain ranges along the India-Asia collision zone swing around the plate margin, from the Chaman and Sulaiman-Kirthar ranges of western Pakistan up to the Hazara and Nanga Parbat syntaxes, where the mountains swing around along the Himalaya to the knot of mountain ranges around the eastern syntaxis centered on Namche Barwa, where they curve south again along the Indo-Burman ranges and out into the Bay of Bengal and Andaman Sea. The great 26 December 2004 earthquake off northern Sumatra occurred at about 30km depth on this plate boundary as Indian oceanic crust subducted north under the Sumatra-Java island arc. During this single earthquake, the second largest ever recorded, the Indian plate boundary ruptured 1400 km north as far as the Burmese coast. The sea floor rose up to 10 metres in places, an uplift that was responsible for the most devastating tsunami in human history.

North of the Himalaya the Tibetan Plateau is the largest area of high elevation (5023m average elevation) and thick crust (between 60-80km thick) anywhere in the world. Tibet was almost certainly elevated prior to the Indian plate collision, with southern Tibet probably looking something like the present-day Andes. Following the collision, the entire plateau, stretching from the Pamir and Karakoram in the west to the Sichuan basin in the east, from the Kun-Lun and Altyn Tagh ranges in the north to the Himalaya in the south, rose to its present height of 5km above sea-level.

The collision of India with Asia and the uplift of Tibet dramatically altered the topography of Asia. As the Himalaya began to grow, the crust thickened and deeply buried rocks were metamorphosed or changed as a result of the increase in burial depth, pressure and temperature. Most of the Greater Himalayan ranges are composed of metamorphic rocks that were formed at depths between about 50km and 15km and then thrust southward along giant fault planes. Classic metamorphic minerals such as garnet, kyanite and sillimanite were formed as shales changed to schists and gneisses, and limestones changed to marble. The rocks show spectacular ductile folds and evidence of extremely high strain.

Between about 30 and 20 million years ago, the Greater Himalayan rocks reached the highest temperatures in the middle crust around 750°C, and actually started to melt, creating pockets of liquid molten magma within the gneisses. The melts began to flow under extreme strain and interconnected pockets of magma collected into feeder channels (sills and dykes). These sills and dykes transported the liquid granite magma vast distances along the strike, feeding it into larger channels. Eventually these sills reached the Earth's surface and ballooned out into giant intrusions, folding the country rocks around them as they cooled. The granite solidified and the

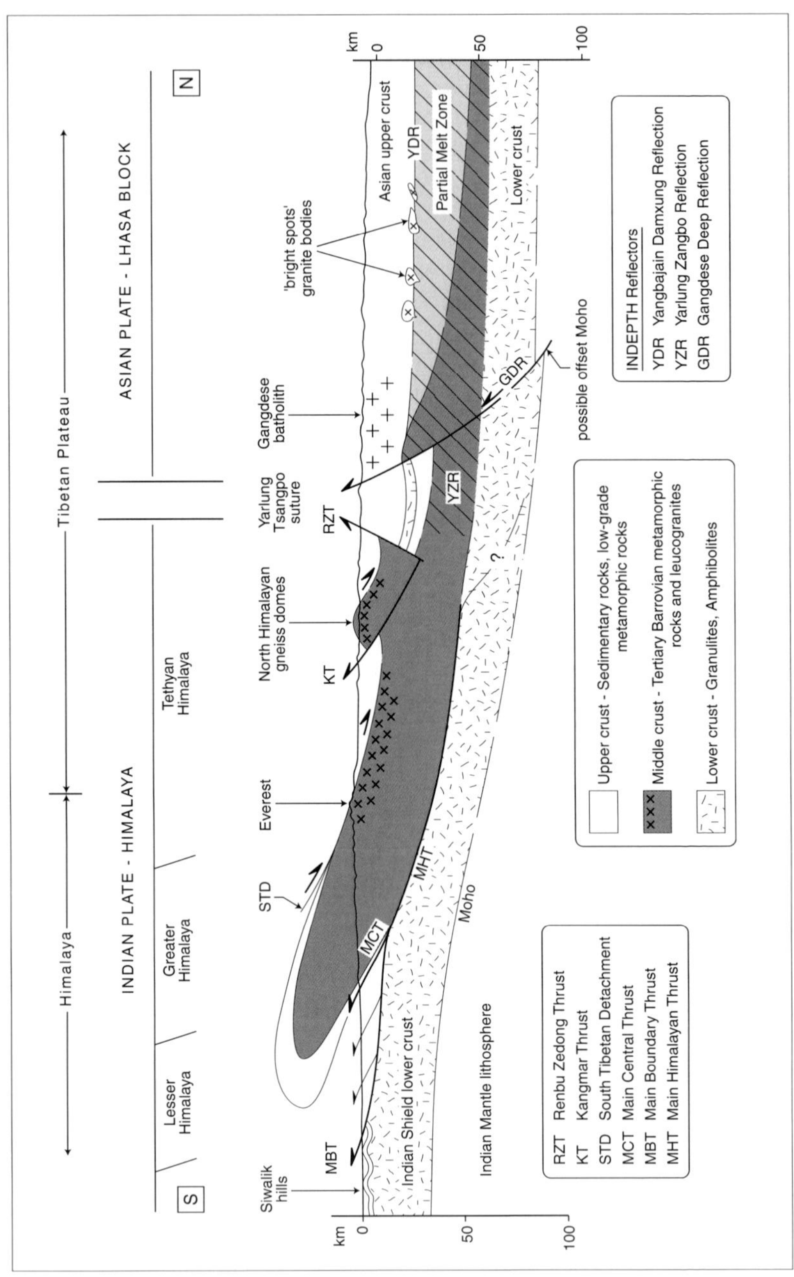

Fig. 3 Model to explain the Channel Flow hypothesis for the southward extrusion of a layer of ductile partially molten rocks from beneath southern Tibet to the Himalaya.

final puffs of gases and liquid magma were ejected out along a network of dykes emanating out from the granite. Some of the finest gems are to be found in these pegmatite dykes, black tourmaline and blue aquamarine to name a few. The south wall of Nuptse shows one of these ballooning sills in the most spectacular three-dimensional form as you walk along the Khumbu glacier towards Everest. This same granite sill can be traced westward into the Cho Oyu region and beyond and eastward to the massive pale granite forming the entire Makalu–Chomolonzo massif.

Geophysical surveys across Tibet

Mapping geological structures across mountain ranges like the Himalaya is painstaking and difficult. Geologists can usually access the valleys and occasionally climb high on some peaks, but much of the terrain remains difficult to access. However, it is only possible to make geological maps and determine the structure of the parts that are exposed. The only way to determine the deep structure of mountain ranges and plateaux is remotely, using geophysical methods, notably seismology. Earthquakes occur when rocks deep in the crust move along faults and spontaneously release energy. Earthquakes release shock waves, which travel along the surface of the earth (surface waves) and cause the ground to vibrate. Shorter period vibrations move through the Earth (body waves) and can be detected by seismometers. The fastest primary waves (P waves) travel at about 6km per second through the crust and somewhat faster between about 8km and 14km per second through the mantle. Secondary waves (S waves) vibrate at right angles to the direction of motion and can only pass through solid material.

Seismic surveys rely on a network of receivers laid out to pick up seismic waves from an energy source on the Earth's surface, usually an explosion of some sort. Various deep crustal seismic surveys have been carried out by Chinese, French, British and US scientists across parts of Tibet, but in the summers of 1994 and 1995 a major survey was initiated called the INDEPTH project (International Deep Profiling of Tibet and the Himalaya).[1] Continental deep seismic surveys are juggernauts of geophysical experimentation. They require large trucks of recording equipment and relatively flat, uninhabited terrain suitable for setting off explosions, both of which are rather hard to find in the Himalaya and south Tibet. The INDEPTH profile found the flattest part of south Tibet to be the large rift valley called the Yadong-Gulu rift, which runs due north of Bhutan, and this is where they laid out the first of a series of north-south seismic lines.

The most prominent feature found on the profile was a large reflector corresponding to the thrust fault called the Main Himalayan Thrust, along which the Indian plate is presently underthrusting the Himalaya and south Tibet. This fault dips gently to the north and runs from the southern margin of the Himalaya, where it reaches the surface. Most of the recent earthquakes in northern India, Nepal and Bhutan have occurred along this fault zone, including the 8 October 2005 Kashmir earthquake. This fault is now the current plate boundary and earthquakes occur down to depths of 80km as it plunges north beneath the Himalaya.

Another fascinating discovery on the INDEPTH profile was the presence of a mid-crustal zone of high electrical conductivity, determined from magnetotelluric studies. These data indicate the presence of pockets of hot fluids at relatively shallow depths in the crust beneath southern Tibet. Together with the seismic data and the high heat flow measured in lakes of southern Tibet, this seemed to fit the picture emerging of a layer between the depths of about 15 to 20km where the crust was extremely hot, had interconnected pockets of fluid-like material, and was partially molten. Fluids at these temperatures, above 600°C, in this sort of tectonic environment are most likely to be granite melts, similar to the granites seen today along many of the high peaks of the Himalaya. The whole of Tibet is known to have high heat flow, with numerous powerful geysers and hot springs erupting all across the plateau.

The results of the INDEPTH project appeared at first to be a real conundrum. How could the vast plateau of Tibet, the highest elevated mass on Earth, support itself above a layer of partially molten crust with pockets of magma at such shallow depth? The seismic evidence seemed to suggest that the crust was almost layered, so instead of buoyantly rising granite magmas, the only place for this partially molten layer to go was sideways, extruding south to hit the Earth's surface at the High Himalaya, precisely the position where the 20 million-year granites were found.

The reflectors on the seismic profiles could be directly linked to the major faults along the Sikkim-Darjeeling profile and the pockets of magma forming today beneath southern Tibet were on a direct link to the granites that form the high peaks of Kangchenjunga and Jannu.[2] Maybe the 20-17 million-year-old granites on Kangchenjunga were the older cooled equivalents of the pockets of liquid melt inferred today beneath southern Tibet. It was rather like a honey sandwich, where the upper crust and lower crust were relatively rigid, and a narrow layer of 'mush' in the middle was flowing as a fluid, rather like thick honey or oil. Gravity acting on the sandwich (Tibet) forced the honey to flow out to the side between the buttered sides of the sandwich – the shear zones either side of the High Himalaya range. Surprisingly, the INDEPTH profile showed that the lower crust beneath the partially melted layer was more solid, and therefore interpreted as the old, gneissic and granitic crust of the underthrusting Indian plate.

Geological mapping of Everest

A major geological mapping was initiated in the Everest region both on the Nepal and Tibetan sides in order to constrain the structure of the Himalaya in more detail. During this work many samples were collected for radiometric dating, geochemical and isotopic analysis and thermobarometric analysis in order to constrain the pressure, time and time of formation of the rocks. One result was the publication of a new *Geological Map of the Mount Everest massif* at a scale of 1:100,000.[3,4]

Geological mapping around the Everest massif has shown that these relatively flat-lying granite sills can be traced all around Everest, from the south faces of Nuptse and Lhotse along the upper Khumbu glacier and upper Kangshung glacier to the northern flanks.[4] These same granite sills outcrop along both flanks of the Rongbuk glacier for some 60km until they eventually disappear beneath the Tibetan plateau. Several generations of granite sills and dykes have been mapped out along these spectacular cliff sections, and these have now been dated, so it is possible to constrain not only the timing of granite melting but also the timing of the ductile fabrics in the surrounding gneisses and the timing of motion along the major faults that cut the granites. Along the Rongbuk cliff sections these granite dykes have been truncated, or cut off at the top by a flat-lying brittle fault. This fault, termed the Qomolangma detachment, forms a passive roof fault to the extruding high-grade gneisses and granites beneath.

Above this fault, unmetamorphosed Ordovician limestones extend all the way south up to the summit of Everest itself. Samples of summit rocks still contain tiny fragments of corals, shells and trilobites that once lived along a tropical ocean shore some 450 million years ago. The famous Yellow Band limestone encircling the summit pyramid of Everest is also composed of Ordovician limestone that has been metamorphosed to low-grade marble. Beneath the Yellow Band on Everest, black shales with thin bands of calc-silicate marbles form the south-west face, and show some spectacular southward-inclined folding on the Lhotse face below the South Col. Another major low-angle fault, the Lhotse detachment, separates these Everest series black shales from underlying granites and high-grade gneisses that form the great cliff ramparts above Base Camp.

Uplift of the Himalaya

We now know that most of the Himalayan granites that form many of the highest peaks crystallized between 24-17 million years ago with a hiatus at around 20 million years. Several dating methods using uranium-lead isotopes, argon step heating ($^{40}Ar/^{39}Ar$ ratios), and fission track dating can be used to constrain cooling histories of these granites. Remarkably similar results were obtained from Zanskar in the west to Bhutan in the east, suggesting that similar processes were acting synchronously along the entire Himalayan chain. Granites cooled very quickly during the period 20-17 million years ago, when the channel was extruding south from beneath Tibet. Erosion rates were incredibly high and there must have been mountains as high as today, if not higher, along the Himalaya at that time. After 16 million years ago the cooling rates declined until the first major glacial periods around two million years ago started with a corresponding increase in glacial and fluvial erosion.

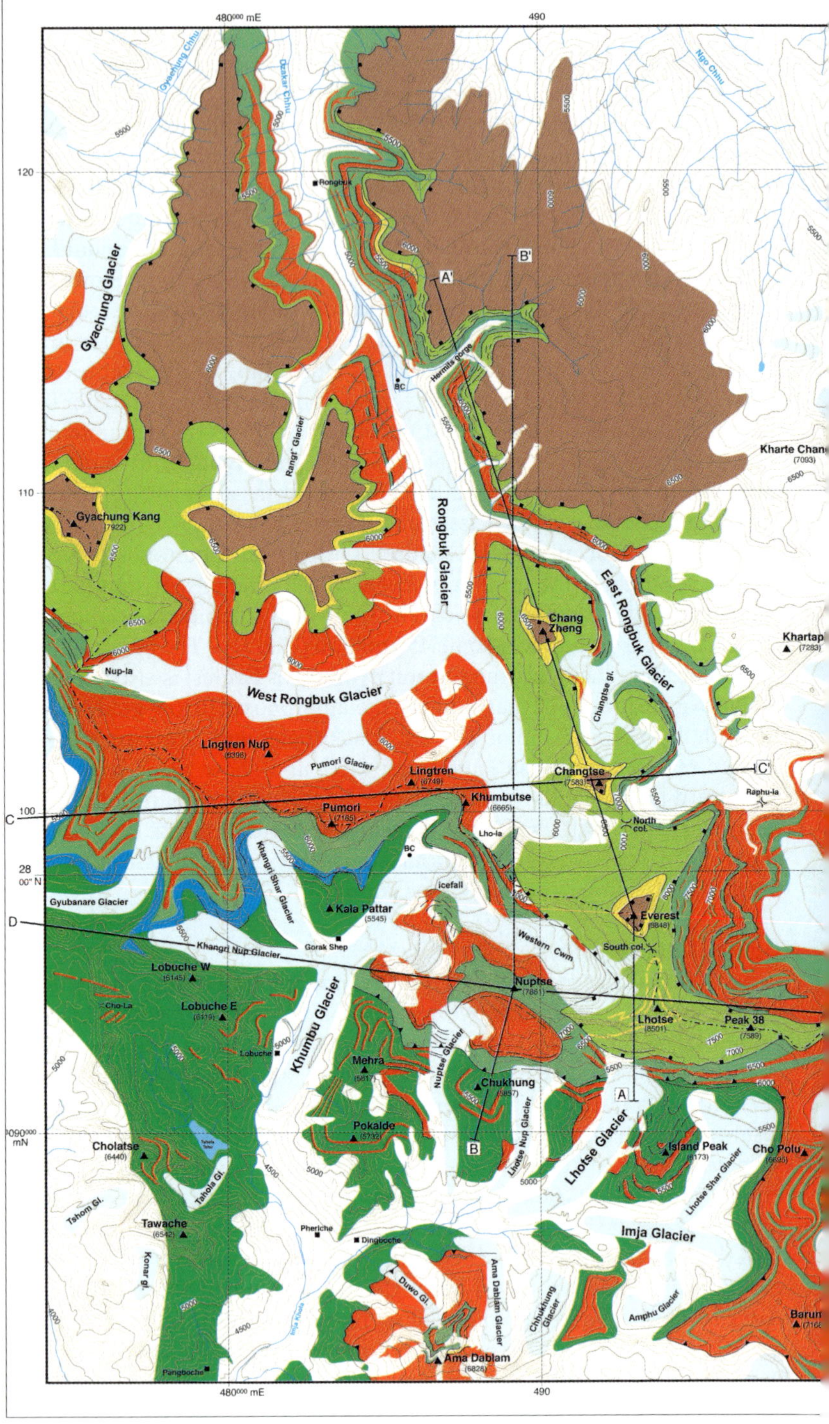

Gyachung Glacier
Gyachung Kang
(7922)
Rongbuk
Rongbuk Glacier
West Rongbuk Glacier
East Rongbuk Glacier
Hermits gorge
Nup-la
Lingtren Nup
Pumori Glacier
Lingtren
Pumori
Khumbutse
Chang Zheng
Changtse
North col.
Raphu-la
Lho-la
Everest
(8848)
South col.
Western Cwm
Nuptse
(7861)
Lhotse
(8501)
Peak 38
Kala Pattar
(5545)
Gorak Shep
Khangri Nup Glacier
Khangri Shar Glacier
Gyubanare Glacier
Lobuche W
Lobuche E
Lobuche
Khumbu Glacier
Mehra
Pokalde
Chukhung
Nuptse Glacier
Lhotse Nup Glacier
Lhotse Glacier
Island Peak
Lhotse Shar Glacier
Cho Polu
Imja Glacier
Amphu Glacier
Cholatse
Tawache
Tshom Gl.
Konar gl.
Pheriche
Dingboche
Duwo Gl.
Ama Dablam Glacier
Chhukhung Glacier
Ama Dablam
(6828)
Pangboche
Kharte Chang
Khartap
Baruntse
480000 mE
490
120
110
100
28 00' N
3090000 mN

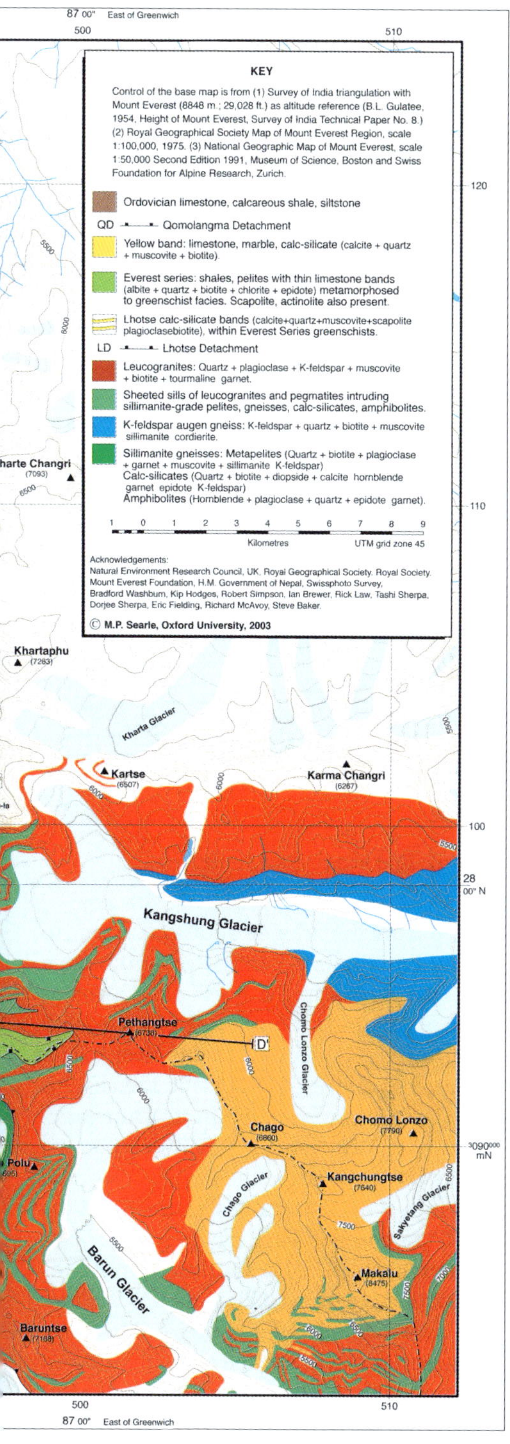
87 00" East of Greenwich
500
510
KEY
Control of the base map is from (1) Survey of India triangulation with Mount Everest (8848 m.; 29,028 ft.) as altitude reference (B.L. Gulatee, 1954, Height of Mount Everest, Survey of India Technical Paper No. 8.) (2) Royal Geographical Society Map of Mount Everest Region, scale 1:100,000, 1975. (3) National Geographic Map of Mount Everest, scale 1:50,000 Second Edition 1991, Museum of Science, Boston and Swiss Foundation for Alpine Research, Zurich.
Ordovician limestone, calcareous shale, siltstone
QD Qomolangma Detachment
Yellow band: limestone, marble, calc-silicate (calcite + quartz + muscovite + biotite).
Everest series: shales, pelites with thin limestone bands (albite + quartz + biotite + chlorite + epidote) metamorphosed to greenschist facies. Scapolite, actinolite also present.
Lhotse calc-silicate bands (calcite+quartz+muscovite+scapolite plagioclasebiotite), within Everest Series greenschists.
LD Lhotse Detachment
Leucogranites: Quartz + plagioclase + K-feldspar + muscovite + biotite + tourmaline garnet.
Sheeted sills of leucogranites and pegmatites intruding sillimanite-grade pelites, gneisses, calc-silicates, amphibolites.
K-feldspar augen gneiss: K-feldspar + quartz + biotite + muscovite sillimanite cordierite.
Sillimanite gneisses: Metapelites (Quartz + biotite + plagioclase + garnet + muscovite + sillimanite K-feldspar)
Calc-silicates (Quartz + biotite + diopside + calcite hornblende garnet epidote K-feldspar)
Amphibolites (Hornblende + plagioclase + quartz + epidote garnet).
1 0 1 2 3 4 5 6 7 8 9
Kilometres
UTM grid zone 45
Acknowledgements:
Natural Environment Research Council, UK, Royal Geographical Society, Royal Society, Mount Everest Foundation, H.M. Government of Nepal, Swissphoto Survey, Bradford Washburn, Kip Hodges, Robert Simpson, Ian Brewer, Rick Law, Tashi Sherpa, Dorjee Sherpa, Eric Fielding, Richard McAvoy, Steve Baker.
© M.P. Searle, Oxford University, 2003
120
110
100
28
00" N
3090000
mN
Kharte Changri
(7093)
Khartaphu
(7283)
Kharta Glacier
Kartse
(6507)
Karma Changri
(6267)
Kangshung Glacier
Pethangtse
(6738)
D'
Chomo Lonzo Glacier
Chomo Lonzo
(7790)
Chago
(6860)
Polu
Kangchungtse
(7640)
Chago Glacier
Sakyetang Glacier
Barun Glacier
Makalu
(8475)
Baruntse
(7168)
500
510
87 00" East of Greenwich

Left

Fig. 4 Geological Map of the Mount Everest area.

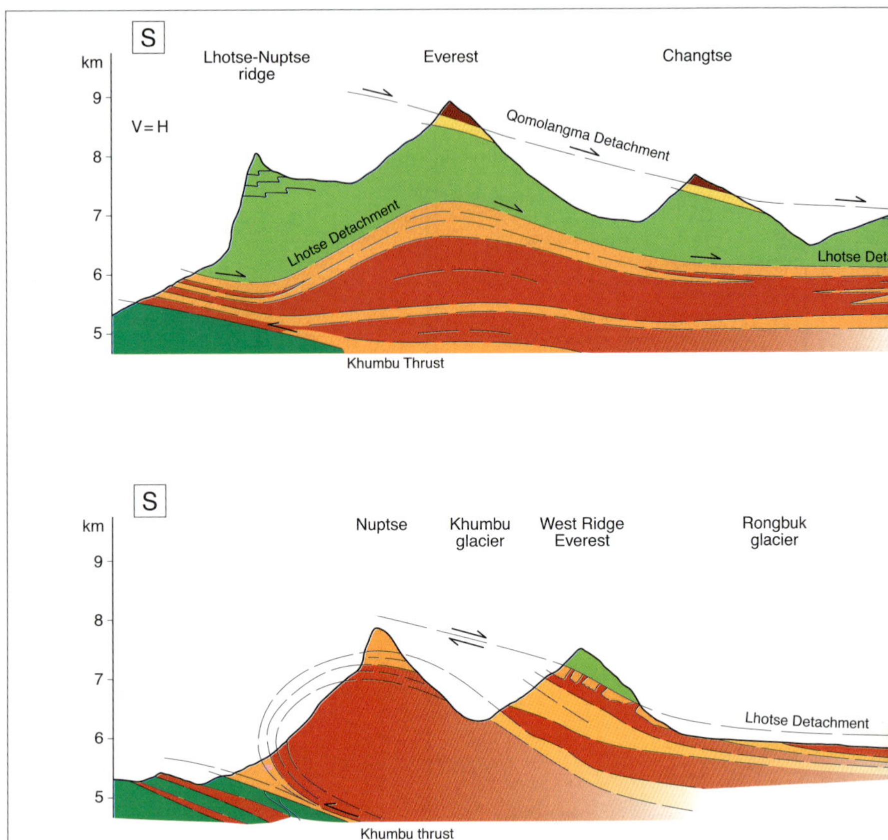

Fig. 5 Cross-sections of the Everest massif. Red layers are granite.

Two areas of the Himalaya have a truly remarkable additional story to tell. At each corner of the indenting Indian plate, centred around Nanga Parbat in the north-west and Namche Barwa in the north-east, a major knot of mountains creates a chaos of contours. Between the 7-8km high peaks of Haramosh and Nanga Parbat the antecedent Indus river cuts a gorge through the Himalaya roughly 5-6km deep. Likewise in the eastern syntaxis between the peaks of Gyala Peri and Namche Barwa, the antecedent Yarlung Tsangpo river cuts a similarly deep gorge between the two mountains. Uplift and incision rates of the river are the highest recorded anywhere in the world. Both the Nanga Parbat–Haramosh massif and the Namche Barwa–Gyala Peri massif are composed of deep crustal rocks, gneisses, migmatites and leucogranites that have been exhumed from depths of 30km or more. Samples of granites collected from 6000m on Nanga Parbat have been precisely dated at ages as young as 750,000 years old. These Quaternary granites, the youngest granites dated, formed at depths around 25-30km and are now at 6km elevation, giving the highest rock uplift rates and the highest exhumation rates known from anywhere in the world.

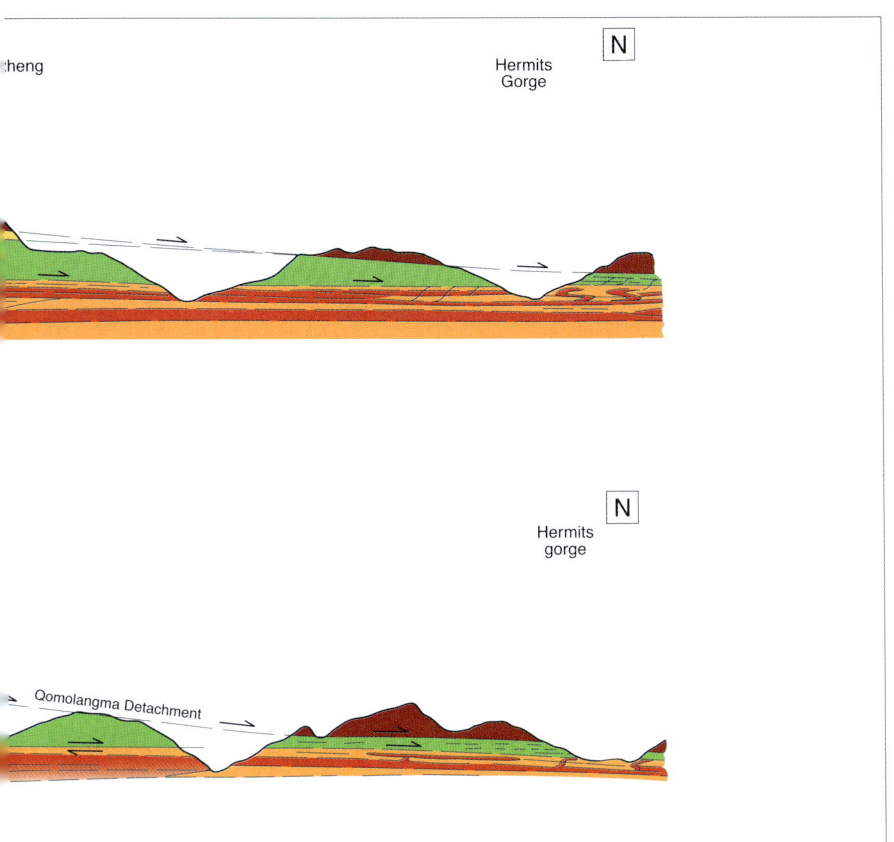

Climatic consequences of Himalaya-Tibet uplift

The uplift of the Himalaya and particularly Tibet affected not only the topography of Asia but also the climate of the northern hemisphere if not the entire world. Due to the Coriolis affect, or the spin of the Earth, the northern hemisphere has a dominant wind flow direction of west to east. The Tibetan plateau was suddenly thrust up into the troposphere, blocking the easterly flowing jet stream. A large high-pressure system sits over the high plateau during the summer months with lows sitting over northern India. This has the effect of sucking in the warm, moist air over the Indian Ocean which is drawn north across the sub-continent. As soon as these moisture-laden clouds reach land they dump their load over India giving the life-giving monsoon rains to India. The ground-hugging monsoon rains lash the southern slopes of the Himalaya but rarely rise over the highest peaks to the dry, arid landscape of Tibet. Heavy monsoon rains result in increased erosion. The Greater Himalaya suffers extreme erosion whereas erosion rates on the arid and relatively flat Tibet plateau are very low. It is clear that tectonic forces created the Himalaya and Tibet, climatic

144. The Rakhiot face of Nanga Parbat (8125m). (*Mike Searle*)

145. The gleaming granite of Makalu (8463m), one of the most stunning, scenically beautiful mountains on the planet. (*Mike Searle*)

consequences followed and now each process feeds off each other to keep the whole tectonic-climate cycle going. The high granite peaks of the Himalaya however, provide not only a geophysical-geological link from Tibet to the Himalaya, but they also provide us with some of best climbing in the world, and certainly some of the most stunning, scenically beautiful mountains on the planet.

References

1. K D Nelson et al, 'Partially molten middle crust beneath southern Tibet: synthesis of Project INDEPTH results' in *Science 274*, 1684-1688, 1996.
2. M P Searle and A G Szulc, 'Channel Flow and ductile extrusion of the high Himalayan slab – the Kangchenjunga-Darjeeling profile, Sikkim Himalaya' in *Journal of Asian Earth Sciences 25*, 173-185, 2005.
3. M P Searle, *Geological map of the Mount Everest massif, Nepal – South Tibet*. Scale 1:100,000. Oxford University, 2003.
4. M P Searle, R L Simpson, R D Law, R R Parrish, and D J Waters, 'The structural geometry, metamorphic and magmatic evolution of the Everest massif, High Himalaya of Nepal – South Tibet' in *Journal of the Geological Society 160*, 345-366, London, 2003.

JEREMY WINDSOR & GEORGE RODWAY

The Use of Closed-Circuit Oxygen Sets in the Himalaya

Any man with a couple of coolies could easily get to Mt Everest, if he were allowed a free hand. To get to the summit is quite a different matter. Altitude will cause trouble.

A M Kellas, 1912

Following A L Mumm's first attempts to use oxygen cartridges on the slopes of Trisul in 1907, mountaineers experimented with a range of different oxygen generators and circuits in order to climb the highest peaks of the Himalaya. However, the success of the open oxygen circuit on the first ascent of Mount Everest in 1953 signalled the end to this colourful period of scientific research and led quickly to the adoption of the set by the wider mountaineering community. Despite this, an alternative 'closed' circuit had also seen action on Everest in 1953. This circuit had considerable advantages over the open device but owing to problems of safety and ethics it was eventually overlooked and consigned to the history books.

In the spring of 2007, a new system will be employed on Everest by the Xtreme Medical Expedition. This group of scientists from University College London intends to develop a system which utilizes the best of both 'open' and 'closed' circuit systems in order to carry out detailed experiments at high altitude. The Xtreme expedition aims to undertake the most comprehensive set of experiments at high altitude on Everest since the 1981 American Research Expedition (AMREE). It will involve collecting data from two groups – the first, a group of up to 200 trekkers heading for Everest Base Camp, whilst the second group of more than 20 scientists will be based in the Western Cwm and will be well placed to take advantage of the new device. By understanding the history of the discarded 'closed' circuit and the experience of those who used it, its role in extreme-altitude mountaineering can best be understood.

The open circuits worn by Tenzing Norgay and Edmund Hillary in 1953 allowed climbers to inspire a mixture of ambient air and oxygen from a pressurized cylinder before exhaling gases directly into the atmosphere. Although this system offers a reliable and effective means of delivering oxygen at high altitude, the open circuit has two limitations. Firstly, the majority of gas that the climber inspires is air from the atmosphere (only 21% oxygen), and thus only small improvements in climbing performance are achieved. Secondly, the open circuit is inefficient, with any oxygen present in expired gas escaping readily into the surrounding atmosphere where it cannot be used again. The closed circuits taken to Everest in 1936, 1938 and 1953, and later to Kangchenjunga in 1955 were designed to solve both of these problems. In a closed circuit the climber is sealed off from the outside world by a tightly fitting mask and a complicated arrangement of tubes and connections. On exhaling, gases are directed through the mask and tubing before passing through a soda-lime filter. This filter absorbs carbon dioxide and directs unused oxygen into a reservoir bag for later use. Any oxygen that is taken up by the climber is then replaced from an oxygen cylinder attached to the circuit. Unlike the open circuit where air is also inspired, the tight fitting closed set only delivers pure oxygen. This high concentration of oxygen overcomes the effects of the low atmospheric pressure found at high altitudes and allows the climber to move more quickly and safely at high altitude.

The first closed circuits were manufactured by Siebe, Gorman and Company Ltd for the 1936 and 1938 Everest expeditions. Although the company had more than 60 years of experience designing sets for fire fighting and mine rescue work, little was known about the performance of closed circuits at altitude. The first tests conducted on the circuit were undertaken separately by Eric Shipton and paediatrician, Dr Charles Warren on Box Hill, Surrey, in 1935. According to Warren, on 'a surface of wet chalk set at a steep angle' Shipton was able to ascend at a respectable rate of 472m/hour. During a further trial, by Warren, a few days later, the apparatus failed to work smoothly and 'the unfortunate subject of the experiment became half asphyxiated and developed a splitting headache.' (Warren 1937) Eventually, after further improvements and tests in England and the Alps, two closed circuits were taken on the 1936 expedition. On the snow slopes below the North Col (7010m), Warren volunteered for the dubious task of testing the set. A witness later wrote:

> He found that although the unit seemed to be in perfect mechanical order it tended not to stimulate but rather to suffocate him. He was actually moving more slowly than the other climbers, and was forced to stop every dozen steps to recover his breath.

Peter Lloyd shared a similar experience two years later. As Oxygen Officer to the 1938 Expedition, Lloyd had tested Warren's closed-circuit set at 3900m and found that it behaved 'satisfactorily'. However after a few minutes on the North Col:

> It soon became evident that there was something very wrong. Mechanically everything was perfect, and the valves were opening and closing like clockwork, but inside the mask I was nearly suffocating and I had to stop frequently to take a dose of fresh air.

On both occasions the closed sets were quickly abandoned.

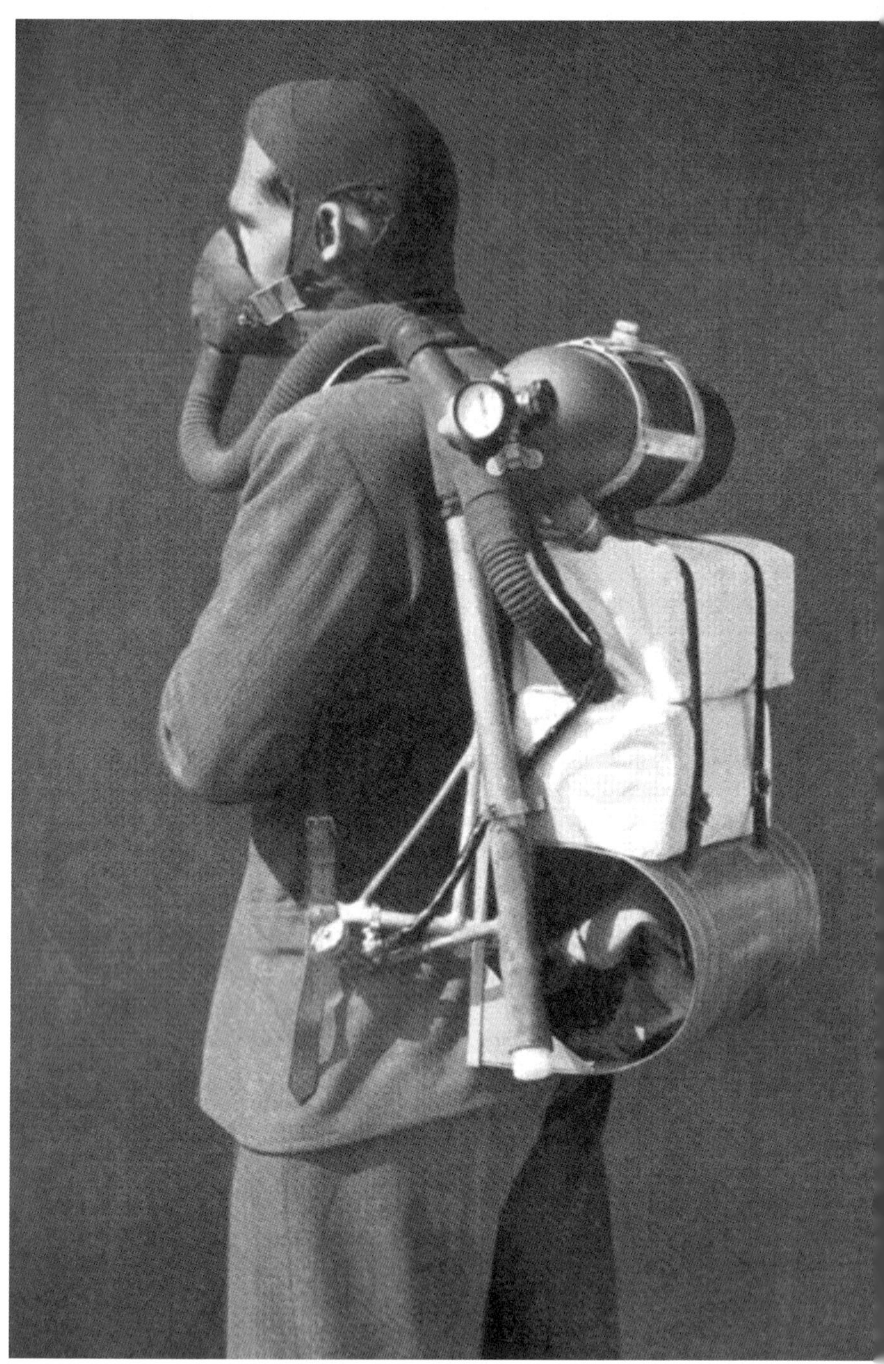

146. The closed-circuit oxygen set developed for use in 1953. (*Alpine Club Photo Library*)

Following his return to England Lloyd conducted further tests on the malfunctioning circuit and soda-lime canister. On a climb in the Lake District, Lloyd found that the components of the circuit were functioning normally and the apparatus, 'worked perfectly well'. Why had the closed circuit failed dramatically above the North Col yet worked so well near sea level?

In a paper presented to the Royal Geographical Society in 1947, H L Roxburgh, a scientist at the Institute of Aviation Medicine, identified a number of potential problems which could explain the difficulties that Warren and Lloyd had experienced. Whilst not ruling out leaks in the system, Roxburgh suggested that the most likely reasons for the feelings of suffocation were due to a combination of back pressure inside the circuit, insufficient absorption of carbon dioxide and finally inadequate oxygen flows which didn't match the oxygen being consumed by the climber.

Despite the failure of the early sets, the potential advantages of the closed system still proved irresistible to some. During the 1952 British Himalayan Expedition to Cho Oyu, the physiologist Griffith Pugh conducted a range of tests with supplementary oxygen on the Menlung La at approximately 6000m (20,000ft). Using a 300-litre rubber bag fitted with a three-way tap, two climbers were able to inspire pure oxygen and therefore simulate a closed circuit. The positive results from a trial on the snow slopes above the camp led Pugh to conclude that there was a 'strong argument in favour of developing closed circuit apparatus for trial on Everest'. Later that year the Medical Research Council (MRC) Oxygen Advisory Committee would support Pugh's conclusions and recommend that both the open and closed circuits should be taken to Mount Everest the following spring. At first, the plan was to use the open circuit for the summit attempt whilst the closed circuit would be kept in reserve for 'research purposes'. However, the manufacture and shipment of eight closed circuits suggested greater ambitions. John Hunt, the expedition leader, would later write: 'If this system, still in an experimental stage in regard to work at high altitudes, should prove successful it might greatly simplify our task ... '

The closed circuit was designed by the expedition's oxygen officer, Tom Bourdillon, and his father, Robert Bourdillon, at the MRC Electro-medical Research Unit at Stoke Mandeville Hospital and manufactured by Messrs Normalair Ltd in Yeovil. Following laboratory tests at Stoke Mandeville, the circuit's components underwent further trials in cold chambers at Farnborough's Institute of Aviation Medicine and on the hillsides of North Wales.

In order for a closed circuit to be effective, the pioneering anaesthetist Ralph Waters had argued: 'The important point is to avoid leaks in the apparatus itself and in the contact of the mask with the face.'

Over the winter of 1952-53 the design team was able to demonstrate that two different RAF pilot's masks could provide between them a tight seal for each of the expedition members. This was important for two reasons.

The first and most obvious reason was that any air that entered the circuit would dilute the concentration of inspired oxygen and reduce the partial pressure of oxygen present. Secondly, if the circuit leaked when low flows of oxygen were used, nitrogen could accumulate and cause what Bourdillon would describe as, 'a most undesirable thing since under these conditions it would be possible to breathe gas containing less oxygen than air'. Unfortunately, this tight-fitting set would come at an uncomfortable price. On a sunny January day in Snowdonia, Hunt wrote with some alarm: 'I tried it myself during a short distance uphill near the hut. I nearly exploded with heat and discomfort… '

The heat was not the only problem. Norman Hardie, a member of the successful 1955 Kangchenjunga expedition, found, 'that after a long session I could hear bubbles blowing through water at each exhalation', making it, 'necessary to drain the outward tube [of] about one quarter of a cup of water' after only a few hours of use.

On the 19 February 1953 four closed circuits were ready for shipment to Nepal. In just four months the research team had designed, manufactured and tested an entirely new closed circuit oxygen apparatus. Although a great deal had been learnt from the earlier circuits, several problems still existed. Could these be overcome?

The closed circuit's finale

Great will be the battle, but greater still the rewards,
of the man who first scales Mt Everest.

G D Abraham, 1912

Following success with both the open and closed circuits on the approach slopes of Everest, Hunt took the decision to use both sets on the final approach to the summit. On the morning of 22 May, Tom Bourdillon and Charles Evans left Advanced Base at Camp IV (6460m) breathing 2 litres/min of oxygen through their closed circuits. Hillary would later write: 'The two men were an awe-inspiring sight! Clad in all their bulky clothes, with their great loads of oxygen on their backs and masks on their faces, they looked like figures from another world.' Over the next two days the pair climbed through the Western Cwm and up the Lhotse Face before arriving at Camp VIII (7930m) on the South Col. Following a day spent resting and preparing the oxygen circuits, they awoke early on the 26 May to the first rays of sunlight on their tent. Already dressed, they slowly laced their boots, drank a flask of lemonade and checked their kit. At 6am Evans exited the tent first and was passed his closed set, 'whose sharp edges caught on every possible piece of cloth'. At temperatures close to minus 20°C, those few frustrating minutes were just enough to freeze the valves shut and force a breathless Evans stumbling back inside the tent. Using a candle, Bourdillon was able to slowly thaw the valves and restore the circuit to life. Now back outside the tent, Evans took a few steps before noticing 'a nasty sensation' and exclaimed to Bourdillon, 'in disapproving tones that it made me feel that I was going to die'. Back in the tent and now already an hour late, Bourdillon began to search desperately for the cause of the problem. Working with bare hands, his fingers began to blister and then bleed as he first checked the circuit's valves before switching his attention to the oxygen supply. Although the valves were moving freely, the reservoir bag was flat and the oxygen flow valve was jammed in its seating and could not be freed. Working quickly, Bourdillon replaced the valve with tubing fashioned from spare parts of an open circuit. Although this would provide his companion with a constant 2 litre/min flow of oxygen, Bourdillon knew 'this was extremely wasteful of oxygen when resting and would limit the maximum effort Evans could make'.

At 7.30am they were both finally ready.

> Our early excitement was now tempered with some gloom, the loss of ninety minutes, the use of some of our oxygen and a reduction in our endurance had severely reduced our chances of reaching the summit.

With their circuits now working well they were soon able to overtake their support group. At 9am they arrived at the site of the 1952 Swiss Expedition's final camp and rested amongst the tent poles and strips of torn cloth. Bourdillon would revise his opinion, later writing:

> The situation seemed promising. We had climbed from 25,800 feet to 27,300 feet in one and a half hours over ground not all easy and were still reasonably fresh.

Despite loads of more than 50lbs, the two climbers were able to ascend at a rate of 284m/hr. Griffith Pugh, the team physiologist, was surprised, as this rate was 'accepted as a reasonable speed for a party climbing under similar conditions in the Alps', and was significantly quicker than Hillary and Tenzing who followed later in prepared tracks at a rate 190m/hr. After a few minutes they began again, this time over a mixture of ankle-deep powder snow and patches of bare rock. At 11am, midway between the Swiss camp and the South Summit, they came across a flat, sheltered area and decided after some muffled debate to change their soda-lime canisters. This was a nervous time, with Bourdillon later realizing:

> If we did succeed in changing them and the valves were to freeze on introduction of the cold canister it might be most unfortunate.

Now with lighter loads, the conditions soon became much easier. However after 10 minutes the situation markedly deteriorated with Evans later

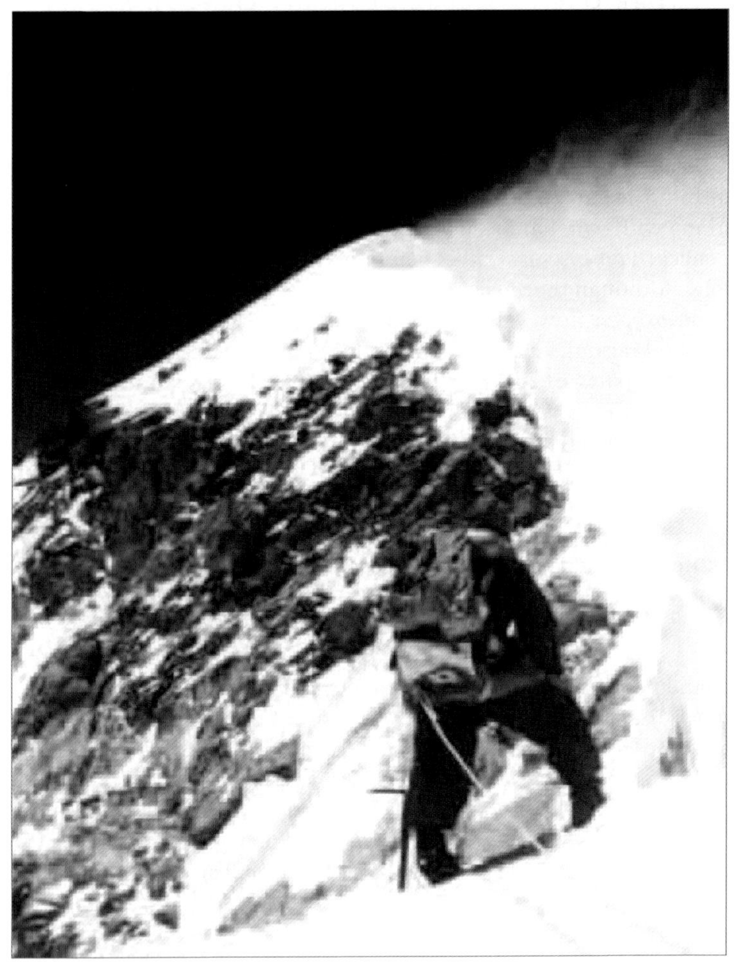

147. Tom Bourdillon standing on the South Summit looking towards the true summit of Mount Everest.
(*By courtesy of the Royal Geographical Society*)

describing how 'I had an attack of breathlessness and all at once felt done in.' On steep, awkward ground Bourdillon tried frantically to identify the problem. The circuit seemed to be working. The reservoir bag was filling and Evans could be seen to be inhaling its contents, yet it was clear to Bourdillon that his partner was breathless and clearly distressed. Writing in his summit report three days later, Bourdillon would conclude:

> It became clear that his second canister had been damaged and severe channelling was occurring. This was a bitter blow…

However, in an article written some weeks later for the *Alpine Journal*, Bourdillon would instead state:

> We did not locate this fault which might have been due to a partially frozen valve, to a distorted valve or a small leak to atmosphere.

At low temperatures the valves and soda lime were both prone to freezing. The expedition members knew that if one or both valves froze shut during inspiration, breathing would cease abruptly and cause what Roxburgh had described years before as 'bottoming'. However if the valves froze in an open position, breathing could still continue but only at enormous expense. Breathing through partially open valves would increase resistance and dead space within the circuit, resulting in a straining climber inspiring large quantities of carbon dioxide. A sudden fall in temperature could also affect the contents of the soda-lime canister. In temperatures close to minus 25°C, Tom Bourdillon described that, 'everything took three times as long to do as it would normally' and gave ample time for the contents of the canister to freeze and affect the absorption of carbon dioxide. By exposing the canister and valves to low temperatures, large quantities of carbon dioxide would accumulate and cause the enormous rise in respiration seen in Evans who was, according to expedition doctor Michael Ward, 'taking up to six breaths per step'. Later, during their descent, Bourdillon converted his partner's set to an open circuit in order to ease this problem. Within seconds Evans found that he 'obtained less benefit than from the faulty closed circuit' and quickly asked for the circuit to be changed back to the original system. If Evans' circuit had been leaking, the change to an open circuit would have either improved the situation or made little difference. However, with such a rapid deterioration it is more likely that damage to the canister and valves was the cause of the problem.

At just after 1pm the pair emerged 'with surprising suddenness' on the South Summit of Everest (8760m). The last 280m had taken more than an hour longer than expected and, with time and oxygen quickly running out, a decision had to be made. Staring hard at Evans, Bourdillon knew that his partner had given 'a wonderful effort, but he and I both knew that there was no possibility of him going on…' And so with just 90 metres separating them from the summit they decided to turn back.

From bitter experience Charles Evans would later recall: 'The 1953 closed circuit set could be put out of action by the freezing of the water in the circuit.' It is therefore hardly surprising to learn that in 1955 two important improvements were made to the set that was taken on the Kangchenjunga Expedition. The first involved fitting it with 'all rubber valves which could be squeezed to free them from ice' whilst the second led to changes in the way the breathing bag was attached to the soda-lime canister such that the chances of water freezing inside the circuit were reduced. Although, according to Norman Hardie, the circuit 'worked well and gave no

route (Abram/Schrott, 1971: VI+ and A2) on the north-west ridge of the Torre Campidel.

On 31 August Dario Segato and Nicola Tondini put up *Il Piccolo Principe* to the left of the 1973 *Leviti-Nemela route* on the south face of Punta dei Larsei. The eight-pitch route is 250m in height with maximum difficulties of 7a+ (crux perfectly positioned right at the top). A week later the same pair climbed a new line *La Mia Preghiera* (7b+) on the north face of the Sass da Putia.

Rather out of character for today's Dolomite ethics was the ascent of *Giuliani* on the Fourth Sella Tower, a little to the left of the *Malsiner-Moroder route*. Two Greeks were the culprits and they completely sieged the 350m line at 6c and A4.

In late September on the south face of the Piz Ciavazes, Giuseppe Ballico and Stefano Michelazzi added *Dulcis in Fundo* (350m: 7a+ or 6c+ and A1 obl) to the left of the classic 1953 *Abram-Gombocz route* on the south-east ridge. This is a partially bolted climb and took the ascensionists four days to open during a spell of unsettled weather.

On 17 July Bruno Pederiva and Mario Prinoth made the second ascent of the *Larcher-Vigiani route* on the south face of the **Marmolada**. In an impressive effort both climbers redpointed every pitch, completing this demanding route, probably the first true 8a on the face, in 12 hours. Larcher's routes, though bolt protected, are known to be bold undertakings and on a previous attempt Prinoth sustained injuries after a big fall.

In July two great names of Dolomite climbing were active on the Marmolada, achieving the second and third free ascents of *Spirit* on the south face of Cime di Auta east peak, which lies directly opposite the Marmolada's south face. The route was put up in 2003 by Massimo Da Pozzo and Danillo Serafini and later freed by Da Pozzo at 7c+/8a, 7b obl. Riccardo Scarian made the first on-sight repeat and was followed a few days later by Maurizio 'Manolo' Zanolla.

Between 27 and 31 July the accomplished Czech climbers Dusan Janak, Pavel Jonak and Vasek Satava climbed an independent finish to *Fram*, Igor Koller's 1991 route on the south face. *Fram* climbs the smooth walls just right of *The Fish*, joining it and *Via Italia* at the fish-shaped niche high on the face. The three Czechs climbed *Fram* completely free except for pitches 12 and 13 on which they used rest points. They didn't bother trying to eliminate these but pressed on to *The Fish* niche, where they climbed out right for five new pitches to complete *Fram – End of Mystery*. Two of these new pitches were IX+ (7c+) with rests and thought to be X– (8a+) for a redpoint. Another was redpointed at IX/IX+. The hardest pitch was a pocketed wall on rock similar to Buoux and one hole less would have made it impossible. Above, much easier ground (following the line of *The Fish*) leads to the summit.

In September Rolando Larcher and Roberto Vigiani made the second ascent of *Sur le fil des Apparences* (Rémy Duhoux/Philippe Mussatto, 2003:

350m: 7c, 7b obl). This route, on the same steep smooth wall as the bold Giordani route, *Specchio di Sara*, was climbed on-sight despite some of the sections being wet.

In the extensive **Pala di San Lucano** on the south-west face of the Second Pala, Lecco climbers Ivo Ferrara and Fabio Valseschini put up *Sorriso* (850m: 21 pitches: VI+ and A2) left of *Via degli Antichi*.

Towards the end of May Marco Anghileri and Raffaele Cargasacchi thought they were repeating an existing line on the west face of the Third Pala. In fact they soon realized they were mistakenly on new ground and went on to complete a new nine-pitch route VI+. The ascent took two days, finishing on 30 April.

On the south face of Monte San Lucana, Ferrera and Valseschini added *Albatros* (385m: VII+) to the right of *Farfalle* (the Butterfly), one of Ferrera's own routes dating from 1999. The climb was completed on 28 May.

In the **Monte Agner Group** on 18 June, Ivo Ferrari made the first solo ascent of the *Fiori route* (800m: VI) on the Spitz dell'Agner (2545m).

Back on great form again was the Italian icon of the 1980s Maurizio 'Manolo' Zanolla. In the company of Walter Bellotto, Daniele Lira and Diego dalla Rosa he put up *Bisogna essere veloci per descrivere le nuvole*, quite a mouthful for a route name and almost longer than the climb, which was five pitches. The new route is remotely situated on the south face of an unnamed 2000m summit in the little-frequented **Feltre Group.** It was graded 8a+, 7b/c obl. It was climbed from the ground up in August using drilled protection and climbed free on 14 September. While completely bolted, protection is very well-spaced and the route not for the faint hearted. Not long after, Rolando Larcher popped in to make the second ascent, found a different sequence on the crux and thought the difficulties more like 8a.

On 1 October Manfred Stoffer linked *Good bye 99* (7b) and *Da Pozzo Vecchio Pazzo* (7c) on the **Tofana di Rozas**, a total of 20 pitches climbed on-sight in one day. Earlier in the summer he had made a ropeless solo enchainment of the classic *Constantini-Apollonio* (6c+), the *Constantini-Ghedina* and the *Spigolo Alvera* to the right in just five and a half hours. That is a total of 2180m of climbing, not including the descents. On the way back down he made a ropeless solo of *Ciapa e Tira*, a 25m, 7c+ sport route on the Pian Schiavaneis. Not long after, having already climbed two routes with a client on the Ciavazes, he made a ropeless solo of *Ottovolante* (360m) on the Brunico Tower, Gardena Pass; 11 pitches from 6a to 7a+ in just one hour and 20 minutes.

In the **Civetta Group** there were several ascents of *Rondo Veneziano* on the Torre Venezia. The 500m, 12-pitch route was first climbed in 2001 by well-known activists Kurt Astner and Christoph Hainz at 7b+, 7a obl. 2005 ascensionists commented on the fantastic quality of this route and felt it could become a real modern classic for those operating at the standard. The route uses a combination of bolt and traditionally-placed protection.

PAUL KNOTT

Russia & Central Asia 2005

Correspondents and information sources used for this report, other than the climbers themselves, were Angara.net, Alpinism Buryatia, Mountain.ru, Extreme Portal vvv.ru, Risk Online, Alpclub Ural, Lindsay Griffin, Sergei Kurgin of Sibalp, and ITMC Tien Shan. The websites listed can be read in English using translation programs available on the internet.

The Caucasus

Only a handful of new routes have been reported in the Caucasus. In July Egor Dul'nev, Andrey Morozov and Sergey Kuznetsov climbed a new 6A route L of the *Forostyan route* on the N face of the NE rib of **Chegem (4461m)** at VI A3 1500m. After route preparation from 29 July to 1 August, they climbed to the summit from 5-7 August. From 2-11 July a team based at the Bezingi alpine camp led by Vladimir Kulikov climbed a new 5B route on the N face of **Pik Pushkin (5100m)**, L of the 1972 *Kudinov route*. Pik Pushkin lies in the Dykh-Tau massif between Dykh-Tau East and Pik Borovikov. The team started by traversing from Borovikov, making 1900m of total height gain. They had considered taking the *Kudinov route* (also 5B), but felt it was avalanche prone and could not find route details even in the alpine camp.

Previously unreported from 2004 was the ascent on 2 August of a new 5B route on **Khimik (3975m)**, a peak N of Adyr-Su mountain that can be approached from the Ullu-Tau alpine camp. The team including DV Savchenko and VL Matekha climbed via the 1000m central bastion of the N face.

The Pamir Alai

Activity in this range seems to be recovering following the easing of security concerns experienced from the late 1990s. In July-August Mark Pretty, David Pickford, Ian Parnell and Sam Whittaker climbed in the **Ak-Su valley**. They climbed two new routes, *The Beast,* 550m E4 6a and *From Russia with Love*, 400m E7 6b as well as freeing an existing aid route and climbing a number of single-pitch routes at E3-E7. Information is lacking as to the location of these routes.

In the Karavshin valley from 6-8 August a team led by Alexander Yanushevich climbed a new 6A route on **Pik Zholtaya Stena** (Yellow Wall). The 600m route involved 375m of VI class climbing with an average 79° angle and took 3 days. Also active in the Karavshin valley in August were Maxim Krivosheev, Denis Veretenin and Andrey Kustov from Irkutsk and

Angarsk, who summited **Asan-Usen (4230m)** by *Pogorelov's route* (6B) in three days of climbing plus another for the 18-rappel descent. They also attempted **Pik 4810** via *Voronin's route* (6B). Another team climbing in the area, from Krasnoyarsk, attempted *Alperin's route* (5B) but were dissuaded by the weather from completing the climb.

The Pamir

Summer 2005 saw another active season on Piks **Kommunizma (Somoni, 7495m)** and **Korzhenevskaya (7105m)**. Out of 156 people from 22 countries, 107 reached the summit of Korzhenevskaya. This is a record number for the post-Soviet period, but according to Vladimir Shataev of the Russian Alpinist Federation, it was exceeded during most of the 1980s, the record being 314 in 1989.

In June-July an 8-member group from the University of Bristol climbed from the **Fedchenko glacier**, a venue little visited since the 1992 Imperial College trip as the access route runs close to the Afghan border. The group travelled via the Pamir Highway to the effective road head at Geolog in the Vanj valley. They returned from Vanj by air, finding this more efficient. Carrying loads up the Abdukagor glacier with the assistance of four porters, they established a base at 5220m on the Fedchenko glacier via four intermediate camps. They made a number of probable first ascents including Peaks **Volodiya (c5847m)** between Tanymas and Paris Commune, **Bronwen (c5550m)** via the E face and NE couloir (50°), and **Pt 5390m** on the Tanymas massif. The latter climb, by Rob Lavin and James Byrne, turned into an epic traverse with ever-present rockfall danger. The expedition ended in tragedy when Ian Hatcher and Simon Spencer-Jones failed to return from an attempt on the N face of **Pik 26 Bakinshikh Kommisarov (6834m)** in the Revolutsii massif.

The Tien Shan

Notwithstanding the overthrow of the country's president early in the year, the most shocking news for mountaineers is that Kyrgystan has ceded two significant areas of mountain territory to China. The agreement remains highly contentious in Kyrgyzstan and has not been widely publicised. One such area is the eastern end of the **Inylchek glacier**. The new border turns N at Pobeda East, following the ridge through Pik Shipilov then crossing the glacier to Khan Tengri. Peaks such as the impressive **Voennikh Topografov (6873m)** now lie wholly within China. A further area of territory has also been ceded at the eastern end of the Western Kokshaal-Too (see below).

Previous visitors to the Inylchek base camps will not be entirely surprised to read that one of the helicopters came to a dramatic fiery demise early in August. Fortunately, no-one was seriously injured. The helicopter, loaded with 16 climbers, crashed 50m from the camp after being hit by a wind gust just after take-off.

148. Pik 5481m (*left*) and Byeliy (Grand Poohbah, 5697m) from the NE. (*Paul Knott*)

149. SE faces of Pik Byeliy (Grand Poohbah, 5697m) and Pik 5481m (*right*) (*Paul Knott*)

On **Khan Tengri (6995m)**, Pavel Shabalin and Ilyas Tukhvatullin made the first 2-man, alpine style ascent of the central N face. Previously, the route has been climbed by large Russian teams and attempted unsuccessfully by about six two-man teams. Earlier in the season, a Polish alpine-style attempt had resulted in a fatality. Starting on 20 August, Shabalin and Tukhvatullin reached the summit on 29 August; theirs was the last ascent of the season. Their ascent began on the *Odessa route* and continued up the *Studenin route*, finishing via a variant of the *Pogorelov route*. Also on Khan Tengri, from 12-14 August a team led by Alexander Moiseev climbed a new 5B route taking the NE rib of the shoulder of Pik Chapaev.

The first full solo traverse of **Pobeda (7439m)** was completed by Gleb Sokolov during August 16-23. He traversed from Chon-Teren pass to Dikiy pass. He had made four previous attempts at the traverse since 1998. Some of the more unusual items in his pack were 1.5kg of fresh cucumbers, 1kg of apples and two cans of beer.

The **Karakol range** E of Issyk-Kul lake sports fine technical objectives that have so far seen little interest from foreign climbers. A team from Nizhniy Tagil and Ekaterinburg led by Sergei Timofeev and including Alexander Korobkov and Mikhail Borich climbed a new winter route on **Dzhigit (5170m)**. The route, on the NW face at around 6A, was climbed using portaledges and was completed to the summit on 6 March.

In July-August Paul Knott, Grant Piper and Graham Rowbotham climbed in the virtually unexplored Fersmana glacier basin in the central part of the **Western Kokshaal-Too**. The mountains here turned out to be composed mainly of the monolithic granite of the western end of the range rather than the crumbly limestone to the east. A reconnoitre of the highest peak **Byeliy (Grand Poohbah, 5697m)** found steep walls on the NE, E and S sides that were mostly overhung by séracs; the route substantially climbed by Mike Libecki's party in 2000 (from China) appears to have been the SW ridge. Eastern outlier of the massif, **Pt.5481m**, was found to be a quite separate and equally precipitous summit.

The team focused on the peaks at the head of the glacier, starting with the first ascent of **Pik Neizvestniy** (Unknown, 5240m) via the snowy NE arête and the sharp corniced ridge beyond (D/NZ 4). The latter required delicate *à cheval* climbing. They were repelled from two further summits by monolithic granite gendarmes. On **Pik Granitsa** (Border, 5370m) they retreated from low on the W ridge. This and other summits in the area sported impressive granite walls on the Chinese side. On **Pogranichnik** (Border Guard, 5220m) in the SE corner of the glacier cirque they were stopped at the summit 'head' after climbing the N ridge. Their final summit attempt, on the W ridge of **Zastava** (Border Post, 5010m) between Neizvestniy and Granitsa was repelled by deep hanging powder on the north-facing slopes.

The approach to this area is affected by one of the areas of territory ceded to China under the new border agreement. This area starts west of the

Bedel Pass, with the new border following the Uzengegush river from the point at which the road meets it from the north to the confluence of the Chon-Tyuekuyruk river. The border then follows the Chon-Tyuekuyruk east of Pik Koroleva (5816m). Because the road up the Uzengegush now runs partly in China, it appears only military vehicles are authorised to use it. As a result, the above-mentioned team had to complete the last 60-65km to base camp on foot.

At the **Kyzyl Asker** end of the Western Kokshaal-Too, an Alaskan party including James Stover found their climbing curtailed by heavy snowfall, frostbite and infection. The conditions parallel the experience of the Knott-Piper-Rowbotham team, which saw conditions on the upper glacier change during August from melt streams and slush to deep powder snow. The marginal 4000m road passes were also snow-covered for their return journey. On the western approaches to Kyzyl Asker, the limestone gorges of the **Sary-Beles** region were reportedly visited by an expedition organised by Joe Metcalfe. No further details are available.

In July-August the US party of Mike Libecki, Andy Libecki, John Burcham and Heath Jarrett climbed on the Chinese side of the range, in Xinjiang Province. Approaching via Ak-su and Ahqi, they reached the untouched valley of granite that Mike had seen from the ridge of **Grand Poohbah** in 2000. From this valley the Libecki brothers made the first ascent of Tombstone Tower in capsule style, naming their route *Libeckistan* (5.10d A3+ 500m). They descended through a thunderstorm.

Two teams visited the **Borkoldoy range**. A Harvard Mountaineering team including Bjarne Holmes, Kelly Faughnan, Corey Rennell and Adilet Imambekov approached from the N via the Chakyr-Korum river. Prevented by strong river flows from driving to their intended area, the Koldmore valley, they climbed instead in the vicinity of the Ayutor glacier. In total they reached nine summits, all likely first ascents, of which they named the highest **Peak of Theoretical Physics (4856m)**.

In September an ISM trip led by Pat Littlejohn, Adrian Nelhams and Vladimir Komissarov visited the well-guarded central area of the range, following the track they had dug out in 2004 to reach a drive-in base camp at 3570m. From here Littlejohn with James Bruton and Ben Box made the first ascent of the highest peak of the range, which they named **Pik Borkoldoy (5171m)**. Taking advantage of better snow conditions than the previous year, they picked a line through the séracs on the NE flank to gain the S ridge at 5000m, grading the route PD+. The group also made the first ascent of several other peaks. From the Ilbirs Glacier West, they climbed **Pik Tansovsitsa** (4911m, AD) via the N ridge and **Alpinistka** (4959m, D) via the W ridge. From the previously untouched 'Hidden' glacier north of base camp they climbed four further peaks, the highest and most difficult being **Pik Koldunia** (4895m) by the S ridge at AD+. (*See 'Adventure Guaranteed', p129*)

Siberia and the Russian Far East

There were several significant developments in this huge but often neglected region. The exploratory and technical climbing potential in the **Altai** was demonstrated by the first ascent of **Peak 3716m**, in the Mushtuajri valley not far from Belukha, by a technical new route. The 6B route was climbed using a portaledge over 16 days in March 2006. The ascensionists Vitaly Ivanov, Aleksey Avdeenko, Maxim Britz and Igor Slabodchikov named the peak **Vektor**. The route is probably the hardest established in the Altai range.

In August the **trans-Baikal** mountains received what was probably their first ascent by a foreign climber, as a team including French climber Andrew Jelly Antibes put up a new route on **Muyskiy Gigant**. The 33-pitch route was named *Ciao Victor*, TD (5c fr. obl.), 24hr, 900m.

Climbers from Ulan-Ude, Blagoveshchenk, Angarsk and Khabarovsk visited the same area in June-July, climbing in the Ul'zykh valley of the **Barguzin range**. They climbed two high-standard new routes on peaks **60 Years of Victory** and **AMGU**, and on **Argada** made the first ascent of a grade 4 route and the second ascent of a 5A route and a 5B route.

In NE Siberia a pioneering new ski traverse was undertaken through the **Verkhoyansk range** by a team led by Aleksey Romanenkov and Anton Chkhetiani. Over a 39-day period the team, from Moscow, St Petersburg and Lithuania, covered over 800km starting from the coastal tundra. First they crossed the Kharaulakhskiy mountains to N Orulgan, where they made the first ascent of **Pik 1000 years of Kazan** and continued to the Dzhardanskiy alpine massifs. They made the first crossing of the dry mountain areas of E Orulgan, exiting onto the Kolosov glacier from which they made a first ascent in the Amkynda range of **Pik V. Shefnera (2055m)**. Continuing south, the group crossed the Tumarinsk plateau to reach the S Orulgan via the Lena, Syncha and Tara-Sala rivers. Around 90% of the route was previously untravelled. Unusual spring weather meant that the snow cover melted in early May, forcing the team to complete the last 100km on foot through the spring onslaught of insects. During the entire journey, covering around a third of the total length of the Verkhoyansk, they met no one.

DEREK FORDHAM

Greenland 2005

The Danish Polar Centre issued 38 permits for sporting, as opposed to scientific expeditions, in 2005. This was about normal but there was a significant drop in the number of expeditions choosing to cross the Inland Ice. Of the 14 having that as their objective, all but two limited themselves to the trade route between Ammassalik and Kangerlussuaq* although a higher percentage than usual opted for the W-E crossing.

Inland Ice

Of those from whom reports have been received, the first to leave the east coast were Erik Hanstein Andersen, Håvard Skuland Pedersen and Hans Aleksander Bjerke (Norway). The team flew to East Greenland in the middle of July 2005 and spent time preparing their equipment before being taken by boat to Nagtivit. Their pulks weighed 80kg and they had to work their way through extensive crevassing before reaching soft snow where they found it necessary to rope up. The snow soon became stronger and they could proceed faster, moving at night to take advantage of the lower temperature of between –10°C and –25°C. They travelled about 32km per night walking for about 8-9 hours. They experienced whiteout conditions which they found 'hard, monotonous and boring and even the mp3 player didn't help!' The snow was a lot wetter and it was harder to travel in such conditions. As expected they encountered melt water; on day 16, it was up to their knees and was much worse than expected. It formed large lakes on the snow, connected by large rivers. It proved impossible to go around the melt water system so they travelled on a compass course, sometimes using skis, sometimes crampons. This took them across deep rivers in the snow, some so deep that it was difficult to get down to the water. One of the rivers crossed was about 45 metres wide, and they were up to their hips in the water. They had to site one camp in the water-logged area before, after doubling their rations and travelling another long day, they were able to look back at the water.

The next days were less wet but more crevassed. They had to move their pulks one at a time through this area and after scouting the route ahead were able to set up their last camp, number 21, on dry land at Kangerlussuaq

* The 'new' spelling of Kangerlussuaq reflects the changing face of written Greenlandic, or Inuktittut. It is the form used by most of my contacts, including the Danish Polar Centre. I have retained the 'old' spelling – Kangerdlugssuaq – only when the name is quoted. DF

610km from their starting point, on 3 August. Morten Lund and Rasmus Boeckman (Norway) started their 'Sommerfugler i Vinterland' (Butterflies in Winter land) expedition on 21 July at Nagtivit and reached Kangerlussuaq 25 days later. They encountered little lying snow until 1000m and then experienced seven days of snow and continuous whiteout conditions with very heavy skiing conditions. From the highest point on the route, 2500m, the weather and snow improved and they reached Dye-2, the abandoned early warning station, on day 19. Melt water lakes were encountered 60km after Dye-2 and did not present any problems other than wet feet. The ice road, established in earlier years to serve a vehicle testing station on the Inland Ice, was met but since it had not been maintained it was of little use. The expedition reached Kangerlussuaq on 15 August. Their pulks weighed 75kg each and the lowest temperature encountered was –20°C.

Magnus Lovold and Bjørnar Gjerde (Norway) started their 'Greenland 2005' expedition on 2 August after being delayed by the late arrival of some of their equipment. They shared the boat to the drop-off point on the mainland and the first camp with the Sami expedition described next. The first few days were warm but the second week was overcast with clouds. Whiteout conditions, described as 'like walking in a huge glass of milk', led them on one occasion to ski for 40 minutes in the wrong, easterly, direction until their GPS brought them into line. Once past the highest point, the team reached Dye-2 and found the complex simultaneously frightening and fascinating, describing it as, 'a piece of dust in the eye of Greenland'.

Shortly after leaving Dye-2 the expedition came to a very extensive area of lakes and rivers on the ice and changed to a more northerly route. (The unusually extensive area of melt water on this part of the Inland Ice in 2005 has been attributed to global warming and was the reason for an expedition organised by Hvitserk, a Norwegian expedition group, who were one day behind the Greenland 2005 team, being air-lifted out.) Considerable effort was needed to get through this area but the party were helped by finding the tracks of the 'Sami-express' expedition who were by now ahead of them. Resorting at times to floating the pulks on glacial streams, the expedition finally escaped from the ice after 25 days on route.

Anne Lajla and Arvid Dahl (Norway) were the 'Sami ekspedisuvdna 2005' and shared the first day (2 August) of the traverse with the previously described group. They were both Sami from northern Norway and wanted their expedition to raise the profile of the Sami people, two of whom, Balto and Ravna, gave much valuable help to Nansen when he made the first crossing of the Inland Ice in 1888. As a token of how valuable the Sami's help to Nansen was, Anne and Arvid, the first Sami on the Inland Ice since Nansen's expedition, wore traditional Sami reindeer skin clothing and eschewed modern expedition rations in favour of dried reindeer meat as had been used in 1888.

As one might have expected from such experts, they completed most of the route quickly and with no problems; hence the nickname given by their fellow Norwegians, 'the Sami-express'. However, as had other expeditions, they found the last 100km extremely difficult due to the melt water problems and reached Kangerlussuaq on 23 August after a journey of 21days.

Danna Corke and Anne-Mette Nørregaard (Denmark) were the 'Ice Queens Expedition', the first Danish women's expedition to cross the Inland Ice from west to east. Both were experienced adventure racers and alpinists. The crossing started from Kangerlussuaq on 30 April and finished at Isortoq on 5 June.They had four days tent bound due to a storm but otherwise no special problems. The weather was very poor with a lot of wind and snowy conditions for the first 12 days but after that there was almost no wind and they enjoyed continuous sunshine.

On day 15 they passed the abandoned radar station Dye-2 and 144km from the east coast Danna's ski boot broke and she had to walk the rest for the way on one ski or no skis! The descent from the ice cap was relatively easy without too much crevassing or melt water. They were picked up by boat at the Isortoq fjord an hour and a half after finishing the expedition. The journey to Tasiilaq took 58 hours instead of the calculated 4 hours but that's a completely different story.

Olivier Pezeron and Arnaud Fauvet (France) left Kangerlussuaq in early June on an expedition to honour the French explorer Paul Emile Victor. They carried a small sculpture made by P E Victor's youngest child and on arrival in Ammassalik/Tasiilaq, where P E Victor had lived in 1934–1936 while carrying out ethnographic research, this was presented to the local 'Mayor'.

They made the 600km crossing with pulks weighing 95kg each in 20 days, experiencing strong head winds for half the journey. They encountered problems with melt water and crevasses at the end of the journey at Isortoq and commented on the fact that their lowest night temperature in June was –20°C in contrast with Nansen's of –45°C in August 118 years ago and that this seemed to support the local Inuit's claim that rising temperatures were responsible for a decrease in their hunting and fishing catches.

Ingvar Sjothun, Olav Tangeland and Thomas Gjesteland (Norway) formed the 'Kangerlussuaq-Isortoq Expedition 2005' which set off from Kangerlussuaq on 2 June in sunny weather and moderate winds hoping that by starting from the west coast they would avoid melt problems. After nine days of skiing, lots of wind and sometimes complete whiteout they reached Dye-2 and had to have a day off due to winds exceeding100km/hr. The weather then improved and they found the best travelling technique was to start skiing at about 0500 and ski for 9-10 hours. High temperatures in the afternoon were a bigger problem than colder nights. The last few days were made difficult by crevasses and icy melt rivers but after 21 days on the ice they reached Isortoq Fjord for a boat pick up.

Paul Landry and three companions (Canada) reached the east coast north of Ammassalik on 14 June having completed a double crossing of the Inland Ice. No further details are available at the time of writing.

Niklas Norman,Trygve Kristiansen and Carl Florence (Norway) left sea level west of Narsaq in South Greenland on the 29 June and, kiting and ski sailing on the western margin of the Inland Ice, reached the head of Bowdoin Fjord, east of Qaanaaq in North Greenland, some 2300km and 21 days later where they were picked up by local hunters by boat.

Their aim had been to rely as much as possible on the wind but initially they had to walk for three days to get through crevasses and gain height. Then they covered a distance equal to five times the standard crossing from Ammassalik to Kangerlussuaq in only 21 days!

The expedition encountered no problems other than poor wind and white-out for most of the first 10 days and two extensive areas of crevassing as they passed the latitude of Kangerlussuaq. These crevasse fields lie full square across the standard trade route across the Inland Ice and are a good example of why the convenient airfield-to-airfield route is really not a very good route to follow across Greenland!

During the nine last days the expedition averaged 210km/day and the longest distance in 24 hours was 442.7km (in 23 hours).The highest speed during normal travelling was 59km/h.

East Greenland

The CUMC Centenary Kangerdlugssuaq 2005 Expedition was composed of eight members led by James Sample and they were in the field in June-July. Bad weather delayed the team's arrival in Greenland and prevented their chartered aircraft from landing in the chosen spot. They made the first ascent of the most significant local peak, before skiing to their planned area, where they made first ascents of further peaks (mostly unnamed). They were fortunate in that following an accident to one of the members it was possible to get the plane in and have the injured party in hospital only 37 hours after the accident.

The British Kangerdlugssuaq 2005 Expedition: Peter Whyley, Carole Feldman, Paul Hawksworth and Cath Walton used Tangent Expeditions to access the region to the south of the Hutchinson glacier during July-August. As far as was known, the exact area had never previously been visited. Climbing mainly at night, they were successful in making a number of probable first ascents of local peaks.

Manfred Heini and six others (Switzerland) formed the 'Swiss AACB East Greenland Expedition' to celebrate the 100th anniversary of the Akademischer Alpen Club Bern. On 11 July the expedition flew into the Sødalen airstrip, south of the Watkins Mountains, with the object of exploring and making ascents in the mountains between Watkins and Jakobsen fjords. A few ascents were made from the airstrip before moving to an advanced base which gave access to the peaks at the southern end of the Frederiksborg glacier several of which were climbed before the expedition was flown out after spending 23 days in the area.

South Greenland

The KMC Tôrnârssuk Expedition comprising Dave Bone, Marylise Dufaux, Dan O'Brien, Carl Pulley and David Whittingham was active on Tôrnârssuk Island in July-August. The island is uninhabited and lies off SW Greenland. The team was subject to much rain and strong wind which limited their activities. A number of new routes of varying grades were made and apart from a team that put up a number of difficult rock routes in 2004, the island appears to have little recent climbing history.

North Greenland

Martin Brice, Glenn Morris, David Key and David Johnson (GB) forming the 'Greenland by the Polar Sea' expedition left Siorapaluk, the most northerly settlement in NW Greenland, in April travelling with local Inuit hunters by dog sledge. Their intention was to travel 300km northwards along the coast and then return alone by another route on the Inland Ice, pulling their own pulks.

They could not get as far north as they had hoped owing to new snow slowing down the dogs. They had only gone a third of the distance when, after a week or so of struggling to get north, the hunters left them and headed off to hunt polar bear.

The expedition then decided to retrace their steps over the sea ice. The new snow slowed progress with the pulks and things were not turning out as planned, particularly in a storm when a fly-sheet was blown away and two expedition members spent a grim several hours in a 30mph gale at –20°C wrapped in the inner of a Quasar. Miraculously, they later found the fly-sheet wrapped round a rock a few hundred yards away. But the new snow had also frustrated the hunters who shortly returned down the coast; when they offered the expedition a lift it was gladly accepted. This was not quite the reflection of Knud Rasmussen's expedition of the same name that the members had undoubtedly hoped for, but they felt it had been a tremendous opportunity to spend time with Inuit hunters, who still travel and hunt largely as their forefathers.

Dennis Schmitt (USA) in September of 2005 led an expedition across the North Atlantic from Svalbard to NE Greenland.

An attempt was made to sail through the East Greenland ice pack at 78°N to land at Ile de France, in support of which the granddaughter of the French explorer Charcot was on the expedition's vessel, as well as the reigning Duke of Orleans. The attempt to make Ile de France failed, but an important discovery was made in East Greenland above 71°N on the Liverpool Land peninsula just outside NE Greenland National Park. Kap Gladstone has always been shown on maps as a peninsula linked to the mainland by a glacial isthmus. On 12 September 2005 it was discovered that the isthmus connecting Kap Gladstone to the mainland had disappeared and a new strait formed. The newly constituted island is 7km across and is significant because it appears to be a clear product of climate change.

150. The new strait adjacent to Kap Gladstone on the Liverpool Coast, seen from the north-west. (*Dennis Schmitt*)

The 'Danmarkekspedition', which took place 100 years ago in 1906-1908, aimed to fill in the last blanks on the NE Greenland map. The expedition succeeded, but paid a high price. Three of the participants, including the leader, Ludvig Mylius-Erichsen, died of hunger and the low temperatures.

In March 2006 Peter Wath (Denmark) set out from the weather station Danmarkshavn with an expedition cast in the traditional mould; six Danes and five native Greenlandic hunters from Qaanaaq and Illullissat, and 72 dogs! The Danish Crown Prince Frederik participated in part of the expedition, the purpose of which was to follow in the footsteps of the original and to make a tv-documentary series for the Danish Broadcasting Corporation. Peter Wath's expedition was air-lifted out from Station Nord nearly 70 days after leaving Danmarkshavn.

Finn Rasmussen and Erling Gai (Denmark) formed the 'Mylius-Erichsen Memorial Expedition 2006' and also celebrated the 100th anniversary of that famous early expedition. This was the sixth of a series of expeditions which have had a dual purpose. The first is to look for traces of The Independence I and II Inuit cultures and map, draw and photograph them. The second is to look for traces of the Danmarkekspedition of 1906-08, a sledge party from which vanished near 79 Fjord in late November 1907. Mylius-Erichsen, his cartographer and their scientific journals and personal diaries were never found. The current series of expeditions hopes to find these journals and diaries and perhaps solve the mystery of what happened in the cold and dark winter storms of 1907.

The 2005 expedition left Denmark on 27July and was taken out to Hagen

Whilst Dave Macleod's ascent of *The Hurting* attracted universal praise, the creation of Scotland's first bolt-protected winter sports route earlier in the season created a storm of controversy. *Crossroads* (M6) was added to the Upper Tier on Beinn Udlaidh in the Southern Highlands in December 2004, when it was equipped and then led by Scott Muir. From a traditional standpoint, placing bolts to protect a Scottish winter climb is the ultimate sin, and the route brought howls of protest.

In other parts of the world bolts are often used to protect mixed routes, but in Scotland there has always been a strong desire to maximise the adventure and uncertainty when climbing on our relatively small crags. As a result, Scottish winter climbers tend to have excellent on-sight mountaineering skills, whilst the technical difficulty of our hardest climbs are several notches easier than the top-end mixed and dry tool climbs in North America and on the Continent. Scott, who has extensive experience of climbing Continental mixed routes, argues that for Scottish climbing to catch up we need to start developing bolt-protected sports-style winter routes.

Scott Muir is a man of conviction and showed great courage in going against established tradition by placing bolts in Beinn Udlaidh. From a diversity perspective it seems perfectly reasonable to create bolt-protected winter routes for those that want to climb them, but there are a number of important issues that need to be taken into account. Firstly there are the arguments about damage to the environment and stealing opportunities from future generations, but the greatest concern is that bolts will erode the on-sight ethic that many believe to be inherent to Scottish winter climbing.

The future of *Crossroads* then lay with other climbers. If the route became popular and attracted repeat ascents it would have paved the way for other bolt-protected winter routes throughout the Highlands. Alternatively, if the bolts were removed and not replaced, the climb would cease to exist, and would be remembered as an interesting diversion in the long and varied history of Scottish climbing. In the event, the bolts were removed later that summer. No other bolt-protected routes have been developed since, and the traditional Scottish ethic of placing gear as you go has been preserved, for the time being at least.

The third stand-out route was climbed in early March 2005 during the International Winter Meet. These meets are held every other year at Glenmore Lodge and are jointly hosted by the BMC and MC of S. Last year more than 40 guests from 25 different countries were hosted by 30 British climbers and the event coincided with the finest winter climbing conditions of the season. Dozens of excellent routes were climbed during the meet, but the clear stand-out route was the first ascent of *Extasy* (VIII, 8) on Creag Meagaidh by Dave Hesleden and Bruno Sourzac from France. This put to bed one of Scotland's last great problems – the huge 300m unclimbed wall between *Smith's Gully* and *The Fly*.

Dave had tried this line 11 years earlier, but had ground to a halt after the first pitch. Since then the climb had been talked about by several activists,

151. Bruno Sourzac on the first ascent of *Extasy* (VIII, 8), Creag Meagaidh. (*Dave Hesleden*)

with some saying that the blank nature of the rock meant that it would not be possible to protect without using bolts. Hesleden and Sourzac had no intention of using bolts, of course, and it was no surprise to hear that the seven-pitch climb was very steep on typically bold Meagaidh mixed terrain, and that five of the seven pitches merited a technical grade of 8. These statistics alone suggest that *Extasy* is the most difficult and sustained Scottish first ascent ever to be climbed on sight, and in my view is arguably the most important new route since Brian Davison's ascent of *Mort* on Lochnagar five years before. Hesleden and Sourzac are no strangers to top end mixed climbing. Dave is renowned for his skill climbing thin ice and Bruno is one of the world's finest mountaineers. As chief instructor at ENSA in Chamonix, he is the guide that trains the guides, and three days before, on the first day of the meet, he had demonstrated his consummate skill by leading *Cornucopia* (VII, 9) as his first ever Scottish winter route.

My enthusiasm for this ascent contrasts strongly with other commentators who maintain that standards of traditionally climbed winter routes have not advanced since the 1980s, and *Extasy* has been singled out for particular criticism. The challenge is that the technical difficulties on *Extasy* were well within the capabilities of many climbers operating in the 1980s and the climb was simply overlooked at the time. With five pitches of sustained grade 8 with only token protection, I don't believe this claim is true; but it wasn't the technical difficulty of *Extasy* that caught the popular imagination.

Unlike the majority of the difficult 1980s routes that were climbed after multiple attempts, summer inspections or by using aid, *Extasy* was climbed ground up and on sight. This is in stark contrast to today's cutting edge routes such as *The Hurting*, which may be technically two or three grades harder than *Extasy*, but have relied upon tactics such as pre-inspection, abseiling the route and cleaning out gear placements for success. The majority of winter climbers can relate to routes climbed in perfect style such as *Extasy*, because this is exactly how they go climbing – walk up to the bottom of the crag, get the gear out and climb the route.

New routes are often used as the gauge for progress in mountaineering, however sometimes second ascents are made in such outstanding style that they take on special significance. Guy Robertson and Pete Benson's repeat of *The Steeple* (IX, 9) on the Shelter Stone Crag was such a climb, and illustrates how standards have also advanced on long and technically demanding routes. The first winter ascent of *The Steeple* fell to Alan Mullin and Steve Paget in a 24-hour push in November 1999. It was an outstanding piece of mountaineering but the climb was marred by two points of aid and the early season nature of the ascent was severely criticised. A clean second ascent in full winter conditions therefore stood out as one of the great prizes of Scottish winter climbing. After a series of blizzards in early March 2006 the high Cairngorms crags were draped in fresh snow, which prompted Robertson and Benson to have a look.

'Conditions were generally superb,' Guy told me. 'There was good snow-ice in places and the turf was like toffee. There was lots of snow and every crack, niche and crevice was utterly blootered with the stuff. Overall it felt very wintry.' Robertson and Benson completed the route in an astonishing 12 hours and finished just as light was fading. They started up the gully and 'fine corner' of the original line of *Postern*, then went right to the Terrace and up the summer crux of *Needle*. They continued up *The Steeple* 'layback cracks', climbed the big *Steeple Corner* in a single pitch and finished up the '5a wall cracks'. The 250m-long route had two pitches each of 7, 8 and 9 and the *Steeple Corner* was led in a single 45m pitch by Benson. The 5a wall cracks provided the second crux and the only flaw to the ascent was when Robertson dangled momentarily from an axe leash round his neck when his right tool ripped whilst he was pulling onto the slab above the final crack. Fortunately the left tool held. 'What a feeling,' Guy enthused, 'locked off in the final corner, the last gear out of sight, pummelling desperately at a foot and a half of rime ice, the wind howling like a Banshee in my face and 1000ft of air snapping at my feet! I was completely blown away by this route, and I doubt I'll experience the like again. The length, difficulty, variety and majesty of the big Shelter Stone routes are simply unparalleled!'

There are many new route possibilities in the Northern Highlands, but a winter ascent of *Pobble*, a summer VS on Lord Reay's Seat on Foinaven, was a clear target. The 160m-high route takes a series of chimneys up the centre of the crag, and had been eyed up by several winter teams over the years. Foinaven lies in the remote far north and does not hold winter conditions well, but it can be a very difficult mountain to reach when the roads are covered in snow. Malcolm Bass and Simon Yearsley had tried the route in November 2004 but had found mounds of graupel below the crag with a totally black buttress above. 'This time the forecast proved too much of a mid-week temptation,' Simon explained. 'Conditions were predicted to be ideal with heavy snow fall, then continuous snow showers during the day to top up the snow cover on the crag which is east-facing and quickly stripped by the morning sun.'

After an epic drive, involving blocked roads and disintegrating snow chains, they left the car at 5.30am, cycled along the approach track and then used snow shoes for the ascent to the crag. They started climbing by 10am, reached the summit at 9pm and finally made it back to the road by 3.30am after 22 hours on the move. 'The route packs a real punch,' Simon explained, 'with a superb mix of strenuous yet helpful chimneys, and technical delicate slabs, finishing on the very summit of Lord Reay's Seat.' Overall the route came in at a sustained VII, 7, with one pitch of technical 6 and five pitches of technical 7. In common with other Yearsley-Bass ascents, this route was the result of imaginative planning and dogged persistence, and the style of their ascent drew many favourable comments from a cross-section of Scottish winter activists. It just goes to show that it's not always cutting edge technical ascents that provide the greatest inspiration.

GEOFF HORNBY

Oman & United Arab Emirates 2004-2006

The SW face of **Jabal Misht** is possibly the most accessible part of this broad and fantastic mountain. It provides a beautiful face that was breached at its left end by the Italians Mario Manica and Antonella Cicogna to give *Via Tindetinix*, 400m TD VI. This route takes the obvious corner system left of the Precht route *Waterworld* to a finish up a steep headwall. Geoff Hornby and friends added two further new routes to this. First with Susie Sammut and Mark Turnbull he added *Sorely Misht*, 500m and D sup, then with Paul Knott he opened a new 500m route entitled *Mishts of Time* at D and V.

Hornby and Knott's biggest contribution to the 2005 season was a new direct route cutting through the original Howard route on the SE pillar. The Howard route avoided the bottom half of the face by scrambling up a low angled ridgeline and then traversing into the face a half height. *Palestine* climbs the lower wall at the right edge of the main face and then crosses the Howard route to climb a beautiful water-worn groove through the upper face (750m TD 5+).

Elsewhere on Misht, a Latvian team consisting of Normunds Lisovskis and Gatis Kalnins climbed a line up the central S face at 1000m and TD sup. However, their line seems to have taken a lot of common ground with the existing routes of Ramsden and Eastwood's *Threading the Needle* and Searle's *Original South Face*.

David Pickford and Andy Whittaker blew through Oman and made some interesting ascents. On Jabal Misht's SE face they linked together the Hornby/Wallis route *Intifada* with the Ramsden/Nonis route *Eastern Promise* and added a 100m finish up the tower on the summit ridge to provide *Inshalla Salam* at 1000m and UK E3 (ED VII+). This part of the face received another independent line up the wall left of the Ramsden, Eastwood and Chaudhry route *The Empty Quarter.* Climbed by Helli Gargitter and Pauli Trenkwalder, *Shukran* is a 1000m of ED VII, climbed in a day. It climbs a straight line up the wall to cross *The Empty Quarter* above the ledges at three quarter height and then finishes up the grooves immediately right of *The Empty Quarter*.

Jakob Oberhauser and Sepp Jochler put up another very impressive new route of the period. This pairing simul climbed much of the great central pillar line on the S face at V+ and pitched some steeper ground through the overhangs in the central section of the route. They think they must have climbed about 1500m of ground and have offered a grade of ED inf VI+. The route is named *Paradies Der Fakiere* after the incredibly sharp limestone that they encountered. The Al Jil face on Misht gave Oberhauser and Christine Zinner *Joy Without Shades,* 450m TD inf V+.

Jabal Misfah received an ascent by Knott and Hornby who both soloed an easy gully and ramp line on the SE face, left of the Sunburst, *Stairway to Heaven*, AD inf. Elsewhere on the W face, Hornby with Sammut and Turnbull put up *Salmana,* 300m D V+, up the slender pillar left of the white waterfall line.

Following many nights camped at the Hibshe oasis, Hornby has always had eyes for the triangular-shaped tower between the N end of the Kawr massif and the bulk of Jabal Misfah. The feature is known as **Jabal M'Saw**. Knott and Hornby climbed its N face following a beautiful line on white rock through the central depression before exiting right to gain the summit ridge. The summit was traversed to descend to the E and then back around from the N. *White Magic*, 570m and TD inf VI–, provided an excellent outing.

Above the village of K'Saw lie the needles of Asala and Asait. **Jabal Asala** has held the attention of the Austrians for some time and Oelz, Fankhauser, Brachmayer and Eisendle added further routes to the N face in *Stand Art*, 520m TD VI and to the West face in *Nashorn*, 445m TD sup VI+. *Nashorn* is regarded as an excellent route. Visiting French climber Alain Bruzy also added the 250m *Pied Rouge* at D sup V+.

Left

152. The 1000m SE face of Jabal Misht with selected routes shown. (*Paul Knott*)
 a *Icarus* (Littlejohn/Sustad 2001, E4 5c)
 b *The Empty Quarter* (Chaudhry/Eastwood/Ramsden 2000, E2 5a)
 c *Eastern Promise* (Nonis/Ramsden 1999, E2 5c)
 d *Intifada* (Hornby/Wallis 2001, E1/E2 5b)
 e *Palestine* (Hornby/Knott 2005, TD 5+)
 f *South East Pillar* (Howard/McDonald 1988, HVS 5a/b)

Jabal Asait still provides a succession of new routes. Hornby and Knott climbed the introductory wall beneath the E face to give *Buzzy Bee* at 200m and D, before climbing the 385m face above to provide *Arch Wall* at TD inf and V+. Left of *Arch Wall*, Hornby with Sammut and Turnbull added *Shamsa* at D sup V. Oberhauser, Zinner with Rudi Mayr and Magda Reischauer added a slanting line up the same face from right to left to finish close to the arch: *Sackgasse,* 350m and VI–. Manica and Cicogna repeated the Austro/British route *Internationale* on Asait's N ridge and confirmed the quality but thought that it was perhaps undergraded at TD sup and was somewhat longer than 500m.

West of Asait lies a complex series of walls and towers forming the eastern edge of Jabal Kawr and the buttress of Jabal Manzoob. **Torre Hibshe** lies on the Shumeila wall, immediately across the ravine left of the 'Gully Arete' of Jabal Karn Hamis, aka Manzoob East peak, climbed by Brian Davison, Hornby and Sammut at ED2 in 2002. The white wall of Hibshe first attracted the attention of Albert Precht who soloed a line up the left side of the slab at 350m and V+. In *AJ110* Hornby reported a new line up the central part of the slabs *Assilla*, TD inf 5+ exposed, which also ends on the shoulder of the peak. Subsequently the Austrian team of Oelz, Fankhauser, Brachmayer and Eisendle added *Langspielplatter*, 600m TD sup VI+, which finishes up the upper tower to the summit. Further up the ravine, the French team of Bruzy with F Salle added *Rosso Salente*, climbing the 450m pillar and tower of Jabal Zeek above in an excellent position at ED inf VI+.

The mighty S face of **Jabal Kawr** provides a number of routes up to 900m in length, predominantly climbed by Hornby and friends, all sporting long approaches and descents. As part of their mammoth traverse of Oman (see *AJ110*), Hornby, Sammut, Turnbull with David Wallis made the first ascent of the 400m high Rigma buttress. *Umbarak Pillar* is named in honour of Thesiger, and provides the easiest route on this section of the wall at D V+. SE of Kawr and in the shade below the hamlet of M'Seeb lies a beautiful 400m wall which Knott and Hornby named Jabal M'Seeb. The N face of this Jabal provides an excellent venue for exploratory rock climbing with Knott and Hornby adding the wall's first route *Juggernaut* D inf.

East of the Kawr massif lie the isolated towers of Al Hamra. Here, Bruzy and Salle climbed the E tower *Zizanie*, 250m TD VI+ and the W tower *Délivrance*, 200m TD sup VI+. To the E again, the Tanuf gorge gave Bruzy and Renaud *Al Faraj buttress,* 300m TD sup VI+. To the S of Muscat lies the Tiwi Canyon. This area has been a favourite for trekkers and provides a beautiful location for exploratory rock climbing. Bruzy with Salle and Standke added *Relais à trois* at 450m and TD VI, whilst on the Mibam cliff they added *Banane citron,* 250m ED inf VII+.

Pickford and Whittaker left Misht behind and travelled up to **Musandam**, where they explored the far side of the 1565m col on the interior side of the range. In Wadi A'Shwarga they climbed a tremendous arête of 400m length called *Pirates of Hormuz* at TD sup (E2 5b). Further up this wadi the pair then climbed a line up a buttress they named the Chicane Buttress via a 3-pitch route graded E6 6a, undoubtedly the hardest free climb in the region. The route is entitled *The Exile of Peshawar.*

In November 2005 Geoff Hornby organised a dhow to explore the coast of Musandam, to the North of Dibba, with a view to climbing new routes and exploring the scuba diving potential. They began by climbing the twin pillars in the bay of Dawhat Adas, probably the first piece of climbable rock N of Dibba. The L pillar gave Jon Lincoln and Nigel Murphy a 115m route at TD inf V+ called *Renate Anne*, whilst Hornby and David Barlow climbed the 210m pillar to the R at D sup V and called it *Mary Rose*. They then sailed N to explore the area around Dawhat Qabal and found many interesting pillars and walls. The prominent peak on the S coast of the bay is marked Jabal Khatamah (or Hatmah). On its N side there is a bay known as Osprey Bay. Above this bay, Lincoln and Murphy climbed a new route on a feature they named Torre Meghan. The 325m route followed wide grooves then corners and was named *The HB Snobs*, TD. In the next bay to the W, Barlow and Hornby climbed the left edge of a tower they named Torre Hurndall. The 300m climb followed a whitewater streak up a system of grooves on excellent rock at TD inf V and was named *Captain Sensible.*

In the Wadi Bih area of Musandam and the UAE, the big news is the production of the area's first guidebook by Alan Stark. The guide covers the areas spanning the Omani/UAE border of Wadis Bih, Louab and Ghalilah and the gorge above Dibba as well as other areas within the UAE. The guidebook is currently on a CD format and is available through alstark@blueyonder.co.uk. Later it will become a published document.

The big new route climbed in this area has always been admired from the UAE-accessible side of the range. Overlooking the machine gun posts of the old interior border post lies a huge N facing limestone pillar. The Swiss climbers Claude Redard and Pascal Sprungli finally solved the difficult logistics of accessing this pillar. Their route *Longue Vie Au Quatre*, loosely translated as *long life to 4th grade climbing*, is 830m long and TD inf. The route is sustained at grade 4 but with odd sections of 5 and a crux of 5+. They approached through Musandam via Khasab and left their vehicle 1km short of the border post. They climbed the pillar in nine hours. The long descent down the W ridge required a pair of abseils and then a nervy sneaking past the machine gun posts and spotlights in the dark. Elsewhere, Hornby with Barlow and Lincoln added another 200m route to the Shadow Wall area. *Shadow of the Wind,* TD VI, takes the smooth looking wall left of the Hornby / Sammut route *Shadow Boxing.*

Recent developments have potentially altered the positions of the Omani border posts, bringing the Omani post further down Wadi Bih and closer to the actual UAE border post. The UAE post is also now closed to non-nationals. It seems unlikely that UAE-based climbers will be able to access the upper reaches of Wadi Bih in the near future. However, it makes the Swiss route *Longue Vie Au Quatre* fully accessible from the Musandam side.

The following information was received too late for the main report. Routes shorter than 150m have not been included.

MISFAH

Jakob Oberhauser and Sepp Jochler added *Afternoon Stroll* on the S face, 400m VI.

NIZWA TOWERS

JO & SJ added *Rasstag*, 250m VI+ (TD), to the 2nd Tower.

JO, Christine Zinner, Magda Reischauer, Rudi Mayer added *Orgasmus*, 250m VI+ (TD) to the Second Tower.

JO and Brian Davison added *Razor Arete*, 150m 5+ (TD inf) to the First Tower.

AL HAMRA TOWERS

West Tower, Jabal Fokha: *Zick Zack Weg*, 300m VII– (TD Sup). JO, CZ, MR, RM.

Middle Tower: *Nageleinriss*, 300m VI+ (TD). JO, SJ.

JABAL ASAIT

E face, *Stop Smoking*, 350m VI– (TD) . JO, Sigi Brachmayer, Wolfgang Thomaseth, Oswald Oelz.

JABAL ASALA: NW face

Asala Geier, 500m VI+ (TD Sup). JO, SJ.

WADI MUAHEDIN

Mondscheinsonate, 1500m VI+ (TD Sup). JO, SJ.

WADI BANI AUF

These guys went crazy adding numerous new routes. Here are the ones over 200m in length:

Snake Gorge *I've lost a friend*, 200m VI+ (TD Sup). JO, Martin Rannger.
Stachelschwein, 200m VI– (TD). JO, Franz Siedler.
Hangover, 250m VI+ (TD Sup). JO, CZ.
Turnschuh, 300m V; *Colour Line*, 300mV+; *Fantastica*, 250m V+. All by JO, Sigi B, Wolfgang T, Oswald O. All TD inf.
S'Zahnburstl, 250m VI+ (TD Sup). JO, SB.
Holraumsauser, 250m VI+ (TD Sup). JO, SJ.

Elsewhere in Wadi Bani Auf

Fluchthornuberschreitung 700m IV– (D). JO, SJ.
Traverse of Jabal Jaru, 2000m, including 1 pitch of VI. JO, SJ, Martin Rannger, Franz Siedler. Ungradable.

HARISH KAPADIA

India 2005

Overall, 46 foreign and 47 Indian expeditions climbed in the Indian Himalaya during the year. This was a lower figure than normal. Amongst the foreign expeditions, more that half climbed the usual peaks like Kun, Kedar Dome, and Nun. Many expeditions faced bad weather in mid-September and some had to give up owing to poor snow and ice conditions in early October. Amongst the high peaks attempted, Changabang and Kamet, now open for foreigners, and Nanda Devi East were important ascents.

Many expeditions complained of problems in Uttaranchal State, where the Government has imposed a stiff new climbing fee structure. There also seems to be much confusion regarding approach routes (only nominated approach routes are allowed), various permits (forest department, Government of Uttaranchal and IMF) and the permit procedures (from various authorities at Dehra Dun, Delhi and locally). This dampened much of the climbing enthusiasm for many.

Of the 47 Indian expeditions, many were to routine peaks. There were attempts on peaks in Spiti, like Khangla Tarbo and Yunam in Lahaul and Sanakdank Jot. And there were attempts on difficult peaks like Papsura. However, the tragic news was the death of several Indian mountaineers. In a major accident, Dr P M Das with Inder Kumar and Ms Nari Dhami died on the peak of Chomoyummo with two Sherpas (see Sikkim report). In another expedition for which unfortunately no reports are available, five men from the Air Defence Regiment are reported to have died on peak Chaukhamba I. On an IMF ladies' expedition to Papsura, one of their members, Malabi Das, collapsed and died at the high camp after reaching the summit. Along with two porters who died on the Gangotri glacier, these brought the total number of deaths in the Indian Himalaya this year to 13 – a disproportionately high number. Though an active year, it was marred by tragedies and covered by more attempts on easier peaks than on challenging ones. In a seminar towards the end of the year it was suggested that some organized rescue facilities and accident insurance should be made available, that satellite phones and GPS should be encouraged and the entire fee structure revamped. But no one knows when this will be done.

The IMF elected a new President, H P S Ahluwalia in November for a term of two years. Major Ahluwalia, who climbed to the summit of Everest in 1965, is an experienced mountaineer and organizer and he leads a newly elected team of the Governing Council at the IMF.

ARUNACHAL PRADESH

In Search of the Old Pilgrimage Route to Takpa Siri

In remote and rarely visited Arunachal Pradesh, much remains to be explored. One such area was the valley of the Subansiri river in central Arunachal. A team from Mumbai (Harish Kapadia, Wing Commander PK Sashindran, Ms Sangeetha Sashindran and Prateek Deo) explored this unique area as one of the first civilian teams to be allowed there. They followed the ancient pilgrimage route of Takpa Siri.

The Takpa Siri mountain, also known as the 'Crystal mountain' is holy to the Tibetans, Monpas and Tagins of Arunachal Pradesh. A pilgrimage was undertaken every 12 years, starting from Chosam in Tibet. It followed the Tsari Chu valley till its junction with the Subansiri river and then went up the Subansiri river valley till Taksing. From here the route turned north along the Yume Chu. The pilgrimage would end at the holy Yume Gompa (monastery). This longer version of pilgrimage, called 'Ringkor', was undertaken over a three-month period and several thousand pilgrims passed on this route, staying in caves and bamboo shelters, which were called 'Tsukang'. The local people stocked these shelters with food and wood for pilgrims who passed through this challenging and difficult route. The Tagins, who stay in the Upper Subansiri valley, were paid yearly tributes by the Tibetans of Longju, and a special large tribute to help this pilgrimage every 12th year. Today, the pilgrimage has stopped at the McMahon Line or Line of Actual Control (LAC) which divides Takpa Siri and the valleys of Arunachal Pradesh. The pilgrim route at Maja enters the Indian territory and from Taksing, along the Yume Chu returns back towards China. Thus this fine tradition is now lost.

This team followed the Ringkor route on both sides, as much as possible from the Indian areas. From Guwahati, road travel of almost 850km was undertaken over four days, via Tezpur, Itanagar, Kimin, Ziro, Daporijo to reach Limiking, the starting point of the trek. The trek began across the first bridge, named after soldier Shere Thapa, with a 600m steep climb, which snaked its way up. At many places the Tagins had erected improvised local wooden ladders, over exposed areas, where a slip can drag you down the slope or into the river. After the climb was Tame Chung Chung (TCC, 'place of snakes'). From TCC the first exploration was along the Tsari Chu valley to Bidak, a little short of Maja, as ahead is Tibetan territory. Later the team explored the Subansiri valley to trek towards Taksing, the last village on the India side. From Taksing one can look towards the junction of the Chayal Chu and Yume Chu and the LAC. At the merging point of these two rivers, the Subansiri is formed which flows down to meet the Brahmaputra in the plains of Assam.

Early explorers such as FM Bailey and HT Morshead visited the area from Tibet and wrote about the pilgrimages around Takpa Siri. F Ludlow and later F Kingdon-Ward also undertook the pilgrimage and observed

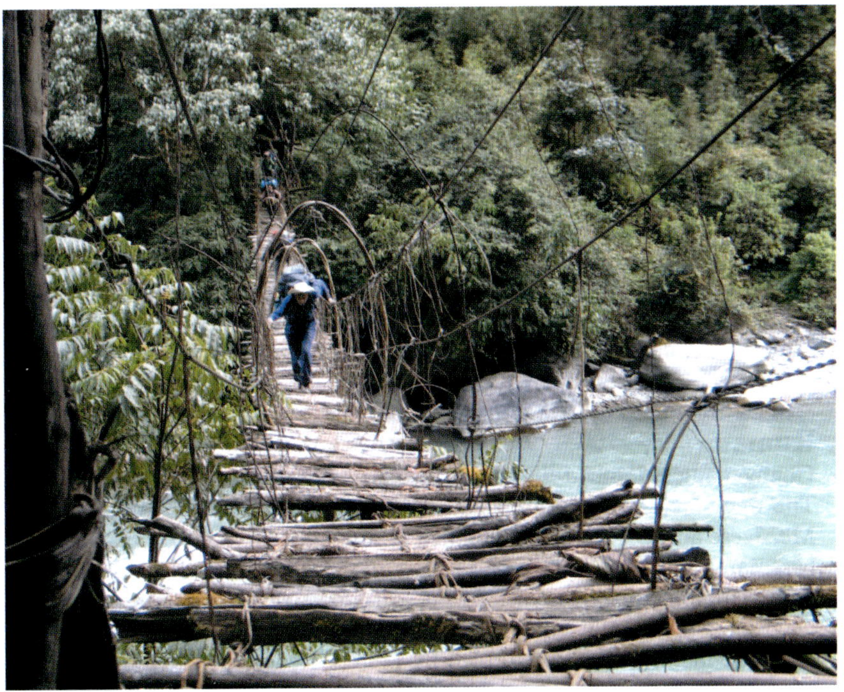

153. Bamboo suspension bridge on the Old Pilgrimage Route to Takpa Siri. (*Harish Kapadia collection*)

and wrote about the traditions and botany of these areas. In 1956, Tony Huber studied the pilgrimage in detail and wrote a thesis for his doctorate called *The Cult of the Pure Crystal Mountain* narrating details of route and various legends associated with it.

SIKKIM

Chomoyummo (6829m)

Situated in relatively unvisited North Sikkim, this peak was attempted by a high profile expedition of nine members, organised by The Indian Mountaineering Foundation and led by its Vice-President Dr PM Das. The team included two Everest summiters and four experienced Sherpas. The party was caught in an avalanche while attempting the summit. Five climbers died, while two survived with serious injuries. The climbers who perished were: Dr Das, Inder Kumar, Ms Nari Dhami (these latter two had summited Everest), Dawa Sherpa and Dawa Wangchuk, Sherpas from the Sonam Gyasto Mountaineering School at Gangtok. Details are sketchy as all the leading members died on the mountain.

Dr Das, as well as being the Vice-President of the IMF, was Hon Local Secretary of the Himalayan Club for Punjab. Hailing from Guwahati,

In the Panmah Muztagh two Spanish teams attempted **Baintha Brakk** (aka 'The Ogre', 7285m). Members included accomplished Basque mountaineers such as Jon Beloki, Alberto Iñurrategi and Jose Carlos Tamayo but both teams recorded failures on the south pillar and *Original British Route*.

The Benegas brothers, Damian and Willie, with fellow Argentinean Matias Erroz were back for another attempt on the highly desirable north spur of **Latok I** (7145m). While they failed low down on this, they did manage to achieve other ascents on lower neighbouring peaks. They climbed the Supercouloir on a c6000m peak on the northern rim of the Choktoi glacier, a little to the right of Biacherahi Towers. This was a 1000m-high 55° névé couloir leading to the summit ridge, on which the pair was stopped 60m below the top by a rock barrier for which they were not prepared. They completed the original line of the *Indian Face Arête* to the summit at 5.10a and A1. This route was first climbed by Sandy Allan and Doug Scott in 1990 but they stopped about six pitches below the summit. The Argentineans also climbed a couple of c10-pitch rock routes at around 5.10 on formations close to base camp.

In the Baltoro, the Trango Group saw huge amounts of activity and some high notable ascents. Jonathon Clearwater (New Zealand), Jeremy Frimer (Canada) and Samuel Johnson (USA) climbed the south-west ridge of **Trango II** (6327m), the major snow-capped peak immediately north of Trango Monk. The 1600m route was named *Severance Ridge* and graded VI 5.11 A2 AI 3 M5. The three spent five days on an alpine-style ascent of 63 pitches but traversed some 150m below the highest point of the snow cap to find a descent route down the south ridge, leaving the summit unclimbed. On 6251m **Trango Tower** several parties attempted *Eternal Flame* and the now standard line of the *Slovenian Route*. On the south-east face, between the *Slovenian Route* and *Run for Cover*, a Korean team engineered a new route, which they christened *The Crux Zone* (A4). This completed a new start, pioneered in 2004, above the approach couloir. Fixed ropes were used throughout but the team completed their line to the highest point of the tower.

Eniko and Iker Pou, together with photographer/journalist Jabi Baraiazarra, climbed *Eternal Flame* to the summit. Their idea was to complete the ascent all free, so they established a line of fixed ropes up much of the route so they could work some of the pitches. In 2003 Denis Burdet free climbed the entire route except for one bolt ladder on pitch 10. The Pou brothers managed to create a variation to this pitch by linking two cracks to the right. The first part, climbed completely free by Iker, was hard. The upper section was only 6c, but because it was wet the Spaniard could not climb it without rests. They estimate it to be 8a. Unfortunately, time did not allow them to free climb the two hard pitches (7a and 7c+) freed by Burdet, but they have proved that a strong climber, finding good conditions, can make an all free ascent.

The major event in the Trango Group was Gabo Cmarik and Dodo Kopold's alpine-style ascent of a new line on the south side of **Great Trango** (6286m), right of the 2004 American route, *Azeem Ridge*. They carried minimal gear, found difficulties harder than expected and endured a very unpleasant bivouac high on the route without sleeping bags in poor weather and the temperature down to –15°C. They reached the summit ridge of the c6250m south-west top on their seventh day, having climbed more than 3000m of rock (*Assalam Alaikum*; 90 pitches; VIII and A2). Unable to reverse the standard route to the Trango approach couloir due to large quantities of fresh snow (the traverse to the couloir can be very avalanche prone), they made a quite remarkable decision to rappel the huge north-west face. For this they had only their rack, five pitons, and eight remaining bolts to make c60 rappels. They rappelled the c2000m face from right to left, crossing through the Russian, American and German routes, taking a couple of serious falls and having a generally epic time before finally reaching base camp.

In the meantime the rest of their team, when not worrying about the safety of this bold pair of young climbers, had been busy themselves. Andrej Kolárik and Erik Rabatin climbed *Mystical Demno* (1400m of climbing, with 34 pitches up to VII+ and A2) to the left of the 2000 Copp-Pennings line, *Tague it to the Top* on the SSE face of **Hainabrakk East** (c5650m). Close by, Igor Koller, Vlado Linek and Juraj Podbradski tried to complete a line on the far right side of the south-east face of **Shipton Spire** that they had attempted in 2004. They completed the route to the notch on the north-east ridge and junction with *Ship of Fools*, from where Koller and Linek made a spirited attempt to reach the summit. Over very difficult ice and mixed ground where they were hit by successive storms, they managed to reach a point 80m below the summit but were thwarted by dangerous snow conditions. *Prisoners of the Shipton* (not to summit) was rated VIII A3 WI 5+.

On the flanks of Great Trango above the Dunge glacier rises the **Trango Pulpit** (6050m), sporting a huge precipitous wall that until last year had only been breached by a Norwegian team in 1999. Sam Beaugey, Martial Dumas, Jean-Yves Fredriksen and Yann Mimet added a second route to the left, climbing for around 17 days in capsule style to create *Azazel* (1500m; VII A3+ M6 WI 4 6a). To say all four completed the route is untrue: three pitches below the top Sam Beaugey donned a winged suit, sized up the prospects of clipping the midway terrace, and launched for a BASE jump. Less than a minute later he was back on the Dunge glacier, where he had to wait three full days for his mates to summit, strip the route and return to base camp.

North of the Baltoro there was a rare attempt on the **Muztagh Tower** (7284m). The original aim was a new line on the imposing north face but when this proved impossible under the conditions, an attempt was made to climb the unrepeated *1956 route* on the south-east ridge. On the last try Bruce Normand (a Scot living in Switzerland) and Philippe Oberson (Swiss) reached an altitude of c6300m, above the great sérac before avalanche conditions forced a retreat. During the expedition, members had made ascents of **Pt 5850m, Pt 6001m** (Tsetse on the Swiss map), and **Pt 6345m** on the Biange-Godwin Austen divide, all possibly first ascents.

On the unclimbed **Savoia Kangri** (aka Summa Ri, 7263m), just west of K2, a Japanese expedition failed at 6300m on the south face, following the couloir climbed by the 1998 British expedition (which reached 7000m on the mountain, the high point to date).

No one summited K2 last year and there is little of interest to report on the neighbouring 8000m peaks except for a most notable new route on **Broad Peak** (8047m). Kazakhstan mountaineers Sergey Samoilov and his partner, currently very much the 'man of the moment', Denis Urubko, made a remarkable alpine-style ascent of the previously unclimbed 2500m south-west face. The pair took six days and on the lower section overcame two steep rock barriers with difficulties up to F6b A2 and M5. At c7400m they were forced onto some rocky ribs, which gave a section estimated to be M6+. The south-east ridge was gained in strong winds and the pair followed the crest over the summit to descend the *Normal Route.*

The Hushe region was again popular with many teams operating in the Charakusa and Nangma valleys. Running north from the Charakusa is the Chogolisa glacier and there a team of strong Italian rock-climbers put up some impressive routes on peaks below 6000m. Hervé Barmasse, Ezio Marlier and Fabio Salini climbed the north face of virgin **Pk 5500m**, via a line they named *Fast and Furious* (700m; V/4, A1). They stopped 10m below the highest point. Two routes were added to **Raven's Peak** (c5300m) above the Beusten glacier. The eight-pitch *Green Tea* was 6b and A1 but the 16-pitch *Up and Down*, on the left and steepest part of the south face, was more demanding. Barmasse, Cristian Brenna, Francesca Chenal and Luca Maspes climbed it using fixed ropes at 6c/6c+ and A1, placing some bolts where necessary in view of a possible future free ascent. This wasn't long coming. Less than two weeks later Brenna climbed it all free in one day at 7c. With a number of other pitches of 7a and 7b, *Up and Down* is a good contender for one of the most difficult free routes in the Karakoram.

Gianluca Bellin and Giovanni Ongaro made the 'first ascent' of the 5500m **Capucin** (originally nicknamed 'The Dru' by Pat Littlejohn and Mick Hardwick, who made the first ascent of Raven's Peak). They climbed the south face (400m; 6b and A2), though it is not clear whether they reached the summit or stopped on the ridge below. Finally, Barmasse and Giovanni Pagnoncelli climbed the north-west face of an unnamed and previously virgin c6000m peak on the long west ridge of **Farol** (only Barmasse reached the highest point). The 1000m route had ice up to 60°. This may be the same as the '**Fiona Peak'** marked on the 2005 Polish sketch map.

Farol Central (c6350m) received its first ascent courtesy of Cedric Haehlen and Hans Mitterer from Germany. The pair climbed the long south pillar at VI A1 M6/M7, avoiding the first big rock buttress via a snow

155. Namika (6325m) rises above the south bank of the Charakusa glacier, close to the point where the Chogolisa glacier flows down from the north. Being below 6500m, the peak is now officially permit free but received its first ascent back in the late 1980s by a British party. (*Luca Maspes collection*)

couloir to the left, which brought them to the crest at around 5600m. They bivouacked once and from the summit made an exciting descent of the snow face to the west, rappelling between séracs and the pillar. They found no trace of any previous passage. Mitterer also joined Canadian Raphael Slawinski and American Steve Swenson for an attempt on the unclimbed **Hassin Peak** (c6300m) on the eastern rim of the Charakusa glacier, north of K6. They had one bivouac but retreated from 6000m when the summit snow slopes became too dangerous to continue. Slawinski and Swenson later attempted **Farol Far East** (aka Righthand Farol peak, c6200m) via a fine-looking goulotte. They enjoyed some intricate climbing before reaching a blank granite headwall. This peak is thought to be unclimbed, though a French team got close in 2004 via a line in the same vicinity as the Slawinski-Swenson attempt. Other parties in the area repeated some of the now quasi-classic routes on peaks such as **Nayser Brakk**.

In the Nangma only one new route has come to light at the time of writing. Polish climbers Jan Kuczera and Tomasz Polok climbed the south-west pillar of the final (lowest) tower on the south-west ridge of **Changi Tower**'s east summit. They called this c5000m formation **Barasa** or Changi Peak. Their route was 500-550m high, sometimes slabby with no protection and graded VII. They named it *Moonlight Pillar*.

DICK ISHERWOOD

Nepal 2005

I am indebted to Elizabeth Hawley, Lindsay Griffin, Bruce Normand, Oliver von Rotz, and Ueli Steck for information included in these notes.

Continuing political unrest in Nepal ensured that the overall pattern of mountaineering activity seen in recent years continued in 2005. Many parties went to Everest, Cho Oyu, the other 8000m peaks and Ama Dablam, but relatively few to the more outlying areas, and several of these encountered Maoist rebels, usually demanding money.

The spring season on **Everest** was marked by unusually bad weather and by forecasts that seem to have been further off the mark than usual. Out of no less than 101 groups, only 53 were successful, compared to 54 out of 64 in spring 2004. It is perhaps a sign of the times that a 50% success rate on the world's highest mountain is considered unusually poor. Most summit climbs were made in very late May or early June, two or three weeks later than the normal peak traffic time. Of these, 21 were made by the original *South Col* route and 32 by the *North Col*; there were no new routes. A Czech party attempted the *Japanese Couloir* but retreated from 7100m. The single autumn attempt was unsuccessful – no one has climbed Everest in the post-monsoon season since 2002.

In the category of comic firsts on Everest, two Nepalese were married on the summit and a South African became the first black person to climb it twice, while the mountain also saw its first Mongolian, Bhutanese, Montenegran and Muslim female ascents. Apa Sherpa climbed it for the 15th time and continues to regard Everest as just a well-paying job. A French helicopter pilot claimed to have landed his Ecureil on the summit and even got out for the view; this got him into some trouble with the Nepalese Government.

Alan Hinkes reported an ascent of **Kangchenjunga** by the original *Yalung Face* route to complete his fourteen 8000ers, and was rewarded by the British Ambassador with a garden party. However, what is good enough for HM Diplomatic Corps is not always good enough for the climbing community and some doubt has been cast on whether he reached the top. Of course no one steps on the actual summit of Kangchenjunga.

Of the other 8000m peaks, **Cho Oyu** had nine pre-monsoon and 37 post-monsoon ascents, mostly from Tibet. **Dhaulagiri** had four ascents by its NE ridge, and several failures, mainly in the spring. **Annapurna** was climbed once, by a multinational party on its N face, which included Ed Veisturs

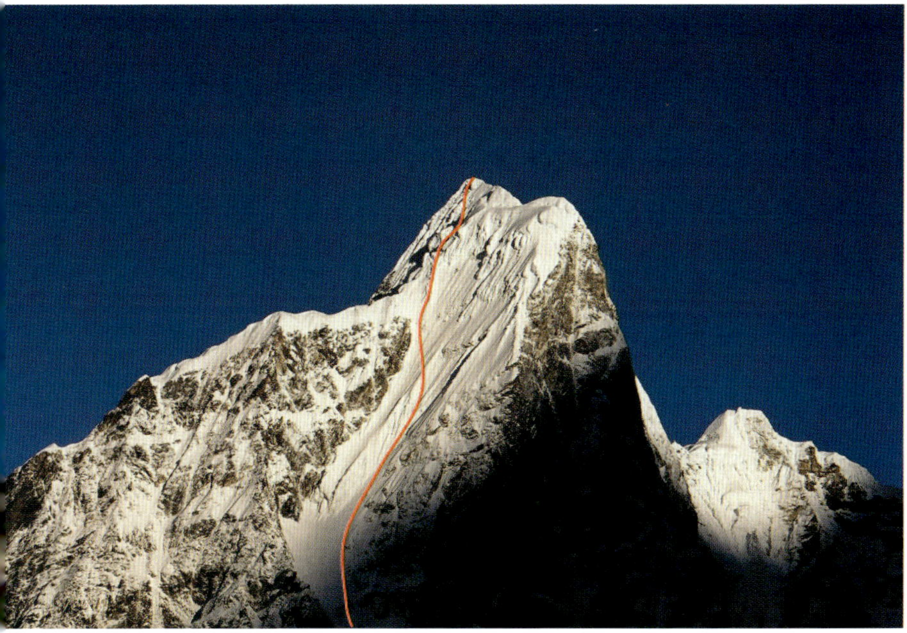

156. Ueli Steck's route on the south-east face of Taweche. (*Ueli Steck*)

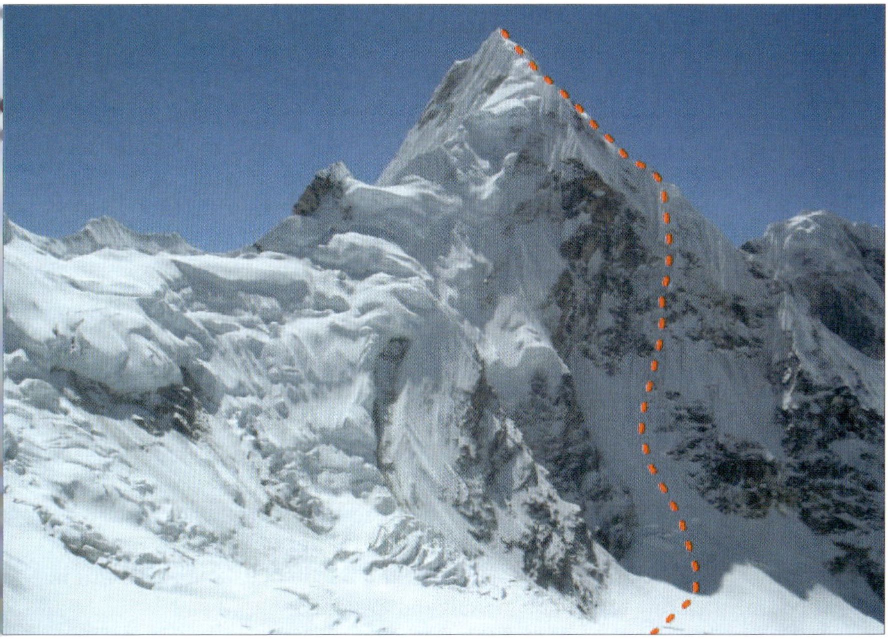

157. The west face of Drangnag Ri. (*Oliver von Rotz*)

who thereby also completed his set of 8000m peaks. On the same expedition a fall of ice killed Christian Kuntner and injured Abele Blanc, both of whom were also on their final 'achtausender'. A Spanish expedition reached 7600m on the W Pillar of Makalu in the spring. In Tibet Ralf Djumovits, Gerlinde Kaltenbrunner and Hirotaka Takeuchi made the first south to north traverse of Shisha Pangma. They reached the main summit on 7 May via the SW face (*British route*) and descended the normal north side route with four bivouacs in total.

In the Phu Khola area north of the Annapurnas a Japanese party climbed **Gyajikang (7038m)** by a possibly new route on its SW ridge. In the autumn this area was sadly the scene of the worst climbing disaster to date in the Nepal Himalaya. A French party of seven climbers and eleven Nepalese employees were killed on **Kangguru (6981m)** when a powder snow avalanche struck their base camp. This peak had only had one fatality in 27 previous attempts, and the camp was apparently placed in the usual site. Not much Himalayan climbing is risk free.

Several more technical climbs were done on lower peaks. Two Korean climbers made the first winter ascent of the N face of **Cholatse (6440m)** in January 2005 by a very steep variant to a previous French route. They had three bivouacs on the ascent, and both were injured and severely frostbitten after a fall into a bergschrund low down on the descent. Ueli Steck climbed another extremely steep variant on this face solo in April, carrying a mere 6 kilos, and taking 37 hours with two bivouacs. The route, a direct finish to the French 1995 route, was graded F5, M6, with 90 degree ice in places. He also soloed the SE face of **Taweche (6501m)** in a largely nocturnal nine-hour round trip in late April. For these achievements he was nominated for the 2005 Piolet d'Or award, though in the end he didn't win. A six-person Korean team climbed the SW face of **Lobuje West (6145m)**, also in April, using some fixed rope on rock up to grade 5.8.

In the Rolwaling valley Bruce Normand and Paul Hartmann climbed the W face of **Drangnag Ri (6801m)** on 9-10 May. The route involved steep ice climbing to WI5 with brief mixed passages. Normand soloed the upper SW ridge from a bivouac as Hartmann was unable to continue due to cramp. This was a new route and probably only the second ascent of the mountain. Normand and other members of his Swiss-based expedition team also made the first official ascent of **Chekigo (6257m)** by a direct route on the W face from a camp on the Menlung La.

Andrej Stremfelj and Miha Haban climbed **Dzanye (6870m)** in the area NW of Kangchenjunga in the autumn season but were forced to retreat from their main objective, the S face of the unclimbed **Janak (7044m)** in the same area due to heavy snowfall and avalanches.

Also in the autumn season, John Roskelley and his son Jess attempted a ridge on the NE (Tibetan) side of **Gauri Shankar (7134m)** but retreated from around 5450m on very loose rock.

JOHN TOWN

China & Tibet 2005

Qonglai

Yasushi Yamanoi of Japan made a solo first ascent on the North Wall of **Potala** in the Siguniang area, reached from the Shuangqiaoguo valley. The route, 'Jiayou', 850m, consisted of 18 pitches at 5.8 A3+.

A Swiss expedition made what is probably the first ascent of **Eagle Rock Peak (c5300m)** via the S face, 700m 7a/A3. Christof Looser, Martin Ruggli and Lukas Durr reached the summit on 14 October. During the same period an American team consisting of Chad Kellogg and four others spent five weeks in the Qonglai mountains. They climbed the west peak of **Luotou (5666m)** before attempting a line to the right of the Fowler/Ramsden route on the NW face of **Siguniang**. Bad weather forced a retreat and they moved to the Chiwen gorge. Here they climbed the north ridge of the **'Angry Wife' (5005m)**, which lies on the ridge north-west of Celestial Peak (5413m). They then crossed into the Shuangqiaoguo valley before climbing the rocky tower of **Daoquo (5466m)** whose headwall provided sustained 5.10 climbing on excellent granite, leading to fragile climbing on the summit block.

Tommy Chandler and three companions visited the nearby Bipeng valley, making an ascent of the NW buttress of **Peak 5202**.

Daxue Shan

In September 2005 a British expedition consisting of Dick Isherwood, Toto Gronlund, Peter Rowat and Dave Wynne-Jones attempted the unclimbed **Gonkala** peaks (5992m, 5928m) near Garze in western Sichuan. The first of these is also known as **Kalawani (5992m)**. Their efforts were brought to an end by a party of 40 monks from the Khur Chong monastery who ordered them off the mountain. The group switched to **Haizi Shan (5833m)** but bad weather forced a retreat. (*See article 'A Cautionary Tale' p71.*)

Nearby, a Japanese expedition consisting of Toshihiko Furuhata and Kazumi Toya conducted a reconnaissance of **Gangga (5688m)** and neighbouring peaks, which lie south of Garze.

Sichuan/ Tibet Border

Two small teams were active in Sichuan in October 2005 in the Jarjinjabo area of the Shaluli Shan, based at the Zophu pasture. Both had ambitions of making the first ascent of **Xiashe (5833m)** but the prize fell to Karen McNeill of Canada and Pat Deavoll of New Zealand who reached the summit via the S face and SW ridge on 13 October after a four-day climb. Ed Douglas and Duncan Tunstall of the UK made the first ascent of the north face, reaching the summit on 16 October and then descending the west ridge in a five-day round trip. They named the line *Don't Cook Yak In Anger* indicating an appropriate degree of stiff upper lip. (*See article 'Xiashe North Face', p35.*)

Key to China/Tibet map

1 Qonglai Shan - Singuniang
2 Daxue Shan - Minya Konka
3 Batang - Dangchezhengla
4 Jarjinjabo
5 Meile Xue Shan - Kawa Karpo
6 Kangri Karpo
7 Nyainqentanglha East - Namla Karpo
8 Nyainqentanglha East - Sepu Kangri
9 Nyainqentanglha West - Samdain Kangsang
10 Nyainqentanglha West - Nyainqentanglha
11 Nganglong Kangri
12 Lunana Himal - Kangphu Gang
13 Chomolhari
14 Everest Region
15 Shisha Pangma
16 Kaqur Kangri

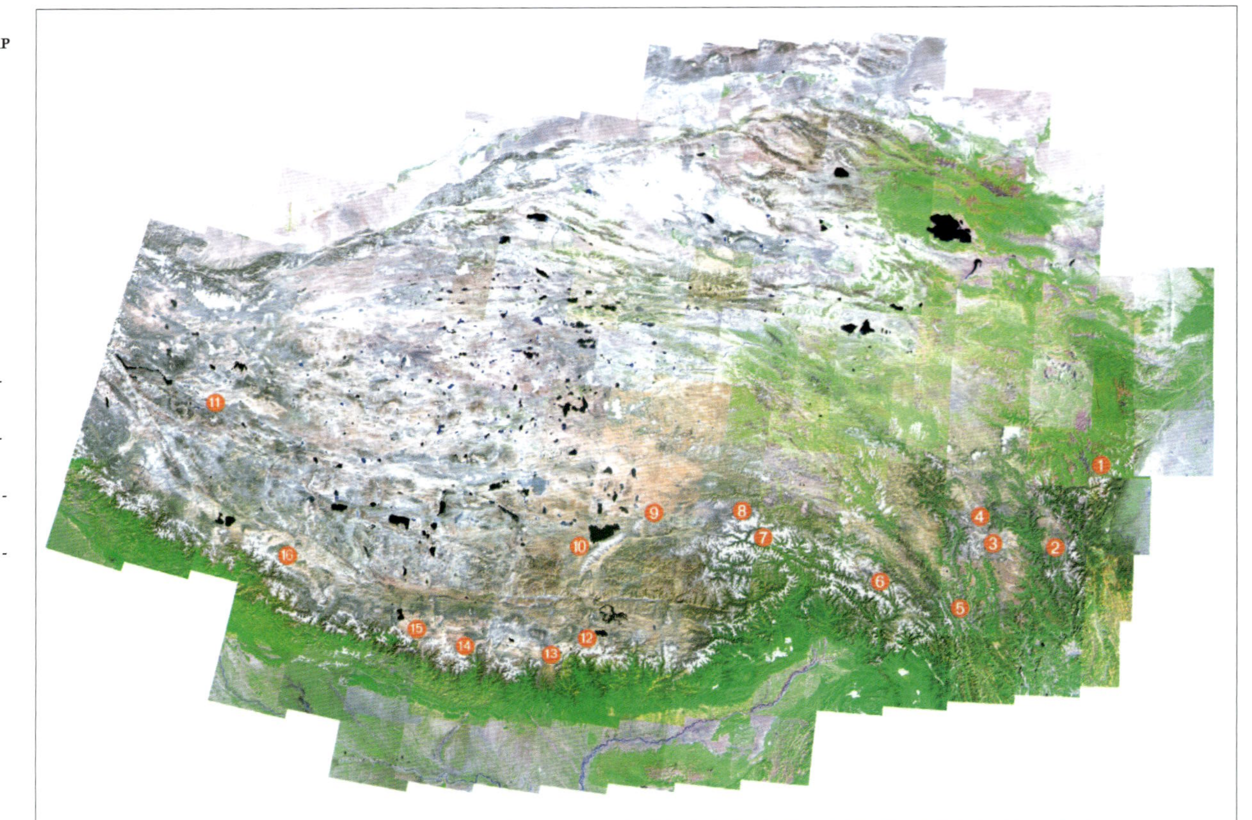

South of the Sichuan-Tibet Highway, a Japanese expedition consisting of Shigeru Aoki and six members explored the massif containing **Xiangqiuqieke (5863m)**, whose highest point is the unnamed **Peak 5870m**. They reached the glacier lake Tsonahou Tso and made the first ascent of an unnamed peak of 5160m.

Nyainqentanglha East

The spectacular peaks of this area continue to attract high class attention. Mick Fowler, Chris Watts, Phil Amos and Adam Thomas attacked the shapely **Kajaqiao (6447m)** and **Manamcho (c6300m)** from the north. The weather in this area once again lived up to its reputation with high winds, incessant snowfall and low temperatures. Fowler and Watts succeeded in making the first ascent of Kajaquio via the W face and NW ridge in a nine-day epic. Thomas and Amos had less success on Manamcho and were turned back by the weather at 5800m. (*See article 'Through Permits and Powder', p2.*)

Sean Waters and Jo Kippax of New Zealand had their sights on the unclimbed peaks at the head of the Lawa valley, in particular **Birutaso (6550m)**. Reaching base camp on 6 October 2005, they experienced heavy snowfall for much of the next month as they placed a series of camps. The final push lasted 16 days, the summit being reached at 10pm on 5 November via the east ridge.

Tamotsu Nakamura continued his explorations of the eastern **Nyainqentanglha** travelling in the steps of Kingdon-Ward up the Yi'ong Tsangpo valley from Gongtsa on the Yi'ong Tso, to the village of Bake, bringing back yet more spectacular photos of unknown, unexplored peaks. (*See article 'A Journey to the Forbidden Yi'ong Tsangpo', p19.*)

Nyainqentanglha West and Central Tibet

Qizi (6206m) is only half a day's drive from Lhasa and a straightforward climb. It is becoming an increasingly popular objective. Seven students of Hong Kong University, together with their five instructors, reached the summit on 4 and 5 August 2005 and a large group of young Chinese climbers were on the mountain in September. In July the 'Beauty and the Beast' charity expedition put the supermodel Jiang Peilin, former Miss World Maria Garcia and 19 other Chinese celebrities on the summit.

An expedition consisting of seven 'Old Boys' from the Keio University Alpine Club, average age 66, made the first ascent of **Kaluxung, 6647m**, in the Noijinkangshan massif, south-west of Lhasa. Eiichiro Kasai (64) and Tadao Shintani (61) reached the summit on 28 September 2005.

Himalaya

Amidst the continuing repeats of existing routes from Tibet on Cho Oyu and Shisha Pangma, one particular expedition stood out. A French team consisting of Cristophe Moulin, Christian Trommsdorff, Patrick Wagnon,

Dana Ruddy, who climbed it as *Belzout Direct* (500m, M6 A0 WI5). This was subsequently freed by Raphael Slawinski and Ian Walsted at M8. Slawinski returned later that winter with Ben Firth and Walsh to climb another line to the left naming it *Great White Fright* (500m, M6). While easier than *Belzout Direct*, the route is threatened by a huge cornice.

CONTINENTAL UNITED STATES

A great deal of activity occurred in the North Cascades during '05. Several long-standing objectives were completed by Mike Layton and partners, including the east face of **Southeast Mox Peak**, *The Devil's Club* (730m, V+ 5.11–) and *The Washington Pass Traverse* (VI 5.9+). Wayne Wallace and Josh Kaplan also completed another long-standing traverse project, this time of the Northern Pickets, *The Northern Pickets Traverse* (VI 5.7). Several other major faces also saw new routes. On **Johannesburg Mountain** Lorne Campbell and Jens Klubberud established *The CK Route* (V 5.10b AI3) while Ade Miller and Stuart Taylor added a new winter line, *Murphy's Law* (V 80° mixed), to the elusive west face of **Mount Index**.

El Capitan saw Tommy Caldwell and Beth Rodden free both *The Nose* (5.14a) and *Free Rider* (5.12d) in a single push. Caldwell had previously freed *The Nose*, becoming only the second person to do so. Dave Turner added a rare new solo route to El Cap, *Block Party* (VI 5.9 A4), over three days in June. The line is semi-independent, sharing pitches with *Tempest* and *Pacific Ocean Wall*. This was Turner's 11th El Cap solo.

In Utah several previously unclimbed desert towers saw first ascents: *Tchalkovsky Overture* (130m, IV 5.11 A3) and *Odyssey* (150m, IV 5.11 A3) by Dave Mealey and partners, and *Chimney Rock* (150m, 5.11 A3) by Layne Potter and Sheridan Potter. There was also significant new route activity in the San Rafael Swell area, including the first ascent of **Dreamcatcher Tower** by Paul and Andy Ross, who named their route *Broken Dreams* (IV 5.9 C2).

In The Zion National Park, Michael Anderson and partners freed several existing lines, including *Spaceshot* (9 pitches, 5.13a), *Golden Years* (8 pitches, 5.12d) and *Angel Hair* (11 pitches, 5.13a R/X), and also established *Freeloader* (12 pitches, 5.12d R) on **Isaac**. Elsewhere in the Park, Brian Smoot, Chris Rowins and Dave Jones put up a new line on **Mount Moroni**, *The Road to Cumorah* (IV 5.11 C1). The same team also added *Locksmith Dihedral* (IV 5.11d C1) to the **Gatekeeper Wall**, while Joe Nolte and Simon Ahlgren climbed *Perfect Day for Bananafish* (V A3) in the **Kolob Canyons**.

In Colorado's **Black Canyon,** Kent Wheeler and Jim Howe climbed *Atlantis* (16 pitches, 5.11) next to Wheeler's existing route *Lost Cities*. The canyon's *Hallucinogen Wall* (VI 5.10 A3) was the scene of several speed ascents, finally culminating in Jared Ogden and Ryan Nelson's blistering time of 8'59". In Wyoming's Wind River mountains, Andy Neuman and Chris Barlow climbed *The Neu Low* (IV 5.11– R) on **Warbonnet Peak**.

ANTONIO GÓMEZ BOHÓRQUEZ

Cordilleras Blanca and Huayhuash 2005

Translated by Erik Monasterio

This review of climbing in the Andes summarizes first ascents and significant repeats in the Peruvian Blanca and Huayhuash ranges between June and September 2005. The information is drawn from: written records held at the Casa de Guías (guide headquarters) and the Casa de Zarela in Huaraz, the AndesInfo archives, *The Alpine Journal* 2004 and 2005, *The American Alpine Journal* 2005, *The American Alpine E-News* November 2005, the *Alpenvereinskarte* (*Cordillera Blanca* 0/3a, 0/3b, *Huayhuash* 0/3c); Peruvian National Institute of Geography Maps (Instituto Geográfico Nacional Peruano); discussions with locals in Ancash and from the correspondence provided by Alcides Ames, Aritza Monasterio, Benoît Montfort, Hugo Sifuentes, Kepa Escribano, Lenin Alvarado, Pavle Kozjek, Ramón Pérez de Ayala and Wayne Crill.

According to NASA, 2005 was the warmest year since the end of the 19th century. These magnificent conditions permitted fast climbing in the Huayhuash and Blanca ranges. However, the extreme drought conditions led to significant rockfall on the north face of Huascarán Norte, heavy crevassing and avalanches on the normal route on Huascarán Sur, unstable cornices on the summit of Alpamayo and a lack of ice on the SW face of Taulliraju.

Cordillera Blanca

Cerro Parón (La Esfinge, 5325m)

On 7 July, N American climbers Josh Wharton and Brian McMahon free climbed the previously aided sections of *Riddle of the Cordillera Blanca*, on the E face of the Esfinge. This route (VI 5.10 A3) was first climbed by Davis and Offenbacher (USA) in June 2000. Wharton and McMahon have named the free route *King of Tebas* and graded it 5.12. They also repeated *Cruz del Sur*, which they graded 5.12a (7a+) and the *Bohórquez-García*, graded 5.11 (6c). The last route was climbed by Wharton in one hour 50 minutes. This is the fastest recorded ascent of the E face.

On 8 July the Basque climbers Kepa Escribano and Fernando Ferreras repeated the E face's *Killa Quillay* (*AJ 2005* p.340), which they mostly free-climbed and graded 7a+/ 7b. Escribano provided the following description of the route: 'It is a beautiful line, the final pitches took in some of the original 1985 route and the initial sections of the climb were difficult to protect during the fast ascent.'

Arkadiusz Grzadziel, Boguslaw Kowalski and Jerzy Stefanski climbed the S face by a new route named *Salida desde la oscuridad*, graded VI, 6b+ A2+ and 680m. From 29 June to 1 July they climbed and fixed 170m. After a rest day they continued until they reached the summit on 4 July. They found rotten rock with cracks full of loose stones. This Polish route is to the left of the line climbed by Canadians Beaulieu and Légaré in 2003.

Chopiraju (Andavite, 5513m)

On 28 July the Germans Lochbühler and Moritz Wälde climbed the S face via a possible new route *Fight Club* (800m, WI4, M5, 85° 50-70°), in seven hours. It is difficult to know whether this is a repeat of the route climbed in 2000 by the Peruvian guide José A Castañeda Queda and his Swiss client Catherine Bertui. The Germans descended the route with a single abseil down the S ridge. The route has a two-hour approach from the Cayesh valley.

Chugllaraju (5575m)

On 24 June British climbers Anthony Barton and John Pearson climbed nine pitches (350m, TD–, 50°-85° ice/mixed), of a direct line on the W face, but were unable to overcome the summit schrund. They approached the climb from the Ulta valley, where they reached a bivouac cave in a 24-hour round trip. They state that the cave is to the left of an obvious rock wall and 40 minutes from the glacier. Barton stated that 'once the foot of the face is reached, an obvious runnel is followed over numerous bulges of ice to a mixed rib. A rightwards slanting gully was avoided in favour of a direct finish, this final section being mainly mixed ground containing the crux eventually led to the summit ridge.'

Hatun Ulloc (Ulloc Grande, c4800m)

Please refer to Ulloc Grande in *AJ* 2005, p.342. The reference to the route *Ulloc Grande* should instead be *Karma de los Cóndores*. In the Quechua language, 'Hatun' means 'immense', 'of large size'. 'Ulloc' (according to elders from Huaraz) could mean 'protruding', 'something that sticks out' or 'something that sticks in'. This peak remains unclimbed. Wayne Crill and Kevin Gallagher (USA) returned to the Ishinca Valley to finish and free-climb their route *Karma de los Cóndores*, c350m, A3, 5.12. After nine pitches they reached the first of three rock ledges. On 18 June they completed the route, which they gave IV, 5.11+. They recommend leaving a fixed line on the sixth pitch, which can later be used to abseil the main roof. The seventh, eighth and ninth pitch can be abseiled with a single 60m rope. According to Crill, the route 'is entirely naturally gear protected with a bolted belay'. The route was repeated a week later, probably on 2 July.

James Wood and Andy Wellman (USA) climbed it in a long day and graded it IV, 5.11d. These two climbed beyond the second main step, but excessive dirt in the cracks made it difficult to protect and they rapped off 60m below the summit. Crill believes that Wood and Wellman deviated to the easier, but less protectable, E face.

Various websites that reprint information from the *Gaceta* magazine of the Universidad Nacional Autónoma de México claim that Carlos Macotela, Marco Iván Serra and José B Guerrero reached the summit of Hatun Ulloc via a new route, *Lawak*, meaning 'flag' in the Quechua language. However, the Mexican trio's own written accounts at the Casa de Guías in Huaraz seem to indicate that they reached another summit to the right and near a rock tower. They struggled with loose rock, vegetation and dirt and graded the route 5.11, A1. They wrote on their route topo: 'Lawak, Pa'la bandera, Hatun Ulloc/Q. Ishinca, Junio 23, 24, 25'. This is confusing because they call the route *Pa'la bandera* (for the flag), and they name the rock tower 'Lawak' and seem to believe this forms part of the rock wall 'Hatun Ulloc'. It is worth pointing out that in the Quechua language of Huaraz, flag is 'Lapapa' and 'Lawak' means 'corn soup with pork ribs'!

Huamashraju (5434m)

In July, Peruvians Jorge Gálvez and Manuel Urquiz climbed four pitches on the rocky NW face, to c.4900m just below the N ridge. They called the route *Directa Monodedo*, 230m, 6b/6b+. On 14 July, Basque climbers Kepa Escribano and Fernando Ferreras climbed a new nine-pitch rock route on the NW face. They then followed the N ridge to the summit. They called the route *Matxinsalto*, ED–. Escribano comments, 'This was a fast climb, with some risks on poorly protected granite slabs up to 6b and with steep cracks.'

Itsoc huanca (c.4800m)

From 12-23 July Ramón Pérez de Ayala, Jorge Barrachina, Daniel Gutiérrez, Jorge Ferrero and María López opened *Dominguerismo vertical* (650m-675m, ED– 6b A2) on the NW face. They descended by abseiling the entire route. They took 13 days; ten and a half of climbing, with five bivouacs of which four were on consecutive days. This is the first ascent of the crag group called 'Risco Ayudin' (4650-4700m) by a Spanish group of that name. However, this name is out of keeping with the geographic naming conventions used by the Peruvian authorities. The original name of the crag is 'Itsoc huanca' derived from the Quechua *itsoq* 'left' and *huanka* 'big rock'. The crag is found on the right (south) side of the Rurec Valley. This granite 'big rock' is L of another crag locally known as 'Chopi Huanca' (refer to P. 4800m in *AJ* 2003, p.287), which has dirt chocked cracks (map *Cordillera Blanca, Süd,* No.0/3b German Alpine Club 1939).

159. West face of Nevado Cayesh (5721m). (*Antonio Gómez-Bohórquez*, 1999)

On 18 August, Italians Roberto Iannilli and Giulio Canti climbed a new route *Libertad es partezipacion* (c600m+c1000m easy rock, A1 6c+), with a single bivouac to the right of the Spanish route. The Italian team was joined by Enzo Arciuoli, and over the course of several days equipped and climbed the NW face of the **Pumahuagangan** peak. On 12 August they completed *Pietrorrago Vaffanculo* (440m, 6a). This route is on the right-hand rock wall at the entry point of the Rurec Valley.

Nevado Cayesh (5721m)
On 10 July, USA climber Steve House and his Slovenian partner Marko Prezelj approached the peak via the Cayesh valley and climbed a new rock and ice route on the W face. The route took 15 hours and required 11 pitches with a technical grade of M8, 5.10 (6a).

Nevado Huascarán Norte (6654m)
In June, Jordi Corominas solo-climbed the NE face by the 1973 *French route* pioneered by Barrard, Desrivières, Narbaud and Ricouard. The Catalan climber took a direct (variant) approach to the route and added a further variant (single pitch, M5) to exit the wall on the E ridge close to the final rock headwall. He reported good snow conditions along the entire

route, which he climbed in 12 hours' round trip, and graded the route MD.

Pirámide de Garcilaso (5885m)

The SW face route climbed on 18 July and recorded in the Casa de Guías de Huaraz by the German team of Tobi Lochbühler and Moritz Wälde (*Marilin*, 300 m, 70º-80º, UIAA IV) appears to take the same line as that climbed by the British team of Wolf and Clark in Aug 1996. The British team gave the grade TD+ (V 90º). The German team were forced to cut left below the summit séracs to descend via the *Renshaw-Wilkinson route.*

Nevado Rataquenua 5336m (Nevado Portachuelo, 5340m)

In July the Peruvian team of Eleazar Blas Blas and Edegar Laveriano López climbed a route they christened *Vía de los Cóndores*. This is a possible new route, located E of Portachuelo between the Illauro and Honda Valleys. Page 19-i of the Peruvian National Institute Map classifies this as P.5536m. The German Map names this peak 'Nevado Portachuelo' (5340m). The *Revista Peruana de Andinismo y Glaciología* 1978-1979 states that the name Rataquenua means 'hidden flower' in Quechua.

Nevado Santa Cruz (6259m)

In June, Jordi Corominas solo-climbed the NE face route originally climbed by Ecuadoreans Navarrete and Suárez in 1984. The ascent took 6 hours, and the descent 3 hours via the 1977 *German route* of Gloggner, Janner and Müller.

Shacsha Sur (5697m)

In June four members of a team of ten, César Rosales, Miguel Martínez, Elías Flores (Perú) and Tiziano Orio (Italy), climbed a new route on the SE face (350m, D+ 70º-75º). They took eight hours' round trip, from a camp on the N side of the Rurec Valley.

Nevado Ulta (5875m)

On 14 August, French climbers Pierre Labbré and Benoît Montfort climbed the NNE ridge, which they christened *Toy's band* (600m, TD+ V+ 90º). Montfort reports that they climbed from the eastern slopes and reached the summit from a high camp on the col (c4900m) near the **Punta Olimpica** (AKA Pasaje de Ulta). According to their description, the col appears to have been between Alco (**Alco, 5375m**) and Ulta. It may be a variation of the NE summit ridge, climbed in 1961 by the Germans Bogner, Kämpfe, Hechtel and the N American Liska. This same summit ridge was also climbed by Earl and Cordes (USA) in August 2003.

Cordillera de Huayhuash

Puscanturpa Norte (5652m)

On 25 June from the head of the Huanacpatay (Huanacupatay) valley, Basque climbers Kepa Escribano and Fernando Ferreras climbed the NW face by the French route *Macanacota*. They made small variations toward the 1984 *Italian route*. They reached a high point an easy rope length beneath the summit and the overall grade was ED+. This may be the fourth repeat of the route and the first time it has been climbed in a day.

Puscanturpa Sur (5550m)

From 17-20 July, the Catalan climber Oriol Anglada and Mexican Marisol Monterrubio climbed 16 pitches (670m, 7c/6c+) which they called *El guardián de la Pachamana*. They approached their route from camps at c4650m on the Huanacpatay Valley and at the foot of the basalt N face at c4800m. They reached a high point at 5300m before abseiling the entire route. According to the tourist map of Felipe Diaz *Cordilleras Blanca & Huayhuash* and the Martin Gamache Topographic Map (1:50,000) *Cordillera Huayhuash* (2004, 2nd Edition) this ascent may be of **Cuyoc**. The new Gamache map gives the summit the name of Cuyoc with an altitude of 5550m. The 1939 Alpenvereinskarte Nr: 0/3c, *Cordillera Huayhuash,* calls it Puscanturpa Sur.

Nevado Sarapo (6143m)

In June, Jordi Corominas solo-climbed the NW face via the 1979 *Gocking and Sisson* (USA) route. The route, graded MD– took 3 hours and the 2-hour descent followed the 1984 *Dutch route* of van Sprang and Veen.

Trapecio (5653m)

On 10 July, Slovenians Pavle Kozjek, Miha Lampreht, Branko Ivanek and Huaraz resident Basque climber Aritza Monasterio repeated Jeff Lowe's (USA) unfinished route on the SE face. They managed to complete the final 250m to the summit. The total length of the route was 800m and the grade given was ED+ (AI6 M5 A2). Following his 1985 ascent, Lowe graded the route V WI6+ VS. It appears to have had significantly more snow cover at that time. On the lower section, the Europeans found overhanging rock and ice-steps at A2 and M5. The middle section of the climb was easier and then they reached a vertical headwall (AI5-6 80º-90º). Kozjek comments that 'Due to bad ice conditions in the last steep pitch we traversed 30m to the right and climbed an overhanging rock chimney (VI–) that opened the way to the upper snowfields. With two more steep pitches (AI 4-5, 60-75°) we reached almost directly the top of Trapecio at 5pm. We descended down the N face using headlamps and reached base camp at 2.30am.'

160. South-east face of Nevado Trapecio (5653m) showing the line of the Lowe route to the blue point, followed by the Slovene-Basque line to the top. (*Antonio Gómez-Bohórquez*)

Yerupaja Sur (6515m)

French climbers Julien Laurent, Benoît Montfort, Pierre Labbré and Françoise Nadal climbed a new route *Furieux mais romantiques* (1200m, ED– 55°-90°), following the left side of the S spur, the left side of the S face, and finally the SW ridge. From Sarapococha they fixed the route to 5500m. The final assault and descent took place from 1-3 August. On day one, they bivouacked at c5600m above the SSW spur. On the second day they reached the SW ridge 300m below the summit, which they finally reached by climbing ice-flutes, 14 hours after setting off. They bivouacked during their descent of the July 1981 *Italian route* of Arcari, Fedeli, Bramati, Besana, Simonetto and Fumagalli.

MARK WATSON

New Zealand 2005 - 2006

This report covers new routes climbed in the Southern Alps during the period April 2005 to April 2006. The grades quoted are 'Mt Cook' alpine grades and Australasian (Ewbank) rock grades.

Darran Mountains

Despite their isolation and high level of rainfall Fiordland's Darran Mountains are New Zealand's current forcing ground for rock climbing — both alpine multi-pitch (free and aid) and sub-alpine crag climbing. The rock quality and virtually unlimited quantity of future lines provides an ample venue for those looking to push their own and New Zealand's standards. A driven few have made the season just past a productive one, and now there are even more quality routes to tempt the motivated.

One of the areas of activity has been the rock massif of Mt Moir (2072m) and its outlier peaks the Mates Little Brother and Moir's Mate. Already the site of a number of high quality lines, the Mate's Little Brother had some notable progress over the summer. Derek Thatcher and Jonathon Clearwater returned to a project started the previous summer and between bursts of rain succeeded in establishing another pitch on a route that cuts straight through the prominent overlaps of an existing line, *Second Coming*. Still unnamed the route has a pitch of 28 (freed by Thatcher), and is so far the hardest pitch freed 'up-high' in the Darrans. Further right on the same wall Craig Jefferies and Kester Brown added the five pitch *New Jersey Drifter* (24, 21, 21, 21, 17). The line was rap-bolted, requires some natural pro and is apparently of the highest quality. Kester Brown also further investigated, and climbed some new pitches leading to the prominent roofs on the right side of the N face of Mt Moir – watch this space.

During a sustained fine spell in late March, Richard Thomson, Richard Turner and Dave Vass walked into Lake Turner via the Donne Valley and Taoka Icefall. They developed a cave, discovered on an earlier visit by Turner, into a good four-person bivvy. Turner's Eyrie, perched on a cliff on the N flank of Karetai at around 2000m, was named in keeping with many of the nearby features. They also climbed a new rock route on the superb red wall that runs between Te Wera and Karetai. *Statue Bro?* is six pitches, crux 19, finishing just S of Karetai Col.

Also in late March Mark Watson and Tom Riley fired up their petrol drill and initiated the development of the NE face of Barrier Knob (1829m) around the corner from the Labyrinth wall, spending six days establishing some single and multi-pitch routes, most notably: *Quiet Earth* (21, 21, 100m), *Sleeping Dogs* (22, 50m), *Goodbye Pork Pie* (23, 50m), and with Allan Uren, the six-pitch route *The Navigator* (18).

Winter was typically quiet but a keen few ventured out. Matt Quirke and Allan Uren made the fifth ascent, in thin conditions, of *White as a Sheet* (300m) in Cirque Creek.

Brit James Edwards teamed up with Gary Kinsey and Andrew Young to climb a new line on the SE face of Mt Talbot (Psychopath Wall), named *Actions Speak Loudest* (4+, 400m). The route tackled a mix of turf, rock and snow.

Queenstown

Queenstown's Wye Creek became New Zealand's focal point for the sport-mixed climbing movement over the past winter. A number of climbers based themselves in the Wye valley cirque for periods of time and mixed climbs up to grade M11 were developed. First to fall was an already bolted project *Greypower* (M8), by Kester Brown. Some more bolting ensued to provide three more routes: *The Rebirth of Cool* (M7), Kester Brown; *Pippi's Polish Circus* (M8), Johnny Davison; and the area test piece *Northern Exposure* (M11), by Kester Brown (*see Frontispiece*). These routes point towards a shift in attitude and opening of horizons with New Zealand mixed climbing and hopefully the development will continue.

Reminding us that the mixed climbing scene isn't all about bolts, Kester Brown and Jono Clarke ticked off an old two-pitch project with shaky protection on the Telecom Tower (Remarkables), naming it *The Fastest Indian* (rock crux 20). Also on the Telecom Tower, Andrew Mills and Rupert Gardiner climbed a new five pitch line at a grade of about 3+.

In the summer Rupert Gardiner, Dave Bolger and Cris Prudden ventured into the Stoneburn, climbing a five-pitch rock route on an outlier to Stoney Peak, *The Sentinel* (17).

Barron Saddle – Mt Brewster Region

It's tempting to call the North Buttress of Mt Hopkins (2678m) one of the 'last great problems' of the Barron Saddle – Mt Brewster Region, but that would be a bit misleading as it's more the fact that it's isolated and long, rather than technically hard, that has kept climbers off its heights for so long. Whatever way you look at it, it presents a strikingly obvious and compelling rock ridge and it was great to see it finally climbed in January this year. Paul Hersey and Kynan Bazley took the honours, taking 10 hours to reach the summit from the valley floor and taking another two days to walk back out. They graded the route 5+ with rock crux of 17. The twist to this story is that a month later Guy McKinnon and Steven Fortune also climbed the route and subsequently returned to Christchurch, believing they had made the first ascent. Severe disappointment came when McKinnon eagerly opened the latest issue of *The Climber* about a week after their return ...

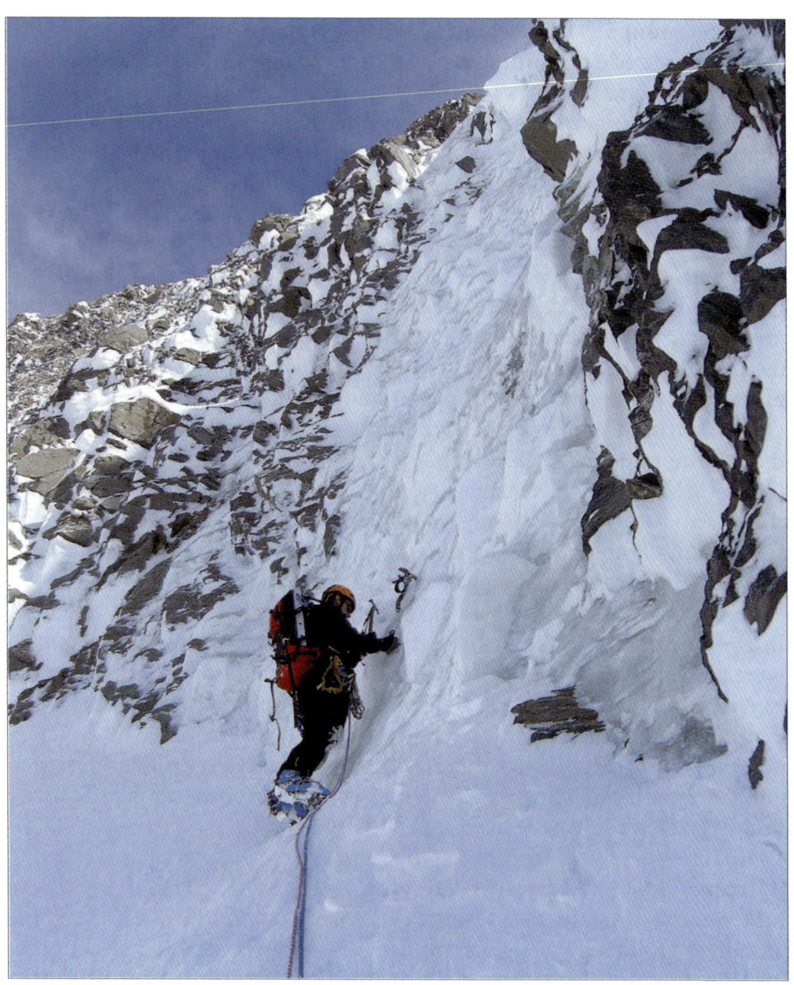

161. Johnny Davison at the start of *Stealing White Boys*, Mt Haidinger east face headwall. (*Marty Beare*)

The winter saw a couple of prominent new lines climbed. On Mt Huxley (2505m) James Edwards and Sam Barron climbed an 800m route on the W face, spending the night in a hole near the summit. Edwards also teamed up with Steven Fortune and Paul Warnock for an 1100m route on the SE face of Mt McKerrow (2650m). The route is called *Fortune Favours the Bold*. In July Paul Hersey and Mat Woods climbed a grade 3 gully route on the S face of Peak 2200m.

Aoraki Mount Cook and Westland

The west side of the Divide has been relatively quiet for new routes this past year, with only two climbs to report. In the summer Allan Uren and Craig Cardie climbed an obvious and reportedly good quality route to the right of *Moonshine Buttress* on Conway Peak (2899m). *Sunshine Buttress* follows a direct rock buttress with a grade of 16. In March 2006 Andrew Rennie and Graham Zimmerman climbed a new route on the SW face of Mt Matenga (2665m), Franz Josef Névé. *Mixed Blood* is a mixed route and went at Grade 4, M5, WI3 (4 pitches). The route is apparently 'short and sweet' and provided 'some very good, hard and interesting climbing'.

The other side of the Divide has not seen much more going on. In March 2005 Michael Madden and Tshering Pande Bhote (Nepal) climbed a direct and obvious new line on the S face of Aoraki Mt Cook (3754m). *Sherpa-Kiwi* is graded 5. In late October Johnny Davison and Marty Beare climbed the prominent right-hand ice fang on the Mt Haidinger (3070m) E face headwall, high above the Tasman Valley. *Stealing White Boys* is graded 5. A parallel left-hand line was climbed the previous winter (2004). Just down the road from Mt Cook Village, three new ice routes were climbed up the Bush Stream valley by Mal Haskins, Jason Tweedie, Thomas Evans and Nina Conradi. January 2006 saw Mark Watson and Nico Hudak head into the Reay valley, east Tasman valley in search of quality red rock. The pair climbed a prominent stepped buttress *Max Johnson* (17, 7 pitches) on an outlier peak (2235m) to *Mt Johnson*, and later the same day a classic, sharp arête *Tim Fin* (15, pitched and simul-climbed).

Canterbury

Showing that there are still plenty of new things to do in the Southern Alps if you are motivated, Guy McKinnon ventured alone onto the NW face of Malcolm Peak (2512m), making the first ascent of this 500m greywacke face (14). Malcolm Peak is on the Main Divide between the Lyell glacier and the Heim plateau.

Mount Everest Foundation Expedition Reports

SUMMARISED BY BILL RUTHVEN

AMERICA – NORTH AND CENTRAL

British Buckskin 2005 Paul Ramsden with Rich Cross. September-October 2005

It is well known that the weather can have a major effect on mountain areas. Hence this team was unable to land on the Buckskin glacier due to poor surface conditions (unbridged crevasses covered by powder snow) and even though they managed to land on the Upper Ruth glacier were unable to make any progress towards climbing either of their objectives – the NE face of Bear Tooth (3069m) and the N buttress of Moose's Tooth (3156m). The rock on both peaks was also covered with powder snow with no ice, causing dangerous avalanche conditions. The moral – don't go to Alaska in the autumn after a record dry summer! MEF 05/08

'A Slice of Ice' – Alaska 2005 Stuart McAleese with Nick Bullock and Mike (Twid) Turner. March-April 2005

This strong team hoped to make the first ascent of the west face couloir on Middle Triple Peak (2693m) in the Kichatna Spires (aka Cathedral Peaks) where there is still much to be done. Unfortunately, weather conditions dictated otherwise. Although Talkeetna ('a small drinking town with a climbing problem') was virtually at a standstill owing to deep winter snow, they were surprised to find during their flight into the mountains that very little ice was visible. This was due to extremely low temperatures (–15°C in the sun on the glacier at midday) which would also preclude technical climbing, which is inevitably very slow. The intended objective – normally a continuous 1200m ice-line – was actually bare rock. During the next week continuous snow and strong winds hampered all movement and added to the avalanche risk, so although they explored much of the Tatina glacier, virtually no climbing was achieved. MEF 05/13

British Ruth Gorge 2005 Tom Spreyer with Mark Walker. May 2005

Mount Wake (2755m) and London Bridge (2250m) are peaks facing one another across the Ruth gorge, and generally offer good scope for mixed routes. However, unseasonably warm and unsettled weather had cleared most of the ice in the area, which necessitated a change of plan. They therefore 'moved into rock climbing mode'. After several failures they climbed *Ham & Eggs* (900m, V 5.9 WI4) on the Moose's Tooth, continuing to its west summit, and then made a one-day ascent of *Dream in the Spirit of Mugs* (1100m, V 5.10c) on the west pillar of the Eye Tooth. Few other expeditions to the area achieved as much this spring. MEF 05/23

Scottish Pantheon Range Simon Richardson with Mark Robson. August 2005

The main objective of this team was to make the first ascent of the 600m NW pillar of Athena Tower on Mount Zeus (2959m) – described as the 'Bonatti Pillar' of the Pantheon Coastal Range (British Columbia). Unfortunately, at about one third height they encountered a 50-metre wall which, having no obvious cracks or other features, stopped further progress. They therefore turned their attention to the hitherto unclimbed 2km NW ridge of Zeus, which provided an excellent alpine route (at TD) and the first ascent of the mountain's West Peak, as well as the first N-S traverse. With the weather holding, they then crossed the Ragnarok glacier, and made the second ascent of the NW ridge of Mt Fenris (2896m) at AD. MEF 05/28

Yorkshire Tokosita Glacier 2005 Andrew Saxby with Jago Trasler. May 2005

Although the summit of Peak 3512m above Central Alaska's Tokosita glacier had been attempted by several climbers over the years, all had failed. Bad weather delayed this team's flight to the Mount Huntington landing site, but they eventually established a base camp at 2620m below their chosen peak. Unfortunately Coley Gentzel and Seth Hobby from the USA had the same objective, and in fact climbed it whilst the UK pair were getting established. Nevertheless, they continued in the hope of making the second ascent; but after climbing 300m of ice and mixed ground on the NW ridge (Scottish grade V), they were forced to retreat when Saxby suffered severe stomach pains, possibly due – at least in part – to hanging from belays in his harness. Frequent heavy snowfalls with whiteout conditions and avalanche danger precluded any further attempts. MEF 05/29

Yukon 2005, Kluane Glenn Wilks with Jonathon Wakefield. May-June 2005

In recent years, the Yukon has received considerably less attention from British climbers than Alaska but, as these men discovered, there are still rich pickings available. From a base camp on the Donjek glacier in Kluane National Park, they made first ascents of eight peaks between 3300m and 3700m, including Donjek 3, 4 and 5 at Scottish grades 2 and 3. MEF 05/37

AMERICA – SOUTH AND ANTARCTICA

British South Georgia 2005 Julian Freeman-Attwood with Rich Haworth, Crag Jones and Skip Novak. January-February 2005

After sailing 1300km from Port Stanley to land at Larsen Harbour on Novak's yacht *Pelagic*, this team skied up the Philippi, and eventually onto the southern Spenceley Harmer glacier, to start a very committing 17-day south-north traverse of South Georgia. En route they tried to climb the north ridge of Mt Baume (1912m) but were repulsed by bad weather some 400m from the summit. However, they were successful in making the first ascent of Pk 5680 (1727m) to its north-west, before completing their traverse at Royal Bay, where they were reunited with *Pelagic*. MEF 05/01 (*See article 'Strictly for Aficionados', p143.*)

Rio Turbio, Lost Valley of the Andes Leo Houlding with Jessica Corrie and Kevin Thaw from UK plus Vicente Banate and Tommy Hienrich from Argentina and Mark Karhl and Tom Koiesk from USA. March-April 2005

Despite the presence of big granite crags, the Rio Turbo valley in Argentina's Lago Puelo National Park (close to the Chilean border) had not previously been visited by British climbers. Unusually heavy rain and a flooded river initially prevented access by the present team, but after nine days, the level eventually dropped and they were able to get across on horseback. Although two hours from base camp they were able to see their prime objective – an 800m granite wall dubbed the Mariposa – there was insufficient time to attempt it. However, their exploration revealed that this was an impressive location with plenty of scope for first ascents, and they therefore plan to return in 2006. MEF 05/05

British Antarctic Peninsula 2005 Phil Wickens with Alan Geer, Alastair Gunn, Tim Hall, Alun Hubbard, Andy Kerr, and Colin Souness plus Nico L'Homme from France/Poland. December 2004-March 2005

This team sailed from S America on Alun Hubbard's yacht *Gambo* to Anvers Island, where they hoped to complete a traverse of Mt Francais (2825m) via its SE and NE ridges. A 1000m new line on the SE face took them to the S ridge, but from here they retreated due to Category 5 avalanche danger. A second attempt via Mt Rennie was also abandoned owing to bad weather (only five and a half clear days whilst they were in the area) and dangerous snow conditions. Moving to Wiencke Island, they made three attempts to climb and link the challenging Seven Sisters of Fief (c1430m), but again bad weather prevented success. However, they climbed a new gully route on the NW side of Noble Peak (c760m) at AD+ and a new route on the SE face/N ridge of Mt Wheat (1095m) in the Wall Range at AD–. As an 'expedition within an expedition' Hall made the first successful 'paramotor' flight (defined as foot-launched powered paragliding) in Antarctica. MEF 05/11

South Georgia '05 Alun Hubbard with Tom Chamberlain, Alistair Gunn, Tim Hall, Dan Haywood and Rory Williams plus David Fasel from Switzerland. February-May 2005

With a change of team, this was to some extent a continuation of 05/11, using *Gambo* to access South Georgia. The bad weather continued, with a pressure drop to 930mb causing 'unbelievable winds'. In 13 days on Mount Paget (2996m) they only experienced two weather windows, each of about six hours. Both attempts to reach the summit were unsuccessful, but they did achieve the first ascent of its subsidiary peak (c2100m), which they named Buzen Point. MEF 05/12

Stoats Apolobamba 2005 Carl Reilly with Tom Bide, Graeme Schofield and Sam Walmsley. June-August 2005

Although Japanese climbers visited the Acamani region of the South-Eastern Cordillera Apolobamba during the early sixties, little is known of their achievements and recently published Bolivian maps do not cover this part of the Apolobamba. These young explorers – all past or present members of the University of Birmingham Mountaineering Club – planned to extend the well-known 'Paul Hudson Map' whilst making first ascents of some of the local peaks. They actually climbed five (assumed new) routes which they graded from D– to TD; two (including a traverse) on Casalala (5650m), two on Huelanacalloc (5847m) and one on Canisaya (5652m). MEF 05/20 [*For further information see website:* www.apolobamba.com]

British Cordillera Oriental 2005 Tony Barton with Tim Riley. May and August 2005

Although the Cordillera Oriental is relatively easy of access and the majority of its peaks are of moderate height, it is one of the lesser-visited areas of Peru. However, the vulnerability of a two-man team was brought home to this pair when Riley injured his back soon after arriving in Peru in May, forcing him to take a prolonged rest. Fortunately he recovered sufficiently to allow a return to the mountains three months later, when they climbed a new route on Nevado Nausacocha (c5150m) and several other previously unclimbed peaks. MEF 05/27

Welsh Western Patagonia 2005 Chris Smith with Steve Hartland and David Hillebrandt. September-November 2005

These stalwarts with short memories returned to Patagonia in the hope of at last making the first ascent of Cerro Aguilera (2500m). During some of their previous attempts they had not even set foot on the mountain, but in 2004 [MEF 04/17] they found what seemed to be a satisfactory approach from the south-east, so this year were hopeful of topping out. Alas, the elements were against them once again with only two days of 'good' weather during four weeks in the area. The wind was so strong at one stage that their tent 'exploded'. MEF 05/41

Tepui 2005 John Arran with Anne Arran, Miles Gibson and Ben Heason from UK, Alex Klenov from Kazakhstan and Ivan Calderón and Alfredo Rangel from Venezuela. March-April 2005

Following their success two years earlier [MEF 03/27] the Arrans returned to Venezuela with an augmented team hoping for similar results in 2005. Unfortunately they found that access to other unclimbed tepuis was virtually impossible owing to the thick jungle terrain surrounding them. They therefore turned their attention to the 1000m main face of Angel Falls. On this they were successful in making the first ascent of a route which they called *Rainbow Jambaia*. The 31 pitches up to E7 6b/Fr 7c/7c+ took 19 days, with 14 nights spent on the wall. Anne Arran, as an individual, was joint recipient of the Alison Chadwick Memorial Grant for 2005. MEF 05/43 (*See article 'Rainbow Jambaia: A First Free Ascent of Angel Falls Face', p121.*)

Rondoy West Face 2005 Gareth Hughes with Tim Darlow, Myles English and Oliver Metherell from UK and Robin Deplante from France. July-August 2005

For the leader this was a return to an area that he had visited 12 months earlier as a member of Iain Rudkin's expedition MEF 04/37. Their prime objective was a new route up the obvious ice funnel on the west face of Nevado Rondoy (5879m) in the Cordillera Huayhuash. Unfortunately there had been little snowfall in the area since May, so conditions were dry and the glacier had changed considerably, making the approach dangerous and the route unjustifiable. Conditions on Jirishanca (6094m) were no more encouraging, but the summit of Cerro Mexico (5040m) was reached via its west ridge (D). They therefore decided to carry out a thorough exploration of the east side of the Copa Massif in the Cordillera Blanca. Here they had more success, reaching the summits of Copa (6188m), Artesonraju (6040m), Tocllaraju 6025m), and Chopicalqui (6534m) by routes up to D+, and reconnoitring various other peaks. In the light of their experience, they now feel that conditions would probably be safer earlier in the climbing season, eg May-June. MEF 05/46

GREENLAND

CUMC Centenary Kangerdlugssuaq 2005 James Sample with Alex Cowan, Matt Harding, Ali Ingleby, Leah Jackson-Blake, Jenny Marshall, Mike Moss and Tom Stedall. June-July 2005

Bad weather delayed this team's arrival in Greenland and then kept them tent-bound for three days 60km short of their intended landing area. However, once the weather improved, they made the first ascent of the most significant local peak, before skiing to their planned area, where they made first ascents of a further 11 significant peaks (mostly unnamed) via routes from PD to TD. MEF 05/10

KMC Tôrnârssuk Expedition Dave Bone with Marylise Dufaux, Dan O'Brien, Carl Pulley and David Whittingham. July-August 2005

Tôrnârssuk Island is uninhabited and lies off SW Greenland to the west of Pamiagdluk, an island visited by a Karabiner MC expedition in 2004 [MEF 04/20]. This team planned to explore and establish new rock and mountaineering routes in the northern half of the island. However, their arrival coincided with the end of a long dry spell, and they were subject to a series of active depressions with much rain and strong winds, which limited their activities. Nevertheless, they climbed a number of new routes, varying from F to E1 and up to 1000m long. Apart from a strong European team that put up a number of difficult rock routes in 2004, the island appears to have little recent climbing history, although the team was surprised to find an automatic radio/TV/mobile repeater station complete with diesel generator, helipad etc. MEF 05/26

British Kangerdlugssuaq 2005 Peter Whyley with Carole Feldman, Paul Hawksworth and Cath Walton. July-August 2005

This group of teachers used Tangent Expeditions to access the region to the south of the Hutchinson glacier in order to explore and reach the summit of as many unclimbed peaks as possible in the time available. As far as was known, the exact area had never previously been visited, and the only available map proved to be inaccurate. Climbing mainly at night, they were successful in making 11 probable first ascents of peaks between 1480m and 1905m. MEF 05/47

HIMALAYA – INDIA

N Wales Changabang '05 Nick Bullock with Stuart McAleese and Olly Sanders. September-October 2005

The plan to climb a new route on the west face of Changabang (to the right of the Boardman-Tasker route) originated with Twid Turner and Louise Thomas, who heard that the Nanda Devi Sanctuary had reopened. Unfortunately the couple had to withdraw from the team when Louise became pregnant, and on arriving in India, the others found that the Sanctuary was still closed. They were therefore forced to approach from the north via the Bagini glacier and 9km of the 'moraine from hell'. As they started the climb the weather broke and after heavy snow flattened their base camp, a Dutch team came to their assistance and lent them tents. However, the bad weather continued, so with food running out and a tooth abscess making its presence felt, they abandoned the attempt at 6200m. MEF 05/24

British Sikkim 2005 Julie-Ann Clyma with Roger Payne plus Kunzang Gyatso Bhutia and Sagar Rai from the Sikkim Amateur Mountaineering Association. March-April 2005

Although the fact that Sikkim has borders with Tibet, Nepal and Bhutan means that all visitors have to obtain an 'inner line' permit, this is not difficult, and the authorities have recently designated a number of peaks in the area around the Talung glacier as 'trekking peaks'. Having seen some of these during 2004, Clyma and Payne returned to explore the glacier and hopefully to make first ascents in the area. Despite poor and very cold weather throughout, two peaks were climbed: the north summit of Lama Lamani c5650m received its first ascent via the NW flank and W ridge (AD+) and then Tinchenkang (6010m) by its NW ridge at D– (probably its first 'alpine-style' ascent and third overall). MEF 05/49

(*See article 'Early Season Alpine Summits in West Sikkim', p139.*)

HIMALAYA – NEPAL

British Machermo Owen Samuel with Andy Turner. October-November 2005

Machermo (aka Phari Lapcha) (6017m) in the very popular Gokyo valley is one of 33 peaks recently given 'trekking peak' status by the Nepalese authorities. Although one route (*Bonfire of the Vanities* ED1) has already been climbed on its north face, these two prospective guides felt that there was scope for another. Unfortunately, an unseasonably cold period meant that snow conditions were poor with little ice, making the face unclimbable. After reaching 5300m on a rising traverse, theyAla Dwere forced to abandon their attempt. MEF 05/21

Ngozumba Glacier Research Project Doug Benn with Steve Keene from UK, Jason Gulley from USA and Endre Gjermundsen from Norway. November-December 2005

This unusual expedition was set up to study the role of high-altitude ice caves in the evolution and drainage of ice lakes, and assess the feasibility of cave diving within them. Basing themselves on the Ngozumba glacier between Cho Oyu and Gokyo they succeeded in exploring and mapping five caves at altitudes between 4900m and 5300m (the longest of them extending to 905m), achieving the record for the world's highest surveyed cave in the process. They exhibited a wide variety of morphologies ranging from high, narrow 'canyon-like' tunnels to wide, low-roofed caves occasionally opening out into large chambers. MEF 05/48

CHINA & TIBET

British Gongkala 2005 Dick Isherwood with Toto Gronlund, Peter Rowat and Dave Wynne-Jones plus Nona Rowat as base camp doctor. September-October 2005

In a brief visit at the end of a previous expedition to Western Sichuan, Isherwood realised the potential for exploration and first ascents in the Gongkala Shan area, so lost no time in arranging this return. In particular it was hoped to climb the two principal peaks – Kawarani I & II (5992m and 5928m respectively) (aka Kawaluoren). With no obvious easy routes from the north, the team concentrated on the southern approach where, after initially supporting – and even blessing – the expedition, monks from the local monastery suddenly became aggressive and insisted on them leaving. With little time remaining, they returned to Haizi Shan (5833m) in the hope of completing the route previously attempted [MEF 04/33] but once again were repulsed by bad weather. However, Rowat and Wynne-Jones made what was probably the first ascent of a consolation peak of 4800m. MEF 05/04 (*See article 'A Cautionary Tale' p71.*)

2005 British Habuqung Shan Derek Buckle with Alasdair Scott, Martin Scott and Bill Thurston. September-October 2005

The Habuqung Shan mountain range lies west of Lhasa and north of Sangsang and is believed to contain 16 peaks over 6000m, the highest being Dobzebo. Although British climbers visited an area a little to the north in 2002, it is thought that no climbing has ever taken place in the range. This team explored the area, and made the first ascent of Dobzebo North (6412m) via its south face and of Dobzebo South (6429m) via its south-west ridge, experiencing no technical difficulties on either. MEF 05/16 (*See article 'Dobzebo and the Battle of the Mountains', p55.*)

British Kajaqiao 2005 Mick Fowler with Phil Amos, Adam Thomas and Chris Watts. October-November 2005

Although located in an area of Tibet officially closed to foreigners, in 2004 Fowler received a permit for an attempt on Kajaqiao (6447m) in the Nyainqentanghla East Range. However it was 'the wrong sort of permit' and was withdrawn at a late stage. Fortunately a new (correct) permit was issued for 2005, and the team took full advantage of it. Despite very cold conditions (–15°C at BC) and 1.5m of snow falling while they were on the mountain, Fowler and Watts were successful in making the first ascent of the peak via its W face and NW ridge at a grade of Scottish V. They took six days to climb and three days to descend. Meanwhile, Amos and Thomas concentrated on the area to the south of Kajaqiao and reached a height of 5880m on the NW ridge of Manamcho (6240m). MEF 05/17 (*See article 'Through Permits and Powder', p2..*)

Imperial College Shar Kangsum 2005 Daniel Carrick with Naomi Bessey, Ben Gready and Joe Johnstone. July-August 2005

There are about 15 peaks above 6000m in the Shar Kangsum range of Tibet, and this University expedition planned to explore and make first (official) ascents of as many of them as possible. Although they had to abandon an attempt on their main objective Purba (aka Shahkangsham, 6822m) at c6000m due to avalanche risk, they were successful in making the first ascents of three other others: Peak 6603, Peak 6210 and Peak 6390, each being climbed 'alpine style' at grades up to PD+. MEF 05/25

British Xiashe Ed Douglas with Tom Prentice and Duncan Tunstall. October 2005

It is rumoured that Xiashe (5833m) in the Quionglai Shan of West Sichuan had been attempted once before by a Korean team, but this 'illegal' expedition was unsuccessful. Two New Zealand women pipped Douglas and Tunstall to the summit by a few days to claim the first official ascent. However, the British pair established a fine new route on the hitherto unclimbed 1300m north face, then descended by the west ridge. They called their route (which was graded Scottish IV/5) *Don't Cook Yak in Anger*. In the meantime, Prentice opted for a solo reconnaissance of the area (the mapping of which leaves a lot to be desired) during which he made an unsuccessful attempt on Pt 5690m by its long north-east ridge. MEF 05/36. (*See article 'Xiashe North Face', p35.*)

New Zealand Unclimbed Tibet 2005 Sean Waters with Jo Kippax. September-November 2005

Although a permit for a similar expedition was issued in 2004 it was withdrawn at a late stage. This year they were luckier, and although hampered by heavy rain, the team was able to access the Lawa Valley in the Nyainqentanglha East region of Tibet, where the precipitation continued in the form of snow, which made all progress difficult – impossible without snowshoes. After 12 days of effort, they established a camp on névé below the southern aspect of Birutaso (c.6550m). From here a full day's climbing took them 900m up steep snow/ice couloirs followed by snow arêtes and ramps to the summit, but necessitated an unplanned bivouac before descending next day. MEF 05/44

Hong Meigui Yunnan 2005 (caving) Richard Bayfield with Maxine Bateman, James Bruton, Louise Dugan, Simon Froude, Katie Froude, Ruth Kerry, Martell Linsdell, Alys Mendus, Hugh Penney, Ben Stephens, Jon Wichett and Steve Whitlock plus local contact Liu Hong. July-August 2005

This was a follow-up to recent expeditions [*including MEF 03/49 & 04/54*] to the Zhongdian limestone plateau at 4300m in Yunnan Province which seemed to indicate massive caving potential. In particular they planned to explore many of the high level entrances discovered in 2004 in the hope that they might improve on the previous area's depth record of 120m (in Dawa Dong). Sadly, the area did not fully live up to expectations, but nevertheless, aided by local yak-farmers, the team found some 30 new cave entrances and a massive resurgence of ice cold water that awaits investigation by a team of hot-blooded cave divers. (*For further information see website:* www.hongmeigui.net) MEF 05/51

PAKISTAN

British Kero Lungma 2005 Peter Holden with Bill Church and Colin Morton. July-August 2005

This trip was originally proposed by Dave Wilkinson, but he was unable to participate owing to a climbing injury incurred beforehand. The intention was to return to the Kero-Lungma glacier (visited by two of them in 1996) to explore its north-east branch and climb some of the biggest peaks at its head. They were successful in making what was probably the first ascent of 'Twin Peak I' (c5500m), but had to retreat several times from high camps on 'Twin Peak II' (c5450m) and Peak 6123m due to poor weather and dangerous conditions. They warned future expeditions to the area that indicated heights varied from one map to another, and rarely agreed with their own findings. MEF 05/31A

International Uli Biaho 2005 Jay Piggott and Jonathan Clearwater from NZ, Jeremy Frimer from Canada and Samuel Johnson from USA. July-August 2005

This team hoped to make the first ascent of the stunning 2000m line on the NE buttress of Uli Biaho (6109m) in pure alpine style: however, on arrival at its foot they realised why it remained unclimbed – a 60m summit mushroom avalanched down the face several times each day, making the route completely unjustifiable. An attempt on the mountain's south ridge took them within 400m of the summit before a storm forced a retreat. Three expedition members then made the first ascent of a 1600m rock route (VI, 5.11, A2 AI3, M5) on the SW ridge of Trango II (6327m), which they named *Severance Ridge*. MEF 05/35

CENTRAL ASIA & THE FAR EAST

2005 Ak-Su 'Free and Clean' Mark Pretty with David Pickford, Ian Parnell and Sam Whittaker. July-August 2005

Since access to the eastern bloc countries is now so much easier, the granite spires above the Ak-Su main and subsidiary valleys of Kyrgyzstan have become a popular destination for technical rock-climbing teams. The area has been likened to the 'Yosemite Valley in the 1930s with terrorism'.

This team planned to repeat some existing routes but also make some first ascents. Despite being plagued by bad weather they were successful in climbing two completely new routes, *The Beast*, 550m, with pitches up to E4 6a and *From Russia with Love*, 400m, up to E7 6b, the latter possibly ranking as one of the current hardest on-sight routes. They also freed an existing aid route and climbed a dozen one-pitch (up to 45m) routes between E3 and E7. MEF 05/02

Grand Poohbah Paul Knott with Grant Piper and Graham Rowbotham. July-August 2005

Maintaining his reputation for visiting remote mountain areas, this year Paul Knott chose the Fersmana glacier basin in the central region of Western Kokshaal-Too. The aim of his team was to explore and climb, and in particular to make the first ascent of the highest peak in the area – Pik 5697m, nick-named 'Grand Poohbah' in 2000 by Mike Libecki. After experiencing a number of problems in accessing the area – a vehicle breakdown, a closed road and a changed border – they were delighted to find the area populated by elegant spires and steep granite walls. Unfortunately, Grand Poohbah itself was defended by overhanging séracs and they could see no feasible route. They therefore turned their attention to other peaks, making the first ascent of Neizvestniy (Russian for 'Unknown', 5240m) and attempting others to which they gave appropriate Russian names, viz: Granitsa ('Border', 5370m), Pogranichnik ('Border Guard', 5220m) and Zastava ('Border Post', 5010m) but without reaching their summits. Being stranded for several days at the road head whilst trying to get out made them seriously consider taking a satellite 'phone on future trips.

MEF 05/18

Cambridge Mongolia 2005 Alan Dickinson with Tom Lambert. July-August 2005

The best laid plans oft go awry, especially when conditions on the ground fail to match their appearance on maps and satellite photographs. When this duo eventually reached Monhh Khiarhan (4202m) (Mongolia's second highest mountain) in the Altai Nuruu range, they found that a 70km ridge traverse that had been their prime objective 'looked rather tame' so they turned their attention to the peak itself. This they climbed from the north over a subsidiary peak (spotting footprints of what may have been a snow leopard en route) and returned the same way. After moving to the Tavanbogd National Park, they attempted a route on Huiten (4374m), the highest peak in Mongolia, but turned back 150m from the summit because of bad weather. However, they did complete what may be a new mixed snow and rock route on a peak of 3542m to its south-west. (*For further information see website*: www.mongolia2005.org.uk) MEF 05/32

University of Bristol 2005 Tajikistan Simon Spencer-Jones with Ed Bailey, James Byrne, Ian Hatcher, Rob Lavin, Amy Marshall, Stevo Nicholls and Sam Smith. June-July 2005

This team of past and present students of Bristol University with varied experience planned to explore the southern end of the 70-80km long Fedchenko glacier in the High Pamirs. Climbing in groups of two to four, they soon made first ascents or new routes on Peak Volodiya (5847m), Peak Bronwen (5550m) and Tanymas (5900m). The most experienced pair, Ian Hatcher and Simon Spencer-Jones, then set off to attempt the expedition's principal objective – a multi-day traverse of Peak Bakinshikh Kommisarov (6834m) and Peak Revolution (6948m). Unfortunately, the weather rapidly deteriorated, with strong winds and heavy snow, and the pair were never seen again, despite a number of air and land searches. We would like to express our deepest sympathy to their families and friends.

MEF 05/33

MISCELLANEOUS

Benarat 2005 (caving) Dick Willis with Tim Allen, Andy Atkinson, Mark Brown, Richard Chambers, Andy Eavis, Robert Eavis, Rich Gerrish, Martin Holroyd, Matt Kirby, Dave Nixon, Pete O'Neil, Robbie Shone, John Volanthin and Mark Wright. September-October 2005

The Mulu area of Sarawak is one of the most significant karst areas in the world so has long been popular with British cavers. This team proved that the Terikan caves formed a single 32km system: they also extended the Whiterock caves by 17km to a total of 20.9km and connected them to the Clearwater caves, making this the tenth longest system in the world, at 130km. There is obviously much more work to do in the area.

MEF 05/52

Book Reviews

COMPILED BY GEOFFREY TEMPLEMAN

Achttausend drüber und drunter
Hermann Buhl
Piper-Malik, 2005, 360 pp, price Euros 22.90

Why should the *Alpine Journal* carry a review of Hermann Buhl's life-story published in German when English-speaking readers have long been familiar with its classic telling in *Nanga Parbat Pilgrimage*? The answer – for completeness. Readers of *Nanga Parbat Pilgrimage* can only follow Buhl's life up to his legendary solo first ascent of the 'Naked Mountain'. There the book ends and anyone who wants to know more has to grab my own *The Kurt Diemberger Omnibus* (Bâton Wicks 1999) or my old *Summits and Secrets*... unless, that is, the reader is content with a couple of short chapters in Höfler and Messner's *Hermann Buhl – Climbing without Compromise* or can track down a fine piece of psychological research in the first edition of Chris Bonington's *Quest for Adventure*.

Hermann Buhl fell to his death with a collapsing cornice on 27 June 1957 on Chogolisa's summit ridge. In Germany, after the tragedy, I, as his last companion, wrote an epilogue-report for a 1958 memorial edition of Buhl's own book on his life, telling of our common experience and making a couple of subtle corrections to the events as described in the official expedition book by Marcus Schmuck.[1] These pages by myself about the Broad Peak climb and the fatal attempt on Chogolisa have been retained in this latest edition of Buhl's story.

So what is it that has turned this old bestseller into such a 'hit' five decades after its first appearance – for a 'hit' indeed it is in German-speaking Europe. Since *Achttausend drüber und drunter* ('Eight thousand – above and below') appeared 'new born' last September, it has already sold out and has gone into its second print.

The 'cherries on the tart' are Hermann Buhl's complete expedition diaries, published worldwide for the first time in this new-old book – unfortunately so far only in German, but that will change. Now in his diaries, beyond any art of 'shading' by later interpretation,[2] the grand man speaks with his own voice about his impressions at the very moment, day after day, page after page, written on the spot with his own hand! Here he is on Nanga Parbat in 1953 and on Broad Peak and Chogolisa in 1957, till the day before the fatal attempt. One can follow the gruelling climb up the avalanche-prone Rakhiot-face of Nanga Parbat and get an idea of the

Hermann Buhl (*Kurt Diemberger*)

tensions between Herrligkoffer and Buhl's sworn-together crew on the mountain before Hermann's incredible solo ascent. He also deals with the difficulties with the high-altitude porters, a reason for his later adoption of *Westalpenstil* – the first form of Alpine style – for Broad Peak. He wished to dispense with the help of porters and oxygen for the climb and rely just on a small team of friends.

The pages of his diary for Broad Peak reveal a critical Hermann Buhl, aware of the difficulties within his team, which was not composed of his originally chosen friends Hugo and Luis Vigl and himself, but had turned for various reasons into a 'foursome' together with Marcus Schmuck and his partner Fritz Wintersteller and a young Kurt Diemberger on his first expedition experience. (It is so long ago I feel the third person is only appropriate!)

At this point, as an additional 'cherry' to this edition, there is a memorandum by Buhl about events before the start of his last expedition, when he and Schmuck were caught in a tug-of-war over the leadership. Buhl's writing reveals clearly that he was the initiator of the enterprise – but finally, with the Austrian Alpenverein against him, accepted as a compromise to be the mountaineering leader – and overall leader on the mountain – whilst Schmuck was given the official general leadership. This was hardly a fortunate solution, bearing in mind that there were just two more members, Wintersteller and myself.

In spite of a couple of sermons delivered to me by Buhl for my education – for he considered himself my 'expedition-father' – we became friends and stood together on the top of Broad Peak at sunset – about two hours after Schmuck and Wintersteller. At this point the fragile unity of the team, held together by the common target, finally crumbled and the great achievement of this first ascent (which Buhl, as his diary shows, tried desperately to save for the eyes of the world as the unique common success it was) became split into a battle of small-minded considerations over individual merit – including the time of the first steps in the summit snows on 9 June 1957. As a result each pair then went for a separate peak, each on its own and without telling the others.

On Chogolisa, the sensitive Buhl, released now from the nervous tensions and pressure of the 'double leadership' with Schmuck, found again his great drive and enthusiasm. He was – as his last page of diary tells – 'in good shape', breaking trail in an enterprise where he found himself to be much more of a pioneer than on Broad Peak. Hermann Buhl enjoyed a spiritual high even on his last day, as if on Nanga Parbat. Then, in the fateful blizzard, he walked out of his life…

The first half of the 'new' book leads up to Nanga Parbat – telling of Buhl's multi-faceted experiences in the Alps; his youth in Tyrol, climbing the Dolomites and the western Alps, the Eiger, Walker Spur, his Badile solo and an involuntary bath in the Inn river when he fell asleep on his bicycle. And all written in great style, never boring. This is just as it was in the English language version, in a masterly translation by Hugh Merrick.

When Ken Wilson republished *Nanga Parbat Pilgrimage* in 1998 he looked back to its first appearance in English in 1956 when, as he said, the book 'struck an immediate chord with the ambitious young climbers of the day…Perhaps they were subconsciously preparing themselves for the obvious challenges of the Greater Ranges that were already beckoning as the first ascent phase drew to an end.' The book's present success confirms that for another generation nothing has changed.

And of Nanga Parbat, at the climax of Hermann Buhl's lonely pilgrimage? 'Buhl's solo… is now confirmed as one of the greatest mountaineering feats of all time,' says Wilson. But why does he wait to publish the second part of the book in English? At least the Buhl-diaries! Here, after Nanga Parbat, is the second high point of Buhl's life… one that even today is still exerting its influence on mountaineering in the Himalaya. 'Hermann Buhl has transferred the *Westalpenstil* into the Himalayas,' said Messner in his book *Die Herausforderung* (The Challenge), 1975, in a caption of a portrait of the great climber. In something of a contradiction, Messner, in another caption 25 years later, suggests that Buhl's 'rise to fame' ended with Nanga Parbat: 'His fall began, when he returned to Base Camp,' says Messner in *Climbing without Compromise*. Also in the German edition, below a picture of Buhl looking towards Chogolisa in the Höfler/Messner-book there is a comment, ascribed by Höfler to Messner, that 'Buhl's will of life was finished/emptied'. If that was so, how for Heaven's sake, could he have reached the summit of Broad Peak in spite of his frostbite?

Such contradictions, with Buhl's death on Chogolisa seeming to confirm the pessimists' view of Buhl's failing will, caused me to mount the barricades of the mind in a defence of my friend's memory. My case is set out in a six-page note or *Schlußbemerkungen* at the end of this book. Unfortunately my old Broad Peak companions, Schmuck and Wintersteller, felt cheated of their glory as first ascensionists – being a couple of hours ahead of Buhl and myself. Yet I, whom they branded a 'street urchin' and 'egomaniac', had reached the pair on the snow slope of the summit even before they left it. Handing their diaries to the writer Richard Sale[3] and his interpretation skills, they helped spin an account that is barely penetrable for anyone who wants to find out the historical truth about this expedition.[4]

Samantha Sacks from Toronto in an essay 'The Revision of History' published in *Alpinist* magazine (14) in 2005, after phone calls, interviews and having read *Summits and Secrets* as well as the 'treated' version of our companions, concluded: 'When I compare the two stories, it's hard to know whether the truth lies in one or in the other – or somewhere between them.' Greg Child, in the same article, points out that climbing histories are by their very nature personal accounts and therefore intrinsically subjective. This certainly is true – and gives the reader the possibility to live the climbers' experience, fears, happiness and fulfilment. It is that which counts in a book, not painstaking details like who was it that packed how many sandwiches in whose rucksack! It must be a certain type of writer, who loves to dig out the number of footsteps and weight of rucksacks of each climber as well as each word that was (perhaps) said, five decades earlier.

Far better then, to read a book like Hermann Buhl's *Nanga Parbat Pilgrimage*, whether the old or new version, that truly comes from the heart and the spirit of a climber. And let us hope that Buhl's diaries – his *Tagebücher* – are published in English soon.

Kurt Diemberger

NOTES

1 Marcus Schmuck died in August 2005, aged 80.
2 'Shading' is a reference to the 2005 International Festival of Mountaineering Literature (*AJ* 110, 414, 2005) when the theme was biographies and differing versions of climbing history. Jim Perrin remarked that the matter of shading had been crucial in his biography of Don Whillans. 'And the shading is as I wanted it to be,' said Perrin.
3 Also at the festival was Richard Sale whose *Broad Peak* (Carreg 2004) highlights Marcus Schmuck and Fritz Wintersteller as the driving force of the Austrian 1957 first ascent and casts Diemberger in a distinctly unflattering light. Diemberger, of course, has a strong personal interest in this latest version of Buhl's autobiography (as well as having written an accompanying commentary and provided many of the fine photographs) which makes him a slightly unusual choice as a reviewer. However, who better to comment on Buhl's Broad Peak and Chogolisa diaries than his rope mate on those climbs? The review also provides him an opportunity to respond to Sale's account.
4 Richard Sale's *Broad Peak* was reviewed in *AJ* 110, 369-371, 2005.

The Longest Climb - Back from the Abyss
Paul Pritchard
Robinson, 2005, £7.99

Paul Pritchard shot to climbing literary fame when his book *Deep Play*, published in 1977 by Ken Wilson's Bâton Wicks press, won the Boardman Tasker Award. In it he related a classic rags to riches story (I'm speaking metaphorically here – no one ever gets rich simply by climbing hard) of a talented British climbing bum, from humble beginnings in his local Lancashire quarry to mind-numbingly scary deeds on the likes of Gogarth and Sron Ulladale, then on to even more desperate adventures in Patagonia and the Himalaya. He excelled at every aspect of climbing and with the publication of his first book was hailed as the Joe Brown for our times. He famously blew the prize money on a round the world climbing trip and on the tick list was that fantastically improbable-looking Tasmanian sea stack – the Totem Pole. Here, his life was altered forever when his abseil rope dislodged a block that stove in his skull and left him paralysed down the right side. His second book *The Totem Pole* (Constable 1999) graphically related the horrendous story of the accident, heroic rescue by Celia Bull, and slow rehabilitation. It won him a second Boardman Tasker.

The Longest Climb takes up the story where *The Totem Pole* left off. Now married to his Australian nurse Jane, Pritchard has moved back to North Wales. A life that has been so besotted by climbing must be hard enough to lead when for whatever reason one suddenly finds one can no longer climb, but couple this with an inability to control your erratic right leg or use your right arm, not to mention a myriad of other difficulties, and it is hard to understand why Pritchard does not come over as bitter and twisted. To be sure there is the occasional lapse into expecting special treatment because of his disabilities and then damning those who treat him differently, but such occurrences are rare and are totally overshadowed by his determination as he gathers 'together some semblance of a life again... It was never going to be my previous life, full of mountains and cliffs and high living, but a life nevertheless'.

Things had to change; as Pritchard says, 'Before my accident I was never much of anything except a climber.' Now the climbing gear is sold off and the Climbers' Club guidebook project for Gogarth – a crag he 'loved more than girlfriends' – abandoned. In place of climbing, Pritchard sets about a gruelling regime of pushing himself through what would have been, in his previous life, absurdly simple tasks. Walking up a local hill is transformed from a pleasant easy hour or two in the fresh air into a nightmare struggle of logistics and grim determination that (only just) succeeds in overcoming despair. The same dogged characteristics that once got him to the top of *The Super Calabrese*, a new E8 on Gogarth's suicidally loose Red Wall, see him to the summit of Moel Elio (all of 726m).

No longer able to get an adrenalin rush from climbing 15 metres of unprotected 6a from a single RP belay, he resorts to racing a recumbent tricycle down Llanberis Pass. It wasn't really a race, it was a charity ride, but such is his competitive nature that to Paul it was still a race, and a 45km one at that. More such milestones are passed, from walking up Snowdon to moving the little finger of his right hand, and gradually Pritchard ups the ante, pushing himself into everything going, cycling, hiking, swimming, bowling, photography, even golf. Attempting to climb a 4000m-plus peak, he finally succeeds on Mount Kenya (5199m) in the company of professional mountaineering minders and a film crew. The culmination of these ever increasing efforts (for now at least) is his ascent of Kilimanjaro, at 5895m the highest peak in Africa, and anything but a picnic. The climb was achieved in the company of fellow disabled mountaineers, Jamie Andrew, Pete Steane and David Lim, respectively a quadruple amputee, a partial paraplegic, and the victim of a paralysing nerve disorder respectively. Add in too a fair dose of bad weather. Paul has to battle with his own self-doubt that at one point sees him turning back only to change his mind and make the summit.

Comparisons with all-round nice guy Jamie Andrew are inevitable, but in his stubborn, bulldog-like personality Pritchard comes across as closer in attitude to Norman Croucher or even more, that legless hero of a previous generation, Douglas Bader. It seems a very tough way to learn to temper your arrogance with humility but Pritchard is facing this too: 'I cringed. It was painful to see how others must have seen me once. OK, so I was never so rude but I still thought I was more important than many other people just because I could climb better than they could.'

Paul Pritchard has turned a personal tragedy into a personal triumph. He writes well and has produced a very readable story, full of odd twists of humour that lift up what could otherwise be a very dark tale indeed. A few silly proof-reading errors are irritating, and it seems odd to publish it in paperback without an initial hardback run, but this is a good book and is thoroughly recommended, as indeed are all his books.

Stephen Reid

Learning to Breathe
Andy Cave
Hutchinson, 2005, pp 276, £18.99

On Thin Ice
Alpine climbs in the Americas, Asia and the Himalaya
Mick Fowler
Bâton Wicks, 2005, pp 224, £18.99

I have known both Andy Cave and Mick Fowler for many years now and been fortunate enough to spend time with them both socially and in the mountains. For these reasons and out of respect for their climbing achievements, I eagerly awaited the publication of these two books. I am pleased to report that I have not been disappointed.

These are important works written by two of Britain's finest climbers. Coming as they do on the heels of titles by respected commentators who have chosen to focus on the more negative and dark sides of the sport, their appearance is doubly welcome. Here to restore the balance are books written by dedicated protagonists, who have managed to convey the challenge, adventure and sheer joy of our sport (admittedly, tinged with sadness at times) with few axes to grind. I for one would like to raise a glass to that.

It is a tough job to review these two books alongside each other, as, like their respective authors, they are markedly different in character. Each of the writers has set out with a different agenda, and while one is a first book, the other is a second. To the armchair reader, *On Thin Ice* will probably come across as the memoirs of an amateur enthusiast, and *Learning to Breathe* as a pit to the pinnacle tale of professional climbing self-development. However, the reality is somewhat more complex, as Mick does derive some income from climbing and Andy complements his professional climbing with academic work.

In *On Thin Ice* a more measured, mature and thoughtful Mick Fowler emerges than from his first book *Vertical Pleasure*. The format is essentially the same – a collection of climbing adventures snatched over weekends, short breaks and annual leave from his nine-to-five job with the Inland

Revenue. What has changed, however, are Mick's circumstances – he is now married with two children – forcing a reassessment of risks and absences.

For those readers who missed the first helping, Mick provides an introductory chapter, summarising earlier climbs, before going on to chronicle his climbing from 1988 to 2002. Visits to Wadi Rum in Jordan, the Lofoten Islands in Norway, Etratat in Normandy and Scotland in winter provide light entertaining interludes between expeditions. However, it is the series of trips to the greater ranges that are the historically most important and powerful passages. It is quite a list: Ak-su traverse, Taweche north-east buttress, north face of Changabang, Arwa Tower, north buttress of Mount Kennedy and Siguniang's north face). Most professional mountaineers would be happy to amass a series of such significant first ascents over an entire lifetime. The fact that they are the output of a little over 10 years and done while holding down a conventional job and tending the needs of a young family makes them incredible. Mick's enthusiasm, humour and understatement shine through the narrative, countered by more reflective passages as he tries to juggle his climbing with ever increasing commitments and responsibilities. This reflection gives balance to the book, makes it more accessible to the general reader and ultimately a much finer read than *Vertical Pleasure*.

In *Learning to Breathe*, Andy Cave has set out with great ambition to tell us a number of complementary stories. At its heart lies a classic 'rags to riches' theme. A boy from Royston born into a mining family follows in his father and grandfather's footsteps into the local pit. Soon he is on strike with time on his hands. What had been a weekend passion becomes an obsession. Climbing acts as a catalyst and broadens Andy's horizons, empowering him to leave the world he was born into and to educate himself academically. It is an extraordinary personal journey and in the telling admirably and amusingly describes two very different worlds and the people who inhabit them.

Learning to Breathe is also a piece of social history detailing the miners' strike of 1984-1985 and its effect on the communities involved. As it turned out the strike, its end and the ensuing pit closures were a pivotal moment in recent British history, ushering in a decline in union power and heavy industry, followed by a shift to a service-based economy. Andy's life has mirrored this time of momentous change, which together with his gifts as a writer placed him in a great position to document it and its effect on pit communities. Moving on, well-described climbs at home and abroad become increasingly difficult and demanding, driving the book to a powerful conclusion on Changabang.

By far the most telling chapters of both books deal with the ascent and epic descent of Changabang's north face in 1997. This is hardly surprising. The difficulty, effort, time and suffering involved during the ascent of the face itself were considerable enough, yet were eclipsed by what followed.

Steve Sustad took a tumble near the top, plucking Mick with him. The fall nearly cost them their lives and injured both climbers (Sustad sustaining a number of painfully broken ribs, Fowler a gashed nose). Then, on the descent Brendan Murphy, Andy's partner, was swept to his death by an avalanche. The rest of the descent and protracted trudge back to the safety of base camp over several high passes stretched the remaining climbers to their limits of physical and mental endurance. Their very survival hung in the balance, starkly illustrated by Andy abandoning his tent before crossing the final pass. Sheer will-power wins through in the end, leaving both authors to reflect movingly on the price paid. Obviously this expedition and its aftermath was difficult for everyone involved, but one gets the impression that as Brendan's climbing partner it was particularly hard on Andy.

I expect and look forward to further works from both authors. Andy has quite wisely been selective of the material used in his book, leaving many more adventures from his climbing career to date to be documented should he wish to do so. Mick is showing no signs of slowing his output of world-class first ascents in the greater ranges, and in a few years' time will doubtless have amassed enough new experiences for another instalment to share with us.

To conclude; two of Britain's finest climbers have produced two of the most notable pieces of recent British mountaineering literature. Personally, I feel that *Learning to Breathe* is a finer work of literature, but as a record of contemporary mountaineering achievement *On Thin Ice* is unparalleled. Both books have rightly won mountain literature prizes and therefore hardly require my endorsement, but for those of you who have somehow overlooked one or both of these titles, I recommend you make amends with a trip to your local bookstore.

Simon Yates

Mountain Rescue
Chamonix – Mont Blanc
Anne Sauvy
Bâton Wicks, 2005, pp 368 £14.99

When I saw the red rescue helicopter homing in to me (broken legged below the Glacier du Tour on the AC's 2005 Chamonix ice meet) I knew I would write the review for this book. I had gone out to Chamonix intent on press-ganging a Valley resident, or at least a regular visitor, into the task. However, a boulder beneath soft snow and a ski binding that failed to release dictated otherwise. The mountain rescue service – the PGHM – had suddenly shot up greatly in my estimation and during the coming weeks, with my right leg immobilised, I would have time to digest this intense and lengthy tome.

Anne Sauvy is respected as the author of finely crafted short stories set in, or more usually above, her beloved Chamonix. In 1997 she spent the summer at the helipad of the rescue service at Les Bois, near Les Praz, watching, listening to the gendarmes and doctors as they returned from missions, sometimes hazardous, often routine, and gradually becoming a part of the helipad family. This book is the chronicle of that season.

In bald statistics, it was a 'normal' season for the busiest rescue service in the world – 415 rescues, 36 deaths (three more than the previous year), 1 missing, 84 ill, 281 wounded and 183 unhurt. Sauvy is careful to emphasise how relatively few this is compared to the hundreds of thousands who have found joy in Chamonix's mountains during those same three months (June, July and August).

Thankfully, though, Sauvy is rarely concerned with statistics and for all the bureaucratic plainness of her title, this is the most human of books, both in its portrayal of the rescue crews, whom she invests with a quiet grandeur, and of the pain, physical or emotional, suffered by those whose fun in the mountains has been dashed so abruptly. Layered between the call-outs, for example, to pick up a victim of altitude sickness from Mont Blanc or pluck an injured climber from overhanging slabs on the Aiguille Pierre Allain, is the banter of crews, their fixation with the Tour de France on the TV, and Sauvy's progress reports on the redstarts that nest in the roof of the helipad chalet.

While Sauvy's short stories have a polished elegance, a veneer almost, her observations here have, at times, a harrowing nakedness, most particularly when the helicopter brings back the body of one of the rescuers, Régis Michoux, killed while descending the Whymper Couloir after a training ascent of Grand Montets Arête with fellow team members. As the tragedies mount, Sauvy resolves to abandon the book, but is persuaded that rescuers' story must be told.

There are one or two oddities in the translation, most irritating of which is the word 'mechanician' for the second member (besides the pilot) of the helicopter crew. Maybe the word 'mechanic' was thought to have too much of the oily rag about it (there is an unconvincing footnote that hints at this) but it would have made more sense, as would 'flight engineer' or possibly 'winch-man'.

Much more distracting, though, is Sauvy's tendency, as the modern phrase has it, 'to go off on one', railing against the madness of this 'dismembered and crudely savage world' – politicians, television, taxes, permissiveness, second home owners, architects and (endlessly) journalists. Sauvy is incensed by the media's regular invasions of the helipad, their intrusive behaviour in trying to film bodies, and their focus on death and the sensational. There is a certain irony then, when on 10 August, Sauvy decides to dispense with the sprains and minor cases of altitude sickness etc and keep to 'dramatic, novel or significant events'. What is sauce for the goose becomes sauce for the gander.

Yet it is the personal nature of the book (for all the digressions that implies) that is its strength. There are several extraordinary pages where the body of a young Russian woman climber is being transported, suspended way beneath the helicopter on a rope, that are among the most beautiful I have read. The victim of rockfall on the Dru, Elena performs an aerial ballet, seeming to come back to life through mysterious grace. It is as if her body, 'for the space of a moment, wanted to appear in its full beauty, before leaving us for ever,' says rescuer Olivier Fernandez. Whether the poetry of this passage is really Fernandez or Sauvy exercising licence, it is surely born of the bond of trust and friendship the author had won with the team.

And after all the sniping at the journalists (I am, of course, sensitive in this matter) it is interesting to find buried in the appendices the admission, in the words of Captain Jean-Claude Gin, then commander of the PGMH, that: 'If the PG has survived, it is thanks to the press coverage.' Good or ill, the media keep the service in the eye of the politicians who allocate the funds. And I for one have reason to be profoundly grateful to all concerned. Even as I was being winched from the slope in a maelstrom of spindrift whipped up by the helicopter rotors, the words were beginning to form: 'Thanks guys!'

Stephen Goodwin

Mountain Rescue

Bob Sharp and Judy Whiteside

Hayloft, 2005, pp 264, £20

The year 2005 has brought a classic example of the immutable law of public buses: you wait for ages for a good book on mountain rescue and then two come along together.

It was my pleasure to introduce authors Bob Sharp and Judy Whiteside at the launch of this book last November during the Kendal Mountain Book Festival. The pair were surrounded by smiling friends and colleagues, fellow rescuers mainly I think, a cheerful group that somehow exemplified what is special about the rescue service in the UK. They could have been the parents of a junior football club or charity fundraisers; that is, 'ordinary' people (no one really is) prepared to turn out and help others for no material reward at all.

Sharp and Whiteside start from a similar premise to Anne Sauvy, that the press and TV frequently sensationalise or misreport the business of mountain rescues. However their approach to correcting the record is entirely different. While Sauvy opts for reportage and digressive opinion, Sharp and Whiteside have gone for straight completeness, telling the story 'from the inside out', explaining how the service in the UK is organised, how it is trained, the wide variety of call-outs, the hardships, risk and subtle rewards. Rescuers, casualties and family members all have their say. 'When that bloody bleeper goes off – so does he…' tells of another dinner gone cold.

Both the authors speak from experience – Sharp is team leader of the Lomond MRT and a veteran of some 250 rescues – and have clearly taken great pains to present an accurate, readable and well-illustrated account of the UK service. When the pager bleeps, off they go, not knowing for how long or at what cost. Why? A challenge, an adrenalin high, a chance to test one's mettle, banter and camaraderie; all play their part. The common thread is a willingness to help others, often fellow climbers or walkers.

But don't let any of this scare you off the hills. Apparently slips are more common around the house than in the mountains. As the authors observe, if you want to slip and bang your head on something, then stay at home.

Stephen Goodwin

Breaking Trail: A Climbing Life
Arlene Blum
Scribner, 2005, pp 330, US$27.50

Breaking trail is what Arlene Blum does. Not just as a Himalayan climber, for which she is well known, but also as a scientist, explorer and speaker. Her first book, *Annapurna: A Woman's Place*, like the 1987 Annapurna expedition she led, brought her immediate and well-deserved acclaim. But writing a memoir is also a high-risk activity, and Blum doesn't shrink from this challenge either. This volume offers a much broader context of her adventures, as well as a tantalizing glimpse of her motivations, some of which are surprising.

The surprising bits open each chapter, with deeply personal flashbacks to her childhood, revealing a vulnerability that is startling in such a formidable woman. Blum admits that in writing the book, more than 90 per cent of her time was concentrated on the early family research. Having grown up in such an overly protective family, she could almost be expected to title her book *Breaking Free*.

But *Breaking Trail* it is: from the American Pacific North-west to Denali, from Africa to the Pamirs, from Afghanistan to Everest, from Bhutan to Ladakh. She treks and skis and climbs her way onto an impressive number of expeditions and adventures around the world, many of which are described as nail-biting page-turners.

Some of Blum's most impressive achievements are her all-female ascents: Denali, Annapurna and Bhrigupanth. Her reasons for mounting all-women expeditions spring from her experiences of discrimination as a climber, be they real or perceived. Her story is written firmly from the position of an 'outsider', at least relative to the established American climbing fraternity of that time. Undoubtedly, there was a certain amount of chauvinism in the '60s and '70s, and Blum often felt the brunt of it. A common criticism she heard was that she, and other women like her, were attempting to overstep their bounds in order to prove themselves. But we also know that other women climbers were not having quite so tough a time. The close-knit climbing communities loosely associated with Harvard, the American Alpine Club and the Pacific North-west treated other leading female climbers such as Molly Higgins and Marty Hoey a little more gently. Why? It's hard to say conclusively, but this book is clearly an attempt by Blum to unearth some of those demons.

Her explanations of these situations are necessarily one-sided. As she explained on a memoir panel at the Banff Mountain Book Festival in 2005, an autobiography is only one 'take' on the truth – one's own. And although she stresses that her main goal was to provide some good personal storytelling, much of the book is also an apologia on the history of climbing attitudes towards women climbers – quite a convincing one. Ironically, in the process of defending her perspective to readers – and, in person, to some whom she perceives as the worst offenders of the time – she breaks new ground, this time within herself. Freely admitting the cathartic value of writing about her personal mountaineering history, she equally freely admits the therapeutic value of finally confronting some of the characters she has resented for so many years, and having an honest conversation.

Blum is a high achiever, in everything she does. While training and apprenticing hard as a mountaineer, she was also successfully pursuing a PhD in biochemistry at top American universities. And here too she breaks trail; her research results in the banning of two cancer-causing chemicals and opens up an entirely new area of biophysical research. She's also a charismatic leader and successful motivational speaker.

Blum's style is compelling in its juxtapositions: the worlds of academe and high-altitude camps; her amazing self-confidence accompanied by a sense of victimization; her triumphs and tragedies. Her style is very personal, as Chris Bonington notes in his foreword: 'Arlene … is courageously open about her private life.' The reader cannot help but be absorbed by her family struggles, her humiliations, her deeply felt losses of death in the mountains, and her unabashed pride at success. Arlene Blum bares her soul.

The fact that she doesn't quite solve all her personal problems in this volume leaves the impression of a memoir of *this* part of her life, not her *entire* life. That life is still a work in progress and I, for one, hope to see the next memoir instalment in another few years. Not according to Blum, who says that this book was terribly difficult to write, and swears that there will not be another one: '*Annapurna* took me one year to write. I've been working on this one ever since – almost twenty years!' Let's hope she changes her mind.

The book is well illustrated with black-and-white photographs throughout. Its lack of an index makes it less valuable as a research tool, which is unfortunate since there is an impressive amount of material on a great number of significant expeditions that took place at an interesting point in the history of mountaineering. Perhaps in the next edition – or the next instalment.

Bernadette McDonald

Kangchenjunga
Imaging a Himalayan Mountain

Simon Pierse

School of Art, University of Wales, Aberystwyth, 2005, pp 128

Kangchenjunga has long fascinated not only climbers but tourists, botanist and plant-hunters, artists, photographers and travellers generally. Lying on the border of Sikkim and Nepal, the mountain is clearly visible from the hill station of Darjeeling. Indeed it seems to dominate the view from there, drawing all eyes towards it. As such it was the subject of intense scrutiny and speculation long before it was first climbed in 1955.

Believed to be the highest mountain in the world until the mid-19th century (at 8586m it is in fact the third highest) it is a distinctive presence; instead of the classical pointed peak of popular imagination, the massif appears as a vast castellated and crenulated fortress. Such is the difference in height between the peak and the viewpoints in Darjeeling that it sometimes appears to float above the clouds or mist, a seemingly disembodied and enchanted kingdom. Joe Brown was awestruck when he first saw it:

> The sky was steaming with vapours and I could just discern the outline… I was looking at a gigantic unearthly shape, boiling inside a tissue-thin bank of cloud. This was truly an incredible sight. I seemed to be looking up at an angle of 45 degrees at the mountain, yet it was nearly 50 miles away….

Simon Pierse has not set out to write a conventional history of mountaineering on Kangchenjunga but to attempt something more interesting and ambitious – an account of the ways in which the mountain has been perceived and subsequently depicted in prose, photography, paintings and prints. As he suggests, Kangchenjunga 'has been a topographical feature to be sketched, mapped and surveyed; it has been seen as an embodiment of the sublime, a picturesque motif, a mountaineering challenge, a peak conquered but left untrodden; and recurrently throughout all of these, a sacred mountain and symbol of the spiritual. Added to all of these is the religious significance of the mountain to the Nepalese and Sikkimese people who live in its shadow, and to whom the mountain is symbolically the residence of a god.' The name Kangchenjunga can be translated as *The Five Treasuries of Great Snow*, referring to the five principal peaks of the massif. Not only intensely poetic and evocative, it seems particularly appropriate, suggesting not just size and majesty, but something sacred and otherworldly.

The breadth of Pierse's enquiry is thus apparent. This is a potentially enormous subject, given that probably no other Himalayan mountain apart from Everest has attracted such attention over such an extended period, and Pierse navigates his way through a complex and fascinating narrative with admirable clarity and concision.

In the event, he does get sidetracked by the mountaineering history of the mountain, retelling the fascinating stories of the various expeditions; including Sir Douglas Freshfield's circumnavigation of 1899, the ill-starred 1905 expedition that included Aleister Crowley, the self-styled 'Great Beast 666', the German expeditions of 1929 and 1931, and the International Expedition of 1930 that included Frank Smythe.

While it can seem, as his narrative develops, that his stated purpose has been somewhat lost in the desire to account for the exploration of the area around the mountain and the many different attempts on it prior to 1955, what actually emerges is a realisation of just how important a role mountaineering has played in defining the image of the mountain, especially in the 20th century. What also becomes apparent is the way that mountaineering and mountain travel are just one aspect of a complex matrix of creativity; plant-hunting expeditions yield wonderful topographical paintings, exploration produces ground-breaking and astonishing photography, climbers bring back from high altitude subtly different ways of seeing the world.

The question of the degree to which mountaineering might itself be designated an art is a fascinating notion and one that we continue to debate. To a mind conditioned by contemporary art – in particular its conceptual manifestations – Freshfield's circumnavigation of the massif seems now to recall the carefully structured walks of contemporary artists such as Richard Long and Hamish Fulton, and vice versa; one might suggest parallels between the process of climbing the peak and conceptual projects involving journeys by younger artists such as Pierre Huyghe, who recently travelled to Antarctica, or Tacita Dean. On the mountain decisions about the route are both practical and creative; one yearns not only to create an achievable route to the peak, but one that is also aesthetically pleasing. Climbers are creative people. Climbing is creative.

I would have welcomed further discussion of such ideas, which lurk in the background of Pierse's account, for when he does hypothesise his analyses are both interesting and convincing. For example, of the phenomenon of the disembodied mountain, in which the peak hovers above a sea of clouds or mist, he suggests: 'This, along with Kangchenjunga's name, which when freely interpreted, can be taken to mean a kind of sacred space, has helped to fix in the imaginations of generations of westerners the idea of the mountain as an ethereal realm, disembodied from the world and periodically revealed in the same manner as a vision.' Are Himalayan climbers then visionaries, seeking the purity, the sanctity, the cold brightness of the high altitude world?

Pierse's assessments of the value of the images of the mountain he discusses are also convincing. The painter Edward Lear (perhaps better known today as the writer of nonsense verse) visited Darjeeling in 1874 and on his return to Europe produced a series of large oil paintings. These are fascinating and impressive pictures – and possibly the only examples of a major European painter of the 19th century working on Himalayan subjects. But Pierse is correct in identifying an awkwardness, a contrivance to them, which one does not seem to find in Lear's wonderful topographical watercolour sketches, made before the subject. Pierse also rightly praises Vittorio Sella's exquisite photographs, made during the 1899 circumnavigation with Freshfield, which set an extraordinarily high standard for high mountain photography. Pierse suggests that 'the term that Sella himself used to describe his rigorous technical and aesthetic standards: *la realta severa* (severe reality) might also be used to sum up the quality of rare beauty that is found in the images themselves.' He rightly calls Norman Hardie's photograph, *The Untrodden Summit of Kangchenjunga, 26 May 1955* 'an outstanding image of mountaineering history.'

Kangchenjunga was, of course, first climbed in 1955 by Charles Evans' British expedition, and the mountain has continued to occupy a special place in British mountaineering. That expedition was exemplary in so many ways, not least for the due respect accorded to the beliefs of local people, which meant that Band and Brown stopped short, just 20 feet or so away from the final summit. One wonders how many subsequent ascensionists (almost 200 are listed in *AJ* 2005) have acted with such due care and attention to the culture of the region in which the mountain lies.

Pierse's book is a valuable addition to the literature of both mountaineering and the art of the mountains. It is essential reading for anyone interested in the position that mountaineering occupies in the interface between culture and nature, and the products of that interface. It serves to remind us that while, as far as the general public goes, Everest has inevitably become the focus of attention, Kangchenjunga is absolutely key both to the development of mountaineering in the greater ranges and to the meaning that such places occupy in our imaginations.

Ben Tufnell

Mount Everest: The Reconnaissance 1935. The Forgotten Adventure
Tony Astill
With foreword by Lord Hunt
and introduction by Sir Edmund Hillary
Published by the author, 2005, pp 359, £30
email: alpes@supanet.com tel: 0044 (0) 23 80293767

The fact this book has a foreword by John Hunt, who died in 1998, is a good illustration of just how long this project has absorbed Tony Astill. His task was to fill the front-tooth gap on the shelves of Everest literature that left Eric Shipton's 1935 reconnaissance as the only pre-war expedition without a full account and also, I would guess, the only expedition without a book well into the 1980s. Such a monumental effort deserves serious consideration.

There's no doubt that this book is very welcome, which is more than can be said for several recent Everest books by modern climbers who seem to gather up the richest material and convert it to dirt. Astill has made a strenuous effort to weave together the contrasting, often delightfully so, diaries and recollections of the different protagonists. He was quite right to delay publication when he gained access, at a late stage, to Michael Spender's glorious diaries, since these add a literary richness that is often absent from the other diaries.

They all have their own voice, however, and Astill lets them speak in their own words. New Zealand climber Dan Bryant's likeability shines through; Tilman's miniaturist entries offer a stark integrity in comparison with Spender, and are often more revealing than their brevity might suggest. There is one entry in particular from Spender, for 20 June, which he spent alone at the village of Phuru. Woken at midnight by conch shells and oboes, he gives the musical notation for the racket, and a description of his terror at hearing it. Early that morning, trying to leave the village, he is struck down with a stomach illness and has to return, but completes his survey work first as best he can. 'Fetched by Dzongpen [the local official],' he writes, 'to his best couch where I spent some crazy hours thinking I was a Chinese puzzle. The Dzongpen was charming. His room was clean, he burned tapers and incense, fetched me water and showed the greatest concern, keeping the house quiet and the room empty of the curious.'

The doctor, the inestimable Charles Warren, is brought to the village, and the two men agree on a diagnosis of malaria. Spender takes sleeping powders and collapses into sleep. 'Dreamt very vividly that E. [his wife, Erika] brought forth an incredibly healthy child of indeterminate sex and was immediately afterwards enormously healthy and we went out together the same evening.'

Here in one brief diary entry is the surreal intensity of mountain exploration: the determination to work despite illness, the exoticism he revels in despite his misery, the acknowledgement of human kindness from a stranger, the interjection of powerful and hallucinatory imaginings of home. It is intoxicating stuff.

Astill's book is studded with revelatory moments like this, reminding me of what an epic encounter it was for the first humans coming against such a remote and inhospitable terrain. 'This 1935 expedition,' Astill writes, 'was to experience some of the same romance of the reconnaissance of 1921.' I adored references to tents made of 'aero-canvas' and baths taken at the Tollygunge Club. The comprehensive detail of the book does not make it an effortless read, and at times I found myself wishing Astill had pushed his analysis further at the expense of sometimes repetitive narrative. But the sheer weight of evidence made me rethink several things.

Dan Bryant, the rugged New Zealander whose inclusion led to Ed

Hillary's inclusion in Shipton's 1951 reconnaissance, and H W Tilman were dropped for the 1936 expedition to Everest. The nature and scale of Bryant's afflictions – boils, carbuncles and rope-burns that became badly infected – suggest to me that he was suffering some systemic problem other than chronic altitude sickness. Tilman too, who had previous experience at altitude and would climb Nanda Devi the following year, could also have been suffering from another illness. Ironically, it seems, his poor performance ultimately proved to his benefit.

The exhaustive descriptions of what people ate on the expedition also made me wonder. It clearly fascinated the team itself. My medical knowledge is protozoic, but Astill offers the raw material for an interesting analysis by an expert of how well or ill-prepared the pre-war expeditions were. As it happens, no amount of good food or tough New Zealanders would have made any difference in 1936, when the expedition met an early monsoon.

You could argue that such questions are now dryly academic but I don't think so. As Shipton's biographer Peter Steele acknowledges, Shipton is a pin-up for the modern generation of lightweight Himalayan mountaineers, particularly in America. If climbers know one thing about him, and it often is one thing, it's his 'back-of-an-envelope' planning style. Astill calls Shipton's lightweight approach 'slightly obsessive'. All my climbing life I have found it inspirational, without ever examining why that should be. This book made me feel a re-evaluation is overdue. Shipton was after all sacked from the 1953 show because his organisational skills were slapdash. But I don't think, on the evidence of this book, that the allegation is fair. Not that he didn't inflict organisational hiccups on his co-campaigners. Bryant and Tilman, in Darjeeling days before the rest of the team, had no idea exactly who was coming to join them.

Modern climbers should revere Shipton, I believe, not for some putative alpine-style guru status, but for his philosophical approach to mountaineering. After all, their equipment and knowledge base, along with fast approaches, make this world profoundly different from Shipton's. It is his restless passion for unexplored terrain, his need to cut away the cultish waffle that he could see surrounding Everest like afternoon cloud, that is so appealing.

There are occasional blips in Astill's research. He recounts the story, first told in Tenzing's autobiography, that his father Mingmar crossed the Nangpa La to give his son a surprise visit. While it's true that Tenzing's father traded across the Nangpa La in the 1920s, he never left Tibet and was living in 1935 at Tsa, where his wife was a servant. In fact, Astill recounts how the expedition stopped here, and bought food. (Tenzing would bring Earl Denman to the same house in 1947.) This is not a major error but it did provoke in me thoughts about the relationship between Sahibs and Sherpas. I think largely the expedition members were curious, often paternalistic, sometimes patronising. They didn't, however, have the means to understand intimately the tensions and concerns of their Sherpa friends. I sometimes wonder if the Italians, who seemed to have combined exploration with cultural academic enquiry in the shape of Fosco Maraini, had attempted Everest, they might have packed an anthropologist instead of, or more likely alongside, a surveyor. I suppose the RGS wasn't like that in those days.

No matter, the care, thought and effort of this book deserve great credit. It is fabulously illustrated, with some wonderfully eccentric shots. Here is Kempson, clearly bouldering en route for Everest, a pad person to his fingertips. We see Tilman in his Homburg and Rinzing propping an umbrella over Kempson's head. Warren's portrait, all raffish charm, put me in mind of the North Wales rock climber Noel Craine. Nothing, it seems, changes much, perhaps not even Everest.

Ed Douglas

I'll Call You in Kathmandu. The Elizabeth Hawley Story
Bernadette McDonald
The Mountaineers Books, 2005, pp 25, US$24.95

The Hawley Story is fascinating stuff for anyone with an interest in the chronicling of Himalayan mountaineering and that perennial favourite, climbers' gossip. So what does this acid-tongued interrogator really think of the procession of climbing big shots, quiet achievers, and dissembling pretenders who have trooped through Kathmandu this past 40 years?

That Elizabeth Hawley's opinion came to matter is without doubt. After the Russian ace Anatoli Boukreev (subsequently killed in an avalanche on Annapurna I) reached only the secondary summit on Shisha Pangma, he lamented to a friend: 'I've got to go back – Elizabeth says I didn't really climb it.'

A serious-minded, middle-class girl from the American Midwest, Hawley reached Kathmandu in February 1959 by way of Baghdad, Tehran, Karachi and Delhi at the end of a two-year round-the-world tour, having quit *Fortune* magazine at the age of 34. It was only a short visit but she was captivated by the place – then still very much in its mediæval time warp – and in September 1960 returned for good, working as a part-time newswire reporter, though 'journalist' was only one of several hats she wore.

Hawley's worldwide reputation rests largely on her role as a reporter on mountaineering in the Nepal Himalaya, with particular emphasis on ascents and failures on Everest. Over the decades a vast archive has accumulated – thankfully published on disc in 2004 by the American Alpine Club as *The Himalayan Database: The Expedition Archives of Elizabeth Hawley*. The data has been extracted from a process better described as 'interrogation' than 'interview'. A team would barely have settled into their Kathmandu hotel when there would be a message that 'Miss Hawley' had arrived in reception. AC president Stephen Venables likened it to being called to see the headmistress.

Ironically, 'Liz' Hawley has no direct experience of climbing at all and has never even trekked as far as Everest Base Camp. But analysis has not been her intention. Hawley prides herself on reporting facts rather than opinion – a chronicler rather than an historian. However for *I'll Call You in Kathmandu* McDonald has skilfully drawn her out on generations of mountaineers. Bonington she judges the 'most outstanding climber of the seventies' and Messner in the 1980s 'the supreme star of the Himalayas'.

Others she is less charitable about, but I wouldn't want to blunt your sense of anticipation by naming names here. Nor will I reveal the answer to McDonald's probings over rumoured affairs with, among others, Jimmy Roberts, Eric Shipton, Andrzej Zawada and Don Whillans (the mind boggles!). Hawley declares she is 'not the marrying type', but one senses she would have said 'yes' to Ed Hillary whom she regards as the finest person she has ever met. Hawley has been a tireless worker for Hillary's Himalayan Trust and the pair became close following the death of Hillary's first wife and daughter Belinda in a light aircraft in the Khumbu.

McDonald's 'Hawley Story' is comparable to Ed Douglas's biography of Tenzing and Jim Perrin's of Don Whillans in that it tells the story not just of one individual but of a whole milieu. In her chronicler's role, Liz Hawley must have quizzed thousands of climbers – myself among them – yet she herself has remained, to most, something of an enigma. McDonald has succeeded in turning the tables on the inquisitor. When, at the end of their conversations, Bernadette pinned Elizabeth on the affairs and marriage stuff, Hawley couldn't duck it. 'You cunning vixen,' she chided McDonald. But the biographer's job was done and the result is this sympathetic and insightful portrait.

Stephen Goodwin

Recollections 1915-2005

Edward H Peck

Published privately, 2006, pp 315

The Alpine Journal may not seem an appropriate place to consider the privately published memoirs of a diplomat. But Sir Edward Peck's distinguished career, culminating in his appointment as High Commissioner to post-colonial Kenya, Chair of the Joint Intelligence Committee and, finally, the UK Permanent Representative to Nato, was embroidered throughout by his deep passion for mountains and mountaineering. *Recollections* is peppered with accounts of small-scale expeditions to mountain ranges made available to Peck during postings and official visits abroad, particularly in Turkey and during his time in Africa.

Not all readers will necessarily be interested in all the diplomatic detail, but most of this is readable and entertaining. Peck's attendance or involvement in some key moments in recent British history – the Cicero spy scandal, for example, during the war, or his experiences in Berlin – are told well and offered this reader at least a leg-up in his learning. The cast list of his contemporaries includes the former Foreign Secretary Denis Healey, and the current US Secretary for Defence, Donald Rumsfeld.

Perhaps the most engaging passages are about his childhood, particularly those early years spent in Switzerland where his love for mountains developed. He recalls meeting Charles Bruce on the Dents du Midi in 1924, and the affection for what seems now a distant age is matched with a keen eye for the revelatory detail. I almost laughed out loud as he remembered the clacking of mating tortoises that enlivened his walk to work in Ankara.

He was a friend of Robin Hodgkin, and they climbed together in the Ala Dag, Peck recovering a swastika flag from the summit of Demirkazik which was presented to the AC's archives. He skied with John Hunt in Greece in 1947, and long into retirement he was still travelling around the globe, while enjoying his relocation from Kent to the Cairngorms.

I doubt all those awarded the GCMG – 'God Calls Me God', as the joke has it – are quite so good-humoured and down-to-earth, and I couldn't help wondering whether a lifetime contemplating the enormity of nature on Peck's days off had a beneficial influence during sticky negotiations at the office; a likeable book from a remarkable man.

Ed Douglas

High Endeavours
The Life and Legend of Robin Smith
Jimmy Cruickshank
Canongate, 2005, pp 384, £16.99

It is 44 years since Robin Smith died at the age of 23, but for those who knew him the memory of his life is fresh. Jimmy Cruickshank's biography, *High Endeavours: The Life and Legend of Robin Smith* is a testament to an extraordinary life and talent and to the lasting impression he left on Scottish climbing and climbers.

The account is in three parts. The first is devoted to Smith's early life from his birth in Calcutta, the second son of emigrant Scots, to his separation from his parents aged eight to be educated at boarding school in Scotland, and his growing exposure to and love of the hills. The second part covers his rapidly maturing talent both academically and on steep rock and ice in Scotland, the Lakes and Wales, and the Alps. The last section covers the ill-fated joint Russian British expedition to the Pamir and Robin's death in a fall with Wilfrid Noyce.

The book draws heavily on the accounts of those who climbed with him in winter and summer on Scottish cliffs, Alpine faces and ridges and finally, tragically, on Pik Garmo. Unusually for a work of this nature, the author is not a mountaineer, but a childhood friend. Cruickshank met Robin at

George Watson's school in Edinburgh, and over the next few years the pair began to explore the hills through the tutelage of Archie Hendry, their French teacher. Cruikshank's direct climbing involvement with Robin only lasts as far as a trip to Skye, after which he decides that cricket is more to his liking and gives up climbing.

One would think that this would be a considerable bar to writing such a biography, and certainly there is an air in the book of the author observing exploits with which he has a diminishing understanding and sympathy. Countering this lack of direct knowledge of Robin's later career, he has drawn on the accounts of many of Robin's later climbing companions and on extracts from Smith's diary and his writing, particularly from the journals of the Scottish Mountaineering Club and Edinburgh University Mountaineering Club. This gives the book a rather disjointed progress and at times it takes on the feel of an anthology with little attempt to explore psychology and motivation or to deal critically with others' contributions. Nonetheless, the biography covers the main events of Smith's short life and his rise to climbing superstar and one has to admire the author's perseverance in drawing together written sources from most aspects of Robin's career. In this he had the advantage of earlier work done by an SMC member, John Inglis, who was killed in a fall from *Parallel Buttress* Lochnagar in February1994. Inglis's article was published posthumously in the 2002 SMC journal.

Smith was a complex character, as becomes clear from the contrasting accounts in this book. Some, such as Malcolm Slesser who led the Scottish contingent on the Pamir expedition, found him intolerable while recognising his talent. And it is hard to sympathise with Smith's reported behaviour, at one time holding Slesser underwater until he nearly drowned and later pissing into his tent; though on a later occasion he delighted Slesser by bringing him breakfast in his tent on a cold and miserable morning. Others, particularly women, thought him a most courteous and sensitive individual.

My own dealings with Robin were wholly pleasurable. We climbed together on a number of occasions, some of which are covered in the book. Like many of us, he delighted in scruffiness and the inadequacy of our equipment and provisions. He had a rather cavalier attitude to danger, but then most of us had at an age when we believed ourselves immortal. Early in our acquaintance we sat at the top of Rannoch Wall on Buachaille Etive Mor after a hard climb. It had started to drizzle and I coiled the rope while Robin told me of falling solo from the crux of *White Ghyll Chimney* and only crushing an orange in his pocket after the one hundred foot drop. I was impressed but even more so when instead of slanting off to descend the easy *Curved Ridge*, he strolled to the edge of the wall and started down *Agag's Groove* with me a reluctant follower on the steep greasy rock. With Robin, the day was always tending towards the epic, especially in winter when a struggle back to the hut down ice-glazed rock lit by a failing torch while the driving snow blinded the eyes, would be the highlight of the climb.

He could occasionally appear distant, especially when in the company of Dougal Haston, who was frequently unpleasantly arrogant to lesser mortals. And at times, perhaps in an attempt to prove himself to Haston, he was a rebellious hellraiser. Of course, these traits are not uncommon in the climbing fraternity. There are enough examples of Robin's sensitivity and courteousness in the book to counterbalance his other side. Certainly, my experience, as a little bit of a hellraiser myself, was that Robin was more thoughtful than most of my contemporaries. Letters he wrote to me include an apology for completing with Haston a first ascent we had explored together, and an account of the crux pitch on *Point Five* in which he explained how the conditions had made it so easy compared to my five-hour struggle. Nowhere did he allude to the truth that his talent far exceeded mine. A lesser man would have crowed.

So I'm sure that this book for all its faults of style, for all its taking of others' reminiscences and reworking their writing, will be welcomed both by those who knew him and by those who have come across his original writing and his magnificent routes. Rock climbs such as *Shibboleth*, *The Big Top* and *The Bat*, even with modern gear, are serious while his winter routes on the Comb and Orion face of Ben Nevis in the days of step-cutting were truly wonderful. In the Alps as a member of the Alpine Climbing Group he was responsible for the first British ascent of the Walker Spur and the north spur of the Fiescherhorn. The fall on Pik Garmo cut short a talent which would have shone for many years in world mountaineering .

Jimmy Marshall, in his obituary for Robin in the 1963 SMC Journal, quoted at length by Cruickshank, captured both his spirit and our sense of loss. 'He delighted in impromptu, unexpected incidents which would carry the adventure far into the night, to impress one's memory indelibly with a sense of satisfying fulfilment and a wild belonging to the mountain world. ... He is, and always shall be, greatly missed by his friends and can certainly never be forgotten by the climbing world.'

High Endeavours is by no means an objective book. It is an affectionate account by a schooldays friend and as such has flaws of selection and interpretation. However, it is redeemed by the first-hand tales of Smith's contemporaries and by Robin's own writing in journals and his diary. The result is an enjoyable and important biography, capturing the anarchic excitement of an era before advances in protection and equipment that have transformed the pursuit of mountaineering.

Robin Shaw

Todhra

Dennis Gray

Flux Gallery Press, 2005, £9.95

Dennis Gray's novel mingles hard mountaineering with the perils and compulsions of being gay. An uneasy mixture you might think, even though public attitudes towards homosexual relationships have surely moved on from the harsh experiences suffered by John Firth, the central character in this saga set in the days before gay pride and more tolerant public attitudes.

Todhra is a challenging gorge in Morocco where Firth emerges as a hard man among the climbing fraternity but also as an individual coming to terms with his true sexuality and the impact this has on those who know him or admire his prowess as a mountaineer.The story moves through a variety of climbing locations ranging from Otley Chevin to Nanga Parbat. Gray builds his characters well, describing the high tension of moving among the top extremes of rock in masterly style, although occasionally in language that would have bewildered Whymper and his generation. For example, Firth tackles a particularly testing stretch of rock: 'with an almost one-arm front lever, he locked over and pushed hard, brought his right toe to his left hand and stood up.' As you do.

To cries of 'Vive le Rosbif' he triumphs on the most difficult problems on the Fontainebleau boulders. A winter route on the Grandes Jorasses and new routes on Nanga Parbat and the Ben secure his place as a mountaineering celebrity. But in contrast to all this macho action are the guilt-ridden promiscuous encounters with rent boys and cruising gays, an urgent visit to a clinic for sexually transmitted diseases, the taunts and violence of Big Ernie, an archetypal homophobe, the trauma of being outed and the culminating humiliation of being sodomised by a bi-sexual Berber and being asked to pay for the privilege.

Throughout all this travail Firth maintains rapt admiration for his own sex. Of one encounter he recalled: 'The kid was truly beautiful with a fine athletic body, skin like fired porcelain and hair straight and black as strands of coal. His dark eyes were child-like and trusting'. So off he goes again with many an embrace and much fumbling in the boxer shorts. By contrast with his climbing descriptions, Gray spares us most of the physical detail and Todhra is no more sexually explicit than a Rubens nude upon which a wisp of gauze has strategically landed. For which we can only be thankful.

Ronnie Faux

Playing. Robin Hodgkin's Mountaineering Letters 1937–47

Ed. Adam Hodgkin

Published privately by Adam & Christopher Hodgkin, 2005, pp.x+100

It is good to have all Robin Hodgkin's writings on 'playing' – as he termed mountaineering – assembled in one book, instead of being scattered through articles in the *Alpine Journal*, *Climbers' Club Journal* and letters to his mother and others. These have been put together, with a masterly introduction, by his son Adam, with glimpses of Robin's early days and illustrated by some of Robin's own photographs.

Robin's early promise of being a first-class climber and mountaineer was justified when, on the 1938 expedition of young graduates to the Caucasus, he cracked a new route on the south ridge of Ushba by making use of a sensational ledge. The subsequent expedition to Masherbrum ended in near-disaster – when only 600ft short of the summit of what would have been the highest mountain climbed at that date. Robin lost most of his fingers and toes after spending a night in a crevasse after their tent had been blown away. But the experience did not diminish his ability to climb well despite this handicap.

Appointed to the Sudan Education Service, perhaps in the mistaken belief of his relatives that this flat country would offer few temptations, Robin nonetheless sought out the few mountains available on the edges and made a successful first ascent of Jebel Kassala. His wartime leaves were spent in neighbouring mountainous countries. In 1941 he was in Uganda and Kenya making an inevitably damp way into the Ruwenzori and successfully beating a way up the overhanging corniches of Margherita. He was disappointed a few hundred feet from the Nelion summit of Mount Kenya, which he reckoned to be a 'real' (ie difficult) mountain. In 1943 Robin looked for mountains in Turkey and I introduced him to the Ala Dag, where we made a number of second ascents following a pre-war German party, removing a swastika pennant from the summit of Demirkazik.

Returning to the Alps in 1947, Robin saw his friends John Jenkins and Nully Kretschmer fall to their deaths on the Brenva side of Mont Blanc. This, followed closely by his marriage to Elizabeth and a growing family, quenched his enthusiasm for more adventurous climbs, but he never lost his love for the mountains which he was able to share with his friends and impart to his pupils when headmaster at Abbotsholme.

Edward Peck

Danger on Peaks
Gary Snyder
Shoemaker & Hoard, 2004, pp 112, US$22

In case you don't read any further than this, let me offer you a conclusion first. The further we get away from our earliest mountain climbs, the more we realise how much they were actually embedded in the very life they might have been apparently escaping. When the poet Gary Snyder first climbed Mount St Helens in August 1945 he read of the atomic bombs dropped on Hiroshima and Nagasaki on the morning of his descent in a newspaper at the forestry office on the slopes of the mountain, 'my heart still one with the snowpeak mountain at my back'. Standing on a volcano, the young Snyder was so shocked at the 'cruel destructive power' unleashed in the volcano of the newspaper photographs that he vowed to fight against such cruelty for the rest of his life. But the young Snyder vows 'by the purity and beauty and permanence of Mount St Helens'. At 8.32am on

18 May 1980, volunteer geologist David Johnston reports from Coldwater II Observation Post that Mount St Helens is erupting, before being vaporized with his station. This viewpoint is now known as Johnston Ridge, Snyder tells us in his footnote to '1980: Letting Go'. Know the nature of your mountain, he is suggesting, but also, know the meaning of its language.

Gary Snyder believes not only that metaphors are real, but that every tiny bit of reality can be a metaphor. The problem with this is that many of the poems in this collection are expected to carry a significance that is less than obvious. 'Honour the dust' is a fine imperative with which Snyder has chosen to inscribe my copy of this book, but some bits of dust are more interesting than others, just as some metaphors are more powerful, insightful and more accurate than others. Different dust: different dangers. Different peaks: different dust. Different girls: different legs. Actually the title of this book is taken from a poem about Snyder first seeing his future wife, Carole, and his memory of 'her lithe leg' that has, he knows, been trained as 'proud, sceptical, passionate' by 'the danger on peaks'. Many of these poems are about dangers and joys below and beyond the peaks. Any book by Snyder is about the whole world and its specific signs. Politics, passion and peaks are embedded in each other in this thought-provoking collection of very material metaphors from the mountaineering Buddhist master-poet of America. At the reading in Oregon where Snyder signed my book, he began by saying that these were not actually his mountaineering poems because they would be too intimate. I'm still pondering what he meant by that.

Terry Gifford

Durchs Jahrhundert: Mein Leben als Arzt und Bergsteiger

(Through the Century: My Life as a Doctor and Mountaineer)

Lutz Chicken

Edition Raetia, Bozen, Italy, 2003, pp135, 15 Euros

Born in Bozen, South Tyrol, at the start of the First World War, Ludwig 'Lutz' Chicken was the son of an English father and an Austrian mother. Bozen was then a part of the decaying Austrian empire, but South Tyrol was ceded to Italy in 1919 and its prosperous provincial capital is today better known as Bolzano. Beautifully illustrated, *Durchs Jahrhundert* charts (in German) Lutz's life through a turbulent century.

Lutz's early love for nature determined his two passions of medicine and mountaineering. As a member of the Himalayan Foundation, he was unexpectedly chosen to take part in the Nanga Parbat exhibition of 1939 together with Peter Aufschnaiter, Heinrich Harrer and Hans Lobenhoffer. The outbreak of the Second World War turned this abortive adventure into years of internment in India. At Dehra Dun, Lutz was able to use his medical knowledge in the camp hospital. His passion to heal proved stronger than his wish to escape. When Harrer and others fled, he declined to join them and continued his hospital work.

Returning to northern Italy, Lutz finished his studies within the year and, after some difficulties, started a private clinic, devoting his life to his patients and his newly wed English wife, Ursula. He never lost his enthusiasm for climbing and *Durchs Jahrhundert* combines vivid descriptions of Lutz Chicken's experiences on mountains around the world with stories of internment, post-war reconstruction and his way out of the Germanic nationalist lure towards an enthusiastic pan-Europeanism.

Bettina von Reden

The Ice Maiden.
Inca Mummies, Mountain Gods and Sacred Sites in the Andes
Johan Reinhard
National Geographic, Washington, 2005, pp 384, US$26

Llullaillaco. Sacrificios y ofrendas en un santuario inca de alta montana
Constanza Ceruti
Ediciones Universidad Católica de Salta, 2003, pp 347, npq

In the last three or four decades a number of publications have occasionally appeared, offering the incredible information that the Incas were some 500 or 600 years ahead of contemporary climbers and, furthermore, that those stalwart hill peoples conducted a systematic form of mountaineering that would enable them easily to claim the first ascent of no less than 120 Andean peaks between 4000m and 6739m. Nearly all these publications had hitherto appeared in Spanish. Now, after his very successful expeditions in Peru and northern Argentina, American archaeologist Johan Reinhard has poured into a single work all his first-hand knowledge and research accumulated in 20 years of dedication to this form of archæological mountaineering. The title of his work sounds like a counter to the several *Ice Man* books that have been appearing in Europe. Reinhard's contains 12 chapters, systematically covering his findings on elevated mountains such as Copiapo (6052m), Ampato (6288m) and Llullaillaco (6739m). Among the descriptions of his many climbs he inserts veritable debates on related topics such as the meaning of mountains for hill people everywhere and human sacrifices on mountains in many places.

For a number of years before Reinhard began his activity, several Argentinian mountaineers were busy climbing and inspecting Andean summits, aiming to locate some lofty shrines. In 1973 they founded CIADAM, initials for Centro de Investigaciones Arqueológicas de Alta Montana. Its present Director is a young woman who has recently gained her doctorate, Constanza Ceruti, who was co-leader on several of Reinhard's expeditions. Her volume, *Llullaillaco*, is the published form of her doctoral dissertation. The book contains seven chapters about Llullaillaco (the highest archæological site in the world), minutely detailing all findings, including the discovery in 1999 on its summit of three Inca subjects and some 100 diverse burial objects. Ceruti, like Reinhard, takes pains to explain the peculiar form of sustained mountaineering that the Inca practised. Both suggest that 'mountains and ancestors' and 'mountains and fertility' were, among others, the main reasons for the existence of Andean summit shrines. Both works contain numerous illustrations in colour and black and white, line drawings and sketch-maps.

The old and well-ingrained belief that the ascent of mountains everywhere – for whatever reasons – began with and evolved from a 1492 spectacular rock climb or the deeds of some eccentrics two centuries ago is slowly being set aside. With their solid contribution, sportive scientists like Johan Reinhard and Constanza Ceruti have laid a firm foundation for the new endeavour of summit archæology.

Evelio Echevarría

Key Issues for Mountain Areas

Editors: Martin F Price, Libor Jansky and Andrei A Iatsenia

United Nations University Press, 2004, pp 280, US$32

I have a new and somewhat dubious label. According to this enlightening work of reference I, and thousands of others who have concluded that life is better in Cumbria, am an 'amenity migrant'. By the same token, I suppose when I went south to the big city decades ago in search of fame and fortune (failed on both counts) I was an 'economic migrant'.

Amenity migration is defined as 'the movement of people to a particular region for the vision of life in a quieter, more pristine environment and/or distinct cultural attributes'. Its effect cuts both ways, putting pressure on local resources, pushing up land and house prices, eroding cultural diversity, while also, hopefully, bringing in capital and fresh entrepreneurial initiative, creating jobs. The phenomenon is being felt in mountain areas in both developing and industrialised countries, according to one of the papers included here, concluding that the cultural effect of this new class of mountain resident and their role in conservation and sustainable development deserve future attention.

'Further study', the cynics might say, is the academics' answer to every problem. In fact what is impressive about this series of papers on preserving mountain ecosystems while improving the lives of those who live there, is not just how much study has gone into these complex issues but how much has been done on the ground since mountains sidled on to the agenda of policy makers at the Earth Summit in Rio de Janeiro in 1992.

At the time I wrote a feature for *The Independent* headlined by an enthusiastic sub-editor, 'Man's abuse of the giants'. That abuse had been highlighted in a 400-page report *The State of the World's Mountains* edited by AC member Peter Stone. Another, Roger Payne, at the time national officer of the BMC, urged climbers not to view native people as 'just an ethnic backdrop for our adventures'. It was, as the phrase goes, 'a wake up call' and although the snooze button is an ever-tempting option, there is no doubt we are all now much more aware of the impact of our actions – whether on a personal mountain holiday level or as part of society generally – on environments and communities far away.

At a fairly local level this book offers plenty of heartening case studies, from the revival of the native Hutsul horse in the Carpathians for transport and trekking to numerous kerosene depots and self-help conservation and income generating schemes in the Himalaya. However as principal editor, Martin Price – yet another AC member doing good works – emphasises in his introduction, the future of mountain regions is inextricably woven into the global fabric of interlinked markets, institutions and policies within a biosphere that is experiencing rapid change. One thinks immediately of global warming and glacier retreat. The Chinese Academy of Science, for example, predicts that Tibet's 60,000 square miles of glaciers will halve in size every decade at current rates, turning yak pasture to desert.

The evidence is abundant, indeed for TV and newspapers eco-warnings have become a daily staple, but the bold political steps to address this most fundamental 'Key Issue' are still awaited. Keep banging the drum.

Stephen Goodwin

100 Jahre AACB

Akademischer Alpenclub Bern, Bern 2005, pp 307

This fine volume, which has been presented to the Alpine Club by the Akademischer Alpenclub Bern, provides a detailed and fascinating account of this small but very active University Club since it was formed in October 1905.

In addition to a general historical review the reader finds information on every aspect of the members' activities including ski mountaineering and hut management: the Bietschhorn, Engelhorn and Schmadri huts are owned by the Club. Another section contains biographies of prominent members such as Hans Lauper of Eiger fame and Albert Eggler, the leader of the successful Everest-Lhotse Expedition in 1956. It is pleasant to note that two members of the Alpine Club – Captain J P Farrar and Sir Arnold Lunn – were elected to honorary membership of the AACB.

This comprehensive and well illustrated work is a worthy record of the Club's history and achievements.

Christopher Russell

Memories of Surveying in India 1919-1939

Gordon Osmaston

T G Osmaston

91 Windermere Park, Windermere, Cumbria LA23 2ND, 2005, pp56, £5

Gordon Osmaston, a founder member of the Himalayan Club and formerly Director of the Survey of India, was born in India in 1898. He was commissioned into the Royal Engineers at 18, winning the MC in France, before being ordered out to India with the Third Sappers and Miners. After two years he obtained a position with the Survey of India, hoping for lots of work in the Himalaya, his interest in climbing having been aroused in the Lake District by climbs with Heaton Cooper.

Many years were to pass before this aspiration was fulfilled, however, and the early chapters of this short memoir recount surveys in Burma, India and Assam. Osmaston's chance came in 1936 when he took charge of a new survey in northern Tehri Garhwal, exploring the Gangotri and Chaturangi glaciers. The most interesting section for AC members, however, will be the description of his surveys in the Nanda Devi Sanctuary in the autumn of 1936 when he persuaded Eric Shpton to act as his guide into the area. Young Tensing was one of the party, and they met Peter Lloyd and other members of the first ascent party returning from the mountain. The advent of the Second World War brings to an end this fascinating personal account of surveying in India.

Geoffrey Templeman

Travels Amongst the Great Andes of the Equator

Edward Whymper

Ripping Yarns.com, 2005, pp 394+xviii

The latest offering from Ripping Yarns differs from its predecessors in that it is in hard covers and printed in facsimile. Apart from its overall size, the book is identical to the 1891 edition but with the scientific appendices and fold-out maps omitted. The latter are available on-line, however. Whymper's main interest was in studying the effects of altitude on climbers, but as there was unrest in the Himalaya and troubles in Peru, Chile and Bolivia, he decided to go to Ecuador and climb Chimborazo and Cotopaxi. Accordingly, he set off in 1870 accompanied by his old colleague/adversary Jean Antoine Carrel and the latter's cousin Louis Carrel.

This book, complete with the many excellent sketches and drawings reproduced here, is a classic of mountaineering literature, although I would imagine that the number of people who have read it right through, compared with *Scrambles*, is probably comparatively few. This reissue gives you the chance.

Geoffrey Templeman

Walking in the Alps
Kev Reynolds
Cicerone, 2005, 500 + xii, £20

A revised edition of Kev Reynolds's invaluable 1998 hardback, with updated information, revised maps and many more superb illustrations.

Classic Norway. Climbs, Scrambles and Walks in Romsdal
Tony Howard
Cordee, 2005, pp144, npq

It is 35 years since *Walks and Climbs in Romsdal, Norway* first appeared, this being the fourth revised edition, produced in response to continued public demand for up-to-date information. The opportunity has been taken to include more walks and many more colour illustrations.

Seton Gordon's Scotland. An Anthology
Compiled by Hamish Brown
Whittles, 2005, pp330 + xviii, £25

Seton Gordon (1886-1977) was one of Scotland's most prolific writers on natural history subjects, publishing a total of 27 books. Hamish Brown has undertaken the Herculean task of sifting through them and extracting the most interesing and worthwhile pieces.

Thailand. A Climbing Guide
Sam Lightner Jnr.
The Mountaineers Books, 2005, pp 336, $21.95

The latest climbing guide from The Mountaineers is also a travel guide to Thailand, giving comprehensive information on accommodation, sight-seeing, history, ecology, etc, as well as details of over 350 climbs. It is fully illustrated with topos and action shots.

The Andes. A Guide for Climbers
John Biggar
Andes (Castle Douglas), 2005, pp 304, npq

The third edition of John Biggar's comprehensive guide to the Andes for 'the average mountaineer'. All 102 6000m peaks are included, plus over 210 lower peaks. In full colour. An indispensable guide.

In Memoriam

COMPILED BY GEOFFREY TEMPLEMAN

The Alpine Club Obituary		**Year of Election**
Matthew Christopher Faulds		1994
David Stuart Brinkman		1992
John Angelo Jackson		1953
George Cubby		1967
Michael Boos		2002
Robert William Milne		1993
Michael Phelps Ward	Hon 1993	1952
Edward Hugh Jackson Smyth		1962
David Pasteur		1959
Anthony Gosselin Trower		1952
Heinrich Harrer		Hon 1999
Ian Roger Jarratt Angell		1975
Rosemary Greenwood		1985
Michael Holton		1966

After last year's remarkably short In Memoriam list, we have lost 14 members in the past year. Obituaries for just over half of these are included here. Also included is one, for John King, from a previous year, and one for Eric Langmuir, a former member of the ACG, who was known to many of us. I shall be interested to receive tributes for any who have not been included here.

Michael P Ward CBE FRCS 1925-2005

A formal portrait painted in 1995 for the Worshipful Society of Apothecaries of London. Michael was Master from 1993-1994.

Michael P Ward CBE MD (Cam) FRCS 1925–2005

Michael Ward will be remembered mainly for his being the Medical Officer on the successful British 1953 Everest Expedition though, for serious students of Everest history, his role in the 1951 reconnaissance trip will be remembered as of more significance.

Born in 1925 in London, his father was a senior civil servant in Malaya and, as was usual in those days, Mike was sent back to England for his education. He was fortunate in having a proxy family of guardians with children around his own age. His father was interned during the war and so Mike saw nothing of him for almost six years. His mother got out of Malaya just in time before the Japanese invasion. She settled into a cottage in the Cotswolds and Mike then spent his holidays there. This was in some ways more traumatic than the separation from his parents, since he was then separated from the family he had grown into. He was educated at Marlborough, where his housemaster was Edwin Kempson who had been on Everest in '35 and '36.

Mike's mountaineering began in 1939 when he was 14 with a guided ascent of the Wetterhorn with a Dutch family. In 1943 he went up to Cambridge, joined the University Mountaineering Club and met such inspirational characters as Geoffrey Winthrop Young and Wilfrid Noyce. In the next few years he developed his rock climbing, making a number of new routes in North Wales including a hard direct finish to *Longland's* on Cloggy (with Menlove Edwards as second) and the ever-popular *Wrinkle* on Carreg Wastad. In 1947 he was in the Ecrin with Bill Murray and John Barford when they were hit by stone fall. They fell 150m-180m, Barford was killed and both the other two suffered fractured skulls. He recovered from this accident and got back to climbing with trips to Harrison's Rocks.

After qualifying in medicine in 1949 and doing the statutory pre-registration year in hospital, he had to join the army for national service. As a medical officer in Woolwich he found himself with time on his hands. Spurred on by reading of a party going to reconnoitre a route to Everest from the south, he started to research such a route. Delving in the (then) chaotic archives at the Royal Geographical Society he unearthed photographs, some taken clandestinely during the war by RAF pilots, and an unpublished map. The photographs revealed key features of the Nepal side of Everest, and thus encouraged he set about organising an exploratory expedition with Murray. They had difficulty, at first, in convincing the Everest Committee of the feasibility of the project but eventually, with Shipton as the invited leader, the 1951 Reconnaissance Expedition took off.

This first expedition must have been fantastic for Mike, not only to find the route up the Khumbu glacier and icefall and to find his research vindicated, but then to go exploring with Shipton into the unknown area west of Everest, find those famous Yeti footprints and escape from the Chinese border guards. This love of exploration stayed with Mike throughout his life. In 1964 he was able, with Fred Jackson, a cardiologist, to get into Bhutan and explore remote regions north and east towards the border with Tibet. In 1980 he got permission to reconnoitre Mount Kongur in Xinjiang, China, with Chris Bonington and Al Rouse before leading a successful expedition to climb it the following year. In 1985-6 he was on the Royal Society's expedition which made a South-North traverse of Tibet.

His interest in maps and the history of exploration of the Himalaya was also life long, from his discovery in 1949 of the Milne-Hinks map to the publication in 2003 of his scholarly book, *Everest: A Thousand Years of Exploration*. Between these dates he wrote numerous geographical, historical papers, including an article for the *Alpine Journal* on the Pundits who worked for the survey of India in the late 19th and early 20th centuries. In fact he had been asked to author a book on these Pundits, whose work is still not widely recognised, and had completed about two thirds of it when he died. Before that he had been closely collaborating with Tony Astill on a book about the 1935 Everest Expedition. Tony tells how he admired Mike's continuing wonderful enthusiasm for exploration both on the ground and in archives, especially of the RGS, of which he had an encyclopaedic knowledge.

The story of the 1953 Everest Expedition is so well known that I will not repeat it. Mike played his part both as medical officer and as a climber. The expedition's health was good, especially compared with that of the Cho Oyu expedition of the previous year, perhaps, in part, due to Mike's efforts. A story (from Mike Westmacott) from 1953 illustrates his approach to preventive medicine (or dentistry) as well as illustrating his wry sense of humour. He was giving a health talk to the team before setting out for Nepal. He impressed upon them the importance of visiting their dentist well in advance of the expedition and getting any required dental work done. 'Because,' he said, 'I *can* pull teeth – but I'm not very good at it!'

After the '53 Expedition, Mike concentrated on his surgical training which involved, in those days, swotting for post-graduate exams whilst working in very busy junior hospital jobs with plenty of night duty. He duly climbed the surgical career ladder and was appointed a consultant surgeon to St Andrew's Hospital, Bow and later at Newham District Hospital, also in the East End of London. He was highly regarded as a teacher and an all-round surgeon ready to undertake the management of injuries to head, chest, abdomen or limbs as well as the usual round of elective surgery. He was asked to stay on after the statutory retirement age of 65 for another three years, as increasing specialisation and keyhole surgery made it impossible for one surgeon to take on his work load. For mountaineers unlucky enough to get frostbite he was the first choice for referral. He never took on private practice, believing that the NHS should provide a sufficiently good service to render private practice unnecessary.

I first got to know Mike in 1960 when I was working with Griffith Pugh preparing for the Silver Hut Expedition. I was somewhat in awe of Mike, five years my senior and already famous as an Everester. Mike was Griff's first choice for his team for the Silver Hut Expedition. They had met when Mike was preparing for the 1951 Reconnaissance Expedition. Of this meeting, Mike wrote:

> The first meeting was characteristic. Griff was sitting in a free-standing Victorian bath in water with ice cubes floating on the surface in the middle of a self-imposed hypothermia experiment. He had forgotten our meeting. At the next encounter he looked at the photographs of the proposed route on Everest and said that he could ski down it and if he could do that, we could climb up it. The mountaineering difficulties were thus disposed of and we turned to the scientific problems.

These problems were the provision of a satisfactory oxygen system and the importance of adequate fluid intake for climbers high on Everest, factors which Mike later believed had been crucial to the success of the '53 expedition. Griff gathered important data on these topics in 1952 on Cho Oyu but it is interesting that he and Mike had discussed these matters even before the '51 trip.

It is clear they hit it off well. They both considered themselves outsiders and not part of the medical or mountaineering establishments. They had little time for the niceties of social conventions or small talk. Mike admired Pugh and was a great champion of his contribution to the success of Everest 1953. There is no doubt that through his writing and lecturing he helped establish Pugh's reputation.

The Silver Hut Expedition, 1960-61, was a wonderful, unique experience. Led by Sir Edmund Hillary with Pugh as the scientific leader, its aims were to study the long-term effect of really high altitude on the human physiology of acclimatisation. We were nine months out of Kathmandu, most of the time at altitude in the Everest region. The winter was spent in the Silver Hut at 5800m. We were a very mixed team of climbers and scientists drawn about equally from New Zealand, USA and UK. Mike trekked out in December with John West, each successfully carrying a Lloyd-Haldane apparatus, a delicate thing of blown glass for measuring oxygen and carbon dioxide in gas. These were crucial to many of our projects and the original ones had both been broken. Mike was official medical officer to the 22-strong team, many of whom were also medics. He was senior to most of us in both years and certainly in mountaineering experience. I think, to the New Zealanders and Americans, playing the part of 'rough Colonials', his background of public school and Cambridge and his accent suggested that he belonged to the aristocracy. Mike played up to this role and I remember him addressing them as, 'My dear chap', much to their amusement.

By late February the Silver Hut was getting crowded and so Griff was quite happy to agree that Mike, Mike Gill, Wally Romanes (New Zealanders) and Barry Bishop (USA) should go off and attempt Ama Dablam. The ascent of this most beautiful of mountains was probably the highlight of Mike's mountaineering career. The boldness of this unassisted, technical climb was years ahead of its time. It remained unrepeated for about twenty years.

In the spring we moved over the Barun Plateau to attempt Makalu and continued our physiology at advanced base camp (6300m). Mike and John West even made a couple of measurements of VO2 max, using the stationary bike, on Makalu Col (7400m) still, 45 years on, the record for the highest altitude at which this has been measured.

In the 1960s, Mike was appointed leader of an expedition to Shisha Pangma, the last unclimbed 8000m peak. However, there were difficulties in getting permission and before they were able to get it, the Chinese themselves made the first ascent and the expedition was cancelled. In the later 1970s, he and I planned a number of trips which failed to come off but then started a series of studies, in this country and later in Switzerland, on the effect of exercise on fluid and electrolyte balance in ourselves. These were field studies with full metabolic control on a fixed diet, the exercise being hill walking for eight hours a day for five consecutive days, bracketed by four control days. We collected a group of enthusiasts including a professor of nuclear medicine, an orthopaedic surgeon, a naval surgeon and a gynaecologist and two medical technicians, as well as we two. We called ourselves 'The Worshipful Company of Gentlemen Physiologists' but to keep us on the straight and narrow we included one card-carrying professional physiologist. Over the years we conducted four, two-week studies in North Wales, the Lakes and Switzerland and made some quite important findings that we hoped might have a bearing on high-altitude pulmonary oedema.

In 1975 Mike published *Mountain Medicine*, the first textbook of its type in the world, and probably ahead of its time; unfortunately, there were then few people interested in the subject, so sales were small. In 1984, when we were on a scientific expedition to Pikes Peak in Colorado, I asked Mike if he was thinking of a second edition of *Mountain Medicine*. He had not considered it but did so soon after and asked me to collaborate on the project. At the publisher's suggestion we asked John West to join us and so was born *High Altitude Medicine & Physiology* by Ward, Milledge and West, now the standard textbook on the subject. The third edition was published in 2000. Mike was not a technophile. He not only eschewed the computer, he hadn't even got into the typewriter age! The result was that for all his chapters, he wrote the draft in his 'doctor's' handwriting! This I reduced to a computer Word file, and posted the printout to him for correction. On its return I would e-mail a final draft to John West in California. In this way all his papers and articles were produced. He was fortunate to have Johanna Merz, former editor and now production editor of the *Alpine Journal*, to do this job for him for his many articles and his Everest exploration book.

In the latter part of his surgical career he began to take a more active part in the Worshipful Society of Apothecaries and after retirement became

Master of the Society. In this capacity, he not only attended the very numerous social functions required of the role but helped develop courses and examinations in areas such as the management of disasters.

He was justifiably proud of the house in Lurgashall that he and his wife, Jane, largely designed and built, together with the garden and grounds. He was proud too of their son Mark's achievements, gaining a music scholarship to Eton, a scholarship to Oxford and, nine years ago, presenting him and Jane with a granddaughter. His last few years were dogged by ill health, first serious kidney trouble, then a horrendous car accident and ensuing major operations. Jane nursed him back from each critical situation. It is ironic that just when he seemed to be gaining health again he should be struck down by sudden death due to a ruptured aortic aneurism.

Mike was, in many ways, a very private man – a typical English Gentleman. But he clearly was a deeper and more complicated person than appeared on the surface. He had an abiding love of mountains and landscape and would have subscribed to much of Geoffrey Winthrop Young's philosophy, I believe. He chose a quote from Young's most famous poem, 'The Cragsman', as the title of his mountain memoir *In This Short Span* (1972). In his first book, a commissioned anthology entitled *A Mountaineer's Companion* (1966), Mike included five pieces by Young. One was a poem I had not come across before. The first verse is:

I have not lost the magic of long days;
I live them, dream them still.
Still I am master of the starry ways,
And freeman of the hill.
Shattered my glass, ere half the sands had run -
I hold the heights, I hold the heights I won.

The poem was written by Young as a comparatively young man after he lost a leg in the First World War. It could stand as a sort of epitaph for Mike.

James Milledge

Michael Westmacott writes:
I had met Mike before 1953 but hardly knew him except by reputation. Indeed, he was not very easy to get to know well until one was engaged in some joint enterprise. Then he was a splendid colleague and a true friend. Jim Milledge has mentioned his role in the 1951 reconnaissance of Everest. If it had not have been for Mike, it would never have taken place. He had spent many hours at the RGS, combing through uncatalogued material, and then had the enthusiasm to engage Bill Murray and Campbell Secord in the job of persuading a reluctant Himalayan Committee to authorise the reconnaissance in 1951 and Eric Shipton to lead it.

This trip was very much on Shipton lines – small, modestly funded, living off local food. Tom Bourdillon, quizzed subsequently on the radio about expedition food, could only say, 'Well, there should be some.' (Tom was not a rice eater.) The story is well known. Braving the monsoon, with the accompanying rain, mud and leeches, they trekked the unknown trail to Khumbu from the hills above Jogbani. They arrived at the foot of the icefall on 29 September. After a break of 10 days spent exploring and getting acclimatised, they climbed the icefall as far as the huge crevasse that barred the way into the Western Cwm. They hadn't the equipment for bridging it or climbing down and across, so returned to the valley having had a closer view of much of the Lhotse Face and established that there was a possible route to the South Col.

On his return to England, Mike was 'incandescent with rage' to find that the Swiss had obtained permission for Everest in 1952, ahead of a tardy British application – though it was later found that the Swiss had applied for permission months before the reconnaissance had left. This proved to be a blessing in disguise, as the extra year made possible vital research, much of it on Cho Oyu, into the medical problems of high altitude. This was carried out largely by Griffith Pugh, but with Mike keenly interested. He did not go to Cho Oyu, as he was working hard on the FRCS Primary Examination.

He was an obvious choice for 1953 and was appointed medical officer and a member of the climbing team. In the event, he played a full part in the 'build up', in particular working on the Lhotse Face with George Lowe, but was denied the chance of going to the South Col, as John Hunt needed him as a reserve and also available in case of any medical emergency. At the same time, he attended to the numerous, luckily minor, ailments of the Sherpas and sahibs, and helped Pugh with his research – which could be somewhat unpopular. There is a scene in the 1953 film showing George Band stepping up and down on a box while wearing a face mask and having his exhaled air sampled for subsequent analysis. George was more co-operative than most of us.

In those days the training of doctors, in any specialism such as surgery, was long, arduous and poorly paid, but Mike resisted the temptation of well-paid lecture tours and concentrated on his profession. By 1960, after a year's exchange spent at a hospital in Canada, he was a senior registrar at the London Hospital, and in touch with Griffith Pugh and Jim Milledge who were developing plans for a major medical/scientific expedition to Nepal. Jim has already described the research programme. This was combined with an expedition headed by Ed Hillary with a variety of objects – hunting the elusive yeti, building a school for the Sherpas and climbing Makalu.The medical side of this expedition was ground breaking and it was larger and better resourced than any similar venture in the past. Mountaineering objectives had generally predominated, research being side-lined whenever there was any conflict. This time the medical side was largely independent, though its finances were greatly helped by Ed Hillary's success in getting generous financial support from World Books. But most of the doctors and their assistants were climbers too, and took the opportunity of skiing or climbing when free to do so. Indeed, their performance after prolonged exposure to altitude was one of the things to be measured, and it was important that they should stay fit.

The most notable climb was the first ascent of Ama Dablam, which was achieved in mid-March by Mike, with Barry Bishop, Mike Gill and Wally Romanes. In the days before modern ice gear, this was a considerable achievement. But then there was disaster. Descending from a high camp, Gumen Dorji fell and badly broke his leg. Mike straightened the leg and bound it to an ice-axe, cushioned by cardboard. Gumen was large for a Sherpa, and could hardly be carried by his smaller companions. The two Mikes, belayed in turn, carried him down steep ground until at last help arrived from below.

Up to this time, Mike and his companions were obviously strong and well acclimatised, but the subsequent attempt on Makalu brought further disasters, no doubt due largely to physical deterioration at altitude. The first such disaster involved Ed Hillary. He had gone back to New Zealand during the winter, and on return had to go to Kathmandu to try to pacify, and pay, the government for the 'unauthorised' ascent of Ama Dablam. Too soon after that, going up high on Makalu, he had a stroke, and had to be taken down by the Sherpas, with Mike in attendance. Ten days later, Peter Mulgrew, at 8300m above the Makalu Col, suffered a pulmonary embolism. Incapable of descending to the Col, he spent four days above 8000m, and was very badly frostbitten, subsequently losing both legs below the knee. The account of his evacuation is agonising. At the same time, four of the Sherpas lost their footing and narrowly escaped a long fall; two of them were hurt, and Ang Temba unable to walk unassisted. Then Mike himself, no doubt exhausted by his efforts above the Col and the care of the casualties, became desperately weak, and then delirious. After two days more or less unconscious on the Col, he recovered enough to stagger down with the help of John West, carrying only his diaries.

As Jim has recorded, this gruelling experience was not enough to deter Mike from further expeditions. He remained very active in his profession and in his interest in Central Asian exploration. But I end on a more personal note. I treasure the memory of a week with him in the far north of Scotland, when we had both been unable to join other friends with whom we normally climbed every year. The weather was mixed, and for some nights we bivouacked in a ruined shed, with the rain coming down a few feet away. We walked strenuously over the hills, talking on every subject under the sun, taking in summits or rock climbing en route. Then we went south, Mike insisting on driving every mile of the way – a commentary perhaps on my driving, but also on his stamina. He was totally reliable, and good company, and will be greatly missed by all who knew him.

John Jackson 1921-2005

John 'Jacko' Jackson was a member of the British expedition that in May 1955 made the first ascent of Kangchenjunga, third highest mountain in the world. His love of the Himalaya had been kindled 10 years earlier in Kashmir and was to endure for the rest of his life. He was trekking on the verdant Singalila ridge in his eighties and partying with Sherpa friends in Darjeeling only last February. When he died, some five months later, butter lamps were lit on his behalf in the gompas of the former hill station.

Born in Nelson, Lancashire, John Angelo Jackson had on his doorstep the 'Brontë' moors. He started rock climbing at the age of 12, exploring the gritstone outcrops with his older brother Ron. When Ron purchased a motorbike and sidecar for £5 – an old side-valve Ariel – the pair extended their activities to the crags of the Lake District and then in 1938 to the Isle of Skye. It was a classic apprenticeship for the all-round mountaineer that Jacko was to become.

Joining the RAF in 1940 he flew with 31 Squadron as a wireless operator and air gunner in Dakotas over Burma. In 1944, however, he got a dream posting, assisting Wilfrid Noyce, another climber in uniform, as an instructor at an Aircrew Mountain Centre in Kashmir. Rather like the institutions John would run years later, it was recreation with a purpose. Over a two-year period, he made numerous ascents of peaks in the 4500m-5300m range in Kashmir and undertook many mountain treks, including in neighbouring Ladakh.

After the war, John trained as a pharmacist, but switched to teaching, first in his home town and later in Redcar, North Yorkshire. He taught science and geography and in an extra-curricular role introduced youngsters to the hills. In 1946 while on a climbing visit to Buttermere in the Lake District, John met an army officer who questioned him extensively about his experiences in Kashmir. It was John Hunt, who would later head up the awards schemes that Jackson implemented while director of Plas y Brenin, the national mountaineering centre, from 1960 to '76.

Three post-war alpine seasons in Switzerland were followed by an RAF expedition to the Garhwal Himalaya in north-west India, including an attempt on Nilkanta (6596m), rebuffed high up by the arrival of monsoon weather. John's experience secured his selection as a reserve for the 1953 British Everest expedition and he became heavily involved in the testing of oxygen equipment, much of it carried out at Helyg, the Climbers' Club hut in the Ogwen Valley. He was elected to the AC that same year.

Disappointment at not actually getting to Everest, was fully compensated when he was invited to join the 1955 expedition to Kangchenjunga, led by Charles Evans. It was, by comparison, a modest affair, largely free of flag waving and national expectation, however in climbing terms Kangch' was a much more unknown quantity than Everest and is today regarded as one of the hardest of the 8000ers.

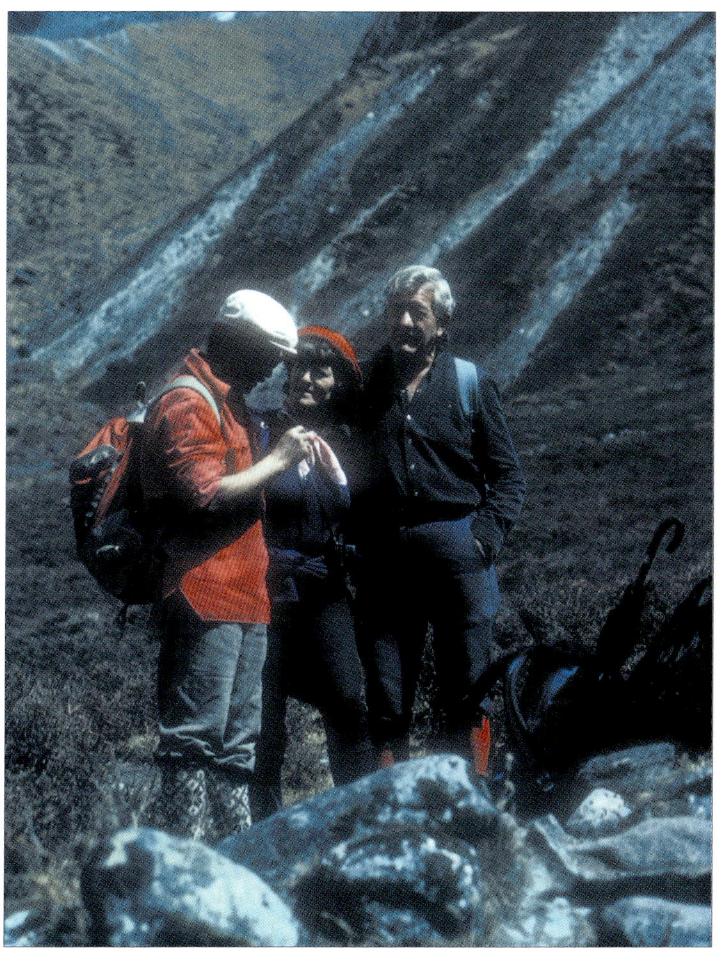

John Jackson (right) with his wife Eileen and Tenzing Norgay in the Onglathang valley, Sikkim, in 1986. This was a joyful chance reunion. The Jacksons were trekking with John Noble, who took the photograph, heading up towards the Goecha La when they met Tenzing returning from Kangchenjunga with his own private trek group. Tenzing had visited the National Mountaineering Centre, Plas y Brenin, on several occasions while 'Jacko' was Director, and during Noble's own time there as an instructor in the 1970s. (*John Noble/Wilderness Photographic Library*)

Jacko reached Camp V, at 7710m, the penultimate camp on the mountain, but did not see much of it due to snowblindness. For the final push he and Tom MacKinnon had been assigned the task of leading Sherpa teams carrying vital supplies. On the carry to Camp IV he rather overdid the practice of pushing up his goggles, which tended to fog up when wearing an oxygen mask.

He spent a sleepless night in agony. 'I felt as if powdered glass had got under my eyelids,' he recalled. Still in acute pain next morning, he nonetheless insisted on continuing up, roped between two Sherpas. He could barely see where they were going but encouraged the team on through deep soft snow.

Expeditions were an integral part of John's life for more than half a century, most frequently to the Himalaya. Elsewhere, he went with Hunt on expeditions concerned with the Duke of Edinburgh's Award scheme to the Staunings Alps in Greenland and to the Pindus mountains of Greece. In the Staunings he and Hunt climbed a 6500ft peak, topped by a rock tower. They named the peak Beaumaris – both having adopted Wales. Approaching his 70th birthday he made an ascent of Kilimanjaro and also of Point Lenana on Mount Kenya.

John's love of mountain travel was shared by his wife Eileen whom he first met at a cricket match, another shared enthusiasm. In 1976, after retiring from Plas y Brenin, the couple drove a campervan overland to India and Nepal on a nine-month spree of trekking, climbing and skiing. They celebrated their 55th wedding anniversary four days before he died.

The National Mountaineering Centre underwent many changes during John's tenure, responding to a need articulated by Hunt for well-trained mountain leaders. There was much concern over the high percentage of mountain rescues in Snowdonia involving young people. Taking over as director in 1960, John introduced a range of leadership courses and oversaw the creation of Wales's first dry ski slope. The first Mountaineering Instructor's Certificate courses were run at the centre in 1969 and hailed as a great success, however it was not long before a row broke out within mountaineering over whether the certificates route had not gone too far and was endangering the game's freewheeling nature.

Soon after the campervan trip, the Sports Council for Wales asked John to be their consultant for a National Outdoor Centre for Wales. A site was chosen at Plas Menai, not far from his Anglesey home, and Jackson stayed on as director until 1983, seeing the centre through its formative years, the emphasis being on sailing rather than mountaineering.

Revealingly, John entitled his first book *More than Mountains*. His fascination with the Himalaya was not limited to headline summits or new routes, he wrote about the flowers, including a short essay on the breathtaking beauty of blue poppies, the birds, the geology and scenery, and about the inhabitants, including the yeti. In 1954 he had been the mountaineering leader of a yeti hunt organised by the *Daily Mail*. Thankfully none was found and Jackson came to the view that prints sighted over the years might be those of the equally elusive Tibetan blue bear.

John was a regular contributor to the *Alpine Journal* and despite failing health – he suffered from leukaemia – accepted my invitation to write an account of a 50th anniversary journey by Kanchenjunga veterans to India in February 2005. Sherpa hospitality in Darjeeling was lavish, from those friends who subsequently would light butter lamp candles for him, and Jacko got one more chance to see Kangch'. He described it thus:

'The final morning of 13 February was clear with blue sky. Would we see the Kangchenjunga massif at last? We did! Jannu and Rathong stood out boldly, then the summits of Kabru began to show. Further east, Pandim and Tingchenkang were impressive. But the 'Five Treasures' were playing hide and seek so that only fleetingly did they show themselves. It was enough.'

Stephen Goodwin

George Band writes:
I have very warm memories of 'Jacko'. He and Tom McKinnon proposed and seconded me for membership of the Alpine Club in 1955.

One of the pleasantest diversions on the Kangchenjunga Expedition was when Jacko, Neil Mather (who also sadly died in 2005) and I undertook an 'Easter shopping trip' over the hills to the delightful village of Ghunsa, to order more potatoes and dried vegetables to augment the expedition's supplies. My diary records 'idyllic walking through pine woods banked with snow'. It was just the kind of trip Jacko loved. He had passed through that village the previous year when he made a unique journey, with just Sherpa companions, leaving the *Daily Mail* yeti hunting expedition in Solu Khumbu, and following the Himalayan chain eastward, travelling discreetly partly in Tibet until twenty days later he met up with his brother Ron, at the end of John Kempe's 1954 Kangchenjunga reconnaissance party, of which Ron was a member.

Jacko was also an excellent photographer and, with his broad interest in natural history to complement his mountaineering, he was a popular speaker and must have enthused thousands of young people to take up adventurous outdoor activities. He told me, after one presentation, that a well-heeled businessman came up and said, 'I wish I could just take off several months to travel in the Himalaya.' 'You could,' replied Jacko, 'it just depends on how determined you are to want to do it.' Throughout his life Jacko showed no lack of determination, and was fully supported and, whenever possible, accompanied by his vivacious and energetic wife Eileen.

Despite failing health, what a fantastic last six months he had: accepting the Himalayan Club's invitation to speak in Mumbai and Kolkata, including a visit to the Sherpas of Darjeeling and a last view of Kangch'; attending the team's private 50th Anniversary gathering at Pen-y-Gwryd, and joining the speakers on the platform at the public celebration arranged by the Mount Everest Foundation at the Royal Geographical Society on 7 June. He and Eileen also celebrated their 55th wedding anniversary and, as a lasting gesture to posterity, thanks to prompting from his good friends Harish and Geeta Kapadia, the Indus Publishing Company, New Delhi, produced in May his second volume of memoirs encapsulating 60 years of *Adventure Travels in the Himalaya.* These are the dreams he won.

Nigel Gates writes:

In December 1957, some two years after taking part in the successful Kangchenjunga expedition, John Jackson became Chief Instructor at Plas y Brenin under Director 'Gim' Milton. Two years later, in March 1960, he was appointed Director, a position he held until retirement 15 years later.

'Jacko' was an inspirational leader. He attracted a group of outstanding permanent instructors, such as Roger Orgill (his Chief Instructor/Deputy Director), Ray Greenall and David Humphreys, and an annual succession of one-year temporary instructors. These were supported by short-term voluntary instructors and it was in this capacity that I began working for John. Although one did not always agree with John's decisions at the time (in retrospect they were usually correct), I never saw any indication of lasting rancour. The plain fact was that John was an outstanding leader and he knew how to get the best out of those who worked for him.

Under John's leadership, Plas y Brenin became a centre of excellence, renowned for high-quality training and certification courses; its clientele ranged from those with experience undertaking assessment courses to groups of physical education students sent by institutions on a week's introduction to mountain activities. As a former teacher, John was a strong proponent of the philosophy and the value of outdoor *education* – rather than merely outdoor activities. John was, furthermore, an outstanding photographer; those who attended his illustrated lectures rarely failed to be impressed and inspired by his magnificent slides.

When John left Plas y Brenin in 1975 he did not fit into a normal retiree's pattern. Within a month he and his wife, Eileen, set off on an overland trip to India and Nepal. He continued to travel to a variety of destinations, such as the Galapagos Islands, Machu Picchu and the Himalaya, and he lectured widely.

In 1978, John was appointed consultant, on a part-time basis, to advise on the planning and construction of Plas Menai (originally named Plas y Deri) the Welsh Sports Council centre near Bangor. John's part-time commitment eventually became full-time and in July 1980 I became John's first instructor when he ran two pilot courses before the centre's full opening some months later. John retired from Plas Menai in 1983.

John influenced me in many ways. In my teaching and lecturing career I've made frequent use of class management techniques that I learnt from him – and they've always worked effectively. John guided my first faltering steps on skis, on the artificial ski slope at Plas y Brenin, and I have skied regularly ever since. John also introduced me to gluhwein – and what a mean gluhwein he made. His recipe stipulated a quarter bottle of brandy for every bottle of wine and the resultant potion had a kick like a horse!

Jacko's long-lasting and outstanding legacy is that he has inspired thousands of people – myself included – many of whom have been motivated to engage further in the mountain and other activities he introduced them to at Plas y Brenin, Plas Menai and elsewhere.

Heinrich Harrer 1912-2006

When Anderl Heckmair died, aged 98, in February 2005, I wrote to Heinrich Harrer asking if he would write a tribute to his Eiger rope mate for the *Alpine Journal*. He responded with enthusiasm, telephoning immediately then quickly turning round an affectionate piece in which he quoted Heckmair's words: 'First we were opponents, on the wall we became partners and afterwards friends for a lifetime.' It appeared in the 2005 *AJ* published just a couple of months before Harrer's own death at the age of 93.

With his passing, all four of the 'heroes' (for so they were fêted) of the first ascent of the north face of the Eiger are now gone. Harrer's partner and fellow Austrian Fritz Kasparek fell to his death in 1954 on Salacantay, Peru; Heckmair's companion Wiggerl Vörg was killed in the war, on the Eastern Front. Gone too, as if in a kind of sympathy though we know it is really a victim of global warming, is the notorious ice-field that gave Harrer the title for his second bestseller – *The White Spider* (1959). The first, of course, was *Seven Years in Tibet* (1953).

Born in Hüttenberg, Carinthia, in July 1912, Harrer had a thirst for success. With an athletic body honed from childhood running errands for his postman father around his native hills, he excelled at skiing and mountaineering. He studied geography and athletics at the University of Graz, gained a place in the Austrian ski team for the 1936 Olympics and a year later won the downhill in the World Students' Championship. Two decades on and he was still picking up medals, as the Austrian National Amateur Golf Champion.

But there are shadows in Harrer's youthful past – as there are regarding much of what happened in Austria in the 1930s – and question marks over Harrer's own closeness, or otherwise, to National Socialism. In 1997, he was forced to admit a brief membership of the SS but strenuously denied any involvement in Nazi activity. The timing was cruel. Harrer's second great adventure, his Seven Years in Tibet, had just been turned into a Hollywood epic with Brad Pitt as the good-looking hero who escapes from internment in British India to become a tutor to the Dalai Lama. Harrer was portrayed as a real life Indiana Jones, which in many ways he was, but for once he would have preferred anonymity.

While the film was in production, a radio journalist from Salzburg, Gerald Lehner, had obtained documents in Washington taken from the Berlin state archives after World War II. Harrer's marriage application stated he had been a member of the Sturmabteilung (SA) – Nazi thugs – from 1933 and joined the SS in 1938. Confronted, Harrer denied membership of the SA, claiming that a 'false' declaration had been made in order to speed up his marriage. His bride was Lotte Wegener, daughter of an eminent geophysicist, Alfred Wegener, and well connected to the Nazi elite. Harrer was in a hurry, not only to get married, but also to do so before rushing off to Nanga Parbat. In his 2002 autobiography *Mein Leben* he protested: 'Was it youthful opportunism or blind determination, to subordinate oneself for sporting objectives? It was, in any case a mistake.'

Hollywood dropped the beleaguered Austrian like a hot brick and he was hurt not to be invited to the US premiere of Seven Years. Harrer was concerned also that the revelations should not rebound on the Tibetan cause he had espoused, and China certainly did try to exploit the disclosure to smear its exiled adversary the Dalai Lama.

The whiff of controversy was still in the air when Harrer addressed the Alpine Club as guest of honour at our dinner in the splendour of the Great Hall at St Bartholomew's Hospital in 1998. Though 86 years old, he was still an erect and imposing figure and had only recently stopped skiing in the hills of Carinthia. At Bart's he was among mountaineers with a keen appreciation of the audacity and climbing genius deployed over those four days on the *Eigerwand*. Some knew the route first hand. Mind, at the time of the first ascent the AC old guard viewed the Eiger game with Olympian distaste, decrying its high mortality rate and the use of 'cheating' aids such as pitons and crampons. In 1937, my redoubtable predecessor Colonel Strutt declared the north face to be 'an obsession for the mentally deranged'. Sixty years later, here was one of them addressing us.

Such is the classic status of *The White Spider* that the story of the climb hardly needs retelling. Four previous attempts on the face had ended with eight deaths and two climbers retreating from Death Bivouac. Early on, Harrer and Kasparek joined forces with the faster and better equipped German pair Heckmair and Vörg. Heckmair led every pitch. Harrer, who unlike the others had no crampons and was relying on nailed boots, generally brought up the rear, increasingly weighed down by retrieved pitons.

Battered by stone-fall and avalanches they reached the summit in a howling storm and shook hands without a word. Harrer and Kasparek had been on the face for 85 hours and all four had been perilously close to joining the roll of the so-called *Mordwand* victims. Harrer had felt certain that avalanches cascading over him on the Spider would hurl them all off the face. One suffocating mass followed another. "I seemed to have been standing in this crushing, sliding Hell for endless ages," he wrote.

The image of Germans and Austrians united in struggle was a gift for the Goebbel's propaganda machine, coming, as it did, just months after the *Anschluss*. The four were whisked to Breslau, now Wroclaw in Poland, and presented to Hitler at a rally where they were cheered by a crowd of 30,000. 'Boys, boys,' the Führer said to them. 'This thing you have done.' Harrer was reportedly moved to tears by Hitler's praise and told him: 'We have climbed the Eiger *Nordwand*, over the summit and beyond, to you our Führer.' He later vehemently denied saying any such thing, blaming the words on a 'total simpleton of a ghostwriter' appointed by a Nazi publishing house.

He did not dispute, however, his enlistment in the Styrian SS as an Oberscharführer, a rank equivalent to sergeant, explaining that he was 'invited' to join as a sports teacher after the Eiger ascent. 'I wore my SS uniform only once, on the day of my marriage,' he said. SS membership was an 'aberration' but he had to just 'grin and bear it'. The party card, however, was a useful passport to Nanga Parbat. He might not otherwise have been selected.

When Harrer sailed from Antwerp in spring 1939, he would not see Europe again for 13 years. Lotte was pregnant with their son Peter, though, contrary to Hollywood's version of the departure scene, Harrer was unaware of it. She gave up waiting for her missing husband. Under Peter Aufschnaiter, the expedition reconnoitred the Diamir flank of Nanga Parbat and returned to Karachi where the team was shadowed by British agents. War was looming. Harrer and two Germans made a break for Persia in a ramshackle car but were arrested for their 'personal protection'.

Harrer fretted away almost five years imprisoned at Dehra Dun (see article 'Prisoners of the Raj', page 213 of this *AJ*), in sight of the Himalaya, before, third time lucky, an escape bid succeeded and he and Aufschnaiter slipped into Tibet. It was one of the greatest adventures of the 20th Century. Fugitives without papers or money, wind and cold their 'permanent companions', they marvelled at Everest and received unexpected hospitality from nomads. After 18 months they arrived in Lhasa, two blistered vagabonds begging for food, who found favour with the Tibetans and settled into an idyllic life. Harrer became a tutor to the young Dalai Lama, instructing, as he said, 'this clever lad' in the ways and sciences of the West and arguing about religion. But with Chinese troops pressing on Lhasa, Harrer took to the road again, and with heavy heart crossed via Sikkim into India in March 1951 – shortly before the Dalai Lama himself was forced to flee.

He returned to Austria and married Margaretha Truxa but she did not see much of her wandering husband. Trips to the Andes, Alaska, and the Ruwenzori followed and the marriage was dissolved in 1958. Four years later, he married Carina Haarhaus and this time it lasted, despite almost continuous globetrotting. Harrer met the Xingu Indians of Brazil's Mato Grosso, the Bush Negroes of Surinam and the Andaman islanders; escaped death in an horrific fall over a waterfall in New Guinea and shared a near-fatal bout of malaria with his explorer friend King Leopold of the Belgians. Accolades started to flow. He was awarded the title 'Professor' by the President of Austria, the Golden Medal of the Humboldt Society and the prestigious medal of the US Explorers' Club. He was made an honorary member of the AC at the time of the Bart's dinner.

The mementoes of this adventurous life are on display at a Heinrich Harrer museum in Hüttenberg, officially opened by the Dalai Lama in 1992. When the Nazi stains began to show, the Dalai Lama remained constant and reassured his old tutor if his conscience was clear, then he need not fear. And Harrer always insisted it was. In a message of condolence to Harrer's widow, the Dalai Lama expressed deep sadness. His 'Austrian English teacher' had been a personal friend, he said, who had, through his writings, done much to raise awareness about Tibet and the plight of its people.

Stephen Goodwin

Eric Duncan Grant Langmuir MBE 1931-2005

Eric Langmuir died, aged 74, at his home near Aviemore, on 18 September 2005. A natural but entirely unassuming leader, he inspired the respect and deep affection of both the mountaineering and wider outdoors communities of his era. A member of the Alpine Climbing Group, the Scottish Mountaineering Club, the Climbers' Club and also an Honorary Member of the Club de Montagne Canadien, Eric was probably most widely known for his book *Mountaincraft and Leadership*. First published in 1969 under the title *Mountain Leadership* and thrice painstakingly revised, it is now referred to by many simply as 'Langmuir' and has for years been the indispensable bible for all who would take parties of young people into the hills, or for those simply aspiring to climb for themselves; indeed, it is a thoroughly readable and enjoyable guide to all aspects of the mountain scene.

The early war years saw Eric evacuated from his home in Glasgow to Achiltibuie on the Wester Ross coast. Later he was to move to secondary school in Callander before gaining admission to Fettes College. National Service followed with a commission in the Royal Artillery before he went up to Peterhouse, Cambridge, there to read for the Natural Sciences Tripos and join the University Mountaineering Club. The year was 1952 and the CUMC was enjoying a run of success under a line of notable presidents: Brasher, Smith, Band, and Chorley, to which in two more years, Eric's own name would be added. He was already a competent VS leader with more Scottish winter experience than most, and soon found himself climbing with, among others, Geoff Sutton, the next president, and contemporaries Bob Downes and Mike O'Hara. In that company his climbing blossomed and he went on to play a significant part in the exploration of Scottish rock, notably Trilleachan Slabs at the head of Loch Etive. In 1954 he pioneered *Spartan Slab* which still ranks as one of the most popular climbs in Britain.

At the end of his CUMC presidency in 1955 Eric joined Geoff, Bob and Alan Blackshaw for what was to be an outstanding alpine season. For Eric the plums were the République Arête of the Grands Charmoz with Alan, and, with all three, the *South Face Direct* of the Punta Gugliermina and the *Cassin route* on the north-east face of the Piz Badile, both graded ED and both first British ascents which did much to augment the post-war renaissance of British guideless alpine climbing. In his final season, 1957, before family responsibilities took over, Eric added the Roc-Grépon traverse and the Bonatti route on the east face of the Grand Capucin, climbing with George Fraser.

After Cambridge he was employed for two years as a field exploration geologist in Canada, where he also met his future wife, Maureen Lyons. Returning to England he taught briefly in Wimbledon, before taking up the post of Principal at Whitehall Centre for Open Country Pursuits, the ground-breaking initiative of Jack Longland, then Director of Education for Derbyshire. This naturally led to his next appointment as Principal at Glenmore Lodge, the National Outdoor Training Centre near Aviemore. Under his guidance, the centre was to gain an international reputation, attracting a stream of volunteer instructors. The whole question of safety in mountains concerned him deeply. As an original member of the Mountain Leadership working party under Longland in the early 1960s, then in launching a parallel scheme for Scotland in 1964 and in due course, through his book, he made an outstanding contribution to this all-important topic. His responsibilities at the Lodge also included mountain rescue, initially as leader of the Glenmore team, then as co-ordinator in the northern Cairngorms, later as a member of the Mountain Rescue Committee of Scotland and finally as its Chairman from 1968. For this voluntary service he was made MBE in 1986. It was also at Glenmore Lodge that Eric first became interested in avalanche prognosis and, working with the late André Roch at the Swiss Avalanche Research Centre in Davos, he developed ideas for setting up an avalanche forecast and warning system, the foundation for the Scottish Avalanche Information Service. Later he was to instruct SCGB reps courses in this vital subject. Many lives must have been saved as a result of this work, which was recognised in 1987 by his election as a Fellow of the Royal Society of Edinburgh.

Leaving Glenmore Lodge in 1969, Eric moved to Moray House in Edinburgh, there to establish and develop courses in outdoor education before becoming Assistant Director of Leisure Services in Midlothian, responsible for all 'countryside' matters including sailing and skiing at which he was much more than just proficient. Indeed, he held the highest grade as a BASI ski instructor.

After early retirement to his new home at Avielochan in 1988, Eric was soon appointed to the Countryside Commission for Scotland, later to be renamed Scottish National Heritage, and in 1991-93 was a member of its Cairngorm Working Party, courageously entering a minority report that was to play an important role in the eventual foundation of the Cairngorms National Park. At much the same time, enthusiastic and fiercely competitive as ever, he took up orienteering. What began as recreation became a passion as, almost to the end of his life, he competed successfully in events throughout the western world. And he continued hill-walking with his family and many friends. At the age of 60 he made several first ascents in the Bhutan Himalaya, including Wohney Gang (5589m). At 70, his enthusiasm for the hills undimmed, he traversed the length of the Cuillin ridge – and climbed Mont Blanc. But then in 2004, without warning, cancer struck. Yet he made a typically brave and determined recovery and, barely three months after major surgery, climbed from Buttermere to Black Sail to join in a celebration of the life of his friend, Chris Brasher. Twelve months later, in June 2005, he was in Cambridge for the CUMC Centenary dinner. It was to be our last meeting.

Eric's wife, 'Mo', as she was always known, died from cancer in 1980. He is survived by their two sons, two daughters and eight grandchildren and by his fellow orienteer and devoted partner of recent years, Marion MacCormick.

John Peacock

David Pasteur 1931-2004

David Pasteur was born into a family of mountaineers and the mountains were always a part of his life, from the days when he accompanied his family on Alpine trips in his youth during his school holidays to the final year of his life when he climbed the Pic du Canigou in the French Pyrenees and Ben Avon in the Cairngorms.

The family link to the Alpine Club goes back to Henri Pasteur who became a member in 1873 and was vice-president from 1893-95. His son Charles joined in 1890 and also held the position of vice-president. David's father, Hugh, two uncles, a cousin and other members of the extended family were also duly elected. Several ladies were active mountaineers, including Hugh's aunts, sister and cousins Nancy Morse and Joyce Norton (married to Teddy Norton, leader of the 1922 Everest expedition). David himself joined in 1959 and two of his children have been members since 1996.

David was the eldest of Hugh and Grisell Pasteur's three children. He grew up in Kent and was educated at Winchester and King's College, Cambridge where he got a good degree in Classics. He started climbing during childhood holidays, which would usually involve climbing or walking as the family loved to be in the mountains. His first proper introduction to the Alps was a family trip in 1948, when he was 16.

Whilst at Cambridge, David climbed with the university club, and Richard Morgan became one of his principal climbing partners. He had several seasons in the Alps during the 1950s, the south-west ridge of the Wetterhorn and the Shreckhorn-Lauteraarhorn traverse being amongst the more notable routes achieved. Richard Morgan remembers:

'The Schreckhorn/Lauteraarhorn traverse was the longest day we ever had. The year was 1958, starting with a seven-hour approach from Grindelwald to the Strahlegg hut. David asked the warden what time we should get up for the traverse. His response was 'Sechs Uhr am Schreckhorn', and that was only the start of the traverse. So up at midnight, we asked? He didn't correct us. It was torchlight most of the way, up the south-west ridge (D–). We were on the summit not long after six, ready to tackle the mile-long traverse between the peaks. It was one of those alpine crests that is vertical on one side and overhanging on the other, with wholly unstable flanks, graded D+. We got to the Lauteraarhorn summit about midday, so we had plenty of time for the descent, didn't we? The guidebook suggested avoiding the softening south face route and keeping to the shattered rock crest, then over the Strahlegg pass. Somehow, as the day moved to a close, we limped back to the Strahlegg hut by 6pm. Time for an early night, I thought. And then David produced the clinch blow: "I've got to get back tonight to meet the family. We're off to Zermatt tomorrow." I recollect nothing more. But if you'd had David as the most reliable supportive companion for such a climb, you would have refused him nothing either.'

National Service took him to Africa with the 4th (Uganda) Battalion of the King's African Rifles, where he took every opportunity to explore the mountains. His experience of Africa led him to choose a career in the Overseas Civil Service where he was posted as a District Officer in Uganda. Much of his time was spent in the west, close to the beautiful and largely unexplored Ruwenzori mountain range.

David's most important contribution to mountaineering was in the Ruwenzori, where he climbed extensively between 1959 and 1967. He also climbed on other peaks in East Africa, including Mount Elgon, Kilimanjaro and Mount Kenya. He was a member of the Mountain Club of Uganda, being secretary, vice president and then president between 1959 and 1966. Another of his interests was photography, both stills and cine. Andrew Stuart, a fellow Mountain Club member, recalls:

'David always retained the ability to laugh at himself, which was why we all thought so much of him. The time I particularly remember was when we were building, (or actually rebuilding, as we moved it from one site to another) a mountain hut on Sabinio, one of the Virunga volcanoes where the gorillas are. When the hut was more or less finished, David asked us all to congregate inside and then come out of the door bearing our tools, so that he could film the completion of our work. Unbeknownst to him one of the panels at the back was not yet in place, so, as soon as they had been filmed, everyone darted round the back and reappeared through the front door to be filmed, resulting in an apparently endless stream of builders. We would not have done it to anyone for whom we had not the greatest affection.'

On trips to Ruwenzori, David gave great encouragement and training to his regular headman/guide John Matte and his porters. Matte subsequently played an important role in enabling climbing parties to continue visiting the range during the civil strife of the Amin and Obote periods. He later became the chairman of a cooperative, Ruwenzori Mountain Services, which was held up as a model in Africa.

David made a number of first ascents on Ruwenzori including the north-west rock-face of Johnston peak, the glacier route up Vittorio Emanuele and the south-west face of Kraepelin. His unrivalled knowledge bore fruit in the production of the *Mountaineering Guide to the Ruwenzori* which he co-

David Pasteur climbing *Fracture Route*, Crowberry Ridge, Buachaille Etive Mor, July 1955. (*Richard Morgan*)

wrote with Henry Osmaston. This was published in 1972, and although now out of print, remains the definitive guide.

In Uganda he met his future wife, Ingrid, and they were married in 1963. In 1967, they returned to the UK and David joined the Department of Local Government Studies at Birmingham University, where he worked in international urban management, devising and running training courses and conducting research, until his retirement in 1996. He continued to travel with his job, mostly in Africa and south-east Asia. Whilst working abroad, he also pursued his interest in butterfly collecting and his extensive Malaysian collection is now in the care of the Hunterian Museum in Glasgow.

In 1972, David and his family moved to Sugarbrook Manor, a 16th century farmhouse in Bromsgrove, Worcestershire. At weekends a lot of his time was spent on the renovation of the house and maintaining the large garden. Holidays usually involved mountaineering and the family regularly attended the meets of the UK branch of the Mountain Club of Uganda.

His trips to the Alps were not so frequent in later years, but he visited the Pyrenees with the family in 1985 and 2004. In 1992 he organised a family trip to Zinal with Ingrid, his five children, mother and aunt (a summiter of the Matterhorn in the 1930s). David's ascents included the Bishorn (with all of his five children), the Pointe de Zinal and a traverse of the Grand Cornier from south-west to north-west (taking 16 hours). In 1997 he completed the Haute Route from Chamonix to Zermatt with his cousin, daughter and son-in-law. He went on an organised trek to Nepal in 1998. Another family trip to Arolla in 2002 included all of the immediate family, this time accompanied by three spouses and four grandchildren. David was out in the mountains every day in the company of various parties, climbing the Pigne d'Arolla, La Luette and doing several valley and hut walks.

One of David's friends has said of him: 'David was one of the most focused men one could meet; to be taken on his own terms, a man of great integrity, short on prejudice, long on family commitment, intellectually bright, of a deep religious faith, totally disinterested in social trappings. It was a privilege to have known him.' David had a great love of the mountains, where it was always a pleasure to be in his company.

Wiz Pasteur and Chris Pasteur

Robert 'Rob' William Milne 1956 - 2005

On 5 June 2005, Scottish climbing lost one of its favourite adopted sons when Rob Milne suddenly collapsed and died whilst ascending the south-east ridge of Everest, some 350m short of the summit.

Rob was born in Montana, USA, in 1956 and was brought up in Colorado before moving to Edinburgh in the late '70s to complete a PhD in Artificial Intelligence. He immediately fell in love with Scottish winter climbing and developed a strong reputation as a bold ice climber. In January 1980 he teamed up with Rab Anderson for the first ascent of *The White Elephant* (VII, 6), a 300m-long ice route on Creag an Dubh Loch's Central Slabs and one of the greatest winter climbs in the Cairngorms. This was the beginning of one of the most prolific partnerships in British climbing, Anderson and Milne making more than a hundred first ascents in winter together. Notable were *West Buttress Direttissima* (VII,8) on Beinn Eighe, *Inclination* (VII,8) on Stob Coire nan Lochan and *Raven's Edge* (VII, 7) on the Buachaille. Together they pioneered modern winter climbing in the Southern Highlands, opening their account with the first winter ascent of the brilliant *Deadman's Groove* (VII, 7) on The Cobbler. They were also at the forefront of modern mixed climbing in the Northern Corries with first ascents of a string of modern classics such as *Deep Throat* (V, 6), *The Hoarmaster* (V, 6) and *The Inquisition* (VI,8).

To outsiders, the Anderson-Milne partnership looked an uneven one. The famously forceful Anderson appeared to be the driving force, but Rob was the stable backbone of the pairing. Invariably, Rob was the one who wanted to go out every weekend, and it was Rob who approached every route with an unyielding optimism that it could be climbed. This confidence was based on a long series of major international mountain ascents. In 1975 he made the first ascent of the long north-east ridge of Mount Vancouver in the Yukon and three years later came away from the Kichatna Spires in Alaska and with a good clutch of first ascents. In 1980 he climbed the north face of the Eiger, and in 1984 he visited the Karakoram with an all-star American team including Jack Tackle, Galen Rowell and Andy Embick. Here they made the first ascent of Lukpilla Brakk, a beautiful 1100m-high rock spire across the Biafo glacier from The Ogre. This significant ascent drew attention to the potential of Karakoram granite and inspired dozens of further expeditions.

In his private and business life Rob was just as successful. He met his wife Valerie in Edinburgh. They married in 1981 and had two children, Alex and Rosemary. After he finished his PhD, he worked in the USA as Chief Artificial Intelligence Scientist at The Pentagon before returning to Edinburgh to form his own Intelligent Applications company. Rob maintained his links with academia and was made a fellow of the Royal Society of Edinburgh (Scotland's National Academy) and was given an honorary degree by Robert Gordon's University in Aberdeen.

Rob's involvement in the Scottish Mountaineering Club's publications programme was a natural combination of his business and climbing talents. Rob masterminded the latest edition of The Corbetts guide and its accompanying CD before becoming editor of the District Guides. Together with Ken Crocket and Tom Prentice he updated the format resulting in the beautifully produced North-West Highlands District Guide, widely acclaimed as the finest book the SMC has ever produced. Rob then stepped up to become Convenor of the Club's publications. He brought a quiet and efficient tone to meetings, and somehow it never seemed out of place that the premier mountain book publisher in Scotland should be led by a climber with American roots.

When Rob, who was elected to the AC in 1993, climbed a new route on Carstensz Pyramid in Indonesia in 2001 with Steve Sustad, the idea of climbing the Seven Summits (the seven highest peaks in each continent) took hold. He had climbed Denali way back in 1980, so in 2003 and 2004 efficiently ticked off Mount Vinson, Elbrus and Aconcagua. Typically, he also climbed Mount Kosciuszko in Australia (there is sometimes debate as to whether Carstenz Pyramid is in Australasia or not), just to make sure. Everest was to be Rob's last Seventh Summit. He was also about to complete the 219 Corbetts, having already ticked all 284 Munros.

Rob was a man with unlimited energy, and was never backward in coming forward. Whenever we met he would enthusiastically tell me about his latest mountain adventure. He painted such vivid pictures that I wanted to rush out there and do the same thing. Rob always wanted to know what everyone else was up to and delighted in celebrating other people's success. You always felt good after talking to Rob. He will be sorely missed.

Simon Richardson

Anthony Gosselin Trower 1921-2005

Anthony Trower ws born on 12 July 1921 and died on 5 December 2005 at the age of 84. He was known from his schooldays as Cocky, a name which stuck with him throughout his life, but there was nothing arrogant about him – quite the opposite. The word was applied following the older meaning, 'formerly a term of endearment' (OED). He was senior partner in the firm of solicitors Trower, Still and Keeling of Lincoln's Inn, a family firm of which his father and grandfather had been senior partners before him.

He left Eton on the outbreak of war in 1939 and enlisted in the Hertfordshire Yeomanry. He saw service in Political Intelligence in the Middle East and in India. In 1943 he joined the SAS and in 1944 was parachuted into France behind the German lines in support of the Normandy landings. He rarely talked of his distinguished war record, which was clearly one of great courage, but he did manage to describe his parachute landing, with a jeep which got stuck in a tree. His first task was to extricate the jeep from the branches of the tree. He fought with the French Resistance and had a hand in the blowing-up of railway lines. He then moved forward with the Allied advance into Germany, where he was one of the first to relieve Belsen, an event which left him understandably traumatised. At the end of hostilities he was still to be found in Norway, rounding up pockets of enemy troops. In later years he was a stalwart of reunion trips organised by the SAS Association, and he also helped to ensure that all SAS graves had wreaths laid on them on Armistice Day.

I first met Cocky in 1949 at a height of about 12,500ft while descending the Arbengrat on the Obergabelhorn. From that meeting, where he was climbing with Charles Evans, there developed a lifelong friendship which I treasure, strongly linked to our love of mountains. In the autumn of 1951 Cocky visited Kulu with Charles Evans and E Ker, but their plans were impeded by bad weather and restrictions on movement (*AJ 58*, p270). Two peaks of 16,000ft were climbed, but the party was turned back on Deo Tibba (19,687ft).

Cocky was elected to the Alpine Club in 1952, and maintained a strong link with the mountains in later years. In 1981 he joined the AC meet in Nepal, when we completed the circuit of the Annapurna Himal, crossing the Thorung La at about 17,500ft. Cocky was the most enjoyable of companions, and the rest of the party took great delight in calling upon his skill with binoculars and bird book whenever some exotic Himalayan bird was spotted. He was invariably able to identify it. There were later walks, in the Lötschental in 1982 and a circuit of Monte Rosa in 1985. My main recollection of Cocky in all these adventures was of fun and laughter. In 1957 he married Joan Kellett – a very happy marriage which lasted nearly 50 years. He is survived by Joan and their four sons and a daughter, and by 17 grandchildren, to whom the Club extends its sympathy.

J H Emlyn Jones

Colonel Edward Smyth FRCS 1913-2005

Edward Smyth (known to many as 'Teddy Smyth'), who died on 24 October aged 91, lived a remarkably varied life that spanned most of the 20th century. A dedicated and innovative orthopaedic surgeon, he possessed a strong Christian faith which led him to take every opportunity to use his profession in mission work. On top of that his zest for life found outlets in mountaineering, skiing, sailing, trout fishing and writing.

Edward Hugh Jackson Smyth was born in Guildford in 1913, the only son of an ophthalmic surgeon. After Epsom College, he trained for medicine at St Bartholomew's Hospital. Very soon after he qualified war broke out and he enlisted in the Royal Army Medical Corps. Trained as a paratrooper, he was part of the British Expeditionary Force which crossed to France, and he was one of the last to be evacuated from the Brittany beaches with Alan Brooke nearly three weeks after Dunkirk. At the end of the war he was back in Normandy with the Allied Forces, and when France was liberated, and Germany invaded, he was one of the first medical personnel to uncover the horrors of the Nazi concentration camps. In the intervening period he served for three years in West Africa. For many years after the war he was an active member of the Territorial Army, retiring eventually with the rank of full Colonel.

No sooner had peace been declared than he answered a call to serve in the Grenfell Mission in Newfoundland. He was swiftly demobbed and set off with his wife and three young children to the remote outpost of St Anthony at the northern tip of Newfoundland. For the next year, travelling in his own yacht round the coast in the summer, and driving his own dog-team in the winter, he brought every sort of medicine to the villagers.

For the next five years he practised orthopaedics in the Canadian city of Calgary. But never one to stay in the urban areas for long he joined one of the Canadian relief organisations working in the Yukon and frequently took special leave for sorties up the Alaska highway or by small aircraft. In later life he was a splendid raconteur with his stories of children spitting out their tonsils from a makeshift operating table in the village street, or getting the float plane off too small a lake by tethering its rear to a tree and cutting the rope when the engines were flat out.

But his greatest love was the mountains, and gazing out of his Calgary window, the eastern Rockies were always on the skyline. He had climbed most of the highest peaks in Britain before the war and he now turned his attention to Banff, Lake Louise and the Jasper National Park. In the Kananaskas area he found a whole range of peaks over 3000m that had apparently never been climbed. He led a team up each one, subsequently writing up the expeditions for the Canadian Alpine Club of which he became a distinguished member.

In 1951 Smyth, with his wife and five children, returned to England and settled in the Isle of Wight. He soon attained consultant status practising

Colonel Edward Smyth FRCS, 1913-2005

orthopaedics in the Island and at Southampton for the Wessex Regional Hospital Board for the rest of his working life. It was during this period that he invented the 'Smyth triangular pinning method' for hip surgery that was widely used in Britain and adopted in the Groote Schuur Hospital in Cape Town; he wrote regularly for the *British Journal of Orthopaedics* and the *Journal of Bone and Joint Surgery* on this and other topics. He was closely associated with the Lord Mayor Treloar Orthopaedics Hospital in Alton and the Cambridge Military Hospital in Aldershot. During his years on the Island he operated on many famous patients convalescing at Osborne House, and almost as many notorious patients from Parkhurst Top Security Prison.

The Isle of Wight provided every opportunity for yachting; with his children, Edward Smyth sailed extensively in the Solent and across the Channel, owning a succession of 5-ton cruising yachts. Canada had been his introduction to skiing and every winter with his wife he would endeavour to spend two weeks in the Alps, usually at Arosa or Mürren. But climbing mountains was still his passion, and his summer holiday in the Alps usually took pride of place. With medical colleagues, old friends, and his children as they grew up, he found refreshment each year among the 4000-metre giants. The Matterhorn, Dent Blanche, Monte Rosa, Weisshorn and many more became food and drink to him. He became a well-known member of the Alpine Club (elected 1962) and for a period in retirement served as club archivist. And in his seventies he was walking in the foothills of the Himalaya up to 5000m with a group he called the Ancient Britons.

When it was time to give up the National Health Service and private practice he continued at the Cambridge Military Hospital part-time for a while. Despite a heart attack in his early 60s he went to Nigeria in 1977 to do a semester as visiting Professor at the University Medical School and to offer a helping hand wherever he could.

Edward Smyth always enjoyed a deep, but private, spiritual life. He hated being asked to wear his heart on his sleeve and for this reason found it difficult to come to terms with the Charismatic Movement which seemed to him unnecessarily ostentatious. In the last two decades of his life he found ever-increasing solace and camaraderie in the fellowship of Churt Parish Church pastored by the Reverend Colin Pontin.

Colonel Smyth, as he liked to call himself in retirement years, remained extremely active mentally to the end. He had written poetry during the war years and from time to time subsequently, and in 2003 a number of his poems were published in the anthology *Time Standing Still*. A regular column in the *Farnham Herald*, broadcasting on local radio, and letters to the Press provided an outlet for his ever-deepening Christian faith and his strong views on the moral decline of the nation.

In 1939 he married Ursula (née Ross), an extremely happy marriage that lasted until her death 44 years later. He remarried in 1989 to Bunty Keen, a widow, who died in 2001. He is survived by his three sons and two daughters, 13 grandchildren and seven great grandchildren.

John Smyth

John Rawnsley King 1944-2003

When John King died in August 2003 as a result of a summer scrambling accident on the Aonach Eagach ridge, he had been out of contact with all or almost all his former climbing friends and companions for many years. As we now know, this was largely attributable to a depressive illness which dogged him for most of his adult life. He was, however, a man of resolution and purpose and he did not let his illness stand in the way of a demanding and distinguished career in the field of fiscal and development economics. Nor did it prevent him from finding solace in the hills, especially in Scotland, though it does seem to have meant that latterly these were largely solitary expeditions or family affairs.

Born the son of a school teacher and an industrial chemist who worked much of his life in the whaling industry including seasons in the Southern Ocean, John was destined after Fettes to read history at Oxford. A year between school and university spent teaching in Western Kenya, however, sparked in him a desire to change to a more practical subject which included economics so that he might make his career in economic development.

During that year in Kenya, frustrated by the cancellation of a school expedition to Mt Elgon, he made a solo ascent of Kilimanjaro. In a nicely understated letter to his parents, he describes how, although his gym shoes came to pieces and he suffered mild frostbite, he had taken a second set of footwear and the doctor had signed him fit on his return; so all was well.

At Balliol he was an active member of OUMC and made his first forays to the Swiss Alps, establishing himself as a careful climber who was always meticulously well prepared and equipped.

During an OUMC winter meet at the CIC hut in 1967 he was a member of a party which successfully searched for and extricated an avalanche victim who had been trapped for some 12 hours after being caught out on No 4 Gully. They were just in the nick of time. Writing about it afterwards for the Proceedings of the Club's Avalanche Symposium of 1979, John included this memorable passage, 'If you get into a similar fix as casualty or rescuer, remember that there is more hope of a miracle than you will be inclined to believe – because hope itself is a useful commodity.'

Following a Master's degree at the Institute of Development Studies at Sussex University and a year teaching economics in Mauritius, he took a post at the University of Nairobi as lecturer in economics. Here he joined and rapidly became Hon Secretary of the Mountain Club of Kenya, a post which well suited the efficient but retiring person that he was. By now married, he and his wife Anne (who became the Hon. Editor of the MCK Journal) set up home in Nairobi. Many among the mountaineering fraternity enjoyed their hospitality at Arboretum Court.

John invited me to visit him in 1971. Christmas of that year found us first wandering among the satellites of Mt Kenya on peaks Delamere and Coryndon, and then climbing Batian and Nelion via the Darwin Glacier and descending and making a most satisfying circumnavigation of the mountain. John was the ideal companion, knowledgeable about the area and its history, deeply aware of its economic and political problems, uncomplaining when most of our food was stolen and surprisingly full of deep and intriguing conversation. It was as happy a trip as any I have undertaken.

While he was living in Nairobi the seeds were also sown which led to his most enduring economic publication, *Stabilisation Policy in Kenya*, a work which has had a lasting influence as an economic guide in that part of the world.

After Africa and a teaching post at Lancaster University he was offered a job as Economic Adviser to the Inland Revenue, a position which for some years he found congenial and stimulating. However, his real vocation lay with developing countries and he eventually became a consultant economist with the Fiscal Affairs Department of the International Monetary Fund. This led him to numerous developing countries including Bhutan, Nepal, Bangladesh and a spell as Resident Representative of the IMF in Albania for two years, during the most troubled period of the late 1990s. In this work his talents of patience, scholarship and economic wisdom combined to enable him to produce reports on local conditions which were of considerable value to his employers, and to the countries he visited. The work also enabled him to reach more (and more remote) mountain ranges than is given to most people even in this era of easy travel, though he left no record of what were almost all solitary wanderings. In the Albanian context he would, I feel, have particularly savoured Richard Hargreaves' article 'Mountains for Peace in the Balkans' in *AJ* 2004.

The accident which led to his death occurred whilst he was on leave. On this occasion he was accompanied by his younger daughter Elizabeth. He had recently had two separate hip replacements, which probably rendered a minor slip much more serious than it might otherwise have been. After a sensible bivouac – for which he was characteristically well prepared – he and Elizabeth set off on the descent to Clachaig Inn, but suffered a more serious fall on the way down. Despite having sustained a badly broken ankle as well as other injuries, Elizabeth continued down to get help in an epic journey which called for determination, courage and endurance well worthy of her father. But, alas, by the time help arrived John had taken a further tumble and was dead.

Michael Baker

Rosemary Greenwood 1917-2005

To say that Rosemary Greenwood had been born into a mountaineering family would be an understatement. Among her forebears, and their close relatives, were seven AC members, of whom Francis Fox Tuckett (AC 1859), Geoffrey Howard (AC 1907) and T Howard Somervell (AC 1921) became either a President or a Vice President. On her mother's side, her great-grandfather Joseph Fox joined the Club in 1859, and his cousin, Harry Fox (AC 1885) was with Donkin when their expedition was lost in the Caucasus in 1888. Rosemary's elder sister, Jean (Kuhn), was a member of the Ladies Alpine Club during the 1930s, and her younger sister Jen (Solt), and nephew Philip Solt are currently members. Vol 99 of the *AJ* (1994) contains an article by Rosemary setting out the relationships and climbing achievements of her convoluted Quaker family, together with a family tree.

Born a Howard, Rosemary's first introduction to the Alps was through skiing. Her family home was at Loughton on the edge of Epping Forest, but the family also rented a holiday home at Grindelwald. Rosemary's mother, a Fox, was musical and saw to it that all her seven children played instruments – Rosemary studied cello at the Royal College of Music, and played chamber music until she was 85 – and there were occasional opera performances in their large garden. (Their production of Handel's *Xerxes* was the first since Handel's day.) Her father ran a factory in Ilford where he manufactured pharmaceuticals. Howard's was a byword for Aspirin during the first quarter of the 20th century, and the firm was also notable for quinine.

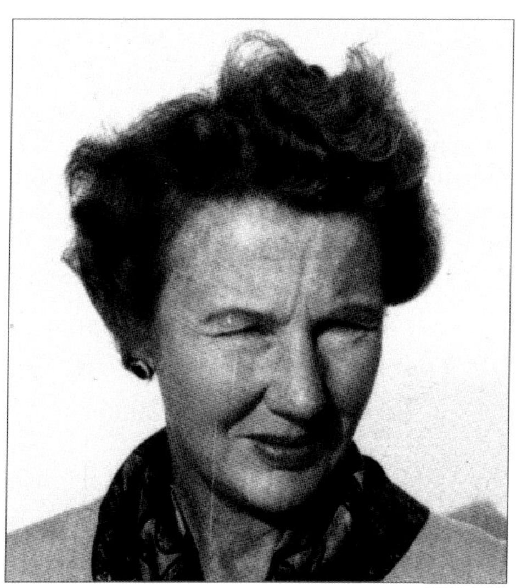

Rosemary Greenwood 1917-2005

The two Fox uncles were pioneer skiers, and the family chalet at Grindelwald was much used for skiing parties. Rosemary later became prominent in the Eagle Ski Club. She did not join the AC until 1984, by which time her climbing list covered seven pages.

Her earliest climbs, during the 1930s, were in Switzerland. Her very first recorded climb was with Ashley Greenwood, then a family friend. Probably the most ambitious at that period was of the Finsteraarhorn in 1939 with her sister Jen and a guide. During the war she continued with rock climbing on Skye and later in Colorado. After the war, in 1950, she returned to Switzerland and concentrated on ski mountaineering. However, in 1954 she led a Ramblers' party to the Julian Alps (having joined it as a participant the previous year) and went on to join Ashley to climb in the Bregaglia. A couple of years later, in 1956, they married.

In spite of Ashley's legal work for the Colonial Office (see obit. *AJ 109*, 2004), which involved residence in Uganda, Fiji, Gibralter and Hong Kong, they climbed, trekked or ski toured practically every year until the mid-1990s. As well as in all areas of the Alps, they climbed in Greece, New Zealand, Norway, Peru, Nepal and India. Always ready for adventure, they returned, after several years in Fiji, by boat to Colombo (Sri Lanka) and thence by bus through India, the Middle East and Central Europe.

After Ashley retired he and Rosemary became very active on Club evenings, and arranged the food before lectures. They also became prime movers in a number of Himalayan treks, including to Lahul, Nepal (Annapurna Circuit), Sikkim and Ladakh where Ashley climbed Stok Kangri (6121m) to celebrate his 80th birthday. Rosemary, aged 77 and in bad weather, decided to call it a day after reaching a high camp at approximately 5000m.

In 1889 one Hubert Fox had initiated the sport of skiing at Grindelwald, and in 1989 Rosemary was invited to represent her family as Guest of Honour at the centenery celebrations. But it was not until she was in her eighties that she began to wind down her walking activities; even so, as recently as the summer of 2005, she proved herself indomitable, albeit on the coastal paths of Devon. She died just before her 89th birthday.

Livia Gollancz

Ian Angell 1939-2006

Ian Angell died on 14 January 2006 just four days before his 67th birthday from a head injury sustained from a fall while hillwalking on A' Chrois in Arrochar.

During his life Ian achieved innumerable ascents ranging from local outcrops close to places where he lived to Mera Peak in the Himalaya. He was generous with his time and many people benefited from being shown the ropes whether on his local crag near Largs on a summer's evening or on an expedition to the higher mountains and their ridges. Ian attained national fame in 1961 when, as 'a slim 22-year-old student', he made a solo ascent of the Hörnli ridge of the Matterhorn in 3 hours 25 minutes, a post-war record. As befitted his modesty he was astonished and suitably embarrassed when it became national news on the front page of the *Daily Sketch*. The headline read 'Mad dog Ian climbs it solo!' The report quoted the Zermatt chief guide Godlieb Perren: 'A splendid effort which only an Englishman would dare. He is a first class mountaineer.'

As with most people who spend time in the mountains, Ian's trips were not without incident. While skiing from the Valsorey Hut, up the Plateau de Couloir on the High Level Route in the mid-1970s he was avalanched and buried along with the avalanche cord he was trailing. Frantic rescue efforts by a following German team revealed his cyanosed, lifeless form; but swift, effective resuscitation restored him in what one companion described as 'the nearest thing he had seen to the resurrection'. Incredibly, Ian restarted the tour only 24 hours later, despite both the trauma and hypothermia, and successfully finished in Zermatt.

Born on 18 January 1939, he was brought up in Sheringham in Norfolk and educated at King Edward VII Grammar School in Kings Lynn. He started climbing when at school where, it is rumoured, his initials are carved at the top of the bell tower. On leaving school he went to Rugby College of Engineering and was a founder member of Rugby Mountaineering Club.

Ian was devoted to his wife Shirley, also a climber, who wrote the definitive history of the Pinnacle Club. In it she relives the first time she set eyes on her husband to be, which was up a tree outside the Vaynol Arms in Snowdonia! As she wrote in her book, 'Later he danced the polka with me up and down the road. It was love at first sight.'

When working for the UK Atomic Energy Authority (UKAEA) in Cumbria Ian established many new rock routes in the area, publishing a guidebook to St Bees Head and a number of magazine articles. Both Ian and Shirley were members of the Wyndham Mountaineering Club, and Ian was a member and later an honorary member of Wasdale Mountain Rescue Team. He became a member of the Fell and Rock Climbing Club in 1972 and from 1976 until 1980 was assistant warden at Brackenclose, in Wasdale. It was in May 1975 that he was elected to the Alpine Club and helped to catalogue the Club library when it was moved to Charlotte Road in September 1991.

Ian qualified as a Mountain Guide in 1978 and served as treasurer for the British Mountain Guides in the late eighties and early nineties. In 1981, now living in south-west Scotland, he joined the Scottish Mountaineering Club serving on the committee from 1983 until 1988 and then as a Trustee of the Scottish Mountaineering Trust. In 1998 he became the SMC Honorary Club librarian a position he held until his death.

In 1992 he first visited the Staunings Alps in north-east Greenland and returned in 1994 and again in 1996, achieving first ascents and naming one Shirley's Peak after his wife. He enjoyed the Arctic and in 1996 also visited Spitsbergen, where he admitted his calm approach was somewhat ruffled by the polar bear tracks circling the camp.

Ian retired from the UKAEA in 1996 and successfully ran his own independent business working in various nuclear power stations. With more free time he climbed all of the VS rock routes on Buchaille Etive Mor and fulfilled an ambition of a winter ascent of *Orion Direct*.

In April 2005 he completed the Munros on Sgor Gaoith in Glen Feshie and was joined by a group of more than 50 family and friends. For once the weather behaved and he was cheered on to the summit as a family of golden eagles flew below over Loch Einich.

Ian cared passionately about the mountain environment and was dismayed by the recent proliferation of radio masts and wind turbines. As a man of principle, he was prepared to take a stand and speak his mind on such issues.

Ian was very involved in the local community and church though he rarely spoke about his strong Christian faith. At his death he was chairman of a group which had successfully lobbied to make his home town Largs a Fair Trade town. At his funeral on 25 January, the church and much of the churchyard were overflowing with family, friends and colleagues paying their respects to a caring, unassuming man, renowned for his youthful enthusiasm and love of the mountains.

Ian delighted in his family, especially his two granddaughters Bethany and Megan. He is survived by his wife Shirley and three sons, Timothy, Adrian and Stephen.

Colwyn M Jones

Alpine Club Notes

OFFICERS AND COMMITTEE FOR 2006

President	S Venables
Vice Presidents	R Turnbull
	P Wickens
Honorary Secretary	R M Scott
Honorary Treasurer (Elect)	R N K Baron
Honorary Librarian	D J Lovatt
Honorary Editor of the *Alpine Journal*	S J Goodwin
Honorary Guidebooks Commissioning Editor	L N Griffin
Committee Elective Members	T J Clarke
	J S Cleare
	R Eastwood
	A E Scowcroft
	A Stockwell
	C Watts

OFFICE BEARERS

Librarian Emeritus	R Lawford
Honorary Archivist	P T Berg
Honorary Keeper of the Club's Pictures	P Mallalieu
Honorary Keeper of the Club's Artefacts	D J Lovatt
Honorary Keeper of the Club's Monuments	W A C Newsom
Chairman of the Finance Committee	R F Morgan
Chairman of the House Committee	
Chairman of the Alpine Club Library Council	H R Lloyd
Chairman of the Membership Committee	W G Thurston
Chairman of the Guidebooks Editorial and Production Board	L N Griffin
Guidebooks Production Manager	
Assistant Editors of the *Alpine Journal*	P Knott
	G W Templeman
Production Editor of the *Alpine Journal*	J Merz
Newsletter Editor	R Turnbull
Website Editor	P Wickens

Assistant Honorary Secretaries:

Annual Winter Dinner	W A C Newsom
Lectures	M W H Day

NO 'MORALITY-FREE ZONE' IN CLIMBING

By Doug Scott

In the Tyrol Declaration on Best Practice in Mountain Sports (2002), which subscribed to the above dictum, it was noted in the foreword that a 'growing callousness in society is making inroads into mountaineering and is causing deep concern in the climbing community'.Thus, in section six, 'Emergencies', delegates came up with the following maxim:

> If a person we meet – regardless if it is a fellow climber, a porter or another local inhabitant – needs help, we must do everything in our power to provide qualified support as quickly as possible. There is no 'morality-free zone' in climbing!
>
> 1. If aid by an official instance – like mountain rescue – is not possible and we are in a position to help, we are obliged to give persons in trouble all possible support if this is possible without unduly endangering ourselves.
>
> 2. Helping someone in trouble has absolute priority over reaching goals we set for ourselves in the mountains. Saving a life or reducing damage to an injured person's health is far more valuable than the hardest of first ascents.
>
> 3. Life-preserving measures should only be stopped if the death of an accident victim or a sick person has been established beyond doubt.

Not all delegates, including Chris Bonington, Roger Payne and myself, could see the point of reiterating what appeared to be self-evident, for was it not a fact that most committed climbers had at some time either given or received such assistance in the mountains – Bonington and Whillans rescuing Nally on the Eiger north face; Bonington with Scott rescued from the Ogre by Anthoine and Rowland; Yates rescuing Simpson from the summit ridge of Siula Grande. There have been, and will be, many more such acts of courage, even above 8000 metres.

In May this year, a bombshell exploded into the climbing world when massive media coverage reported ailing English climber David Sharp had been largely ignored and left to his fate by 40 other would-be Everest ascensionists, 300m from the summit. The response was swift with letters to editors about inhuman mountaineers and this being the antithesis of the Good Samaritan principle. There was outright condemnation from Edmund Hillary – 'It would never happen in my day' – and Chris Bonington who was horrified at such indifference to human life. American climber Ed Viesturs, who has climbed all fourteen 8000-metre summits without oxygen and rescued a woman from just 100m below Everest summit, told the *Seattle Times*: 'If you are strong enough to mount a summit attempt, you're strong enough to attempt a rescue, or at least sit there with him and try to provide a little comfort.' Others rationalised that norms of common humanity could not always be applied in the so-called death zone. Our member, Alan Hinkes, suggested that above 8000 metres it was unlikely that anyone would have the strength to help another ailing climber. 'It is not realistic to expect help or rescue; climbing Everest is very serious and expensive, you have to be prepared to pay the ultimate price,' said Alan. I was also unsettled by the concluding words of an article in the *Daily Telegraph* under the name of our president, Stephen Venables: 'Morally, as well as physically, you are entering a different world – a world with different rules.' However, Stephen's words were apparently toughened up by a sub-editor for a final flourish to an article intended to convey the complexity of ethics and behaviour at high altitude and pointing out that great nobility is possible on mountains too.

Yet the fact remains that those 40 Everest hopefuls assumed at the time that they had the strength and oxygen to go the extra 300m up to the summit and back, and then further down to camp for the night. Why was it that at least a splinter group did not react to Sharp's condition and help him down to the camp, less than half an hour away? It would appear that some of the 40 variously were already exhausted, like Sharp, and mistook him for a dead Indian climber of 1996, or thought that he was resting, that he did not require help, or they never saw him at all.

It seems that the 40 climbers were predominantly from commercially guided organisations, whose organisers called the shots and, like dogs on leads, the clients continued up under orders. Now there is a syndrome that has to be addressed and taken into account, especially on Everest, and that is those who pay the money (up to £65,000) to be taken up Everest, from then onwards often absolve themselves from all further responsibility for not only their own lives but also for the lives of others. This problem of disengagement was made clear by Jon Krakauer in *Into Thin Air* where he described how in 1996, at the south summit, he came across his friend and guide, Andy Harris, who was in a very confused state. '...it's inconceivable to me that I would have neglected to recognise his plight,' wrote Krakauer. 'But on this expedition he [Harris] had been cast in the role as the invincible guide, there to look after me and the other clients; we had been specifically indoctrinated not to question our guide's judgement.' Krakauer left Harris and headed down the mountain. Harris subsequently died, to Krakauer's eternal regret: '...the ease with which I abdicated responsibility – my utter failure to consider that Andy might have been in serious trouble – was a lapse that's likely to haunt me for the rest of my life.'

This 'absolvement syndrome' puts a huge responsibility on the com-mercial outfits and their agents when guiding on Everest. It is incumbent upon them to issue guidelines as to just which emergency procedures should be adopted. The clients should know that the blinkers of ambition may have to be lifted when need arises to be Good Samaritans.

It is worth reflecting that it is predominantly the Sherpas who put in the greater effort when it comes to rescuing the foreigners. Is it simply that they are that much more acclimatised and stronger? Undoubtedly this is a factor. However, the fact that many Sherpas have persevered in their attempts to save the foreigner, to the point of terrible frostbite and even at the cost of their own lives, suggests that there is more to it than physical capability. Way back in 1938, on K2, three Sherpas perished in a vain but extraordinarily selfless and persistent attempt to save the ailing American Dudley Wolfe, abandoned by his compatriots at camp VII.

Ang Phurba, a couple of years after helping us climb the south-west face of Everest, was himself above the Hillary Step, only five minutes from the summit, when he turned his back on the prize to help his altitude-sick Korean companion down to the south summit and, next day, to the south col. He had saved the Korean's life. Sungdare Sherpa, in 1979, remained with Hannelore Schmatz below the south summit after she collapsed and finally died. He lost most of his fingers and toes.

The Sherpas remind us that under our veneer of civilisation and our attachment to fame and fortune, we are all capable of the same heroic deeds when it comes to rescuing others stricken in the thin, cold air of Everest. It is just that sometimes we lose the plot and are only reminded of our obligations after returning. By then a visit to the summit will be forever a hollow victory if we fail another in need.

All people whose lives are intimately connected to the land and are governed by natural processes seem to be able to stay in touch with themselves through generosity, kindness and help to others. This is the common denominator amongst all indigenous peoples. Regrettably it would appear that the more sophisticated we become the less this is so.

KANGCHENJUNGA QUINQUAGENARY 1955-2005

The year 2005 marked the 50th anniversary of the first ascent of Kangchenjunga 8586m (28,169ft) the world's third highest peak, first climbed on 25 May 1955 by Joe Brown and myself, repeated on the 26th by Norman Hardie and Tony Streather, on the expedition led by Charles Evans, who had been John Hunt's deputy on Everest in 1953. The other team members were Tom McKinnon, John Jackson, Neil Mather and the doctor John Clegg. The strong team of high-altitude Sherpas was led by Dawa Tenzing. Sadly, two members of the team died during 2005: John Jackson in July and Neil Mather in December, both after a period of ill health, leaving just the four summiters and John Clegg.

As Everest and Kangchenjunga were the only two of the world's fourteen 8000m peaks to be first climbed by British expeditions, and the Everest Golden Jubilee has been well documented in the Alpine Journal 2003, the Editor has asked me for a brief account of the events associated with the Kangchenjunga Jubilee during 2005.

The Himalayan Club was the first off the mark, arranging special celebrations during February in Mumbai, Kolkata (formerly Bombay and Calcutta) and Darjeeling, recognising that 'Kangch' was India's highest peak. Three of the team were able to participate with our wives, Norman and Enid Hardie coming from New Zealand, John and Eileen Jackson, Susan and myself. There was just time to include Jackson's account of this trip in Alpine Journal 2005, the last article he ever wrote.

Nepal came next, having an equal claim to the mountain. Their government was thrilled that Sir Edmund Hillary chose to celebrate his Everest anniversary on 29 May 2003 with the Sherpas in Kathmandu. The ensuing publicity was so beneficial that they decided to sponsor similar celebrations for the jubilees of all Nepal's eight 8000m peaks. The Hardies, Tony Streather with his son Philip, Susan and I were able to accept the invitation to attend on 26 May, coming just two weeks after a similar event for Makalu, first climbed by Jean Franco's French team. To make the trip more worthwhile, I decided to lead a 14-strong trekking party to visit the Kangchenjunga south-west and north-west base camps, one of Nepal's best – and probably most strenuous – treks lasting 23 days. Just below the south-west base camp we were able to make contact with Alan Hinkes, wishing him luck and sending up fresh vegetables, a few paperbacks, and Superglue to repair his Yeti gaiters. He was impatiently waiting for a break in the bad weather to be able to tackle his last 8000er, the final summit push on 30 May being described in stop press terms in last year's Journal.

We had a nail-biting finish to our trek. We should have been collected from the grass strip at Suketar by a fixed wing aircraft, but the strip was waterlogged for several days and we waited in growing frustration. Even the 24-seat Russian helicopter became grounded in Lukla in thick cloud. We missed an evening reception specially arranged for us at the British

Embassy, and were at risk of missing the Government celebration on 26 May for which we had been invited to Nepal, as well as our international flights home the following day. Frantic phone calls to the Ambassador, who appreciated our position as 'distressed British citizens', resulted astonishingly in not one but two helicopters, a nine and a five-seater, just sufficient to accommodate our party and enable us, after a dawn flight and a quick change, to catch up with the procession, and to be capped and garlanded and awarded commemorative plaques of appreciation in the ancient Durbar Square of Kathmandu. We summiters were then conveyed through the milling throng in the streets of old Kathmandu in open horse-drawn carriages, preceded by squads of soldiers, military bands, and flanked by schoolchildren and civil officials. It felt rather like a coronation. Badly in need of our first cup of coffee, the rest of the day passed in a whirl of lectures and presentations on adventure tourism, conservation and development in the Kangchenjunga region, publication of a new bird book, and a set of commemorative postage stamps. A reception in the presence of Crown Prince Paras Bir Bikram Shah Dev and the lovely Crown Princess Himani Rajya Laxmi Devi Shah was followed by a Royal audience and a Gala Dinner. And so to bed for a few hours sleep before we caught our plane home.

The Nepal Mountaineering Association and the Tourist Board were most generous in their hospitality, and were grateful that I was able to say that despite the current Maoist problems in the country we had been most warmly greeted on our travels and felt entirely safe, and foreigners should not be put off from coming to Nepal.

A week after our return, we gathered at Pen-y-Gwryd for our traditional five-year private party, generously hosted by Jane Pullee. Over 40 members of the extended 'Kangchenjunga family' sat down to dinner. Neil Mather who was now very frail after several strokes was not to be outdone. He and his wife Gill chartered a light aircraft to fly them from Inverness to an airstrip at Caernarvon to be with us. We were distressed to learn that PyG's gong, to summon residents to breakfast and dinner, had recently been stolen, and as a modest thanks for Jane's hospitality over the years, the Kangch' team have now presented the hotel with a new gong of orchestral quality which we hope will remain in place for many years.

The next event was the Club's own informal and most enjoyable party on 6 July to celebrate the quinquagenary. It also served to bring to a close the magnificent exhibition held at the Club on 'Kangchenjunga: Imaging a Himalayan Mountain', curated by Simon Pierse, a lecturer in art at the University of Wales, Aberystwyth. It was accompanied by a superbly researched and scholarly memoire written by Simon to form a permanent record of the exhibition, which explored the differing ways in which the mountain had been interpreted by artists, photographers, writers and explorers from Victorian times to the present day.

The main British event was a lecture evening and supper organised by and in aid of the Mount Everest Foundation, who sponsored the 1955 Expedition. It was held at the Royal Geographical Society on 7 June and compèred by David Attenborough, who had actually produced the original BBC TV programme about the climb broadcast on 18 August 1955, and a clip from the historic film was shown. A souvenir programme carried a message of congratulation from Prince Philip, Duke of Edinburgh, who was the patron of the expedition. But the unique feature of the evening which made it particularly memorable was the combined lecture by the four summiters, which is unlikely ever to happen again. The evening was certainly a financial success, raising £14,100 for the charity – marginally greater than the original £13,652 cost of the expedition, albeit in rather more valuable 1955 money!

A final unexpected event was an invitation by the Government of Sikkim to participate in their annual Festival of the Snows – the Pang Lhabsol – which celebrates the deity of Kangchenjunga. We had originally been invited for 25 May but could not be simultaneously in Kathmandu and Gangtok, so were invited for the Pang Lhabsol on 18 September instead. Only Norman Hardie, his daughter Sarah, and I were able to accept. The invitation was not to celebrate the climbing of Kangchenjunga, but to felicitate us for stopping just short of the top, thereby respecting their particular Buddhist religious principles and leaving the summit undefiled. Slight consternation was caused a few days beforehand when a senior Buddhist monk, who felt we should not have been invited, served an injunction to stop us participating. The judiciary advised the Government to serve a counter injunction which prevailed; the monk was defeated and had to pay costs! We were looked after most hospitably, visiting several fine monasteries and a fascinating exhibition of early photographs at the Namgyal Institute of Tibetology. We made an excursion to the Tsomgo Lake near the Natu La, the pass into Tibet used by the early Everest expeditions which had been closed for many years but we were told would be opening again for limited trade with China on 12 October. Hopefully this may gradually lead to securing permits more easily for mountaineering and trekking in the border areas of northern Sikkim.

And so we come to the end of 2005. Earlier in the year I had been surfing the internet on ExplorersWeb.com looking for ascent statistics. I came across a comparison between K2 and Kangchenjunga just prior to their 50th anniversary years of 2004 and 2005 respectively. By the end of 2003, K2 had 198 individual ascents, but then a record number of 48 in the anniversary year itself. The writer speculated whether the same thing would happen to Kangchenjunga in 2005, but on the whole thought not and came up with an article entitled: Ten Top Reasons for Not Climbing Kangchenjunga – basically it was 'Too long, too high, too cold, too hard!' He was rather perceptive. The only additional ascent claimed in 2005 was on 30 May by our member Alan Hinkes, who thereby became the first Brit to complete the ascents of all fourteen 8000ers, only the thirteenth person ever to do so. So there have now been just 196 ascents of Kangchenjunga to end 2005, compared to over 2250 on Everest to end 2004. Congratulations to Alan, also for his OBE in the 2006 New Year's Honours List. What a splendid way to celebrate the quinquagenary!

George Band

THE BOARDMAN TASKER AWARD FOR MOUNTAIN LITERATURE 2005

The Alpine Club was once again the venue for the Boardman Tasker Award's lunchtime reception on 7 October. Guests included Pertemba Sherpa, who summited Everest with Pete Boardman in 1975 and with Chris Bonington 10 years later. Four of the five shortlisted authors were also able to attend. In his adjudication, chair of judges, Steve Dean, spoke of the high level and diversity of the 2005 entries before going on to comment on the shortlisted titles individually:

Andy Cave *Learning to Breathe* (Hutchinson)
A first book by one of our premier Alpine climbers. *Learning to Breathe* is Andy's recollection of his journey from a school-leaver working down the pit in the Yorkshire coalfield, to becoming a major performer in Himalayan climbing. The book contains tender and often very funny accounts of life in the coalfield and of early days getting into the sport and becoming an accomplished mountaineer, culminating in a gripping, and often grim, account of the first ascent of the North Face of Changabang.

Mick Fowler *On Thin Ice* (Bâton Wicks)
A second book of memoirs from one of Britain's finest and most experienced high-altitude climbers. This is an astonishing account of gripping deeds throughout the world's great ranges by a man who has combined extreme mountaineering with all the demands of a conventional career and of raising a young family. We enjoyed this book enormously; it is written in that British tradition of modest recollection with wonderful and often self-deprecating humour, that serves to take the edge off the great seriousness of the adventures described. A climber's climber if ever there was one.

Jim Perrin *The Villain* (Hutchinson)
Never has a mountain book been so eagerly awaited, with all the consequent pressures on the author. *The Villain* grapples with the complexity and myth surrounding the life of one of Britain's greatest mountaineers, Don Whillans. The reader is introduced to the world Don grew up in, in Salford, and then follows his progress to becoming a superb rock climber and alpinist.

All the triumphs such as the Frêney Pillar and Annapurna are well documented, as are the many problems that confronted what emerges as a troubled genius. At times very funny, at times frustrating and full of sadness, this book emerges as both a compassionate view of Don's life and as a social history of British climbing from the end of the war until the mid-eighties.

Richard Sale ***Broad Peak*** **(Carreg)**
This book was the subject of by far our longest discussions and the decision to include it on the shortlist was not a unanimous one. There was strong disagreement about it both on content and style. Nonetheless, *Broad Peak* made for fascinating reading. It is an account of the first ascent in 1957 of Broad Peak by Marcus Schmuck, Fritz Wintersteller, Hermann Buhl and a young Kurt Diemberger. The book is largely based on the personal accounts of Schmuck and Wintersteller and pulls few punches as to the various pressures and conflicts between the expedition members. Nevertheless one is left in no doubt as to the significance and magnitude of what they achieved in climbing the mountain.

Anne Sauvy ***Mountain Rescue: Chamonix- Mont Blanc*** **(Bâton Wicks)**
This fine book is a documentary following the deeds of the mountain rescue service in Chamonix, through the 1997 alpine season. It brings into sharp focus the stresses and problems faced by the helicopter crews in their difficult and often dangerous work. The tenderness and humanity of Anne Sauvy's insights and recollections draw into sharp relief the often tragic and careless waste of life in a typical season in the Mont Blanc range. Chamonix fans will warm to this book, written by someone with an intimate knowledge of the area, and of its often fatal attraction. This is a humbling and grave book, and one all serious alpinists should read.

Steve Dean made no apology for the fact that, for the first time in 14 years, the judges decided to award a joint prize to **Andy Cave** for ***Learning to Breathe*** and **Jim Perrin** for ***The Villain*.**

The Banff Mountain Book Festival, a month later, doesn't allow itself to award joint prizes. But it is interesting to note that the BT shortlist showed up well in the Canadian Rockies. BT shortlisted Mick Fowler came up on the rails to win Banff's coverted Mountain Literature prize with his *On Thin Ice*; Jim Perrin's life of Don Whillans won the Mountaineering History category; and Andy Cave's *Learning to Breathe* emerged, by some feat of judicial imagination, as the winner of Adventure Travel.

Maggie Body, Honorary Secretary

19TH INTERNATIONAL FESTIVAL OF MOUNTAINEERING LITERATURE

On what felt like the first real day of spring (25 March 2006) we gathered at Bretton Hall Campus, Leeds, in anticipation of the 19th International Festival of Mountaineering Literature. There were elements of 'first' and 'last'. It was the first time I had attended a literature festival of any sort, and the last time this much loved event would be held at Bretton Hall. The hotch-potch campus set amid the Yorkshire sculpture park has been a place of annual pilgrimage for bookish mountaineers for almost two decades, but festival director Terry Gifford is ringing a change. For his Bretton Hall finale, Terry had invited an inspiring selection of writers and speakers from Canada, the UK and the USA. The theme was 'Who Preserves Our Heritage?' and it provided a great forum for debate amongst both the speakers and an audience that appeared to be quite diverse in both age and background.

'Who Preserves our Heritage?' Do we as mountaineers tend to think of this at all, and when we do, do we differentiate between the preservation of 'mountain' versus 'mountaineering' heritage? To set the tone for the day Peter Hodgkiss of the Ernest Press began with a plea to us all, as individuals, to keep and archive any photos, diaries and notes from our mountaineering lives. He reminded us that it is not only the outstanding mountaineers and their achievements that are important, but that the everyday archives of an era may be a significant contribution to our mountain heritage in the future.

A well considered overview and provocation of the theme was presented by Bernadette McDonald of the Banff Centre as well as a reflection on her book *I'll Call You in Kathmandu* (*review, p360*). The book is a fascinating biography of Elizabeth Hawley, a remarkable woman who has become central to the recording of Himalayan mountaineering. Bernadette left us with a number of questions to ponder, challenging us to really consider what the relevance of our heritage is, and to whom it is relevant. We all have some responsibility, whether as individuals or as organisations, to care enough about our mountains to share them, and to want to protect them. As individuals do we make enough effort to record and tell the stories that we see? Do authors, publishers and magazines do their best to tell, and allow to be told, all good stories with honesty? Can book festivals provide some neutral ground for informed debate on some of the great mysteries and controversies of our mountaineering heritage? Do organisations strike the right balance between archiving and acquiring information, and dissemination, research and education?

A major attraction of the day was to hear several of those well-known and well-respected 'outstanding mountaineers' of our own era talking about their lives and their writing. The cast was impressive. Andy Cave gave us some great readings and thoughts on writing his *Learning to Breathe* (*review, p348*). Colin Wells, of *Climb* magazine, is quoted as saying people will be disappointed with what was left out of the book, so perhaps we can look forward to more? The book is written with 'soul' and movingly demonstrates how mountaineering can be anchored within the conflicts, the politics and the joys of everyday life. His advice for aspiring writers was to have a story, a good one, and to then be confident and to find one's own voice.

Arlene Blum talked with great enthusiasm. Her fascinating story is told in a new book, *Breaking Trail* (*review, p353*). You could feel the strength of her love of the mountains. Perhaps from a woman's perspective it intrigued me to hear how she managed to pursue a life in the mountains and to balance it with her career and family life. There is a time for everything, and at different stages of life one will have very different priorities. Her talk, like her book, was both intimate and yet universal.

Mick Fowler gave us an insight into his semi-autobiographical *On Thin Ice* (*review, p348*). It is aptly named, since his life appears to successfully tread the fine line balancing work, climbing and family. Another legend, David Roberts, gave a very honest and frank discussion of his life and his reexamination of it in his book *On the Ridge Between Life and Death* – sincere reflections on deaths, resentments and doubts, leaving us with the thought that heroism is courage in service to others. Arlene Blum and David Roberts also took part 'in conversation' – with Vicki Robinson and Ed Douglas respectively – the questioning admitting us deeper into their thoughts and feelings than might otherwise have been revealed.

Ed Douglas left us with this quote from the mountaineering page of an Italian newspaper ringing in our ears: 'Alpinism won't have a future if it forgets its history.' Mountaineering is essentially living; it is the life that we live – we go to the mountains, because we love to go. But the rich heritage of its past is where the future is born.

Next year the Festival will be held in conjunction with the Kendal Mountain Film Festival. Terry Gifford has promised an enticing day 'in colour' rather than 'black and white' – so perhaps we will have to attend on 10 November 2007 in order to divine for ourselves just what he means by that.

Elizabeth Hawker

The last 'Mountain Lit' Fest at Bretton Hall ended with a special moment when Jim Curran – ever a festival favourite – bade farewell to the campus venue of the first 19 years with a piece of 'verse' in the style of the Scotsman rightly known as 'the world's worst poet'.

ODE TO TERRY GIFFORD

(*with apologies to William McGonagall and Rupert Bear*)

'Twas in the autumn of eighty seven,
That Terry got a sign from heaven
To mount a festival of mountain lit-
erature – (OK, the words don't fit.)

He put it on at Bretton Hall,
(The name for most meant bugger all)
But every year in autumn mist
We all drove up to get the gist
Of Terry's annual list
Of mountaineering's glitterati
Invited here to join the party,
To air their views – sometimes contentious
And one or two downright pretentious.
Taking his cue from Andrew Motion
Terry excels in self-promotion,
Working flat out rain or snow
To change the format of the show
And bring in people in the know.

Half a teacher, half a preacher,
The festival would always feature
Ideas good – a few were bad,
Some were mad and some were madder,
He got Ed Drummond up a ladder
(Though if you want to be pedantic
He used a tripod for this antic.)

The audience was often voluble,
Some impressively knowledgeable,
Until that dreadful moment when
Discussion was upset by Ken,
Who would invariably rant
At any controversial cant,
And always found it quite revolting
When hearing any praise for bolting.

'Twas an event not to be missed,
Though not much chance of getting pissed
With vile red wine a pound a glass
And catering reduced to farce.
Some saved themselves for the slim
Chance of getting drunk with Jim
Who has fond memories of Bonatti
Drinking Stones with this old fatty
Along with Sheffield's illiterati
Who never missed the chance to party.

So today is Terry's curtain call,
Alas, the end for Bretton Hall.
Now is the time for him to send all
You faithful punters up to Kendal.

Jim Curran

ALPINE CLUB LIBRARY ANNUAL REPORT 2005

This report must start with thanks to George Band who has served as Library Council Chairman for 12 years. Despite some recent challenges, George leaves a very strong Club Library which looks after the Club's collection of books and pamphlets, archives, photographs and the Himalayan Index. I am honoured to be following his illustrious leadership.

We have 30,000 books to care for and make accessible to members. Since last summer, you have been able to search on the Club Website for any book. Also we hold recent expedition reports which many members find extremely useful. Jerry Lovatt (Hon Librarian) has been able to select some non-relevant or triplicated books and has sold them well; this has provided £53,500 to start the Club Climbing Fund.

This year has seen the completion of work to catalogue the Archives – letters from famous members, news cuttings of ascents – collected since 1857 (25,000 items). This catalogue is currently going 'on-line'. Thanks must go to Peter Berg (Hon. Archivist) and Margaret Pope for this splendid achievement.

The Himalayan Index under Mike Westmacott and Sally Holland lists ascents and attempts on all 6000m peaks in the Himalayas, and spreading westwards to the Hindu Kush; north and eastwards into Tibet and China. The main Index is on our website.

The Photo Library collection now comprises 40,000 images and the next task is to create a searchable (electronic) catalogue of these. It is also providing many images for the Club's '150 years' book by George Band and is doing work on the images for Peter Mallalieu's book about Artists of the Club's paintings.

Meanwhile, the Library Council is working to solve the many problems of ever increasing costs. For example, it really is not possible to run the Photo Library on a free basis and some charges will become inevitable. Nevertheless, we hope to have a good selection of photo images on the website within the next year.

The Library is open Tuesday to Friday each week; Yvonne Sibbald, our librarian, will be delighted to receive you. If you let her know in advance what you are seeking, she will do her best to have it all ready for your visit; photos and archives can be seen by arrangement.

Hywel Lloyd
Chairman of the Alpine Club Library Council

Contributors

JOHN ARRAN is one of Britain's foremost all-round climbers who has excelled on a wide range of challenges, from the competition circuit to bold new climbs on gritstone and sea cliffs as well as big walls around the world. Among his recent highlights are a new E10 on Curbar in Derbyshire, 536 routes in a single day, and three major big wall free climbs up to E7 in Venezuelan jungles. He is a UN contract consultant working to assist post-conflict countries in holding free and fair elections.

PETER BERG is a retired scientist and Radio Three announcer, now a guide in the cathedral and city of Canterbury. He has written on industrial archæology, early music, food, sailing and mountaineering, though he's never managed to include all these subjects in one piece. A current project is a book based on Edward Whymper's lecture slides.

MICHAEL BINNIE, a retired schoolteacher, was introduced to climbing by the late Sir Peter Holmes AC, then a Cambridge undergraduate. Forty-five years of fairly unspectacular rock climbing throughout the British Isles and a few, too few, modest Alpine seasons have been sandwiched between some very exciting ones to Peru, Bolivia, Mount Kenya, Kashmir and two and a half years living in a village in Chitral.

ANTONIO GÓMEZ BOHÓRQUEZ lives in Murcia, Spain. A librarian and documentalist (information scientist), he specialises in ascents in the north Peruvian ranges. He has written two books: *La Cordillera Blanca de los Andes, selección de ascensiones, excursiones* and *Cordillera Blanca, Escaladas, Parte Norte.* He has climbed since 1967, with first ascents including *Spanish Direct* on the north face of Cima Grande di Lavaredo, Italy (1977), Pilar del Cantábrico del Naranjo de Bulnes, Spain (1980), east face of Cerro Parón (La Esfinge, 5325m), Peru (1985) and the south-east face (1988).

DEREK BUCKLE is a medicinal chemist now acting as a part-time consultant to the pharmaceutical industry. With plenty of free time he pursues his passion for climbing and mountaineering at every opportunity. Provided that there are crags and mountains, nowhere is safe!

NICK BULLOCK was a PE instructor for the Prison Service until he turned full-time climber in 2003. He discovered climbing in1991 on a work-related course at Plas y Brenin since when he has established himself as one of Britain's leading alpinists. He has put up new routes in the Alps, Peru, notably *Fear and Loathing* on Jirischanca (2003), and in Nepal. Last winter he put up two bold new routes in Wales, *Travesty* (VIII/8), and *Cracking Up* (IX/9).

JO CLEERE had never climbed or skied before deciding to move to Chamonix five years ago. She is a freelance translator, which gives ample time for pottering about on bits of rock and snow as well as trips to Pakistan, Nepal and Tibet.

JULIE-ANN CLYMA has a background in public health research, with a PhD from the University of Manchester. She has been on more than 20 trips to the greater ranges and has been able to use her climbing experience for initiatives that promote development for communities, protection of the environment, and freedom with responsibility for mountaineers. She is currently working as a mountain guide based in Leysin, Switzerland.

ROGER CROSTON, born and domiciled in Chester, is an engineer in a family business. His time in the mountains is spent mostly in nearby Snowdonia. He has been finding and interviewing the few remaining western eyewitnesses of the old Tibet before the Chinese annexation of 1950. He is currently engaged on research on the Ernst Schäfer Tibet Expedition to Sikkim and Tibet of 1938/39.

JIM CURRAN, formerly a lecturer at the University of the West of England, is a freelance writer and film-maker. He has taken part in 16 expeditions to the Himalaya and South America and has written several books. He has now returned to his original discipline of landscape painting and has had three successful shows at the Alpine Club and the Kendal Mountain Festival.

ED DOUGLAS is a former honorary editor of the *Alpine Journal*. His books include *Tenzing*, published by National Geographic, and *Chomolungma Sings the Blues*, published by Constable, both prize winners at the Banff Mountain Book Festival. When not flogging his soul as a freelance journalist, he can be found on the gritstone edges near his home in Sheffield.

JOHN DUGGER, IFAI Master Craftsman and Fellow of the Textile Institute, is an American artist who is known for his innovative banner-making. He is a general outdoorsman with a special interest in mountaineering, which inspires his artistic practice. He has made original banners for Buckingham Palace and has artworks in Tate Modern and the UK Government Art Collection. He is an associate member of the AC.

EVELIO ECHEVARRÍA was born in Santiago, Chile, and teaches Hispanic Literature at Colorado State University. He has climbed in North and South America, and has contributed numerous articles to Andean, North American and European journals.

DEREK FORDHAM, when not dreaming of the Arctic, practises as an architect and runs an Arctic photographic library. He is secretary of the Arctic Club and has led 21 expeditions to the Canadian Arctic, Greenland and Svalbard to ski, climb or share the life of the Inuit.

MICK FOWLER works for Her Majesty's Revenue and Customs and, by contrast, likes to inject as much memorable adventure and excitement into his climbing ventures. He has climbed extensively in the UK and has regularly led expeditions to the greater ranges for more than 20 years. He has written two books, *Vertical Pleasure* (1995) and *On Thin Ice* (2005).

STEPHEN GOODWIN renounced daily newspaper journalism on *The Independent* for a freelance existence in Cumbria, mixing writing and climbing. A precarious balance was maintained until 2004 when he was persuaded to take on the editorship of the *Alpine Journal* and 'getting out' became elusive again.

LINDSAY GRIFFIN is currently serving what he hopes will be only a temporary sentence as an armchair mountaineer. However, he is still keeping up to speed on international affairs through his work with Mountain INFO and as Chairman of the MEF Screening and BMC Inter-national Committees.

STEVE HOUSE lives in Oregon where he can frequently be found at Smith Rock enjoying low-commitment sport-climbing. He is an IFMGA-certified mountain guide and works for Patagonia, developing products and consulting with catalogue and web projects.

GEOFF HORNBY is a consulting engineer now resident in the Italian Dolomites. He has made more than 250 first ascents in the mountains outside of the UK and is looking forward to 250 more, inshallah.

DICK ISHERWOOD has been a member of the Alpine Club since 1970. His climbing record includes various buildings in Cambridge, lots of old-fashioned routes on Cloggy, a number of obscure Himalayan peaks, and a new route on the Piz Badile (in 1968). He now follows Tilman's dictum about old men on high mountains and limits his efforts to summits just a little under 20,000 feet.

MARK JENKINS is an author, adventurer, and columnist for the US magazine *Outside*. Hallmarks include the second American ascent of Shisha Pangma (1984), the US Everest North Face Expedition (1986), first coast-to-coast crossing of the former Soviet Union by bicycle (1989), first descent of the Niger River (1991) and first ascents of the south face of Mt Waddington (1995) and west face direct of Margherita (2004), highest peak in the Rwenzori. He lives with his family in Laramie, Wyoming.

HARISH KAPADIA has climbed in the Himalaya since 1960, with ascents up to 6800m. He is Hon Editor of both the *Himalayan Journal* and the *HC Newsletter*. In 1993 he was awarded the IMF's Gold Medal and in 1996 was made an Hon Member of the Alpine Club. He has written several books including *High Himalaya Unknown Valleys*, *Spiti: Adventures in the Trans-Himalaya* and, with Soli Mehta, *Exploring the Hidden Himalaya*. In 2003 he was awarded the Patron's Gold Medal by the Royal Geographical Society.

PAUL KNOTT is a lecturer in business strategy at the University of Canterbury, New Zealand. He previously lived in the UK and briefly in Morocco. Since 1990 he has undertaken nine exploratory climbing trips to Russia, Central Asia and the St Elias Range in Alaska/Yukon. He climbs regularly in the Southern Alps and has an undiminished yearning for exploration.

PAT LITTLEJOHN is known for a 'clean climbing' ethic and adherence to a lightweight, 'alpine-style' approach. His worldwide portfolio of first ascents includes the NE pillar of Taweche (Nepal), Raven's Pyramid (Karakoram), Poi N face (Kenya) and Kjerag N buttress (Norway). He suceeded Pete Boardman as director of the International School of Mountaineering in 1983. Pat is keen to ensure that climbing's unique 'spirit of adventure' is kept alive, both on the rock and in the mountains.

JOHANNA MERZ joined the Alpine Club in 1988 and has devoted most of her energies to the *Alpine Journal*, first as assistant editor, then as honorary editor from 1992 to 1998, and currently as production editor.

ADE MILLER lives and occasionally works in Redmond, Washington. This allows him to spend his weekends climbing in the mountains of the Pacific Northwest, specializing in winter ascents. He has also visited and climbed in numerous mountain ranges but has spent the last few years climbing, British Columbia, the Yukon Territories and Alaska.

ERIK MONASTERIO is a Bolivian/ New Zealand psychiatrist and climber, currently living and working in NZ. Erik has climbed all over the world, but specializes in the Andes, where he has done more than 30 new alpine routes over ice, rock and mixed ground. He is engaged on research into personality characteristics and accidents in climbers.

TAMOTSU NAKAMURA was born in Tokyo in 1934 and has been climbing new routes in the greater ranges since his first successes on technical peaks in the Cordillera Blanca of Peru in 1961. He has lived in Pakistan, Mexico, New Zealand and Hong Kong and in the last 16 years has made 28 trips to the so-called 'Alps of Tibet' in the Hengduan mountains of Yunnan, Sichuan and East Tibet. He is currently editor of the Japanese Alpine News and a councillor of the JAC.

SKIP NOVAK, an American based in the UK, has for the last 16 years been leading combined 'sailing to climb' expeditions from his vessel *Pelagic* to far-flung destinations like the Antarctic Peninsula, the island of South Georgia and Tierra del Fuego. In 2003 he built a successor, a 23m sloop *Pelagic Australis* that is now plying both Southern Ocean and Arctic waters in season, forever in search of unclimbed summits accessible from the sea.

ROGER PAYNE has a background in education and sports administration, first as the National Officer and then General Secretary at the BMC, and then as the first Sport and Development Director for the UIAA. He has been on more than 20 trips to the greater ranges and has been able to use his climbing experience for initiatives that promote development for communities, protection of the environment, and freedom with responsibility for mountaineers. He is currently working as a mountain guide based in Leysin, Switzerland.

SIR EDWARD PECK's enthusiasm for mountains was fired at the age of eight by meeting, in 1924, General Charles Bruce on the summit of the Dent du Midi. Throughout his subsequent diplomatic career, he tackled (in moderation) whatever mountains were available – Alps, Turkey (Ala Dag), Himalaya, East Africa and Borneo (Kinabalu). On retirement, he made a home in the Cairngorms.

SIMON RICHARDSON is a petroleum engineer based in Aberdeen. Experience gained in the Alps, Andes, Patagonia, Canada, Himalaya and Alaska is put to good use most winter weekends whilst exploring and climbing in the Scottish Highlands.

GEORGE RODWAY is an assistant professor at Ohio State University, where he investigates physiological responses to the hypoxia associated with pulmonary disease. Whenever possible, he sneaks away to write about historical aspects of mountain exploration and high altitude physiology. His interest in the high and wild have taken him to the sub-arctic mountains of Alaska and the Yukon nearly every year since 1980 and also to Latin America and the Himalaya.

C A RUSSELL, who formerly worked with a City bank, devotes much of his time to mountaineering and related activities. He has climbed in many regions of the Alps, in the Pyrenees, East Africa, North America and the Himalaya.

BILL RUTHVEN has been Hon Secretary of the Mount Everest Foundation since 1985 and welcomes this opportunity to put something back into the sport that gave him so much pleasure over fifty-odd years of active mountaineering. Now confined to a wheelchair, he considers himself the 'complete social climber', attending indoor events such as conferences, symposia, film festivals etc. At these (and anywhere else) he is always happy to 'talk mountains' with individuals planning expeditions. For his MEF work, Bill has been made an Honorary Member of the Alpine Club.

ERMANNO SALVATERRA was born in Pinzolo in 1955, where he still resides. During the summer he runs the XII Apostoli Hut in the Brenta Group, which has been in his family's hands since 1948. During the winter he works as a mountain guide and as a ski instructor. He started climbing at age 11, and has climbed ever since. Even though he is best known for his many exploits in Patagonia, which include three new routes on Cerro Torre, as well as its first winter ascent, he has also made expeditions to Greenland, Makalu, Yosemite, etc. His other passion is speed-skiing, holding the Italian record for five years with a descent reaching 211 kilometres per hour.

VICTOR SAUNDERS was born in Lossiemouth and grew up in Malaya. He started climbing in the Alps in 1978 and has climbed in the Andes, Caucasus, India, Pakistan, Nepal and Bhutan. Formerly a London-based architect, he is now a UIAGM mountain guide and is based in Chamonix. When not working, he likes to relax on steep little bits of rock and ice. His first book, *Elusive Summits*, won the Boardman Tasker Prize.

MARTIN SCOTT has climbed in the Alps, Greenland, Nepal, Tibet, Sichuan, Bolivia, Ecuador, Peru, Pakistan and Alaska. He has worked in many countries as a field geophysicist and later in computing. He now spends more time on expeditions and is Hon Sec of the AC and Vice-Chairman of the MEF.
MIKE SEARLE is a mountaineer and geologist who combines his hobby and interest in his work as a Senior Research Fellow at the University of Oxford. He has worked for 25 years on Himalayan geological projects as well as in the Karakoram and Tibet and has been on more than 20 mountaineering expeditions.

GEOFFREY TEMPLEMAN, a retired chartered surveyor, has greatly enjoyed being an Assistant Editor of the *Alpine Journal* for the past 30 years. A love of mountain literature is coupled with excursions into the hills, which are becoming less and less energetic.

JOHN TOWN is Registrar and Secretary at Loughborough University. He has climbed in the Alps, Caucasus, Altai, Andes, Turkey and Kamchatka, and explored little known mountain areas of Mongolia, Yunnan and Tibet. He is old enough to remember the days without GPS and satellite phones.

SIMEON WARNER lives in Ithaca, New York, which is too far from any mountains. In the winter he climbs ice in the Adirondacks and elsewhere in the north-eastern US. In the summer he avoids the crowds at his local crags by caving instead. Recent mountaineering trips have been to South America and Alaska.

MARK WATSON works for the New Zealand Alpine Club as editor of both *The Climber* magazine and the *New Zealand Alpine Journal*. Mostly found hanging out at various crags, he can also been seen in the mountains from time to time. Mark's favourite New Zealand area is the Darran Mountains, a wonderland of deep diorite valleys and alpine rock. He has also rock-climbed extensively in the USA, UK, Western Europe and Australia.

JEREMY WINDSOR is an anaesthetist and researcher at the Institute of Human Health and Performance, based at University College London. Despite limited ability, he has climbed widely throughout the UK and the Greater Ranges. As an expedition doctor he has undertaken trips to East Africa, South America, Greenland and the Himalayas.

SIMON YATES has, over the last 20 years, climbed and travelled from Alaska in the west to New Zealand in the east, from the Canadian Arctic in the north to the tip of South America. He is the author of two books, *Against The Wall* and *The Flame of Adventure*. As well as writing, Simon runs his own commercial expedition company (www.mountaindream.co.uk) and is a popular lecturer.

Index 2006

2006 Vol 111

NOTES FOR CONTRIBUTORS

The *Alpine Journal* records all aspects of mountains and mountaineering, including expeditions, adventure, art, literature, geography, history, geology, medicine, ethics and the mountain environment.

Articles Contributions in English are invited. They should be sent to the Hon Editor, Stephen Goodwin, 1 Ivy Cottages, Edenhall, Penrith, Cumbria CA11 8SN (e-mail: sg@stephengoodwin.demon.co.uk). Articles should preferably be sent on a disk with accompanying hard copy or as an e-mail attachment (in Word) with hard copy sent separately by post. They will also be accepted as plain typed copy. Their length should not exceed 3000 words without prior approval of the Editor **and may be edited or shortened at his discretion.** It is regretted that the *Alpine Journal* is unable to offer a fee for articles published, but authors receive a complimentary copy of the issue of the *Alpine Journal* in which their article appears.

Articles and book reviews should not have been published in substantially the same form by any other publication.

Maps These should be well researched, accurate, and finished ready for printing. They should show the most important place-names mentioned in the text. It is the authors' responsibility to get their maps redrawn if necessary. This can be arranged through the Production Editor if required.

Photographs Colour transparencies are preferable. These should be originals (not copies) in 35mm format or larger. Prints (any size) should be numbered (in pencil) on the back and accompanied by captions on a separate sheet (see below). Images on CD are acceptable but must have been scanned at high resolution and must be accompanied by numbered captions that match the serial numbers on the CD.

Captions Please list these **on a separate sheet** and give title and author of the article to which they refer.

Copyright It is the author's responsibility to obtain copyright clearance for text, photographs and maps, to pay any fees involved and to ensure that acknowledgements are in the form required by the copyright owner.

Summaries A brief summary, helpful to researchers, may be included with 'expedition' articles.

Biographies Authors are asked to provide a short biography, in about 60 words, listing the most noteworthy items in their climbing career and anything else they wish to mention.

Deadline: **copy and photographs should reach the Editor by 1 January of the year of publication**.

RATHBONES
Established 1742

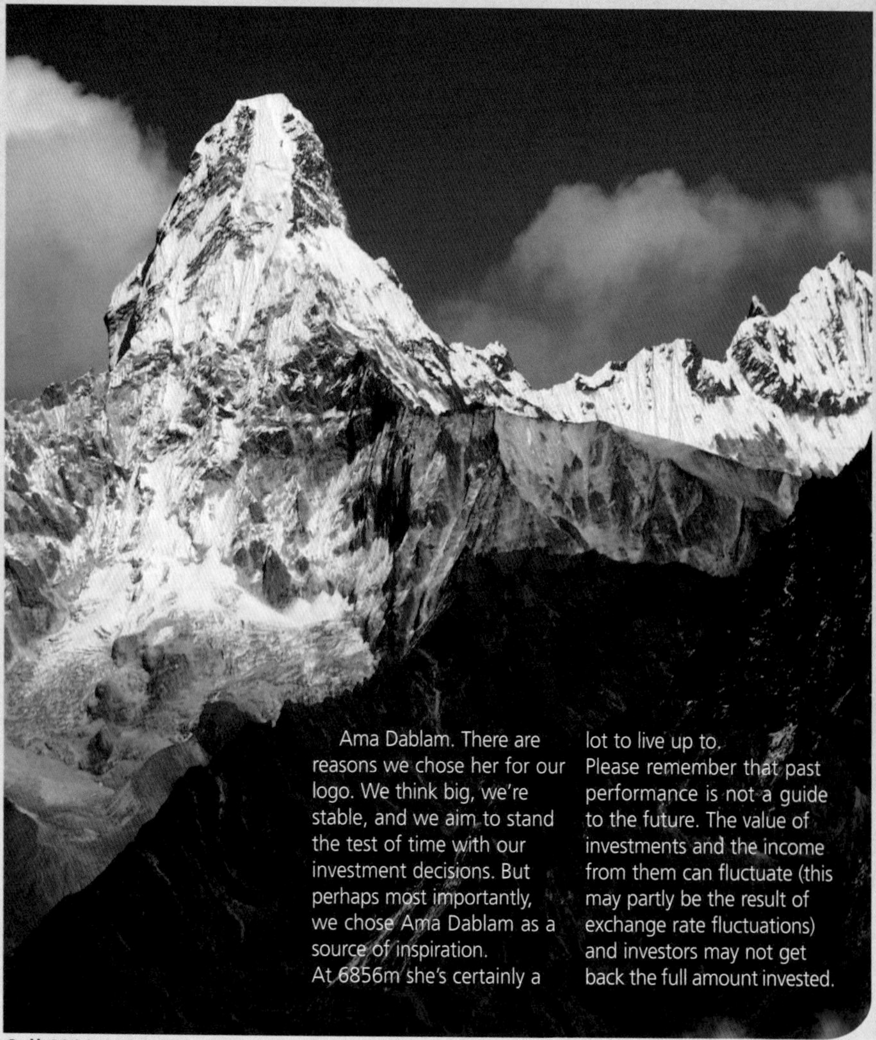

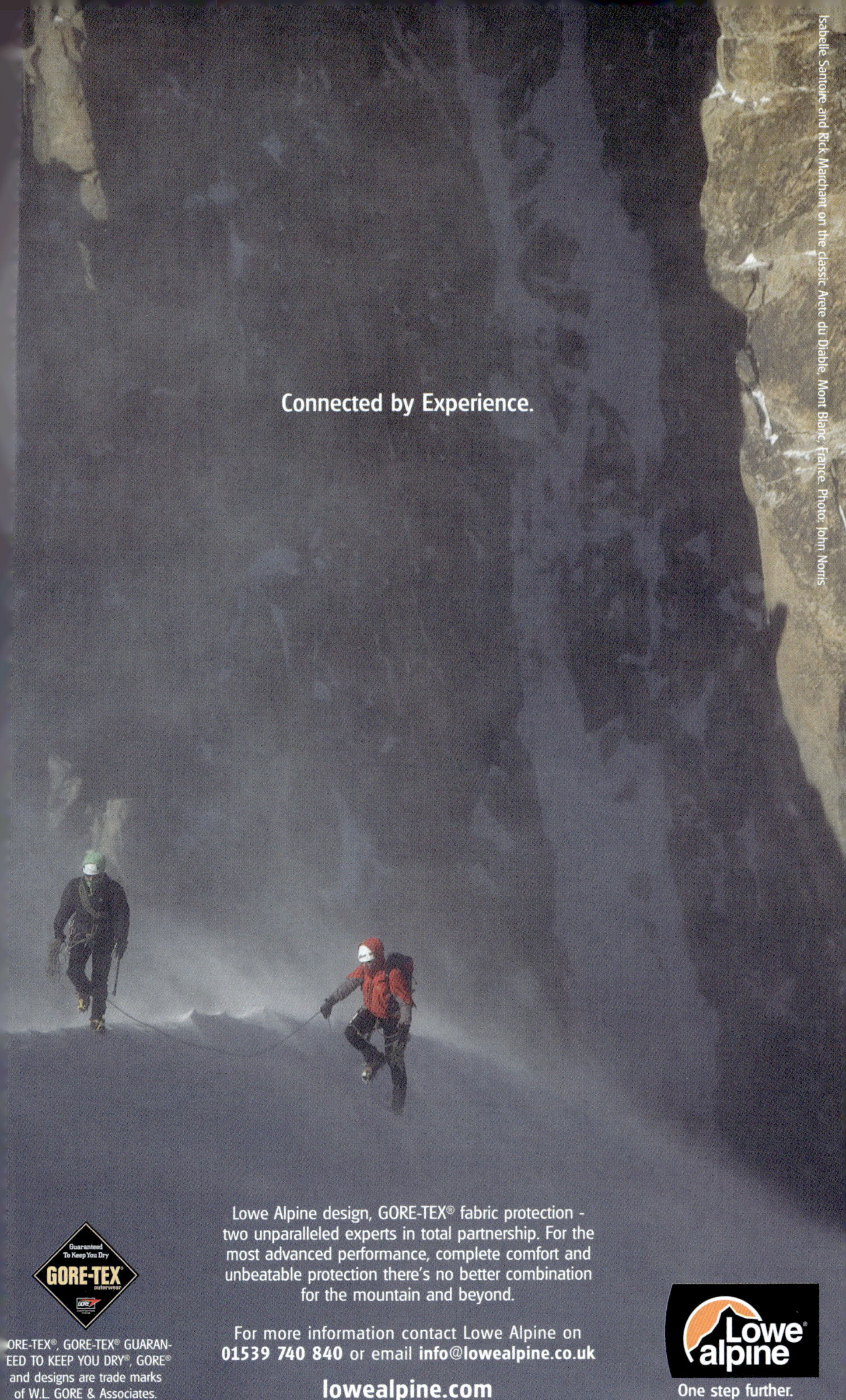
Isabelle Santoire and Rick Marchant on the classic Arete du Diable, Mont Blanc, France. Photo: John Norris
Connected by Experience.
Lowe Alpine design, GORE-TEX® fabric protection - two unparalleled experts in total partnership. For the most advanced performance, complete comfort and unbeatable protection there's no better combination for the mountain and beyond.
For more information contact Lowe Alpine on 01539 740 840 or email info@lowealpine.co.uk
lowealpine.com
Guaranteed To Keep You Dry
GORE-TEX
ORE-TEX®, GORE-TEX® GUARAN-EED TO KEEP YOU DRY®, GORE® and designs are trade marks of W.L. GORE & Associates.
Lowe alpine
One step further.

GRIVEL 100% Produc
0% Blah...Blah..

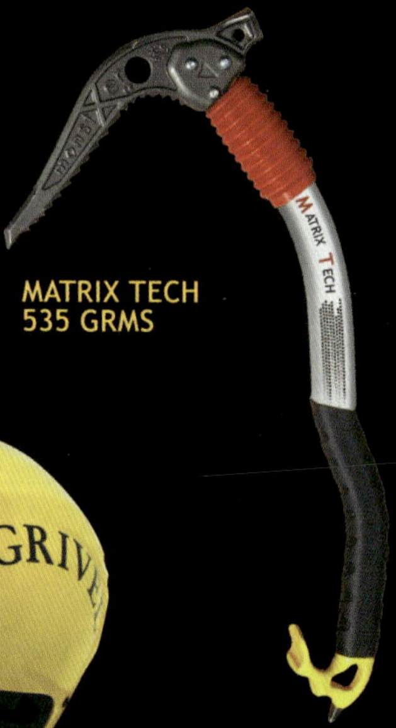

MATRIX TECH
535 GRMS

SALAMANDER
385 GRMS

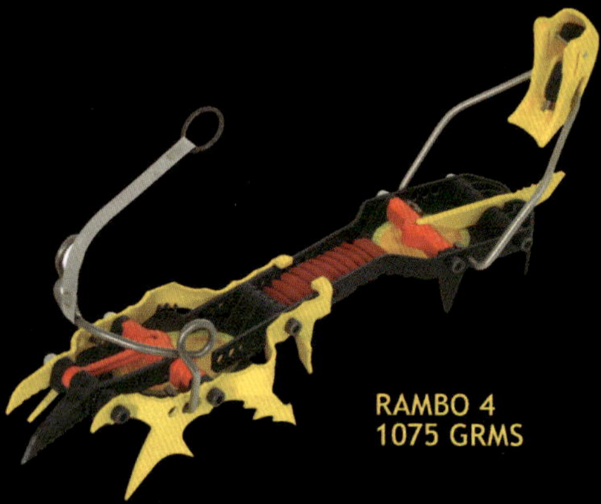

RAMBO 4
1075 GRMS

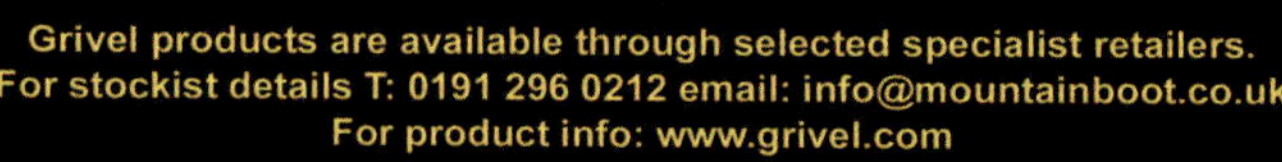

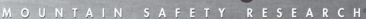

Old castle at Leh